Apostle of Liberation

Apostle of Liberation

AME Bishop Paul Quinn and the Underground Railroad

William P. Quinn

Cheryl Janifer LaRoche

ROWMAN & LITTLEFIELD
Lanham • Boulder • New York • London

Published by Rowman & Littlefield
An imprint of The Rowman & Littlefield Publishing Group, Inc.
4501 Forbes Boulevard, Suite 200, Lanham, Maryland 20706
www.rowman.com

86-90 Paul Street, London EC2A 4NE

Copyright © 2025 by Cheryl Janifer LaRoche

All rights reserved. No part of this book may be reproduced in any form or by any electronic or mechanical means, including information storage and retrieval systems, without written permission from the publisher, except by a reviewer who may quote passages in a review.

British Library Cataloguing in Publication Information Available

Library of Congress Cataloging-in-Publication Data Available

ISBN 978-1-5381-9811-7 (cloth)
ISBN 978-1-5381-9812-4 (ebook)

∞™ The paper used in this publication meets the minimum requirements of American National Standard for Information Sciences—Permanence of Paper for Printed Library Materials, ANSI/NISO Z39.48-1992.

In memory of
Ambassador Ronald D. Palmer
Togo (1976–1978), Malaysia (1981–1983), Mauritius (1986–1989)

Contents

List of Figures		ix
Preface: Why Paul Quinn Matters		xi
1	William Paul Quinn and the Birth of African Methodism	1
2	The Circuit Rider and the Underground Railroad: 1817–1824	17
3	Quinn in New York City: 1824–1828	33
4	Independence in New York City: 1828–1833	43
5	Quinn Returns to the Fold: 1833–1836	57
6	Local Circuits to an International Conference 1836–1844: West to Indiana and Missouri—South to Kentucky and Louisiana—North to Canada	71
7	Bishop Quinn: 1844–1849	89
8	The Tumultuous Years: 1850–1858	105
9	Quinn, the Underground Railroad, and the Civil War: 1859–1865	125
10	Passing the Torch: 1865–1872	141
11	Receiving His Crown	157

Afterword	165
Churches, Chapels, and Institutions Named for William Paul Quinn across the United States	171
Acknowledgments	175
Notes	179
Bibliography	219
Index	249
About the Author	259

List of Figures

1.1	Drawing of Latrobe's "Plan of a Camp Meeting."	10
2.1	Rt. Rev. William Paul Quinn in His Prime.	17
3.1	Mulberry Street Property for Sale.	36
3.2	Announcement and Invitation to Quinn's Sermon.	36
3.3	New York City Map, Mulberry Street.	40
4.1	"The Churches of New York City 1786–1833."	50
4.2	"Pickpockets Rob Quinn."	52
4.3	Quinn's NY Church Is Sinking.	55
5.1	Quinn Meets with President Andrew Jackson.	67
6.1	Excerpt of Siebert Indiana Map.	73
6.2	AME and Underground Railroad Map.	75
6.3	The City of Louisville Map.	78
6.4	St. Louis Harbor Sketch Reduced from Capt. Lee's Map of 1837.	84
7.1	Bishop Quinn.	90
8.1	John Jones and James D. Bonner Advertisement.	117
9.1	Annual Conferences Visited by Bishop Quinn, 1862.	128
10.1	Mary Jane Simms Quinn.	146
10.2	Bishops at the 1868 General Conference, Washington, DC.	149
10.3	Paul Quinn College, Waco, Texas, ca. 1898.	154
10.4	Paul Quinn Art Class.	155

Preface
Why Paul Quinn Matters

Whether within the African Methodist Episcopal (AME) Church or the Underground Railroad, within the courts or the emigration movement, William Paul Quinn prevailed despite pre–Civil War contradictions between race and religion, slavery and liberation. From the birth of the AME denomination in 1816 to Quinn's death in 1873, his dedication to his ministry and to justice and equality never faltered. Carrying his Bible and a saddlebag, Quinn was the first African Methodist circuit rider to mount a horse to preach. The independent Black denomination honed his leadership across the seminal events of American history.

Born of the Black Atlantic, Quinn's life stretched across that global sphere, ranging from his birth of mixed parentage in Central America to his refuge in Europe and his passage to North America. The internationalization of the AME Church in Canada, the Caribbean, and Africa helped Quinn confront the racial power imbalances that impacted his world. His religious work in building Black institutions ensured the overall well-being and protection of enslaved, escaped, and free people of color. Two guiding objectives motivated his activism. In the AME Church, he pushed for religious freedom. His work on the Underground Railroad—defined as resistance to slavery through flight and escape—sought to bring an end to slavery and uphold universal equality.

Born in 1788, he came to America, by all accounts, as an immigrant of mixed parentage. Quinn's contemporaries widely reported Hindustan or India was his birthplace; other AME historians insisted on Honduras. But we can say with reasonable authority that Quinn was born in British Honduras, now Belize, the son of a Spanish mahogany-dealer father and an East African mother. In a sworn 1851 affidavit, Quinn attested to his Honduran birth and his parental lineage. After passage of the heinous Fugitive Slave Act of 1850, he eluded slavery's grasp and illegal capture by claiming British citizenship.[1]

The earliest British settlers at Black River in the Yucatán Peninsula were slaveholders who engaged in a wide range of activities, including mahogany cutting. Eventually, enslaved African mahogany cutters mixed with the Spanish and the native inhabitants. During the late eighteenth century, the Spanish and the Irish also intermingled. The Quinn surname, popular in British Honduras, may have resulted from that combination.[2]

Paul Quinn spent his early life in Belize, where he would have been exposed to his father's business dealings. Most likely, Quinn learned furniture making because of his wealthy family's background in the mahogany trade. In subsequent years as a young itinerant preacher, Quinn was known for making furniture for his grateful hosts. Mixed-race Hondurans were considered "consummate lumberjacks" and excellent woodcutters, according to one expert on the region. Historically, throughout the nineteenth century, English speakers engaged in the mahogany trade, and woodcutters worked the Honduran coast. This could explain later observations suggesting Quinn spoke with no discernable accent. Additionally, the region is known for gold mining and panning, knowledge Quinn later used to his advantage in his adopted country.

He appears to have been among the early Hondurans who came to the United States in the late eighteenth and early nineteenth centuries. One convincing piece of evidence—the immigration of Quinn's first wife, Margaretta Potts, from Honduras to New York City—suggests Central America as his place of birth. The living descendants of his second wife, whom he married much later in life, support this assertion. Dennis Dickerson, a former longtime AME historiographer, named either Central America or the Caribbean as Quinn's birthplace in his recent history, *The African Methodist Episcopal Church: A History*.[3]

In all likelihood, the religious experiences of Quinn's early years in Belize shaped his later multipronged battle against slavery and his penchant for justice. His possibly Catholic merchant father purportedly frowned on his son's religious tolerance and leanings toward Protestantism. A Society of Friends missionary, Elizabeth Walker, first set Quinn on the path toward Methodism by exposing him to Quakerism.

Disowned by his father, Quinn came to America in the early years of the nineteenth century, the golden age of mahogany (the 1720s to the 1820s), when slavery remained enforced in the British colonies. After initially making his way to Gibraltar, Quinn apparently encountered the brother of radical antislavery Quaker, Elias Hicks. Quinn's association with Elizabeth Walker facilitated his immigration to New York, where Long Island Friends, as Quakers were known, welcomed him.

The new immigrant's initial inclination toward Quaker teachings helped shape his outlook and perhaps his compassion and dedication to education. His earliest preaching, however, was among White Methodist Episcopalians. But he soon felt his ambitions crumbling under the caustic moral and spiritual effects of racial prejudice within that denomination. The radical consciousness and upheaval that birthed the AME Church in 1816 revived his soul.

Two decades before, in 1787, Richard Allen had led a sacred and secular revolution. Congregants had followed him and Absalom Jones out of Philadelphia's St. George's Methodist Church, protesting their abysmal treatment. Quinn, a young giant of a man, would encounter Richard Allen at the formation of the AME denomination. After joining with Allen, the preacher planted churches in unfamiliar and unsafe outposts in the United States and Canada before the Civil War. His influence guided missionaries to Haiti and the presence of the church in Africa. He served as vice president of a Black Nationalist Emigration Convention that advocated emigration to South or Central America.

At the moment the seeds of an organized, independent Black church took root, Paul Quinn's life changed forever. Quinn discovered a spiritual home in African Methodism. It yielded opportunities to express his capacity and his aspirations. He seized the chance to lead, although, at times, he came into conflict with Bishop Richard Allen, the denomination's charismatic founder. Quinn fulfilled his life's work as AME's fourth bishop and formed the bridge between the trailblazers and the modern church.

Quinn, AME's original circuit rider, rode half-wild broncos with daring and bravado, catching everyone's attention. Both rough and crude, tender and harsh, he never backed away from a fight. Powerful, dramatic, and compelling, Quinn was down to earth with a prankster's sense of humor. The preacher's stature, muscular frame, and physical strength drew admiring comments during his life. Standing at over six feet tall and weighing 256 pounds "before dinner," this dashing, mustached, ruddy brown man seemed built for "great endurance, persistence and leadership," remembered observers.[4] Despite this and an extensive reputation as a boxer before his conversion, the minister was assaulted, badly wounded, and robbed several times. But his size, strength, and boxing skills did save his life on the untamed frontier as he opened the West to the church. A general nineteenth-century theory held that bulk as well as brains were necessary conditions for an AME preacher and for effectiveness in life. According to religious historians Stephen Angel and Anthony Pinn, most denominational historians thought Quinn "an ideal standard by which to measure contemporary ministers" and the model of "masculine achievement."[5]

Across the country women accounted for the majority of Quinn's supporters and followers. They helped feed, raise funds, mend clothes, and provide shelter for fugitives. Women took active roles in educational efforts. They also confronted Quinn and challenged the church, seeking the opportunity to preach and minister to the faithful. Although Quinn may have been able to lead the laity to Christ, he was unable to sway the men of the church toward women's access to the pulpit.

Quinn's ministry reached north to Canada, Portland (Maine), and New Bedford (Massachusetts); east to New York, New Jersey, and Pennsylvania; and west to Ohio, Indiana, and Illinois, to Iowa, Wisconsin, Kansas, and beyond. His activities in Michigan, while acknowledged, are poorly understood. Remarkably, Quinn either established or helped establish churches in the slaveholding states of Maryland, Kentucky, Missouri, Louisiana, and Tennessee. He sent disciples to California while supporting another's mission to Haiti.

His missionary work on the American frontier best captures his legacy at a time when southern and the midwestern states were firmly committed to the idea of White supremacy. Lawmakers passed Black codes devised to exclude free Blacks rather than merely restrict their civil rights. With the enactment of such laws, the doctrine of racial discrimination bled into legal practices and the social fabric.[6] As Quinn opened the West to the church, he responded with a threefold message: salvation, liberation, education.

Nothing could replace the revelatory light of knowledge. The AME Church and Black educators, some affiliated with other denominations, provided the vehicle. Sunday schools associated with Quinn's churches pay tribute to his lasting commitment to education. Wherever he went, the minister vanquished ignorance and illiteracy. Learning to read the Bible showed the enslaved population the way out of the spiritual and intellectual wasteland intended to keep them in mental darkness. Free Blacks recognized and valued the power of learning and literacy and were quick to see education as a liberating force. Quinn's interest in education was not limited to books alone. From his earliest days as a preacher, the young minister demonstrated by example—financial literacy empowered physical freedom. He taught his followers how to make money and how to save it. At his death, Quinn left an estate of at least $20,000—more than half a million dollars in today's currency.

Quinn and church leaders cleaved to a wider circle, rising above denominational sectarianism. Although ministers routinely worked for the abolition of slavery, their dramatic actions tended to obscure their religious affiliations. Black Baptists, African Methodist Episcopal Zion members, and several other Black Methodists along with traditionally White-denomination members all participated in assisting their brethren out of slavery. Yet religious histories rarely mention ministers playing an active role in escapes from slavery, or at best, they make passing reference to it. Officials, lawmen, and enslavers grew particularly wary of the Black church and its suspected activities in helping fugitives.

Thoroughly suited to carry the banner of the church into the untested terrain of western America, Quinn bridged the chasm between freedom, race, and religion. Once passage was possible, he traveled by train or in his own private carriage. Mostly, he rode his circuit on horseback. Sometimes he brought his dog. Wherever he went, he kept company with radical Black abolitionists and Underground Railroad agents: Theodore Wright and Henry Highland Garnet in New York; Priscilla Baltimore and John Jones in Illinois; Moses Dickson in Missouri; fiery White activists Theodore Weld, Calvin Fairbank, and Augustus Wattles in Ohio, and many others. He usually operated in the middle of the action yet was never visible at its center.

Twenty-five years ago, as a student of the Underground Railroad, my earliest encounter with Quinn and his nebulous activities sharpened my scrutiny. Disentangling his actions and intersections with the movement have been challenging ever since. But he always remained just beyond my grasp—operating on the edges and at the heart of the Underground Railroad at the same time. In 1856, during the last conference the AME Church held in Canada, Quinn cryptically characterized himself as a mole "when it suited his convenience."[7]

Many of the churches Quinn started helped Blacks escape slavery via the Underground Railroad. His reputation and religious authority partially shielded his illegal actions, although he was taken before grand juries under suspicion of aiding freedom seekers in Kentucky and Missouri. The importance of the Black church bolstered his status even as independent African American denominations heightened suspicions among Whites. In those pre–Civil War years, African American preachers had to negotiate between militancy and pious devotion, between conformity and resistance, navigating between slavery and freedom for themselves and their congregants.

Elaine Welch, by specifically using the term "underground railroad" in her 1933 biographical sketch of Quinn's life, alerts readers to his work helping freedom seekers. Welch claims the minister became "interested in the underground railroad in Richmond, Indiana," after he moved there in 1836 and "was a loyal recruit."[8] In fact, he was a well-versed veteran long before his arrival in Indiana. The mechanisms of escape supported by the Black church and its surrounding free Black communities began much earlier than the history of the movement suggests, before suspicions heightened. Welch explains, "He was untiring in his efforts against slavery, and helped many slaves to escape from their masters, and to find an asylum in the north."[9] The AME Church remained silent on the subject of escaping slavery for eighty years. For the centennial history of the denomination in 1916, Rev. Richard R. Wright acknowledged, "Many of the ministers of this church were active in the anti-slavery movement and [the] 'underground railroad,' and much of the actual work of receiving and transporting escaped slaves was done by them."[10]

Although this work focuses on northern escapes facilitated by the AME Church, many freedom seekers escaped through their own initiative, having never interacted with the Underground Railroad. The Society of Friends, Congregationalist denominations, antislavery Methodists, Baptists, and Presbyterians actively offered refuge. Some escapees went by water; others ventured outside the United States completely, having gone south to Mexico or north to Canada. The churches Quinn organized formed an overall pattern, enabling one hidden avenue of hope alongside multiplying tactics for freedom. But Quinn's early years and entanglements with freedom seekers were draped in mystery.[11]

I think of Quinn as the "engineer" of the Underground Railroad, laying out church circuits that became routes for others to follow. We may not fully recognize *how* they did what they did, but the details of Quinn's life help us understand *why* they went where they went. His biography is a revelation.

More a man of action than a man of letters, Quinn, rather than speak or write about himself at length, seemed more comfortable on horseback. He was a storyteller. As a result, we must rely on an occasional letter or report from the bishop coupled with accounts of his life as told by friends—their reminiscences, letters, and retrospectives. Newspaper articles, memorials, and obituaries round out the details of his complex life. His age was as elusive as his life story; he seemed to grow younger as the years passed.

Quinn left a scant written legacy, but he did leave behind a manifesto, as well as the first written episcopal address. He sent an update on his Civil War skirmishes in Kansas to AME's official newspaper, *The Christian*

Recorder. His friend Henry Highland Garnet observed, "A large and an intensely interesting volume could be written, describing the labors and the thrilling incidents of the life of Wm. Paul Quinn."[12] Quinn, however, never spoke about his work on the Underground Railroad. Arrest records, circumstantial evidence, his friendships with legendary Underground Railroad operatives, and the reminiscences of his spiritual family provide the evidence: Paul Quinn and his churches were synonymous with the Underground Railroad.

As the linchpin of the early church, Quinn, the hardy frontiersman, gets lost between Bishop Richard Allen, the forceful and determined founding bishop of the AME Church, and Quinn's successor, Bishop Daniel Payne, the pious and careful educator more suited for modern times. Because Quinn was so elusive in telling his own life story while he was alive, the other ministers' contributions have eclipsed Quinn's central role in ensuring the growth of the church. Both Allen and Payne wrote autobiographies, but we have been left to piece together the details of Quinn's influential life, particularly his early years. The facts of his life were difficult to pin down even while he was alive. Church historians, including Daniel Payne, did their best to pry a full biography out of him. The ninety-year-old biographical sketch by Welch of Chicago's Quinn Chapel revealed his character, personality, and many anecdotal descriptions but no sources.[13] Accuracy surrounding places and dates of his early days eluded most chroniclers. Daniel Payne's observation lingers: "If Bishop Allen, Bishop Morris Brown and Bishop Quinn had kept daily . . . records of their private and public lives, the first part of our history would have been ten-fold more interesting than it is."[14]

History mentions Quinn only in passing, with brief references that hint at his life before his ascent to the bishopric. Combining stories of the emerging public figure from newspaper articles with the historical religious figure captured in AME minutes and Underground Railroad stories has yielded a story rich enough to tell. His many names and titles—William Paul Quinn, W. P. Quinn, Brother Quinn, Elder Quinn, and finally, Bishop Quinn—reflect his ministerial journey. Mostly, he was affectionately known as Paul Quinn, the "Pioneer Bishop of the West," a title given after his ordination as the fourth bishop in 1844. He rose to the position of senior bishop five years later, after the death of Bishop Morris Brown in 1849.[15]

More than any other prelate of the AME Church, Quinn guided the faithful during the perilous pre–Civil War years, sanctioning escape from slavery while seemingly respecting the law. This ardent supporter of the Underground Railroad fearlessly denounced slavery as he moved across the country. Taking outwardly conflicting positions in the face of moral dilemmas and legal dictates, Quinn's life embodies the struggles and challenges that called nineteenth-century Black leaders to greatness.

The AME Church endures because of Quinn's capacity for spiritual wisdom, boldness, and steady guidance reinforced by judicious circumspection. Garnet speaks of his successful maneuvers "over a sea made tempestuous by the warring elements of religious discord, and denominational splits that prevailed in his early ministry."[16] Quinn's brothers in faith remembered that he usually managed to interject humor in the retelling of the dangers he'd faced, withstanding "privations and hardships" that "would have killed half dozen ordinary men."[17]

Quinn met with President Andrew Jackson and remained true to his political convictions. Determination, fortitude, and prudence ordered his steps. Convinced that slavery—and all sins—needed to be denounced from the pulpit, Quinn said of the slaveholder, "May God have mercy on him; I never will."[18] Filled with complexity, grit, and grace, Quinn's story exposes the reality inside the dream of America.

One writer grafted lofty imagery onto this "plumed knight of God," observing that "the early western advance of the Church is synonymous with the endeavors of this flaming herald of the Cross."[19] Writing about a beloved servant of the Lord such as Paul Quinn leaves one searching for balance. What emerges is a man deeply respected, even revered. Few offered criticism, and when it was given, it was brief and fleeting. Daniel Payne admitted, "Like every child of Adam, the Bishop had his faults but he had also his virtues."[20] Still, Quinn repeatedly flouted secular rulings in favor of human rights and higher law. He did not hesitate to use force against his enemies. Payne adds, "He could preach in the pulpit go down and whip the devil, and then go and preach again. He could do more than all the sheriffs and constables put together."[21] He manipulated the truth to his advantage and balked under Richard Allen's control. He was maddeningly elusive about his past.

Paul Quinn rose to lead the AME Church for more than twenty-eight years, serving alone for nearly five of those. He guided the church over the formative moments that often prove disastrous for new ventures, whether religious or secular. One of Quinn's most important contributions to the church was his crucial role in selecting AME bishops between 1849 and 1872, the period during which he led AME as its senior bishop. Fulfilling Richard Allen's vision, Quinn, both directly and in alignment with his disciples, chiseled a lasting imprint on the national and international growth of the church. Years after Quinn's death, Bishop Tanner recognized Brother Quinn's mission to the Western states of Indiana, Illinois, and Missouri as "the greatest Christian enterprise ever undertaken by the African Methodist

Episcopal connection since its rise and progress in our country."[22] Efforts of both the church and its bishops helped the denomination grow in authority and importance. Quinn bolstered the viability and spread of Methodism into the twentieth and twenty-first centuries.

Bishop Allen had left a blueprint for succeeding bishops, including Paul Quinn. Rev. George Singleton, editor of the A.M.E. Review, called the leaders of the church "God-intoxicated men with hearts full of zeal and unconquerable determination."[23] Quinn was and continues to be revered as one of the four horsemen of the Liberation Church: Richard Allen, the apostle of freedom; Quinn, the apostle of liberation; Daniel Payne, the apostle of education; and Henry McNeal Turner, the apostle of expansion. Morris Brown, second bishop of the AME Church and Bishop Allen's immediate successor, must be added to the mighty foursome. It was Brown who exploited Quinn's genius for organizing and laying out circuits and who quickly elevated him after Allen's death. Together these bishops set the resolute course for the AME Church that has lasted for more than two hundred years.

Beloved in life and revered in death, Bishop Quinn left an indelible mark on the AME Church. The measure of success and the magnitude of Quinn's life can be gleaned by the outpouring of love and respect shown at his funeral in 1873. White Methodists and Quakers at his home in Richmond, Indiana, vied "for the privilege of honoring his lifeless form."[24] Each wanted the most important part of the funerary rites performed at one of their beautiful chapels. Love-tinged admiration enveloped his homegoing. His final resting place remains among the Quakers at the elegant cemetery at Earlham College in Richmond.[25] For years the AME denomination held memorials for the bishop on the anniversary of his death. At present Quinn's legacy lives on in the forty-two churches and chapels that bear his name across twenty states, as well as in Paul Quinn College in Dallas, Texas.[26]

Now is the time to introduce this nineteenth-century churchman to a twenty-first-century audience. For the fiftieth anniversary of the church, The Christian Recorder pronounced Quinn, "the Asbury of the African M.E. Church."[27] In 1986, looking back over the two hundred years since the denomination's founding, one writer stressed, "When historians write about the frontier fighters who opened the West—the rugged individualists who had quick fists and unflinching resolve—they rarely mention black preachers," such as Quinn.[28] In Philadelphia in 2016, the denomination celebrated its fiftieth quadrennial session—the two hundredth anniversary of its formal establishment. Quinn and the early bishops helped part the waters to that future. They brought religious salvation to the masses across the diaspora and stood for justice and equality in the oppressive days of slavery.

Harsh circumstances require wisdom and fearless leadership. To stand against hypocrisy, injustice, and immorality required faith and fortitude. For nineteenth-century African American leaders, success demanded courage, strength, and a belief that with God on and at their side, they could move mountains—and they did. If Quinn seems larger than life, it is because he and other Black leaders advanced beyond the expectations of their time. The church Quinn faithfully nurtured has grown to 2.5 million members across the globe, representing thirty-nine countries on five continents, making it one of the largest Methodist denominations in the world.

CHAPTER 1

William Paul Quinn and the Birth of African Methodism

Paul Quinn leaned against a tree, a small bundle tucked under his arm. He listened intently, absorbed by the preaching and ideas that Brother Samuel Collins laid before him. Collins noticed the tall young man's fervor and, as he finished his sermon, extended an invitation to the youth to come home with him to East Point, Pennsylvania. Collins led the local church there. The novice then poured out his heart, explaining his deeply felt calling to preach the gospel.

Quinn's first awakening had come at the hands of Quaker preacher Elizabeth Walker. Female missionaries such as Walker had introduced the world to Quaker ideals and beliefs from the fifteenth to the eighteenth centuries. Walker herself had visited a total of thirty-five countries and public prisons during her missionary travels.[1] AME's first historiographer, Daniel Payne, stated that Quinn had rescued her from a band of threatening young ruffians, who were abusing her as a "damnable heretic" apparently in Honduras.[2] Her *Memorials Concerning Deceased Friends* captured such a moment. In the middle of the violent attack against her, she "held up in her hands a small book . . . stained with the blood streaming from her forehead." She challenged the crowd: "I hold this as a testimony against you." According to Payne, Quinn found "her manner and appearance" so different from what he had expected to see based on all he'd heard "that instantly[,] he felt a sensation pass through him like an electric shock." This awareness caused the seeker serious concern about his responsibility to God, which increased until "he was brought to rejoice in a Saviour's love," the direct result of his encounter with Walker "when he was only twelve years old."[3] In return, she bound him to Quakerism and imprinted Christianity in his heart.

Quinn's support and defense of Walker's religious beliefs provoked his father to disown him. Quinn fled and emigrated from Honduras in Central America. After making friends among the sailors, he was able to obtain passage first to Gibraltar, then to Sheffield England, where he came to the attention of Elias Hicks's brother. According to most sources, Quinn came to North America in the early 1800s as a result of that encounter. Elias Hicks, founder of the Hicksite sect of radical antislavery Quakers, brought the young man to his home in Jericho, Long Island, New York, but few details survive.[4]

Hicks would have been among Quinn's first antislavery mentors. According to Hicks's biographers, nothing aroused his passion more "than the absolute necessity to utterly eradicate slavery and to acknowledge the full humanity of 'the Africans and their descendants.' Half-measures were intolerable—he would accept nothing less than immediate emancipation."[5] Foreshadowing present-day demands, Hicks called for full compensation for the lives and stolen labor devoured by slavery. He advocated for the recognition of the humanity and full equality of African Americans and for sufficient training that would allow the freed men and women the ability to support themselves and their families with dignity. In Quinn's early days in the United States, he may have absorbed Hicks's teachings while he lived with him on Long Island.[6]

After a short stay among the New York Quakers, Quinn moved on to Cecil County, Maryland. Here he confronted the country's northeastern realities of servitude, perhaps for the first time. Quinn barely escaped kidnappers, whose intent undoubtedly was to sell him into slavery farther south. Kidnapping was rampant. Cecil County, so close to the Pennsylvania border, was notorious for the practice. After this early threat of danger, the aspirant fled into Pennsylvania. The near miss taught Quinn an important lesson—caution was always necessary for the traveling minister of color, particularly in the slaveholding states.[7]

In 1808, under the guidance of Bro. Collins in New Hope, Bucks County, Pennsylvania, Quinn worked toward a religious vocation through the White-led Methodist Episcopal denomination. For the next two years, Bro. Collins taught and befriended the religious seeker. In subsequent years Collins helped Quinn obtain his exhorter's license to act as a lay minister, for the Methodist Episcopal Church in 1812, launching Quinn toward his life's calling as a Methodist minister. He divided his time between laboring as a lumberjack and ministering as a local exhorter in nearby towns. With this first step, Quinn began fulfilling his ambitions within the Methodist Episcopal ranks before aligning with the AME Connection.[8]

Quinn's religious path parallels those of other early African American spiritual leaders alive at the time. He, like they, began in the Methodist Episcopal denomination as an exhorter. Officially, Black men who served as licensed exhorters in the local Methodist Episcopal Church ministered only to fellow Black members by holding prayer meetings and performing other nonpastoral duties. Exhorters attended local prayer meetings in churches and private homes. They were expected to arouse nonbelievers and those who had strayed through public prayer and exhortations. They needed zeal for faith-filled, emotional, and intense prayers that could quickly evoke conversion and church attendance.

More than any other group, African Americans swelled the membership rolls of the Methodists, one of America's principal denominations. Unraveling the relationship between early Methodism and its members of color lays the foundation for understanding the origins of the AME denomination. The Methodist Episcopal Church evolved from the old Wesleyan movement, which grew in England and America in the eighteenth century and initially took a clear antislavery stand.

The abiding concern that early White preachers showed for the spiritual lives of Black people accounted for the dedicated support they received from people of color. Early White Methodist preachers were convinced that all stood in need of God's saving grace, and they actively sought Black converts. Whenever possible, Black churchgoers contributed what they could to maintain societies and classes, often working in little gardens until midnight to earn extra money to give to Methodist preachers. The evangelical style and intense Bible-based preaching of the Methodists, when added to their concern for the souls of Black folks, explains why Methodism so appealed to African worshippers.

However, Methodist Episcopal Church policies did not permit Black preachers to speak directly to or systematically treat biblical texts. Whites were sanctioned to become full ministers with wide-ranging priestly responsibilities and to preach at African American religious gatherings. The Methodists did provide some limited precious opportunities for people of color to preach and exercise their homiletical gifts, which few other denominations offered.

This attracted Quinn, who labored among the Methodist Episcopalians.[9] As the paternalism of the racially restrictive church grew increasingly unbearable for Quinn, however, his dissatisfaction mounted, and his zeal eroded under the caustic effects of racial prejudice within that denomination. Methodist Episcopalians generally refused to permit the ordination of Black exhorters to deacons or elders in the church. These were among the church policies that Quinn found galling and that drove AME founder Richard Allen out of the White-led church in 1787. Allen moved ahead that year, establishing, along with Absalom Jones, first the Free African Society and then Bethel Church in Philadelphia.

However, a little-known rule allowed Methodist Episcopal bishops to ordain "local deacons of our African brethren" in those places where Black preachers, such as Allen and Baltimore's Daniel Coker, had built a house of worship.[10] Due to Southern opposition, the rule was never published. The ruling allowed Bishop Asbury to ordain Richard Allen on June 11, 1799. Allen became the first Black preacher ever ordained in the Methodist Episcopal Church.[11] From the inception of the Methodist Episcopal Church in America (1784) until about the 1860s, as few as eight or nine men of color had received ordination. Despite the Methodist Episcopal Church's decision to license Black preachers, its paternalism and racism remained, fueling the movement toward an independent Black church.

Allen continued to work inside the Methodist Episcopal denomination, organizing and working within the Methodist circles that Blacks had formed. Allen observed that "many of the Colored people in other places were in a situation nearly like those of Philadelphia," where racial distinctions were the unchristian, unbrotherly acts of American religious life.[12] A number of White church organizations had stooped to the racial injustices and slaveholding demands of Southern enslavers.[13] Though African Methodists may have found the Methodist Episcopalians' early stance against slavery encouraging, the links between Black ministers and the mother church frayed and then snapped under the growing racial discontent of its Black membership, particularly in the Northern states.

Quinn's future religious path was set in motion in Philadelphia when the situation grew to a breaking point in 1787. Under the influence of Richard Allen, then a local free Black preacher in the Methodist Episcopal Church, and also Absalom Jones, African American membership in Philadelphia's St. George's Church increased dramatically. White members of the congregation, incensed by the growing number of Black congregants in their midst, were quick to announce that their worshipful brethren were in the way. Church historians noted expressions of hostility toward the Black believers among them. Church members removed Black congregants from their regular seats and "officers passed a rule compelling their colored members to sit but one in a pew, and that next to the wall."[14] To the consternation of their White brethren, Black members refused to be discouraged, and the outer ring of the church "soon began to be lined with colored members."[15] Black congregants who worshipped at St. George's Church were then relegated to sit at the back of the church. One writer stated that church members forced members of color "to sit at the rear and participate partitioned off behind wooden screens; the former bondsmen were compelled to observe the services by peeping through eyeholes and not approach the communion table until all whites had been served."[16] Next in this deteriorating situation and escalating racial struggle came the order banishing Black celebrants from the sanctuary. The sexton met African American churchgoers at the door and informed them they had to remove themselves upstairs to the dusty gallery for worship services. From that perch far removed from the altar of God, as Bishop Wayman later recounted, they were required to serve the Lord quietly, "for not an amen" could be uttered by "that sable band."[17]

This mistreatment the Black congregants tried to endure. People of color had recently subscribed to refurbish the church. But these churchgoers could not abide the final indignation directed toward Richard Allen's old friend and fellow preacher Absalom Jones, the first ordained Black Episcopal priest in America. Jones had not been long on his knees when he heard "considerable scuffling and low talking."[18] One of the White trustees physically assaulted the kneeling, praying Jones, dragging him up off his knees, pulling him to his feet, and telling him not to kneel there, Allen remembered.

"You must get up—you must not kneel here!" demanded the trustee.

"Wait until the prayer is over, and I will get up and trouble you no more," Jones responded, measuring his words.

But the trustee beckoned for assistance in helping pull Jones to his feet. In a strike for dignity and self-respect, Allen and Jones led the Black worshippers out of the church and toward their destiny. "We all went out of the church in a body, and they were no more plagued with us in the church," Allen reported.[19] Two congregations emerged: The Bethel African Methodist Episcopal Church, led by Richard Allen, and the African Church of St. Thomas (Episcopal), led by Absalom Jones.

Crossing the line where submission ends and resistance begins, Black believers refused to take a back seat in the sanctuary of the Lord or consent to the passive surrender of their religious rights as the Methodist Episcopal Church members had demanded. One protestant minister warned of "the evil demon of . . . religious discord."[20] In the widening breach of spreading discontent, Black churchgoers linked their religious rights to their civil rights and withdrew from the mother church. Historian Gary Nash and many others recognize the moment the first free Black church in the United States planted "the seed of a [B]lack Christianity unregulated by ecclesiastic authorities and relatively free from the social and psychological domination of white churches."[21] Under the leadership of future AME Bishops and clergy with the support of the laity, this act of "self-assertiveness," as Nash describes it, "signaled the pivotal role" the church would assume in the life of both free and enslaved African Americans.[22]

Richard Allen and Absalom Jones, together with the small band from St. George's Church, formed the Free African Society three decades before the formal beginnings of the AME denomination. The group of dissenters met first in a blacksmith shop that Allen had purchased and then moved to Sixth and Lombard Street in Philadelphia. This society, along with similar congregations taking hold in the eastern United States, formed the embryonic moments of the independent Black church movement that Quinn would help lead.

As Allen sent forth preachers from the AME mother church—Bethel in Philadelphia—Quinn embarked on an itinerant's path that would define his life in Christ and bind the foundations of the church. The success of Bethel as it grew from forty to four hundred members in 1810 angered but also worried White Methodist preachers. Allen's insistence on controlling his own church and owning the land enraged them. White Methodists attempted to take over Bethel.

In a bold move, Allen took the Methodists to court in 1808 and, again, in 1815 to establish Bethel's right to exist independently, free from the control of interfering Methodist Episcopalians. He lost the first lawsuit, which allowed the sale of Allen's hard-won Bethel church, which was built on the land he had purchased. Allen was furious but productive, quickly mounting a well-financed campaign. Relying on good financial planning and solid fundraising, he raised the $10,125—more than $200,000 in today's currency—necessary to buy back the very church he had built and the ground on which it stood.[23] After an eight-year court battle, Allen won the denomination's right to control its fate as an institution independent of White Methodist ownership or supervision. This explains the eight years Quinn itinerated for the Methodist Episcopal denomination and the thirty-year span between the creation of the Free African Society and the formal establishment of the AME Church.

Now the work of organizing the AME denomination could begin in earnest, moving forward with power and confidence, unencumbered by legal troubles and meddling Whites. As the founder of the denomination, Allen became the guiding spirit in the interstate religious organization, as well as the mastermind behind local expansion. After being "vexed, harassed, and embarrassed" for more than a quarter century, notes one church historian, the African Methodists were realizing their yearslong struggle for religious freedom.[24]

Seventeen years after Bishop Francis Asbury had ordained Allen as a local deacon in the White-governed Methodist Episcopal denomination, Allen hosted the first conference of the African Methodist Connection in the United States, held at Bethel Church in Philadelphia. Quinn was there from the beginning. Bro. Collins, Quinn's spiritual father, brought the young acolyte to Philadelphia to bear witness to the birth of African Methodism in April 1816. Richard Allen was determined to unite the five independent branches of African Methodism in existence at the time. Allen organized a general convention of people of color, summoning sixteen preachers from independent African Methodist churches in Baltimore, Maryland; Wilmington, Delaware; Attleboro, Pennsylvania; and Salem, New Jersey, hoping they would unite and join the new AME Connection. Baltimore sent the largest delegation.

The mature, established, and well-respected heads of the various churches and denominations gathered to consider Allen's plan to consolidate into one African Methodist Episcopal denomination. The men deliberated for three consecutive days. Whenever Quinn came into the company of these early organizers, they noted his "tireless zeal among his fellow-workers in the vineyard of the Lord." All seemed struck by Quinn's youthfulness at the time; the old men spoke of Quinn "as making himself generally useful at the convention though not a member"—something church historians would also report. Quinn's friend and later personal secretary, John Mifflin (J. M.) Brown, recounts the story that Quinn's "standing position against one of the pillars of the church when he first came in attracted general attention"; Quinn's pleasant looks and manners drew notice and remarks from many of the old men present, "whose hearts were at once drawn toward him."[25]

As "the door-keeper," the neophyte filled the orders to "furnish the Convention daily with twelve bottles of cider, nine pounds of cheese and a peck of crackers," recount church historians.[26] Conventioneers would take their food with them as they remained in session until the day's business was completed. The limited number of available eating places, inns, and boardinghouses added significance to Quinn's role in helping to feed and sustain the members of the convention, enabling them to focus on the task at hand. It also kept him in contact with them and in the outer ring of their orbit.[27]

Baltimore's Rev. Daniel Coker, one of the most distinguished men at the convention, joined Allen in founding African Methodism. After fleeing slavery in Frederick County, Maryland, in his early teens, Coker escaped to New York City, where he had joined the Methodist Church before returning to Maryland. Francis Asbury ordained Coker a deacon in the Methodist Episcopal Church in 1802, making him the first Black licensed minister in Baltimore. There he led the African Methodist Bethel Society, one of the largest independent prayer meetings represented among those that had gathered with Allen. Coker had planted many of the Black churches in Baltimore.[28]

Like Allen's congregation, Coker's large independent African American congregation withdrew entirely from the White Methodist Church and purchased a church of their own. At the time, Coker and Allen were in frequent contact. Representing his Baltimore church, Coker came to Philadelphia to combine with Allen and the other independent church leaders to form a single denomination. The literate Coker drafted the convention resolutions. Black Methodists of the new denomination initially designated both Daniel Coker and Richard Allen as their first bishops and their national leaders. Allen had not been present on the day of the nominations, but on his return the following day, he voiced his objection. Allen felt that there was no need for two bishops and offered to resign. Coker instead decided to decline the office, and after a second election in April 1816, Allen was elected bishop.[29]

No record of the first convention's proceedings survive. However, church historians sought living witnesses, such as Quinn, who was comparatively young at the time, to provide the names of the sixteen men who participated at this historic gathering. Quinn reliably reported the names of all participants.[30] The young preacher aligned with Bishop Allen's plan for the extension of the AME denomination into new fields and for its consolidation into an effective organization. But not all independent Black Methodists came together to join with AME. Some, such as the Black Methodists in New York and Delaware, remained independent denominations.

During this time of great magnetism for African Methodism, other seekers, such as Jarena Lee, were drawn to it. Assured that she had received a command from God to preach the gospel, Lee was the first known woman to petition the church for a license to preach in 1809, before the formal organization of the denomination. She attributed her conversion to a sermon preached by Richard Allen. Lee again approached Allen for a license to preach in 1817. Her powerful evangelizing convinced Allen, who directed her to hold prayer meetings and to preach, saying she was a woman of God. She traveled with Allen for a time, receiving speaking appointments in several Pennsylvania congregations. Ultimately, Lee exhorted and journeyed alone or in the company of other women to evangelical meetings across the Northeastern United States, but she never received an official license to preach.[31]

This new African Methodism, which Allen embodied and Collins espoused, attracted Jarena Lee and offered Quinn opportunities to fully express his capacity and ambition. He seized the chance to lead. One of the first four men to join the church at the outset, Quinn began his journey when the denomination was confined largely to the East Coast. He and the other AME circuit riders followed the approach and new preaching style of the founder of Methodism, John Wesley. Astride his horse with a Bible under his arm, Quinn fully adopted the practices of the founding ministers.

African Methodism thrived under Allen's leadership. Quinn abandoned the Methodist Episcopal denomination and obtained a license to preach among the African Methodists, although the national organization had yet to formally organize. Bro. Collins, who had converted at the first general class ever held by African Methodists prior to the official formation of the AME denomination, proved an effective mentor. Quinn's spiritual father had walked throughout Ohio, preaching the gospel and planting new societies, before returning to preach in West Chester, Pennsylvania. Collins's stories had captured Quinn's attention and may have ignited his longing for the American West. Bro. Collins had seen something in young Quinn. Even in his youth, Quinn's presence commanded attention.[32]

Collins, preaching at what appears to have been a camp meeting in East Point, initially attracted Quinn to Methodism. In addition to the use of circuit riders, Methodists were among the first denominations to organize outdoor religious worship by introducing camp meetings as a spiritual practice, particularly on the American frontier. In more rural settings, revival meetings, such as the famous Cane Ridge Revival, brought together thousands who sang, shouted, and wept their way to salvation. Camp meetings stirred religious fervor in Black participants as well as in their White counterparts. For many worshippers, revivals inspired their first moments of religious devotion. But in the formative years, faithful Black believers seeking salvation suffered through segregated camp meetings as well as segregated churches (see fig. 1.1). Separate meetings began at least as early as the 1780s.[33]

In 1818, six years after the young itinerant first united with the denomination, Richard Allen ordained him a deacon. Deacon Quinn introduced the first camp meeting of the new AME Connection, holding it in the woods in Bensalem, Bucks County, Pennsylvania, in August of that year, two years before the Bensalem church on Bridgewater Road was erected. The camp meeting was established under the supervision of Bishop Allen, who attended the revival.[34] Quinn led the conversion of nearly one hundred souls.[35]

Quinn, always willing to work across denominational divides, met noted Black abolitionist and founder of the First African Presbyterian Church, minister John Gloucester, at that Bensalem revival meeting. Gloucester let Quinn and Rev. David Smith know that Blacks in Reading, Pennsylvania,

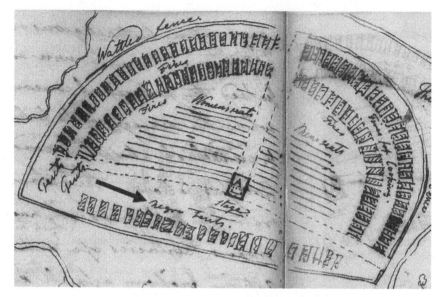

Figure 1.1 Drawing of Latrobe's "Plan of a Camp Meeting." *Note* the arrow (center left) pointing to "Negro Tents," behind the stage. Camp meetings were segregated before African American denominations separated to form their own churches and camp meetings. The sketch depicts the layout of a Methodist camp meeting in Fairfax, Virginia, in 1809. One caption (not shown) reads, "In all there were about 150 tents in the theatre, & perhaps 30 tents & huts of the Negroes." Such racial segregation prompted Black Methodists to withdraw from the denomination a few years later to form their own independent African Methodist churches. A fugitive slave ad in a local newspaper identifies the Fairfax camp meeting, as well as others, as the start of many escapes from slavery. *Journal of Benjamin Latrobe, August 23, 1806–August 8, 1809,* Courtesy of Maryland Center for History and Culture, Library, Special Collections, MS 2009.

were ready to form their own church. The pair of itinerants followed up on Gloucester's suggestion, quickly bringing together the Reading African Society. Later known as the Bethel AME Church of Reading, it, too, would earn a reputation for its Underground Railroad activism. The Bensalem church remains among the oldest in the denomination and traces its origins to Quinn's seminal camp meeting.[36] Deacon Quinn would return to such lovefests—camp meetings or revivals—time and again.

He gravitated to this expressive religious experience throughout his ministry. In the earliest days of the Methodist Episcopal Church, much-anticipated camp meetings offered effective inroads for reaching and converting souls in rural areas. Quinn was able to fully express his captivating preaching style. His powerful sermons at camp meetings brought scores of worshippers to Christ. Outdoor revivals lent themselves to his oratory gift; his powerful singing voice cut through the air. Poetic, melodic hymns, some written by Richard Allen, helped spread Methodist theology among the prayerful, many of whom could neither read nor write. Repeatedly, Quinn would turn to Allen's *Collection of Spiritual Songs and Hymns*. The aspiring preacher could express the multiple facets of his chanted preaching style—exhorting, preaching, and singing—perhaps all at the same time. His own religious depth inspired the devout and roused the doubters.[37]

Camp meetings, usually held in August or September, became a widespread practice. Christians within the various denominations, as well as the curious and unaffiliated, gathered for multiple days of preaching, exhortations, prayer, Bible studies, and socializing. The ministers were hopeful that exhortation and supplication would inspire conversions and baptisms. Families traveled for miles to camp in tents and wagons in shady groves. A central area was generally set aside for the meetings. Ministers and circuit-riding preachers, often with the help of deacons and exhorters, led the gatherings.

A typical day began at dawn with a trumpet blare signaling the time to rise, then prayer in family groups and breakfast. By 8:30 a.m. another trumpet signal brought participants together to begin prayer and testimonials, followed by the main service and sermon of the day. Hymn singing, small sermons, pastoral counseling, and prayer, followed by gatherings around bonfires, lent an emotional and dramatic backdrop to the spirited singing and testimonials. At the day's end, visitors left reluctantly, and participants retired to their tents and wagons for individual and family prayers. The day ended as it had begun, with a blast of the trumpet. The four- or five-day meetings culminated with emotional preaching and baptisms.[38]

Camp meetings were intended to awaken and convert the sinners present. Powerful preaching, drama, and emotional appeal would bring on weeping, wailing, and shouts of joy. Early preachers found in Methodism "an uninhibited freedom of expression which allowed them to shout, dance, sing, preach, pray, and testify when moved by the power of the Holy Spirit," explains one historian.[39] The convocations doubled as social events, adding a festive tone to the spiritual jubilation. The sincerity of expression at Methodist camp meetings and the mesmerizing, soul-stirring effect of rousing preachers appealed to African Americans and their growing sense of religious freedom.

Oftentimes, African American religious camp meetings offered fertile opportunities for physical as well as spiritual liberation. But advertisements seeking the return of fugitives from slavery trained suspicious eyes on camp meetings. An enslaved Missouri woman, for example, who had contemplated escape for several years, finally left for Canada with her husband and son after attending such a service. "[I] made a long camp-meeting of it," she reported and never returned.⁴⁰ When thirteen- or fourteen-year-old Augustus escaped from Hampton Mansion in Towson, Maryland, enslaver John Ridgely noted the teenager's green jacket and corduroy pantaloons in the advertisement. He speculated about the youngster's intentions: "[I] am induced to think he may have been taken off by some of the persons attending the colored camp meeting in the neighborhood which broke up the day after" his escape.⁴¹ Escape ads warned about camp meetings: "[They] left home together to go to Camp Meeting," "It is likely she has gone to the Colored Camp Meeting," and "[She] probably made for the Upper Camp Meeting on her way for the State of Delaware"; one advertisement even advised that "the most probable method to catching him . . . will be at Methodist meetings."⁴²

Camp meetings provided one avenue of escape. Quinn reported holding seventeen camp meetings during his years as a circuit rider. Decades later the *Indianapolis Recorder* left a vivid account of Quinn's preaching. He "was the greatest power in encouraging and helping" African Americans with their burdens. "His power as a preacher in the camp meeting age was felt by all classes of people, for all people crowded his meetings."⁴³

Throughout his ministry, Quinn encouraged fugitivity. The young preacher's lifelong hatred of slavery and injustice fueled his association with the Black church and with the Underground Railroad Movement, another pathway to freedom. Quinn and the Underground Railroad stations he supported operated as sanctuaries for freedom seekers before the movement earned its name. According to local tradition, New Hope, one of Quinn's early charges, functioned as an important haven for escaping slavery at the end of the Underground Railroad line, in Bucks County. Here fugitives crossed the Delaware River into New Jersey to continue their journey north. Quinn most likely learned the inner workings and closely held secrets of escaping slavery during this initial period of his ascending career.

Circuit riders like Quinn, who carried the gospel from place to place in early America, were especially effective in the remote and rugged American frontier. As one writer suggests, these itinerants could turn "a field forest or tent into a temple of God."⁴⁴ Preaching in the open air, exhorters delivered the message of individual redemption in language understandable to the humblest of listeners. Under the AME banner, Quinn, the new exhorter, traveled to eastern Pennsylvania, New Jersey, Delaware, Maryland, and the District of Columbia. Later he entered New York City.

All these factors contributed to the growth and appeal of African Methodism. By 1797, ten years after its introduction, Black Methodism had attracted 12,215 members. Between 1800 and 1815, the number of Black Methodists representing all the denominations, including those that had not joined with

Allen, doubled from twenty thousand to over forty thousand, representing nearly one-third of the American Methodist population at the time. In the quarter century after the American Revolution, all of Methodism grew at a phenomenal rate, reaching a quarter million congregants by 1820, then a half million by 1830. The Methodist and Baptist churches were the largest evangelical denominations. Although John Gloucester organized the First African Presbyterian Church in Philadelphia in 1807, not all Black Presbyterians separated from the mother church, even when they had their separate houses of worship. Quakerism also contributed to the religious development of these early AME preachers, particularly Allen and Quinn. However, "the evangelical style and ethos of Methodism" held greater attraction "than the quiet and mystical character of Quakerism," AME Church historian Dennis Dickerson emphasizes.[45]

Although the Methodist itinerancy can claim responsibility for the phenomenal spread and development of the denomination by bringing "the greatest good to the greatest number" of people, as one observer has stressed, the pastorate is the office that is consistently nearest to the daily lives of the people, "for whose benefit Methodism was primarily intended."[46] The itinerant system delivered intermittent spiritual help whenever and wherever needed.

Adhering to Methodist origins and traditions, Quinn and the early AME preachers reached out to the dispossessed, the forgotten, and the oppressed. This new religion encouraged deep feelings of a personal relationship with God without ceremony, making Wesley's message accessible to everyone. Methodism's spectacular rise, due in part to circuit riders traveling from plantation to plantation and settlement to settlement, thrived on the message of salvation for both enslaved and enslavers.

Methodism offered Quinn freedom to preach in the open air, in the homes of the faithful, and on riverbanks, as well as in houses of prayer. One historian acknowledges that the traveling preacher could build "a special rapport with his temporary audience."[47] Quinn took those temporary audiences, molded them into prayer societies, and then organized them into congregations that built the churches that brought great stability to the denomination.

The AME Church adopted the episcopal office of the Episcopalians, but aligned with the Methodists' structure, particularly its itinerancy system. As such AME would be under the authority of bishops who sustained their lineage and authority through ordination from within. Following the Methodist Episcopal denomination, AME meeting structure calls for quarterly, annual, and quadrennial meetings. Every four years, the AME Church assembles for the General Conference, the supreme body of the denomination. Bishops, delegates, and leaders are charged with the responsibility to discuss, debate, and pass significant legislation impacting the mission and ministry of the church. This quadrennial assembly convenes for the purpose of conducting the church's legislative business, financial reporting, and election of bishops. The motto of the Salem Chapel in St. Catharines, Canada, best captures the AME Church philosophy: "We are Christian in our belief, Methodist in our approach and Episcopal in our organization."[48] And to that one could add, "African in our origin and identity." Quinn lived by the guiding words of Bishop Allen and the denomination: "God Our Father, Christ Our Redeemer, Man Our Brother."[49]

The growth and geographical expansion of African Methodism coincided with a rise in demand by Black protestants for full integration into the Christian community and the right to exercise authority within their own congregations. Until the Denmark Vesey conspiracy of 1822 (discussed later) put a stop to it, there was a distinct movement among large urban Black churches toward the creation of separate churches in the South as well as the North.[50]

Despite the move toward African Methodism, enslavers often demanded that many enslaved Black worshippers remain under the control of the White-led Methodist Episcopal Church. Fearing a split from the Southern church, leaders from the Northern branches of the church retreated from the strong stance against slavery that the denomination espoused in its early years. The political issues of slavery would drive the splintering of the Methodist Church in the mid-nineteenth century. Staunch abolitionists, unable to prevent the breakup, helped establish the Wesleyan Methodist and the Free Methodist Churches, both of which were especially active in working on the Underground Railroad.

Long before this nation devolved into the Civil War over slavery, the social and religious battle raged inside America's churches. One religious historian recognizes Methodism as an integral part of "a gradual unfolding of the process of emancipation."[51] Another wrote that "Allen's church served as a model of Black self-reliance and resiliency in a hostile white world, as well as a purer application of brotherly love."[52]

Theologian James Cone affirms that "The Black Church was founded on the belief that God condemned slavery and that Christian freedom meant political emancipation."[53] Black Methodism began as both a protest and a program that taught its members not to submit to slavery or its effects. The organizers profited from lessons learned during the turbulent founding of the denomination as well as the founding of the country. They understood the persecution of the early ministers of Methodism, the colonists' fight for freedom from tyranny during the War for Independence, and the effects of slavery in the United States. Four years after the end of the War of 1812, the revolutionary sentiments arising from the war's conclusion continued to resonate deeply with enslaved and free Blacks.

Building on AME's guiding liberatory principles, J. M. Brown described Quinn's dedication not only to the sacred mission of the church but also to its secular obligation. Quinn upheld the special purpose of the church: assisting in "relieving the African race from their physical, mental and moral bondage . . . determined to do all in his power to weaken the stronghold of the oppressor."[54] The Lord had sent him to "bind up the brokenhearted, to proclaim liberty to the captives and the opening of the prison to those who are bound."[55]

Quinn found within the doctrine of the church a marriage between his love of Christ, his commitment to freedom, and his love of people of color, enslaved or free. Richard Allen had traveled a mighty path from former slave to his unanimous election as AME's inaugural denominational bishop. Quinn's journey took him from youthful immigrant to deacon in 1818, then to elder and, finally, to senior bishop.

CHAPTER 2

The Circuit Rider and the Underground Railroad

1817–1824

On Christmas Day 1817, a mere eight months after the official formation of the Connection at the Philadelphia conference, Paul Quinn joined as an itinerant preacher (see fig. 2.1). Led by Bishop Allen, Quinn and five

Figure 2.1 Rt. Rev. William Paul Quinn in His Prime. Courtesy of New York Public Library.

intrepid itinerants moved from town to town, village to village, preaching the ideas learned from Bishop Allen: freedom to soul, mind, and body. They spread the gospel, which was infused with Allen's doctrine of "Christian equality, freedom and self-government."[1]

Crossing the Allegheny Mountains, the evangelists traveled along the Monongahela Valley, stopping at Brownsville, Uniontown, and Washington, Pennsylvania.[2] Quinn alone was a circuit rider. Allen, David Smith, and Collins had done this work largely on foot, first as Methodist Episcopal preachers, then later with AME. But young Quinn led the new denomination the modern way: on horseback. Half-wild, bucking, pawing-the-earth broncos were his preference. According to Welch, a sketch could be written about his horses alone. Benjamin Tanner called him "one of the glorious seven who made up at the beginning the whole strength of our itinerating forces.[3]

After the Philadelphia conference in 1818, Quinn demonstrated his true abilities as a worker and organizer. His talents began to unfold with his initial success in laying out the circuit in Bucks County, Pennsylvania. Once adopted, the itinerant system helped the church reach deep into the rural recesses of Pennsylvania's rugged backcountry as well as the urban back alleyways of cities like Philadelphia, to elevate spirits and rescue souls. Quinn found the people in their communities, converted them, and brought them over to the new AME denomination.

The young itinerant kept an impossible pace as he moved tirelessly across the country, always managing to find work as a lumberman when funds ran short. Quinn gathered people living in small Black communities, such as Frederick, Maryland, and Carlisle, Chambersburg, and Shippensburg, Pennsylvania, into prayer societies. In later decades Underground Railroad activists would use these previously established pathways, which often coincided with AME circuits, as escape routes to freedom. Frederick Maryland's Bethel church congregation (later renamed Quinn Chapel) remembers itself as an Underground Railroad "safe house." All three Pennsylvania towns on the circuit lie along interconnected Underground Railroad routes in South Central Pennsylvania.[4]

Towns either had or developed connections to the Underground Railroad and escape from slavery. Howard Wallace, a sixty-year member of the AME Church, penned *Historical Sketch of the Underground Railroad from Uniontown to Pittsburgh*, depicting two major Quinn strongholds. Wallace affirmed that by the 1840s, a recognized escape route out of slavery began in Uniontown and ended in Pittsburgh, where he had physically helped move freedom seekers through. The route undoubtedly developed decades earlier. The author mentions Brownsville, another initial circuit station, as part of the route.[5]

Early churches, such as Frederick's Bethel, occupied a simple log cabin. Humble beginnings in cabins, homes, and blacksmith shops did not herald the mighty future that awaited the denomination. Planting the seeds of Methodism consumed its missionaries. The turmoil and uncertainty that accompanied the missions of the first ministers prepared them to act boldly and decisively as they rose through church hierarchy and battled the demons of racial oppression.

While Allen bound together the church in Philadelphia and Quinn worked in rural outposts, Morris Brown, another true giant of the church, was leading a movement for an independent church for Africans in Charleston, South Carolina. Brown first encountered Quinn when the denomination was in its infancy. Brown stood at least six feet and was "well proportioned, but not corpulent."[6] He would play a major role throughout Quinn's religious life, rescuing the young itinerant at what would be perhaps his lowest moment of despair.

Both Quinn and Morris Brown attended the second convening of the denomination in Baltimore. With no house of worship to shelter the city's burgeoning congregation, members gathered in a home in a room set aside for church activities. Quinn represented Baltimore. Brown traveled there representing his large and flourishing Methodist Episcopal congregation, located in and around Charleston. The South Carolinian came to the conference prepared to bring into the fold one of the most important cities in the nation for the fledgling denomination (after Philadelphia and Baltimore).[7]

Brown stood out as one of the most active clergymen of the meeting. Allen had ordained him deacon at the Philadelphia Annual Conference the year earlier, then elevated him to elder during this Baltimore conference.[8] Brown managed to evade the travel obstacles South Carolina had imposed on Blacks so that he could attend religious gatherings in Baltimore and Philadelphia. With Allen's blessing, Morris Brown returned to Charleston after the convention and emerged as the spiritual light to the thousands who had withdrawn from the Charleston Methodist Episcopal Church over poor treatment and racial strife. Once back in South Carolina, however, Brown and his Charleston church suffered scrutiny and harassment for their antislavery radicalism. A major conspiracy swirled around his church, which altered the relationship between AME and the Southern state, landing Brown on the critical path to Quinn's success.

As a newly ordained elder, Morris Brown would deliver a crown jewel to the Connection by organizing three thousand members of his greater Charleston congregation into an AME church (now known as Mother Emanual)—easily the largest Black Methodist congregation in the Deep South.[9] Brown proved an effective organizer, and the congregation quickly outranked Baltimore as the second-largest concentration of African Methodists in the country. Thousands of members, both enslaved and free, soon appeared on membership rolls. Undaunted by the serious opposition, personal threats, and danger of bodily harm or loss of life that confronted these missionaries, Brown and Quinn remained determined to spread the doctrine of the church throughout the country and to penetrate into the South whenever and wherever they found an opening.

By 1820 South Carolina had prohibited the emancipation of enslaved persons within its borders. Whites in Charleston discovered that Brown had secretly pooled money to buy the freedom of enslaved church members. The offense cost the minister a year in jail. To Whites, Morris Brown's church came to represent the dangers they found so alarming in the independent Black church in the slaveholding South.

After leaving one of Charleston's segregated churches, Denmark Vesey, one of Brown's class teachers, found the freedom to preach his radical beliefs. In his role as class leader, Vesey preached to a small group of Black Charlestonians in his home at night during the week—unsupervised by Whites, as the law required. Vesey scholars acknowledge that he had "a pronounced religious dimension to his character."[10] The literate Vesey is reported to have espoused a radical and new liberation theology quoting the Old Testament. He relied on Exodus 21:16 to warn against kidnapping the people and selling them into slavery. Vesey taught the instructions for warfare given in Deuteronomy 20, the Bible verse where God orders the armies of Joshua to kill every male occupant in the cities of Canaan, sparing no one, including women and children: "You shall let nothing that breathes remain alive."[11]

Vesey and his allies allegedly were planning an insurrection in Charleston, which included recruiting other rebels from AME rolls. How much did Morris Brown know about Vesey's activities? Vesey's biographer, Douglas Egerton, maintains that Brown "must have been aware that *something* of great importance was being discussed.[12] Brown may not have known specifically that Vesey, as the class leader he himself had appointed, was using the wrath and vengeance of the Old Testament to fan the flames of insurrection, though Brown's ignorance seems unlikely. Former AME historiographer Dennis Dickerson, in the recent history of the AME Church, makes a strong argument that Brown, in fact, knew.[13]

By June 1822 Vesey leapt into action. Among other arguments, he supported the need for immediate revolt, urging the rebel members of the AME congregation to join the uprising by reminding them of their own former church, saying, "[It had been] shut up so that we could not use it, and that it was high time for us to seek our rights."[14] Their doomed and ultimately betrayed plot was to burn down the city of Charleston in advance of a massive, coordinated uprising that would liberate the enslaved people and slaughter the city's White population. Then in the aftermath, they planned to escape to Haiti. The well-formulated plot was ultimately betrayed, sunk in part by a recruitment process that assumed the enslaved were equally enraged by their bondage. Vesey and thirty-four others were tried and executed. Much of what is known came from the trial rather than from Vesey himself.[15]

After the executions, Charleston Whites exiled the African Church leaders and, turning their anger upon the site they thought had served as a meeting place for the conspiracy, razed the African Methodist Church and burned the sanctuary to the ground. The remaining 1,400-member, largely enslaved congregation was either destroyed or driven into hiding. Panicked local officials again reverted to strict enforcement of old laws, forbidding Black assembly and imposing other repressive measures.

Morris Brown, given fifteen days to leave the state, fled Charleston. He rushed to Philadelphia and avoided prosecution on the charge of conspiracy. Bishop Allen quickly embraced him and began lifting up the South Carolinian, now safe inside the sanctuary of the newly formed AME Church. Years later this "open, sweet, benevolent" man would prove to be an invaluable asset to the church, plus an important ally for Quinn.[16]

Quinn had no connection with the Charleston uprising and crackdown; instead, during this time, he continued to push the AME denomination into the South and other slaveholding states. He would eventually enter Kentucky, Missouri, and Louisiana, although the denomination would not be a force in South Carolina again until after the Civil War. AME managed to take hold and flourish in these hostile climates. Despite the wariness of Southern Whites, Paul Quinn would grow in power, prominence, and influence in their region.

Reflecting the breadth of now-deacon Quinn's ministry, large crowds of worshippers flocked to hear him preach. David Smith reported Quinn was already considered a great figure in the AME movement. Although "he was not very learned, he was both witty and talented, and these endowments enabled him to accomplish much in the behalf of the Church."[17] J. P. Q. Wallace's article "Unique Biographical Sketch of a Pioneer Missionary" offered a glimpse into Quinn's preaching style: He possessed "a remarkable memory for Bible verses," which he quoted at length. "He preached with great deliberation; there was no trace of foreign accent in his speech." His "clear, full, and rich voice" was one of Quinn's important assets. Its "great carrying power" made him "ideal in the open air where much of his preaching was done."[18] His voice and his rapid, eloquent speaking and preaching caught the attention of seekers. According to another observer, "He possessed large spiritual endowments."[19]

Quinn was literate, although many ministers, including Richard Allen and Morris Brown, struggled with limited literacy. Pastors effective at church administration and organization invented ways to uplift the spirits of their racially and otherwise beleaguered members. The minutes of the early conferences were written by Richard Allen's young teenage son and other scribes; Daniel Payne, a former schoolteacher and future bishop, served as Morris Brown's private secretary. Unlettered ministers relied on long, memorized passages of the Bible to awaken their followers. Quinn, always a firm friend to an educated ministry, realized that church-supported literacy, education, and schools would ensure the future of the denomination.

Quinn's energetic style took hold through the burning eloquence of his words of comfort. AME ministers spread more than the gospel—they carried the good news of Allen's liberation church. John Mifflin Brown (J. M.), Quinn's secretary and longtime friend, provided an intimate view of the man and ranked him among the "giants of the earth" of his day.[20] As Quinn's reputation as a preacher developed, everyone, Black and White, strove to hear him deliver the Word. If White men initially came to scoff at a preacher of color, they "went home inquiring the way of salvation," one AME historian explains.[21]

The deacon's talents were readily evident. The conversion of as many as two hundred souls gave some indication of the promise and ability that lay ahead. In those early days, the circuit rider's meteoric ascent dictated that he would not linger long as a local pastor before being reassigned. This becomes apparent to the observer as we move with him along his circuits. The first discipline instructed preachers "[on] visiting from house to house"—what to avoid and how to assist those under their care.[22] Another historian gives this comparison: "In the spirit of the apostles, who were sent out two by two . . . these colored ambassadors . . . left all to hunt up and unite the scattered colored members of the household of faith."[23]

Always pushing for the growth of the denomination, Allen sent missionaries to establish the first AME mission in New York City in 1818. The bishop's ambition was to bring New York, which had not joined with him at the outset, into the AME Connection in union with Philadelphia, Baltimore, and Charleston. By 1820 eight churches had been established to form the New York conference. A few years later, Allen would turn to Quinn, hoping he would bring great success to the endeavor. The church now reached eastward to New Bedford, Massachusetts; west to Pittsburgh; and as far south as Charleston, South Carolina. Conferences were held in Baltimore in April and at Richard Allen's home in Philadelphia in May.

Whenever these first long-traveling preachers returned to Philadelphia after miles of walking and riding, Allen's wife, Sarah, would be troubled by their bedraggled, seedy appearance. As was the custom in the early nineteenth century, the Allens housed the traveling ministers to the AME annual conferences at their Philadelphia home. After Mother Allen brought the "unbecoming appearance of these ministers" to the attention of the women of the church, they purchased homespun cloth. Sewing through the night, these faithful sisters fashioned suitable clothing for the trailblazers. Sarah Allen described the itinerant preachers as having "ventilators" in their elbows, knees, and "the seat[s] of their trousers." The "sewing brigade" remedied this condition by furnishing the missionaries with new pants and jackets.[24] The women ensured the itinerant force maintained a respectable appearance across the long distances they traveled in service of the Lord. Quinn, unlike his tattered fellow itinerants, would later be remembered for being plain and unadorned, even when dressed in the finest materials: broadcloth and fine-yet-simple boots and gloves. Especially striking was his "plug hat" made of the finest beaver skin.[25]

The circuits that took such a toll on the preachers and their clothing were on the verge of growing even larger. The Baltimore Conference had discussed extending the work of the AME Church to territories of the United States west of the Allegheny Mountains. Always with a vision toward expanding the denomination, Allen and his church leaders decided that this western territory should belong to the Philadelphia conference until it grew large enough to stand on its own as an independent district.[26]

Young deacon Quinn ventured west quite early in his ministerial career, although the definition of "the West" would shift with time. After Collins and other travelers returning from western Pennsylvania and Ohio regaled Quinn with stories of the freedom found there, the deacon resolved to go. J. M. Brown remembered that when Quinn "listened to reports of the land that lay beyond the mountains, his soul was aflame for conquest and victory."[27]

Riding his circuit, Quinn and AME kept pace with the country's westward expansion. At that time, Pittsburgh, sitting on the Allegheny Plateau, was considered the gateway to the West. Upon Quinn's first arrival in the city, he established a church in an old foundry and "set up the banner of the living

God."²⁸ Quinn revisited the city on multiple occasions throughout his life and in different ecclesiastical capacities. When he returned to the conference in Philadelphia in 1819, he gave a favorable report of all his accomplishments. Both Bishop Allen and the conference received the news with great joy.

The vast unchurched area beyond the Allegheny Mountains offered a rife field for missionaries, one where Quinn would eventually have his greatest impact and leave his legacy. Moving on his westward mission, the itinerant preacher traveled all along the valley of the Monongahela River, through the hills, slopes, and primitive forest of the Ohio and Mississippi valley. For many, the grueling work would have been a punishment. Quinn "delighted in riding his long and numerous circuits," his biographer declares.²⁹ Elaine Welch's description of Quinn leaves a colorful impression. Only severe cold weather drove him indoors. "He rode a horse like a centaur, expert as a cavalryman, daring and reckless. He cantered through hill and vale, singing the Songs of Zion, armed with a hymn book and Bible with dauntless courage, a firm belief in God."³⁰

The vast area Quinn covered in his travels required him to keep abreast of the differing racial policies and conventions he would encounter in the various states, towns, and communities he visited. Local realities and national politics forced him and the AME Church to navigate around slavery before the Civil War. On the political side, church leadership contended with the news that Congress had passed the Missouri Compromise. The law allowed Missouri to breach the Mason-Dixon Line and enter the Union as the northernmost slaveholding state. Also known as the Compromise of 1820, it laid the groundwork for the extension of slavery in the West. Until passage of the compromise, Congress had attempted to impose geographic limitations on slavery, intending to restrict the practice to south of the Mason-Dixon Line. Now the Missouri Compromise was introducing slavery into northern latitudes. The compromise prohibited slavery in all states north of the Mason-Dixon Line—with the exception of Missouri. The state stood out like a wart on the body politic.

Quinn would come to know Missouri and its support of slavery well as he helped move the denomination westward. Directly confronting the laws of the state, he and others began planting AME churches in Missouri. The state became the site of his future triumphs and arrests. As Quinn's authority increased, he helped ensure that the AME Church took hold in the newest slaveholding spaces, in the free states, and northward, into Canada, apace with the expanding nation.³¹

Deacon Quinn was perfectly situated to assist with escapes from slavery. He was justifiably mobile, moving from town to town and city to city with access to multiple forms of transportation, including a private carriage later in his life. He would become a property owner. Respectability clung to him and would only increase with the passing years. Most importantly, he proved himself an honorable steward; the people trusted him with their sacred and secular lives. Many churchgoers either had been held in slavery or had relatives still trapped in bondage. Quinn was persuasive, with an incisive mind. All these qualities and conditions enabled the work of the Underground Railroad.

Returning east, Quinn pushed across southern New Jersey, which, at the time, also condoned slavery. Salem, Springtown, and Bushtown, as well as Gouldtown, fell within Quinn's circuit. Most of the first sixteen men gathered by Allen and Coker to organize AME in Philadelphia had returned home to either continue pastoring their independent churches or to help organize AME congregations in their home state, as had Morris Brown. Reuben Cuff, one of the original organizers representing New Jersey, was sent to serve the Salem circuit extending to Cape May.

In Salem, Cuff helped purchase the land for the building of the first Black church, Mt. Pisgah AME, in Snow Hill (now Lawnside, New Jersey), originally organized in 1792. The Black church provided one of the first opportunities for landownership among African Americans in America. Allen's fight for possession of his own church building, early wrangling, and the protracted wresting of control from the Methodist Episcopal Church most likely accounted for the denomination's policy of owning the ground on which its churches stand. The Mt. Pisgah church, one of the five founding churches of African Methodism in 1816, stands out as the oldest AME church in New Jersey. Quinn pastored the Salem church between 1821 and 1822.[32]

However, infighting and disharmony began to bedevil the young denomination. "The cloud of discouragement hovered over the newly organized Connection," church chronicler David Smith reports.[33] Often, the birth of churches ignited quarrelsome exchanges. Problems came to light when the deed for the new church did not conform to the AME discipline. This led to several lawsuits and a bitter church feud. Elsewhere along the circuits, congregants fought over land, ministers, church buildings, and ownership, reflecting the growing pains of a dynamic new religious organization.

Quinn, as part of the itinerant system, helped unite the laity in small rural communities to form the backbone of the denomination, leaving an extensive legacy in New Jersey. By then Springtown AME had been established in Greenwich County, New Jersey. Gouldtown and Salem were also among the early congregations. The small rural churches were the roots that allowed the church body to grow. The Annual and General Conferences, held every four years, organized the ministerial phalanx of which Quinn was also a part.[34]

Quinn's network of churches would soon overlap or coincide with what would evolve into Underground Railroad routes. This arrangement could be seen decades before the invention and practical use of the steam locomotive and before the concept of cooperative assistance to freedom seekers had taken hold.[35] African Americans were either escaping on their own or assisting in the escape of their family, friends, and loved ones during this under-recorded period of history. Quinn's churches were part of this developing infrastructure well before suspicions were aroused or efforts coordinated.

New Jersey was a hub, a transit point—freedom seekers both fled to and escaped from the state. It played an integral role in receiving escapees from upper Southern states, such as Virginia, Maryland, and Delaware. New Jersey's surrounding waterways formed essential outlets. Counties in the state's Southern network included Cape May, Cumberland, Salem, and Burlington. The same pattern can be discerned in Pennsylvania, so much so that the Underground Railroad routes may have formed in part *because* of the location of the AME churches. Both the church and Underground Railroad circuits flourished in previously formed African American communities.

Blacks in Springtown and Swedesboro were operating important Underground Railroad stations during the years of Quinn's ministry at Springtown's Bethel AME Church. The town and its immediate surroundings have a notable Underground Railroad history. One of the most important Black abolitionists in the country, Samuel Ringgold Ward, was brought there as a young child. His mother and father had escaped slavery in Maryland after learning that Ward's mother was to be sold to a slaveholder in Georgia. She came out of slavery carrying Ward in her arms.[36]

Early in 1820 the family reached safety in Greenwich, New Jersey, before settling in Waldron's Landing, where they remained for six years. It is impossible to say whether the family knew Quinn in this early period, but both Quinn and Ward's family were in the same place at the same time. Their paths would intersect again (more directly) in New York City. Each—Quinn and Ward—would go on to become forceful Black abolitionists and Underground Railroad operatives.[37]

The family of one of the most famous luminaries of the Underground Railroad, William Still, also found sanctuary in New Jersey. After escaping slavery in Maryland, the family found a safe haven in the Black community in Springtown, overlapping the years the community formed part of Quinn's circuit. Escape to New Jersey, however, did not guarantee freedom, which was short-lived for the Still family. Slave catchers seized them and sent the family back into slavery in Maryland. In her second escape attempt, Still's mother was forced to abandon two of her four young sons when she fled to Burlington County, New Jersey, and rejoined her husband.[38]

Quinn rode through this critical area as part of his circuit—always near but seemingly not directly involved—bound to the Underground Railroad movement through his churches. William Switala, historian of the movement, identified the Bethel AME Church in the Greenwich-Springtown area as the center of Underground Railroad efforts.[39] Quinn also pastored Salem during the years it was an acknowledged station, but according to Emma Trusty's family history, Gouldtown came on the circuit three years after Quinn's departure to other assignments. By then the itinerant preacher was back in Bucks County, Pennsylvania.[40] Other Underground Railroad churches in New Jersey received his unwavering support. Even here, he was following Allen's footsteps. The founding bishop and his wife unstintingly supported anyone escaping slavery.[41]

Quinn's name is frequently tied to the first, or oldest, church in a particular city or state, and those churches have been almost universally implicated in the Underground Railroad. At the forefront of the westward advance of African Methodism, Quinn left an enduring imprint in Ohio and Indiana as well. In Ohio several churches lay claim to being the first or the oldest organized church body. However, Quinn Chapel, first organized in 1821 in a home in Chillicothe and formally established in 1822, appears to be the oldest AME Church in Ohio, in addition to the oldest west of the Allegheny Mountains. Quinn helped the family of his lifetime friend, antislavery activist Lewis Woodson, and other Chillicothe worshippers organize the Bethel church.[42] Quinn's early involvement with the family and the church shaped the long-lasting friendship he enjoyed with Woodson. The two would team up again in Pittsburgh. Quinn formed and revisited these radical partnerships over the course of his life.

By the first two decades of the nineteenth century—four decades before the Civil War—the African American community in Chillicothe had started helping escapees undermine slavery. The free Black community there, together with its various Black churches, was active in the movement. The history of Chillicothe's Quinn Chapel acknowledges that "members of the church assisted runaway slaves and moved them along to the north or Canada."[43] As part of his work on the Underground Railroad, Lewis Woodson rescued an enslaved man in Kentucky who had been kidnapped from Chillicothe by patrollers. Woodson was driven to fight slavery at every moment and had a profound understanding of the toll that the work of helping fugitives extracted. Two of his brothers had lost their lives in Ohio as they fought to free their brethren from slavery.[44]

Wherever Quinn stopped, one reporter notes, "he planted a church or left the influence there that caused one to spring up."[45] During his travels the deacon would often live in the homes of his associates for a short while, as he had done with Bro. Collins at the outset of his missionary work. Quinn was an outdoorsman. He could hunt and fish on long summer days or when the demands of farmwork were over. On rainy days, according to Welch, his grateful hosts might receive "a useful piece of household furniture . . . a chest of drawers, or a handsome fireside chair" crafted from lumber he had obtained from the surrounding well-timbered forests. Welch claims he understood the use and value of wood, which he'd learned during his boyhood and is perhaps indicative of skills he had acquired from his mahogany-dealing family in Honduras.[46]

Early on, Quinn began a pattern that would define his ministry and his lasting contribution to the church. Once the circuit rider entered a new community, his organizing strategy involved meeting the people and asking about the habits and character of their neighbors. Based on the information received, he would select those best suited to help him organize a Methodist society. At an early age, Quinn had developed a knack for quickly recognizing talent and putting it to work. He encouraged young men to enter the ministry, then trained and prepared them. While exhorting at White Marsh, Quinn came across Richard Robinson and recruited him. Moved by Quinn's preaching, Robinson came under Quinn's guidance. Quinn, only eight years older, had the same effect on Robinson that Bro. Collins had had on him.

At the close of his sermon, Quinn instructed, "All you who wish to be saved, stand up."[47] The entire congregation came to its feet. After enrolling them en masse as members of the new denomination, Quinn announced, "Richard Robinson, you are the leader."[48] The next morning, Quinn was gone. He repeated this formula across the country.

First he would find an existing prayer group or congregation, quickly identify a leader, and then authorize them under the banner of the denomination. Using this organizing strategy, the AME standard-bearer helped build the Connection one small congregation at a time. Welch comments, "Unwittingly he built a bulwark of political strength within the church, that was proud to serve him in the near future."[49]

But the conversion experience was not always smooth, and new converts sometimes slipped back into old habits. When Quinn made his return visit on the circuit, Robinson and "all his members had been to a country ball."[50] One historian states that "Robinson seemed to be a merry participant in activities that commonly passed for sins in the early nineteenth century. That is to say, he loved 'the sound of the fiddle and the dancing of feet.'"[51] Quinn rebuked the wayward flock, and they discovered the grace to begin again. Young Robinson and his class finally found their way to salvation, and he did his best to instruct them. A year later, Robinson was received into the Philadelphia Annual Conference and ordained deacon.[52]

The AME denomination operated on multiple levels. Churches established in small rural communities and city centers brought religion to the African Americans living there, while Underground Railroad routes brought freedom. However, the Underground Railroad work, often driven by Quinn, was internal, invisible, secret, and illegal. Outwardly, AME pushed for broader influence both within the United States and beyond. During this early growth period, the denomination began its international missions as well. AME sent its first missionaries to West Africa in 1817.

The rapid growth of AME caused the 1822 Baltimore Conference to recommend that an assistant to Bishop Allen be selected. Quinn was among three traveling ministers chosen for the selection committee, which revealed his heightened stature in the denomination. During the process a competitor actually received a majority vote over the eventual victor, Morris Brown, but the conference and the committee were well aware that Bishop Allen favored Brown for the position. Morris Brown had risen from an exiled South Carolinian to heir apparent to the highest episcopal office; he had served as the aging bishop's assistant. Allen made it clear: Morris Brown was his designated successor.

In turn, Brown rewarded Quinn's particular genius for planting and organizing churches. Sent back to Pittsburgh, now six years after the launch of the AME denomination, Quinn worked to organize the society he had earlier established into Bethel AME in Pittsburgh, one of the first Black churches west of the Allegheny Mountains—and one of its most powerful. Collins was there, serving as deacon. The Pittsburgh church, strategically located on the receiving end of a major escape route out of Uniontown, originally stood on a hill near the confluence of three rivers: the Monongahela, the Allegheny, and the Ohio. The rivers provided easy access from the waterways, bolstering the church's reputation as a stalwart Underground Railroad station. The Monongahela served as a main pathway from the South to Pittsburgh. Located in the aptly named Hill District, the Bethel AME Church identified itself as a stop on the Underground Railroad and its members, leaders in the region's antislavery networks.[53] The African American sections of the city were well-known for aiding fugitives from slavery. Not only had Quinn's friend Lewis Woodson relocated there, he also helped Quinn establish the

Pittsburgh church. As an AME minister, Woodson went on to pastor the church for several years.

Quinn would leave an indelible mark in Pittsburgh; for years, the AME Church existed as one of the most powerful Black churches in America. Pittsburgh's Bethel AME Church, the mother congregation, planted the seeds for five additional successful churches: Brown Chapel, St. James AME, Chartiers Street, Trinity, and St. Paul's, on the south side. Bethel Church's influence was so significant to the growth of the AME Church west of the mountains that the church maintained constant contact with influential older eastern churches.[54]

Quinn pressed onward, organizing a church in the rough-and-tough pioneer town of Steubenville in 1823, another of the oldest churches organized in Ohio.[55] During the early period of the church, Quinn and the seventeen members of his congregation first met in a small frame house, as was often the custom.[56] They continued meeting from house to house until they were able to build a permanent structure more than twenty years later. The brick church became the center of Black life in Steubenville, functioning as both a school and an Underground Railroad stop during the 1850s and 1860s. After Quinn rose to prominence, he chose to issue a decree from this church, now known as Quinn Memorial African Methodist Episcopal Church, that June 1 be set aside as a day of prayer against slavery.[57]

Quinn moved on to Cincinnati, where he oversaw the organization of the church that humbly began in an old lime shed. Such buildings—blacksmith shops, foundries, private homes, and old sheds—represented the institutional foundations of the growing church. Known as Allen Temple, the antislavery church participated extensively in the Underground Railroad.[58] Pastors of Cincinnati's oldest Black church preached antislavery and "opened the church as a way-station for the Underground Railroad," according to Cincinnati history.[59] Several other churches in Ohio were either organized directly by Quinn or greatly strengthened by his earnest efforts.[60]

The church continued its international pursuits, sending missionaries to Haiti in 1824. Quinn was instrumental in helping to send his young recruit, Deacon Richard Robinson, to Port au Prince, Haiti, as a minister to spread the gospel and plant the denomination in that newly independent island nation. The Haiti mission extended the AME influence in the Black Atlantic. In turn, Haitian emigrants from Baltimore organized the Haiti mission in the United States. In the global circulation of Black liberation theology, hundreds of Pennsylvania's AME members immigrated to Haiti between 1824 and 1827.[61] Young Robinson was among the leaders of the church who "quietly pursued their multidimensional, transnational quest for freedom during an era when the most virulent forms of oppression seemed to have the upper hand," reports his biographer.[62]

Canada, knocking at the United States' international border to the north, had joined the AME Church as a prominent ally of the denomination, establishing branches throughout southwestern Ontario beginning in the 1820s. The first societies appeared in 1826 or 1827 in the towns of Erie, Niagara, Gambia, and Malden, as was reported by the General Conference of 1828. Within a decade the AME Church had spread as far east as Toronto. In the coming years, Quinn's reach would expand into Canada.[63]

Quinn's skill as an accomplished horseman during this early time in his life uniquely equipped him for an effective itinerancy and a broad geographic reach. His horses helped make his extensive travels possible. The minister rode from town to town, converting souls and setting up churches along his circuits. When horseback-riding preachers came to the conferences, neighborhood boys were both delighted to tend their horses and excited by the chance to ride horseback. In return for the boys' care, the circuit riders allowed them to ride the animals to their daily watering. Preparation by the church hosting the conference included not only board and lodging for the preachers but stabling for their horses. The cost of feed appeared regularly in early budgets. A stable stood at the rear of Philadelphia's Bethel Church for the ministers' horses. When conferences were held at Bethel Church, Baltimore, the horses were hitched in the churchyard.[64]

At the end of the conference, Quinn and those who could ride mounted their horses and set off to the next posts. During the formative years of his mission work, he seemed to be everywhere. With little more than his Bible, his horse, and his powerful voice, this missionary brought the AME Church to the people. By 1824 Quinn had moved on to New York City.

CHAPTER 3

Quinn in New York City
1824–1828

Paul Quinn, like Richard Allen, was a man of independent spirit, a resolute organizer and visionary. The quality of their thoughts and actions, coupled with their belief in the principles each man held, reveals their effectiveness and, perhaps, their greatest friction. Welch characterizes Quinn as militant by nature: "A man of strong convictions, aggressive and uncompromising."[1] Both of these men of God were better able to battle the demons of slavery and handle waywardness and in-fighting among the faithful rather than weather their own ecclesiastical or personal disagreements.

Quinn had galloped across New York, Pennsylvania, and Ohio in 1824, either organizing or pastoring new churches. The circuit rider had gained an increasing appreciation for the frontier as he built up the church in the nearby West. When Quinn came back east, Bishop Allen sent him to New York City, most likely to compete with the AME Zion Church and to bring that metropolis fully under the AME banner.

Allen met one of his rare defeats in the city. As the AME Connection struggled to gain traction in the South, the bishop directed his efforts to expanding the denomination in New York in the first decades of the nineteenth century. In the meantime, the AME Zion Church was steadily gathering influence in New York, the city of its founding.

Of the sixteen men responsible for launching the independent Black church movement in 1816, no one had represented the independent Black church that had been organized in New York City. Mirroring the resolve that had erupted around the right to worship unhindered by White supervision in Philadelphia and Baltimore, New Yorkers established the AME Zion denomination. A rivalry between New York and Philadelphia left each city competing as the center of Black life. Sometime during 1819, Allen had entered into considerable private communications with AME Zion leadership in New York, pressuring them to join with AME. Baltimore's Daniel Coker, one of the earliest and most influential AME deacons, had abandoned the AME Zion Connection to join with the Allenites. Francis Asbury had ordained Coker a deacon in the Zion Church in 1802.[2]

Before Quinn, Allen had dispatched William Lambert of the Philadelphia Annual Conference to plant a branch of the AME Church in lower Manhattan by fall of 1819. He found an existing school room on Mott Street, in a section now known as Chinatown.[3] The choice to send Lambert to establish the church proved to be an unwise decision. The Zion Church was vulnerable. Its New York members had scattered as they waited for the completion of their new church building. "The Zionites were resentful of incursions made by William Lambert, a one-time member of the Zion Chapel who had defected to the Allenites and then returned [to New York City] to establish a missionary society of the AME Church," admits Christopher Rush, an early AME Zion bishop and historian of the denomination.[4] This defection in addition to the loss of Daniel Coker to the AME denomination turned the Zionists against the Allenites, and they rebuffed any attempts at consolidation.

AME's Mott Street Church opened on July 23, 1820, three weeks before the New York Zionists voted not to join with the Allenites, their Philadelphia rivals. A general meeting of the Zion Church on August 11, 1820, resulted in two pivotal decisions: first, a refusal to join with Allen and the AME Connection and, second, a refusal to return to White control.[5] Thus began the rocky relationship between AME and New York City Methodists that eventually helped upend the relationship between Allen and Quinn.

The founder of the AME Zion denomination welcomed Richard Allen during the dedication ceremonies for their new church building, but further negotiations between the two denominations did not succeed, and considerable bitterness followed. It is possible that Quinn, like his fellow missionary David Smith, found himself caught in the riptides of the AME–AME Zion organizational struggles in New York City.[6]

Defeat in New York notwithstanding, the AME denomination was building toward becoming a nationwide organization, with Philadelphia as its base. By the end of 1820, eight churches formed AME's New York Conference.[7] Once Quinn arrived in New York City, he served as the third pastor of the African Methodist Wesleyan Episcopal Church known as Bridge Street AMWE, in Brooklyn, throughout 1824. The now-familiar story of racial disharmony led the church to break with the Methodist Episcopal Church and affiliate with AME in early 1818. This, the oldest Black congregation in the Brooklyn–Long Island area, was located in the historic settlement that would evolve into Weeksville once community formed around the church in 1838. In Brooklyn, as elsewhere, Quinn laid a foundation for liberation in the early years, well before the concept of the Underground Railroad had taken hold there. Years after Quinn had moved on, the church gained a reputation for hiding freedom seekers in the church basement. From the safe distance of a century after the fact, Rev. Richard Wright felt free to historicize the activism of the church: "This church has a wonderful history, during the days of the abolitionist, it was one of the stations of the 'underground railroad' and from it colored persons were carried to Canada."[8]

Bridge Street was always a leading institution. Ironically, Jerena Lee, one of the first African American female evangelists, had come to New York City with Bishop Allen and Morris Brown for the 1823 New York Annual Conference. Lee preached at the church on Bridge Street, which she called High Street, a year before Quinn's arrival. At that time the majority of "the one hundred souls" of the church in Brooklyn were women.[9] Inviting Lee to preach placed Bridge Street at the forefront of sanctioning women preachers. After Quinn's elevation to bishop, their paths would cross more directly when AME women challenged him over the church's stance against allowing women to preach.

Women were also active in supporting education for the city's children, and the men of the Bridge Street church would set up an education system for the youth of color a few years in the future. They proudly laid the cornerstone of New York City's famed African Free School.[10] The school, in turn, eventually became the forerunner to the New York City public school system. The quest for education among African Americans, as an outgrowth of Sunday schools or Sabbath Schools, played a large role in the concept and establishment of public education in the United States. Quinn may have ministered to the church only for the remainder of 1824, but his influence was long lasting.

Ever on the move, Quinn was sent to pastor Flushing's Macedonia AME Church. For almost a century, the church had offered sanctuary as the meeting house for Blacks in Flushing, including the surrounding villages. Quinn pastored the church between 1824 and 1826, before he'd tangled with Bishop Allen in East Point, Pennsylvania. Macedonia appears to have been one of the last AME churches Quinn oversaw in New York. The once-loyal itinerant began exploring religious paths that led him away from Allen and AME. The January 1826 *Evening Post* listed a house, a store, and a large academy for sale at 136 Mulberry Street, directly across the street from the all-important African Free School (see fig. 3.1). Quinn may have seen the ad and purchased the property at that time.[11]

> **WORTHY OF ATTENTION.**
> FOR SALE, the House and premises No. 136 Mulberry st. consisting of a store, dwelling house and a large academy. Apply at the premises, which can be seen at any time.
> j4 1w

Figure 3.1 Mulberry Street Property for Sale. This is an advertisement for the sale of the property that eventually became the site of Paul Quinn's independent New York City church. "Worthy of Attention." *Evening Post*, January 7, 1826.

Almost a year and a half later, on May 4, 1827, *Freedom's Journal* announced Rev. William Quinn would preach a sermon in June at the consecration of a house designed for the use of the African Free Methodist Society at 136 Mulberry Street, between Hester and Grand, opposite the African Free School (see fig. 3.2).[12] Forming a society was a standard forerunner to Quinn establishing a formal church congregation.

Bishop Allen must have been livid when he discovered that Quinn was acting independently in the same city that had thwarted his plans for consolidating African Methodists and refused to join the Connection. AME membership numbers in New York were always anemic, hovering around 10 percent in comparison with the numbers in Baltimore and Philadelphia. More galling, however, was Quinn's audacity in naming his society the African Free Society—easily confused with Allen's Free African Society.

Noted historian Charles Wesley's insightful analysis of the personality differences between Quinn and Allen presents another factor. In Wesley's view, "the enthusiastic interest of Quinn was lessened by the aggressive" and somewhat "intolerant, autocratic attitude of Allen." Allen was a man of

> **NOTICE.**
> The Public are respectfully informed, that the House designed for the use of the "African Free Methodist Society," situated in Mulberry-street, No. 136, between Hester and Grand, (opposite the African Free School) will be consecrated on next Lord's Day, the 6th inst. at 2 o'clock, P. M.—SERMON by the Rev. William Quinn.

Figure 3.2 Announcement and Invitation to Quinn's Sermon. This took place at the consecration of the African Free Methodist Society at 136 Mulberry Street on May 6, 1827. *Freedom's Journal*, May 4, 1827.

strong self-will and one who would maintain his personal views against all odds. This quality was "excellent for the task of organization, but it often led to the separation of [Allen's] friends from him," Wesley comments. Richard Newman, another of Allen's biographers, says outright that Allen was stubborn, with a "palpable sense of certitude" and a "rigid determination that some might have seen as obstinacy."[13] Quinn, consistently described as a principled man of great daring, may have chafed under Allen's ironfisted leadership.

The relationship between Quinn and AME in New York City did not rupture immediately. Late in the summer of 1826, *The Long Island Star* carried an extensive report of an AME camp meeting held in Flushing—a meeting conducted with "great order and decorum." Hundreds of souls were converted, and fifty were added to the church roster, which we can assume was Macedonia, Quinn's Flushing church. Deacon Quinn was still affiliated with Allen at that point and was listed among the sixteen preachers who'd delivered sermons. On the eighth day, Quinn preached from Matthew 11:28: "Come unto me all ye that labour and are heavy laden; and I will give you rest."[14]

Quinn's actions during this time are unclear. He appears to have worked within the denomination while steadily building his own independent congregation. He took over the Elizabeth Street church, the first AME congregation that had been organized in the city.[15] As was true for so many of the AME churches, the congregation's women comprised the majority of the local worshippers.

Within four years of the consecration of the African Free Methodist Society, Quinn was listed as its minister. He built the church with a membership of 150 followers. His independent church operated in the neighborhood of one of New York's major pulse points at a key time in the state's history. We know of Quinn's activism in New York in part because of reports in *Freedom's Journal*, America's first Black newspaper. The publication began in March 1827 and lasted a mere two years, overlapping with Quinn's time in New York City. The newspaper reported his activities along with those of other New York leaders. Quinn, though, had yet to make a name for himself, and his presence has been overlooked by most New York historians. These were heady times in New York: not only did Samuel Cornish and John Russwurm launch *Freedom's Journal* in March 1827, but slavery was on the verge of extinction in New York State at that time. It had been a gradual, drawn-out process.

Black New Yorkers, fond of parades and public displays, readied themselves for the life-altering event. The months leading to the imminent passage of the New York State law were filled with well-dressed Black New Yorkers "parading through the streets."[16] Karl Bernhard, a foreign visitor to New York, describes in detail the pomp and color of a formal dress parade by the Wilberforce Society, one of the many benevolent societies operating in the city.[17]

New York City Blacks continued planning their celebrations. Meeting at the Mutual Relief Hall in mid-April, a group recommended that all Black churches in the city "hold services of prayer and thanksgiving on July 4," the day the law took effect. Although we have no record of how Quinn's church celebrated, they were most assuredly full participants, given Quinn's growing leadership role. The African Zion Church hosted the largest Fourth of July celebration in the city. Its walls were adorned with banners of the participating societies and with pictures of Thomas Clarkson, the English abolitionist, along with those of former governors who had pushed for emancipation.[18]

Because the Fourth of July was a national holiday, most people of color throughout the state preferred to postpone their emancipation celebration until the following day. This included the New York City Blacks who, on July 5, paraded through the downtown streets en route to the Zion church. A grand marshal led the procession; his mounted aides dashed up and down the line of nearly four thousand marchers. At city hall the grand marshal saluted the mayor to a roar of cheers.[19] Indeed, the later meeting and oration at Zion Church seemed somewhat anticlimactic to participants.[20]

Through the swirl of historic events, Quinn managed to find stability and was considered a leader in New York City's Black community. By this time he had married Margaretta Potts, who came to the United States from Honduras during a major immigration wave in the first part of the nineteenth century.[21] Quinn and his wife formed a strong partnership, working together, focusing on the education and welfare of children as well as community leadership. Both were intimately involved in shaping and guiding the education of New York's young Black scholars. And both were committed to the African Dorcas Association—one of numerous benevolent societies in the city. Working alongside her husband, Margaretta served as the association's secretary and as a member of its board of managers. Women had been encouraged to form Dorcas Societies, first established in 1824, so that they could "glean in the domestic vineyards."[22] The Dorcas Society along with the Daughters of the Conference were the first exclusively female missionary groups within AME.[23]

Margaretta Quinn and other African American women worked cooperatively. They joined together to let families know about the African Free Schools, to enroll children, and to keep up student attendance. Although governed by men, women organized fundraisers, fed fugitives, and took part in sewing circles. Quinn and the other ministers and leaders considered it "a great blessing for our children, and those of our friends of Colour," to enjoy the advantages of a good schooling.[24] They felt it their duty to use their standing in the community to promote regular school attendance so the rising generation could freely participate in the benefits of a solid education.

For a variety of reasons, an unusual number of children belonging to the African Free Schools were missing school. The Society traced the main cause to a lack of suitable garments, so they consistently sought clothing donations for the girls and boys. Women connected with the African Free School and affiliated with the Society, which also "procured and made garments for the destitute."[25] Now that New York was a free state, the Society could serve an important function: replacing the telltale slave clothing of fugitives from slavery with new garments. Slavery may have been outlawed in New York, but it continued to be legal in at least half the states of the Union. Within a few years, the association had clothed forty-nine boys and twenty-five girls and had distributed a total of 232 garments, including hats and shoes.[26] These items were important necessities for school attendance. "In those days," one minister points out, "going to school was not what the boys of today find it. Negro children, even in the streets of New York, were jeered at and pelted with stones. It was necessary for parents or guardians to accompany the children to and from school, and then they were not safe."[27]

Quinn and his wife ensured access to education for New York's young Black scholars. Freedom and community organizing thrived; societies proliferated. Quinn ascended among the leadership. At another large meeting of women of color, ministers of the various Black Churches, together with members of the Manumission Society, convened at the African Free School on Mulberry Street. Concern about the high number of school absences led the group to form the Fragment Society (a type of benevolent society). Rev. Peter Williams was called to the chair, and John Russwurm of *Freedom's Journal* served as secretary. Quinn was nominated to help with recruitment.

Quinn's New York church stood across the street from the African Free School on Mulberry Street (see fig. 3.3). A number of its students would go on to prominence and fame. One of Quinn's foremost friendships from his New York years was with the Garnet family.

Henry Highland Garnet wrote a brief biography of Quinn for *The Christian Recorder*, the official AME newspaper. Garnet first saw Quinn when he was pastor at the Mulberry Street church, "opposite the African Free School" in 1828. Garnet would have been a thirteen-year-old student at the school. They embarked on a lifelong friendship. Even then, Garnet was impressed

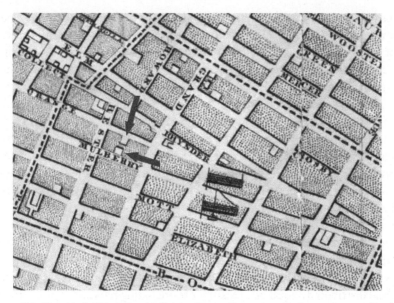

Figure 3.3 New York City Map, Mulberry Street. For a time Quinn was operating in a tight radius. *Note* the two buildings on Mulberry between Hester and Grand. The *right* arrow indicates the location of Quinn's home and independent church at 136 Mulberry St. The arrow to the *left* indicates the African Free School No. 2, at 135–37, which was directly across the street. *Note* Elizabeth Street to the northeast. "New Map of New York City," 1827. Lionel Pincus and Princess Firyal Map Division, The New York Public Library.

by Quinn's stature and his striking presence, his "bright and kindly beaming eye." Rarely could one find "a man of finer personal appearance, even in that populous city." In Garnet's eyes, Quinn's "elastic step, his polished and courtly manners" elevated him to "a ruler and a prince."[28]

Quinn's continuing independence brought with it a level of authority and prominence in the city, where he is said to have begun his lasting association with the Free and Accepted Masons and other prominent organizations.[29] By the end of the year, *Freedom's Journal* reported Quinn among "several respectable men of Colour" meeting with the Manumission Society, again, over matters of poor school attendance.[30] His actions reflect the growing concerns that "many hundreds are spending their time in idleness."[31] To combat the situation, Quinn took a district assignment alongside other participants who resolved to divide the city into seventeen districts, with two persons appointed to each.[32] Between his work with the school meeting and his sermon at the consecration of the African Free Methodist Society, Quinn was a force on Mulberry Street. He allied with prominent New Yorkers, such as Peter Williams, John Russwurm, and Theodore S. Wright, and joined with leading thinkers, such as Christopher Rush, Benjamin Paul, and Samuel Cornish. Wright holds the distinction of being the first Black graduate of a theological seminary in the United States; he graduated from Princeton Theological Seminary in 1828.

Quinn's focus on education and literacy would continue throughout his life. Although his concerns centered on children's education, adults attending night school often sought the gift of literacy as well. At the time, the two highest officials of the AME church, Bishops Allen and Brown, could read, but neither of the two men were able to write their own official correspondence and letters. That duty fell mainly to Allen's fourteen-year-old son and, later, to church historian Daniel Payne, a former South Carolina schoolteacher. Payne, a rising minister in the church, reported that he frequently had the pleasure of conducting episcopal correspondence for Bishop Brown.[33]

Churchman David Smith observed that while Quinn was not particularly learned and perhaps lacked patience for the mundane duties of caring for a flock, he also may have been looking ahead, anticipating higher ground. Although the minister had met with success in New York, Quinn's temperament did not appear well suited for sedentary, sophisticated, metropolitan environments. Furthermore, he had already demonstrated that his organizing skills were highly useful for the rugged conditions of the frontier.

By the late 1820s, one of two possible scenarios resulted from what Allen undoubtedly considered Quinn's betrayal: either Quinn voluntarily withdrew from the AME Connection to concentrate on building his independent church, or Allen, still smarting from the rebuff of the AME Zions in New York and apparently seething over his acolyte's forays into other denominations, finally cut Quinn off from the AME Connection in 1828 and then expelled him for "trying to set up an independent church," according to David Smith.[34]

Other than David Smith, few church historians refer to the incident. Allen appears to have acted unilaterally, leaving no official record. At the time, the discipline had few rules in place governing misconduct. Allen did not hesitate to "read" unruly members out of the Connection. The bishop had expended so much time and considerable energy trying to consolidate the independent Black denominations, and now one of his own luminaries was defecting. L. L. Berry, a later church historian, fills in a bit more detail: "After several years of successful service, because of some disagreement with Bishop Allen, [Quinn] resigned from the Connection and returned to New York City. This was an incident in his career about which he never talked," and it remains difficult to persuade clergymen today to speak of it.[35]

Furthermore, David Smith asserts that "the real cause of so much division" among the African American congregations was the idea that they, too, could follow Allen's empowering example and were at liberty to organize and establish distinct and separate "religious bodies." Smith continues, naming Quinn among the "great many ambitious men" who came to "the front to obtain rule and fame" when he set up a separate church in the city of New York.[36] Moreover, Allen would have known the exact spot where Quinn had opened his church. Three years earlier, in June 1824, the bishop was one of twenty prominent figures visiting and touring the African Free School, directly across the street from Quinn's church location, while the New York Annual Conference was meeting in the city. Jarena Lee was among those who accompanied Allen to the conference.[37]

Quinn was operating in one of the largest and most influential cities in the country at that time.[38] The 1820 New York State census counted almost thirty thousand free people of color, rivaling numbers in Philadelphia, although Baltimore had the largest concentration of free Blacks in the United States. New York City was at the center of the growing American capitalist enterprise. Bringing this prize city fully under the AME banner would have been a true victory for the denomination. It could already boast of its international growth, with seventy-two members in Haiti and an outreach in Canada. Despite Quinn's exile (or defection), Allen persisted as he moved the denomination forward, elevating Morris Brown to bishop on the last Sunday of the General Conference in Philadelphia in May 1828.[39]

CHAPTER 4

Independence in New York City
1828–1833

Quinn was now out of the AME Connection, which had nurtured his spirituality and his growth as a preacher. He may have immediately applied for reinstatement, but it remains unclear exactly what happened. Payne says that by June 18, 1828, Quinn had already made an application to church leaders in Philadelphia to reunite with the Connection, a strong indicator of his expulsion rather than his resignation.[1] The churchmen made no immediate decision on Quinn's request, and the process appears to have dragged on for four years until the New York Conference resolved the problem.[2] In either case, Quinn's defection from AME, the loss of such a great and capable talent, would have been a bitter blow to Bishop Allen.

David Smith reveals, however, that Quinn had not met with great success with his church enterprise and had enlisted Smith's aid. So Smith came to New York and held a quarterly meeting for Quinn. While Smith was there, the congregation grew attached to him and, according to Smith, wanted him "to take charge of their church."[3] And Quinn was most accustomed to riding his circuit, not staying put and pastoring one flock, as Smith suggests.

As further evidence of Quinn's independent streak, which so riled his bishop, the advertising pages of *The Long Island Star* for August 7, 1828, alerted worshippers in Flushing that William P. Quinn had extended an invitation to men and women and all parties to attend another camp meeting in Brooklyn, New York. This one, however, was held by the African Union denomination.[4] Quinn was openly fraternizing with rival independent churches and ministers, such as Delaware's Peter Spencer, founder of the African Union Church. David Smith has also mentioned Spencer as another of those seeking "rule and fame."[5] Peter Spencer, one of the original sixteen in attendance at that first historic convention, had formed the African

Union Church in 1805 in Wilmington, Delaware. Similar to AME Zion Church in New York City, that denomination also decided not to merge with AME. Quinn would have known Spencer from that initial meeting and may have been testing the strengths and limits of the various denominations he served during his time in New York.

Allen moved on without his disciple. Since Morris Brown's flight from South Carolina, he had served as Allen's assistant and business manager, and he was well positioned to lead. Bishop Allen consecrated Brown the second bishop of the AME Church during the 1828 General Conference.

By the spring of 1829, Quinn was acting as an independent pastor when he became involved in two very high-profile events. New York held one of its last public hangings in May of that year. Two people, Catharine Cashiere and Richard Johnson, were scheduled for execution. Two clergymen of color, Theodore S. Wright and William P. Quinn, ministered to Cashiere's spiritual well-being. Her despondent mother accompanied them on the ride to the gallows.

Because of timing problems and delays, large numbers of onlookers began congregating, making it difficult for the procession to move forward. The prisoners and their spiritual counselors boarded a waiting steamboat. Cashiere rued her circumstances as she passed the penitentiary buildings: "That place was my ruin. To it I owe my present situation. I was sent to the Penitentiary many years ago, when I was quite a child, for some trifling offense, and the depravity I there learned, has been the means of my appearing character."[6] Her mother agreed with her daughter's assessment of her ruination. As they neared the gallows, before leaving the steamboat, Quinn and Wright joined in prayer, then sang a hymn at its conclusion.

The somber scene had turned into quite a spectacle. Large numbers had come to witness the executions. The newspaper estimated four or five thousand. "Four or five steam-boats, crowded with passengers, were cruising to and fro; some two or three hundred small boats, equally filled, lined the shore." Boats capsized; people were said to have drowned. When the prisoners reached the scaffold, Quinn and Wright said final prayers, urging repentance for the last time, as well as reliance "upon the merits of the Redeemer."[7] As the moments dwindled, so did the hopes of a reprieve or pardon.

Loved ones said their goodbyes; caps were drawn over the faces of the prisoners. The drop fell, "and they were launched into eternity. Cashiere appeared to have died instantly."[8] The bodies remained suspended for almost three-quarters of an hour before they were lowered into their coffins and finally taken to the Alms House.[9] We are left to assume that Quinn and

Wright accompanied the bodies as they were delivered to friends for burial. This would not be the last time Quinn was there to soothe a suffering soul before execution. He ministered at both the high points and low moments of life.

The country's leading abolitionists were often mentioned in association with Quinn's fellow counselor, Theodore Wright—most frequently, Frederick Douglass, Daniel Payne, and Samuel Eli Cornish, as well as David Walker. Quinn's work with Wright has remained unrecognized. Wright also followed the pattern of Quinn's connections. By 1835 Wright and fellow minister Charles B. Ray, plus other prominent New Yorkers, formed the New York Committee of Vigilance. Wright was active in the Underground Railroad. More than a decade later, he would turn his home into a station. On one occasion he used the committee to help move six freedom seekers through New York City to the Boston Vigilance Committee. Historian Bella Gross dubs Wright "one of the most illustrious 'conductors' of the Underground Railroad in New York."[10] Pulitzer Prize winning historian Eric Foner says a publisher singled out Wright as one of the "originators" of the Underground Railroad in New York City.[11]

As one of the founders of the American Anti-Slavery Society and as chair of the New York Vigilance Committee, Wright reinforced his convictions against slavery. One biographical sketch acknowledges that "Wright dedicated his life to the abolition of slavery and to the dismantling of the prejudice that undergirded it."[12] He used his position with the clergy to hide freedom seekers in his New York church. He and Quinn worked toward the same goals while they were ministering to souls in New York City.

Quinn was moving and operating independently across public and private spheres, political realms, denominations, and independent churches. He was swept up in events that forced him to use the power of the clergy to confront issues around slavery in the New York political system. He landed in the middle of one of the more sensational fugitive slave cases tried in New York City—a notable public incident in the early years for the freedom-fighting minister, which was first captured by *Freedom's Journal*.[13]

Henry Highland Garnet, Quinn's student-friend from the African Free School who was destined to become one of the most famous Black abolitionists in America, reported on the incident years later. Garnet observed that whenever freedom seekers in New York City were in trouble and needed help, the call went out: "'Send for Isaac T. Hopper,' 'send for Quinn,' 'go for Christopher Rush,' and soon, one or all of those heroic and glorious men stood beside the trembling fugitive. The days to which I allude were perilous, and none but true men could stand—and Quinn stood among the truest."[14]

Garnet's *Christian Recorder* article brought Quinn out of the shadows and captured some of his New York City heroics.

Sometime in 1828, Eliza Garnet, Henry's sixteen-year-old sister, was arrested as a fugitive from slavery while attending a party. Now Eliza, who had not been as fortunate in escaping arrest as the remainder of her family, found herself thrown into prison, stirring great excitement around her arrest.[15] Slavery had ended in New York the previous year, but slave catchers continued to operate in the city, and the 1793 constitutional Fugitive Slave clause could be enforced in Northern states. Slave catchers, often referred to as manstealers, roamed the city with the intent of seizing Blacks, selling them, or taking them farther South. Children and young adults, such as Eliza, less able to defend themselves, suffered particular vulnerability. Fortunately, Eliza enjoyed a wide circle of friends and acquaintances, and her parents maintained a good standing in the church.

Quinn, the local preacher-activist, was steadily building his independent church and working on behalf of the local New York City Black community. Eliza's father, George Trusty (now Garnet), served as a class leader and exhorter in an AME church, which may well have been one of Quinn's churches. Quinn was a friend to the family.[16]

After some consideration, concerned New York City African Americans devised a plan of action. First the best legal mind was to be secured. If the legal plan failed, then a rescue was to be attempted "at the hazard of imprisonment and death" for the rescuers. Garnet continues, "On that memorable day at least three thousand colored men and women assembled in the City Hall Park. In the center of that determined crowd, the towering form of William Paul Quinn was seen, and by his side was observed 'the little black giant,' Nathan Thomas. The former was wise in counsel, and fearless in war, but the latter was invincible in conflict."[17]

Eliza's case came before the New York City courts. Richard Riker, the recorder of New York City, was appointed to oversee the trial the day following the arrest. Eliza's counsel relied on a defense strategy aimed at providing a successful alibi. In this case, that meant proving she had been a resident of New York City at the time when witnesses for the prosecution swore that she'd been enslaved in Maryland. All forms of slavery had been abolished in New York State the previous year, and the testimony of African Americans was deemed acceptable in court. The slave catcher, a relative of the late slaveholder Col. Spencer of Maryland, swore to the day and date that Eliza, the alleged fugitive, had escaped from the South, and other witnesses swore to the anxious teen's identity.

Calmly, Quinn rose to testify that he knew Eliza. She had been his wife's pupil for the two years *prior* to the date given by the claimant. Margaretta R. Quinn was called upon to corroborate her husband's statement. Quickly, she produced a sampler stitched by Eliza bearing the same date of the year sworn to by Rev. Quinn. The stitched name and date on needlework samplers, used to learn letters and numbers, served as important historical documents for girls. These moral men and women, determined to defeat an immoral system, were skilled in evasion, omission, and narrow answers, but they made great efforts to avoid the sin of outright lying.

The case was settled in favor of the defendant; with evident pleasure, Recorder Riker gave his decision: "Eliza Garnet, you are free to go where you please." This was an especially important triumph. Foner has written that Richard Riker, along with a group of accomplices, could reap substantial financial gains by playing "a pivotal role in what abolitionists called the Kidnapping Club.... Members of the club would bring a black person before Riker, who would quickly issue a certificate of removal before the accused had a chance to bring witnesses to testify that he was actually free." Decisive action and the speed of the testimony from the Quinns and Nathan Thomas saved Eliza from being ensnared by Riker and his gang and being remanded back into slavery.[18]

Amid the triumph, Eliza was escorted from the courtroom, supported on one side by Quinn, "who looked as calm as a summer's morning," and on the other, by Nathan Thomas. Garnet claims that "three thousand colored people intoxicated with joy over a signal victory won for liberty and justice greeted them as they emerged from the courtroom."[19] Quinn and Black New Yorkers interrupted business as usual for the Kidnapping Club. Vigilant Committees emerged in New York, Philadelphia, and Boston to help combat the problem.

The entire Garnet family had indeed escaped slavery in New Market, Kent County, Maryland, in 1824, two years after the death of their enslaver, William Spencer. As part of the escape plan, eleven members of the extended family, including nine-year old Henry and his older sister Eliza, received permission to attend a family friend's funeral at some distance away. And they never returned.

Escaping through the woodlands and tidal swamps of Maryland, the families followed the traditional escape strategy of sleeping by day and traveling throughout the night. At one point during the family's arduous escape, young Garnet became so exhausted that he had to be carried on the backs of other family members. Once in Wilmington, Delaware, the group came into the network of staunch Quaker abolitionist and Underground Railroad agent Thomas Garrett. There the families separated; seven went to New Jersey.

Garnet's immediate family ventured to New Hope, Pennsylvania, on the banks of the Delaware River in Bucks County. Remember that as a newly ordained deacon, Quinn had held the first camp meeting of the AME Connection there, in the woods at Bensalem, under the direction of Richard Allen. There had been a strong AME presence in Bucks County since the days of Bro. Collins and Quinn's camp meeting. The Bensalem church maintained close ties to Quinn, as well as an impressive Underground Railroad pedigree.[20]

After resting and gathering their strength, the Garnets moved from Pennsylvania to New York City, where they eventually settled in 1825 (during the time when Quinn pastored his independent church there), before the official end of all slavery in New York State. During the wider slave-catching raid on the family, Eliza's father, George (Trusty) Garnet, narrowly escaped by jumping from a window in their home and fleeing; their mother barely eluded her captors. Since escape did not ensure lasting freedom, abolitionists would later purchase her freedom.[21] Kidnapping was nothing new in New York City. It had been a bane for people of color since at least 1785, and throughout this later time period, kidnappers had been quite active in the city. Undoubtedly, the plan had been to kidnap the entire family, return them to the Spencer estate in Maryland, and claim any bounty offered.

Quinn had been active in Garnet's life. Henry Highland Garnet entered the African Free School in 1826. He first encountered Paul Quinn, whose independent church was across the street, while in school. Young Garnet remained at the school until 1828. From there his extraordinary group of schoolmates went on to lead lives of great accomplishment. They included Alexander Crummell, an Episcopal priest and a leading Black intellectual who was Garnet's neighbor and close boyhood friend; Samuel Ringgold Ward, a celebrated abolitionist and a cousin of Garnet; James McCune Smith, the first Black to earn a medical degree; Ira Aldridge, the celebrated actor; and Charles Reason, the first Black college professor in the United States and a longtime educator in African American schools. Quinn's fellow clergyman, Theodore S. Wright, would also mentor Garnet.[22]

Quinn had helped Garnet's sister out of an impending crisis that would have ended with her re-enslavement had he not intervened. The Garnet family's escape from slavery years before and the run-in with the slave catchers left a powerful impression on young Garnet and would shape his radical abolitionist stand as an adult. He had been away, working as a cook and cabin boy at sea, during the raid on his family. Garnet made two sea voyages to Cuba in 1828. After another voyage to Alexandria and Washington, DC, in 1829, he learned of the attempted capture and separation of his family upon his return home. The raid on his family left Garnet with an undying and bitter hatred of slavery that fueled his eloquence and directed his rage. Garnet was at the forefront of the generation of African Americans who pushed the abolition movement away from moral suasion toward immediate political action.[23]

The end of slavery in New York fueled a hope that the loathsome practice would finally die out across the country. During the 1830s, Northern abolitionists, inspired by successful British abolition examples, organized rapidly on local and regional levels, stepping up their proselytizing and propagandizing. In Southern states, however, antislavery societies withered, proslavery advocates stifled criticism of the "peculiar institution," and elaborate arguments justifying slavery's perpetuation swelled. More and more Black bondsmen fled slavery to areas of freedom, such as New York, Philadelphia, and Baltimore, among other cities.[24]

Quinn moved between the sharpening sectional lines and appeared to have gone west for a year or so, possibly to be out of Bishop Allen's orbit during these turbulent years. Newly ordained Bishop Morris Brown adopted a more appreciative attitude toward Quinn and may have suggested Quinn's westward sojourn. During his exile years, Quinn headed back out to the near west, close to the western Pennsylvania-Ohio border. Quinn churches dotted rural outposts in those states. Records of St. Paul's AME Church in Uniontown, Pennsylvania, indicate that Paul "Quin" [sic] pastored the church at times throughout the 1829 to 1830 period.[25]

Quinn emerged in dramatic fashion on the other side of the Alleghenies, in Brooklyn, Illinois, in what is now East St. Louis, where he found a disciple in Priscilla Baltimore. She had purchased her freedom in St. Louis and crossed the Mississippi River with eleven Black families. Together they started the Brooklyn settlement. Mother Baltimore, as she was affectionately known, first saw Quinn coming up the road as he approached on horseback. She thought him a very tall, odd-looking man. He called out to her, rode up to her home, and dismounted. Coming through her gate, the evangelist inquired, "[Could] a fellow could get something for his horse and himself to eat?" As Mother Baltimore headed off to prepare the food, Quinn headed to the stable with his horse, "Bill."[26]

When he returned, he and Baltimore spoke for a time before she invited him to the table to eat. "I never eat till 'Bill' is fed," Quinn assured her.[27] Dinner had to wait. Baltimore showed the itinerant where to find food for his horse. With his horse well cared for, Quinn sat down to enjoy a hearty meal and satisfied his host's curiosity, describing who he was and why he was there. Quinn asked about opportunities for finding space to preach. Baltimore offered her home—she would gather the congregation. News spread, and later that night, her yard filled with listeners anxious to hear the Good News. Quinn sang and prayed and imparted, "I have heard my people's cry and have come to deliver them" (Exodus 3:7). "The people were wild with delight and begged him to remain with them a while and hold meetings. He consented and made his home with this same good woman," a local newspaper later reported.[28]

The Bethel AME Church in Brooklyn, Illinois, was established at the home of Priscilla Baltimore sometime after "1829 but before 1832," according to historian Sundiata Keita Cha-Jua.[29] Since a Quin is listed in the New York City directories as the pastor of the Independent New York Methodist church for 1831 and 1832, we can narrow the dates when he could have traveled west to Brooklyn to 1829 and 1830 (see fig. 4.1).

These represent the years Quinn was out of the Connection but apparently continuing to work on its behalf. Reverend Jordan Early, one of

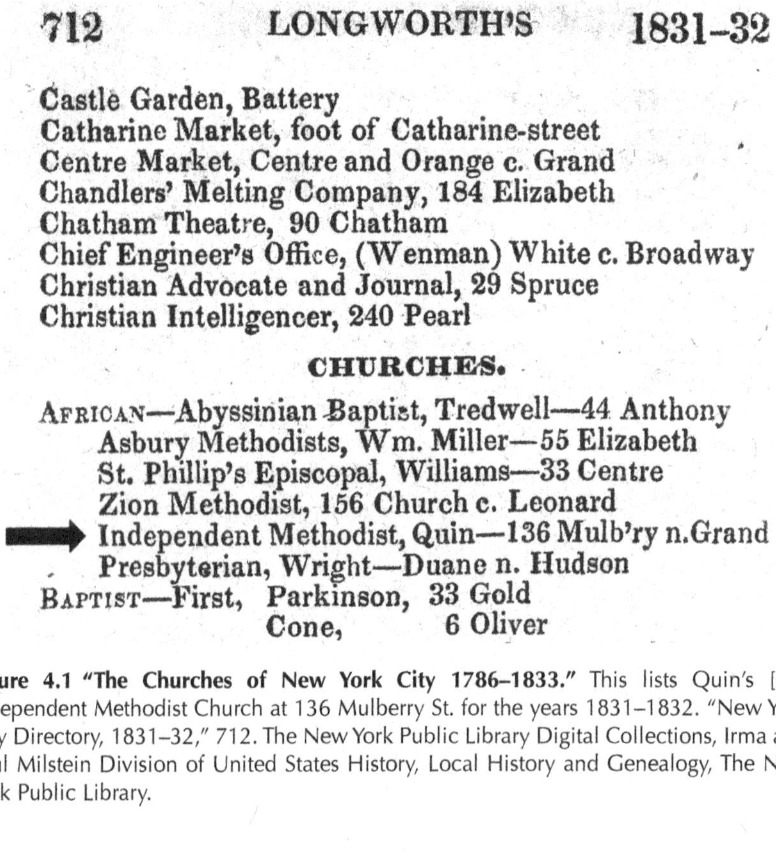

712   LONGWORTH'S   1831–32

Castle Garden, Battery
Catharine Market, foot of Catharine-street
Centre Market, Centre and Orange c. Grand
Chandlers' Melting Company, 184 Elizabeth
Chatham Theatre, 90 Chatham
Chief Engineer's Office, (Wenman) White c. Broadway
Christian Advocate and Journal, 29 Spruce
Christian Intelligencer, 240 Pearl

CHURCHES.

AFRICAN—Abyssinian Baptist, Tredwell—44 Anthony
    Asbury Methodists, Wm. Miller—55 Elizabeth
    St. Phillip's Episcopal, Williams—33 Centre
    Zion Methodist, 156 Church c. Leonard
➤   Independent Methodist, Quin—136 Mulb'ry n. Grand
    Presbyterian, Wright—Duane n. Hudson
BAPTIST—First, Parkinson, 33 Gold
        Cone,   6 Oliver

Figure 4.1 "The Churches of New York City 1786–1833." This lists Quin's [sic] Independent Methodist Church at 136 Mulberry St. for the years 1831–1832. "New York City Directory, 1831–32," 712. The New York Public Library Digital Collections, Irma and Paul Milstein Division of United States History, Local History and Genealogy, The New York Public Library.

Quinn's acolytes, also suggests that Rev. Quinn introduced African Methodism in Brooklyn, Illinois, and in St. Louis, Missouri. Initially, the people had no houses of worship and met in private houses, following Quinn's example. The minister transformed the group "from an informal gathering of individuals into a formal church community."[30]

Brooklyn, Illinois, was not Quinn's only westward stop. Following his familiar pattern in conquering the western states for the church, Quinn and six freedom seekers first organized a Colored Methodist Society in Cleveland, Ohio. The new society members had recently escaped slavery and entrusted the missionary with their newfound freedom. That initial gathering of freedom seekers grew to become Cleveland's St. John AME Church.[31]

Although the original charter was issued in 1836, the *Cleveland Call and Post* furnished the undocumented history. "Rev. William Paul Quinn, an itinerant preacher, led in prayer a little group of fugitive slaves who were jubilant in freedom from their master." The six members, led by Quinn, met on an early winter evening in 1830. Using a house near the corner of Bolivar and Erie Streets, they formed the first religious body for people of color in Cleveland, St. John's African Methodist Episcopal Church, the oldest African American church in Greater Cleveland. Quinn, epitomizing the work of an itinerant preacher, had called them together into a prayer group, "where they could manifest freely their impassioned spiritual emotions."[32]

Quinn left few narratives of his travels. Although it is not possible to keep up with all of his movements during this crucial period, he appears to have been as active and effective in New York City as he was in Ohio and Illinois during his years as an independent preacher. New York City continued to be his home base, however, and a Wm. P. Quinn is listed in the 1830 census as the twenty-four- to thirty-six-year-old head of a two-person household in Ward 14 in New York City, most likely with his wife Margaretta.[33] Sorrowfully, by February 1830, his wife and helpmate had died, felled by consumption. The minister rarely, if ever, mentioned her again.

Four days after his wife's death, Quinn filed probate papers. She died without a will, which enmeshed Quinn in what may have been the first of his many legal entanglements. Margaretta left a personal estate of $2,222, worth about $70,000 in today's dollars.[34] Five months after the death of his wife, early on the morning of July 15, Quinn withdrew $1,800 from the City Bank of New York, only to meet with misfortune. Pickpockets robbed the minister of the money while he slept at his Mulberry Street home. This sum may well have reflected a portion of the money he had inherited from his wife's estate. The *Evening Post* speculated that he had been watched from the moment he'd withdrawn the money (see fig. 4.2).

> *Pickpockets.*—On Thursday Mr. Quin, a colored clergyman of the African Church, was robbed of $1800 at his residence in Mulberry street. One of the bills was for $1000, one for $500, and three for $100 each. He had drawn them out of the City Bank in the early part of the day, and was probably watched by some person who knew he had it, until the theft was effected by abstracting the bills from his pocket whilst he slept.

Figure 4.2 "Pickpockets Rob Quinn." Quinn's church and home sat at the edge of Five Points, one of New York City's more notorious neighborhoods. The newspaper suggests that Quinn had been watched and followed before the robbery. *Evening Post*, July 15, 1830.

Quinn's church and his Mulberry Street home stood at the northern fringe of New York City's notorious Five Points neighborhood—often included among the most dangerous areas in New York history. The lurid conditions gained international infamy, possibly because Five Points was home to one of America's first integrated neighborhoods. Free Blacks and freedom seekers, newly arrived Irish, and Jews mixed in with all types of street culture to form a rich and vibrant but dangerous and notorious community.[35] Mulberry Street, with the African Free School and Quinn's church across the street, operated a block and a half to the north (see fig. 3.3).

Quinn's final years in New York City also marked an important moment for the growth of the AME Church. Bishop Allen had been unable to attend the Philadelphia Annual Conference the year before. With Allen quite frail and ailing at seventy years old, leadership of the denomination passed to Bishop Morris Brown. With Quinn's help, Brown established the Ohio or Western Conference in Pittsburgh that year. Fifteen members attended. The rising leadership of the denomination was already in place. Bishop Brown presided, and Rev. Edward Waters, who would become the third ordained bishop, assisted him. Lewis Woodson served as secretary. Both William Paul Quinn and Daniel Payne were there. Quinn's old friend and mentor, Deacon Samuel Collins, also attended.[36] Unlike the conflicts with Allen, Quinn enjoyed a dynamic growing relationship with Morris Brown, which may have led to the establishment of the Ohio Conference. Quinn had helped lay the foundation with his recent western mission trips. It certainly led to the transformation of the church.

Quinn might have stayed on indefinitely as a local independent preacher and activist in New York City had it not been for one life-altering event: the death of Bishop Richard Allen, "the most distinguished man of color in the United States of America" at that time, according to his biographer. On March 26, 1831, our Lord summoned Bishop Allen to enjoy "the saints' everlasting rest." With the death of "the apostle of freedom," as Allen was known, the world lost "one of the leading lights of African Methodism."[37] Morris Brown preached his funeral, which was a lofty homegoing attended by a huge gathering of sincere mourners.[38]

Quinn had been thinking of returning to the mission field when the news of the death of Bishop Allen reached him. Church historian L. L. Berry reports that Quinn had become "very much discouraged"; the death of his wife may have contributed to his dejection.[39] He quickly met with Bishop Morris Brown and presented his application for readmission to the Connection. This 1831 request appears to have been Quinn's second petition. Although he had been working on behalf of the denomination in the West, no action had been taken at the time of the first request, around 1828.

The founder's death left Bishop Brown to preside alone over the 1832 General Conference, which opened on May 10 in Philadelphia. At that time Brown signaled that the most important business before the conference was the readmission of Reverend Quinn to AME membership, "he[,] having withdrawn and organized an independent church in New York City." The matter was referred back to the New York Conference in the following resolution: "Resolved, that we proceed no further in Brother William Paul Quinn's case, that he return to New York and consult the people whom he now serves, and amongst whom he now belongs and hear what they say on the subject, and get their consent for him or them to join the Connection one way or the other."[40] But Quinn had to wait; his readmittance would take some time.

Besides reinstating Quinn at the conference, a three-member delegation from a Methodist Society in Elkton, Maryland, came to petition the gathering. Southern states and racial restrictions continually plagued the denomination and threatened its churches. The town, the northeasternmost county seat in Maryland, may have been only fifty miles southwest of Philadelphia, but the slaveholding state of Maryland set it worlds apart. The delegation came to the conference, requesting that something be done on behalf of the churches in Maryland belonging to the Smyrna circuit. Payne reports that the Black Codes of the state as he understood them "forbade any colored minister, as well as other colored people belonging to another state, from entrance there, unless they went in the capacity of slaves, or servants of some white person."[41] The law forbade religious gatherings unless conducted "by a white licensed or ordained preacher or some respectable white person or persons of the neighborhood."[42] Attempting to get around the code, the

Maryland delegation came to the conference to request that a local Maryland preacher be ordained who could assume oversight of the church in question and serve the society.

Delegates from Delaware also came to the General Conference to ask that the church intervene there. Delaware authorities had prevented AME ministers from nonslaveholding states from entering the state to take charge of churches. This ruling forced a change in all the ministerial appointments going into Delaware. State laws, Black codes, and other restrictions give an indication of the trials facing the rising Black churches. The codes were not restricted only to the South, but the western states, particularly Ohio, Illinois, and Indiana, had also instituted codes and laws restricting education for African Americans, including their mobility and rights of assembly.

The General Conference also noted the death of Daniel Coker, one of the two primary founders of African Methodism responsible for the denomination's establishment and intellectual formation. As one historian points out, Coker had been interested in Christianity as an antislavery doctrine. After his thwarted election as AME's first bishop, Coker emigrated to West Africa to evangelize and spread Methodism. He became a leader in the African colonization project led by the Society for the Colonization of Free People of Color.[43]

As Quinn sought to return to the Connection, he continued his various duties and responsibilities in New York, his home at the start of 1833. A list entitled "The Churches of New York City 1786–1833" lists an independent Methodist Church at 136 Mulberry Street at Grand (see fig. 4.1); Quinn (misspelled as Quin) is recorded as the minister for both 1831 and 1832.[44] David Smith's observations notwithstanding, Quinn's popularity as a preacher continued unabated. As late as January 1833, Quinn's church was attracting an "immense crowd." William Lloyd Garrison's newspaper, *The Liberator*, explains that the church had sunk nine inches as a result of the weight of the crowds in attendance (see fig. 4.3).[45]

Handling enormous gatherings was commonplace for Quinn, but the structural problems of the church would have been another complication that, as pastor, Quinn would have had to address but not necessarily remedy as a circuit rider.

His disconnecting and unwinding from New York City was gradual. Quinn and his church continued to minister to souls in the city, and the African Free School continued its influence over the future leaders of America, such as Henry Highland Garnet, Alexander Crummell, and James McCune Smith, as well as Theodore S. Wright, Samuel Cornish, and others—all

[For the Liberator.]
TO THE PUBLIC.

The African Methodist Episcopal Church, situated in Mulberry-street, under the pastoral charge of the Rev. Wm. P. Quinn, owing to the immense crowd, was lately discovered to have sunk about 9 inches, but no particular damage was done. Due notice will be given when the house is repaired.

GEORGE WILSON.

New-York, Jan. 1, 1833.

Figure 4.3 Quinn's NY Church Is Sinking. The writer refers to Quinn's Mulberry Street church as an AME church in 1833, although technically, he may have been operating an independent Methodist church. Due to the crowds attracted to the church, the building had sunk nine inches and needed repair. *The Liberator*, January 5, 1833.

who would go on to become forceful abolitionists, Underground Railroad activists, and major historical figures in their own right. Samuel Ringgold Ward, whose mother had carried him out of slavery in her arms to freedom in New Jersey, crossed paths with Quinn again on Mulberry Street. Ward attended theAfrican Free School No. 2 from 1826 to 1833, overlapping the years Quinn pastored his independent church across the street. When Ward wrote his autobiography, he was forthright in explaining his involvement with assisting freedom seekers. He "had the honour" of being one of "the humblest conductors" on the Underground Railway.[46]

Given Quinn's relationship with the school and its scholars, he may have been disheartened to learn that a couple of years after he had left the city, the Public School Society of New York took over the New York African Free Schools, as it did hundreds of schools throughout the city. The society dismissed all the Black teachers and administrators.

In tandem with his pioneering work, through all the trials and suffering, opportunities and setbacks, Quinn maintained a relationship with New York City and its benevolent societies, with his independent church, and with AME in the early 1830s. He continued his attentiveness to his spiritual and civic duties while awaiting a response to his application for readmission to the Connection.[47]

Blacks, particularly in the free states, consistently organized into conventions and societies. Quinn and *Freedom's Journal* editor Samuel Cornish functioned as agents of the Phoenix Society. The "1833 Minutes of the Third

Annual General Convention of the Free People of Color" reports that some of the wealthiest and most talented men in New York City had gathered to launch the society. Education comprised their core concern. Several Black leaders, directed by founder and AME Zion bishop Christopher Rush, formed the society to promote the education of not only the city's African American children but adults as well. The intention of the interracial group was to unite people of color for their own improvement in morals, literature, and the mechanic arts. The society fostered classes, lectures, lending libraries, job centers, and the mutual support needed to fulfill their goals.

Quinn, a director of the society, operated among the leading abolitionists and thinkers of his time. He again worked with Presbyterian minister Theodore Wright, Quinn's fellow counselor during the execution of Catherine Cashiere. Wright was elected vice president. Other New York notables included Episcopal priest Peter Williams Jr., noted restaurateur Thomas Downing, Rev. Simeon S. Jocelyn of the American Missionary Association, and Boston Crummell, father of noted abolitionist Alexander Crummell. Philanthropist, businessman, and abolitionist Arthur Tappan served as treasurer.

The society was one of various autonomous institutions that developed as an outgrowth of the colored convention movement, which reported on its formation and progress. Although young men of color dominated its membership, the society hoped that the entire population in New York City, along with their friends, would benefit from this "Mental Feast," which would survive more than thirty years in some parts of Pennsylvania and the West.[48]

Finally, Quinn's request was answered after the New York Conference took action. Bishop Morris Brown presided at the New York Annual Conference on June 18, 1833. Reverend Quinn was officially and formally readmitted to the AME Connection, and he regained his standing in the church. The matter was referred to the mother church for final resolution. Quinn had been separated for five years from the Connection he loved dearly. David Smith reports, "At a love feast in Philadelphia, Quinn applied to join the Connection again. Bishop Brown brought the matter before the people. They consented to receive him with this proviso: that he should go West and speed the Connection. This he agreed to do."[49] Immediately after his reception, Brown gave Quinn the credentials of a traveling missionary and evangelist, then transferred him to the newly organized Ohio Conference. Quinn started off the next morning. Apparently, all he needed, Welch reports, was a good night's rest, his saddle, and his horse. With his white dog, Bill, and his white horse, Bill, he left New York and the East behind.[50]

CHAPTER 5

Quinn Returns to the Fold
1833–1836

The wilderness has always inspired reverence in Christian thought, and Quinn was eager to embrace the West with all the possibilities it held for the church. The missionary's earlier efforts in the late 1820s had laid the groundwork for the future direction of the denomination after Bishop Brown transferred him to oversee the Pittsburgh circuit within the Ohio Conference. Quinn turned to Pittsburgh, considered the gateway to the West, as his new home and settled there. Steamboats, canals, turnpikes, and railroads had helped turn the city into a busy and thriving trade center that doubled as a vital artery of the Underground Railroad. Quinn welcomed the opportunity to work alongside his mentor and spiritual father, (now deacon) Samuel Collins.

The work of strengthening the church and enlarging its borders fell to Quinn. His wisdom and endurance, as Payne argues, were key to making the expansion an outstanding success. Quinn's evangelist activities marked a turning point in the history of the church. His work, according to one church historian, ushered in the "new age" in African Methodist missionary history and "the beginning of the organized period of missions."[1] As the only AME evangelist west of the Alleghenies, Quinn traveled familiar ground. Mounted on his large, spirited bronco, cantering over hills and through the Monongahela valley, he often sang the Songs of Zion, although mostly off key. He delighted in riding his long, numerous circuits on horseback, jumping hurdles, fording rivers, and scaling hills.

One of the more effective organizers and preachers, Quinn inspired tremendous growth of the denomination in rural areas of the sparsely populated, often dangerous Midwest. To avoid the prejudice and mob violence that existed in areas such as the southern Ohio circuit, clergymen and circuit riders traveled through mountain bypasses offering greater safety.

Bloodshed centered on racial issues was erupting from Philadelphia to New Orleans in 1834. Competition for jobs among free Blacks, newly arriving Irish, and disgruntled Whites fueled the violence. Cincinnati, then part of Quinn's circuit, experienced three such violent eruptions, one each in 1829, 1834, and 1841. Henry Highland Garnet wrote that early in Quinn's ministry in Western Pennsylvania, the circuit rider came to assist Bishop Brown at a camp meeting near Hookstown, about thirty-five miles east of Pittsburgh, on the banks of the Monongahela River near the Ohio border. As the clergy assembled at the home of a local friend, ruffians tried to break up the gathering, expressly targeting Quinn.

"Bring out Quinn!" they cried.

"We want that man Quinn. Fetch him out! If you don't, we will tear the house down."

The rowdy men yelled similar threats until they were hoarse, but Quinn had not yet arrived in the city. A week later, the mob returned, still intent on punishing Quinn, whose fame as a "fearless preacher . . . determined not to be silenced by the devil" preceded him.[2] The mob was hell-bent upon disrupting the camp meeting and driving Quinn out of town.

Trumpets signaled the opening of the camp meeting; people emerged from their tents. As they lifted prayers, songs, and incense to the Lord, the hooting, yelling mob descended. Quinn looked on quietly and remarked to Bishop Brown that he could handle the "disturbers of the peace." Brown, seeing that his own "gentle means" were no contest for the situation, told Quinn to handle it his way. Quinn rose from his seat without speaking a word and seized an "ample green stick" about the size of a young sapling. Armed with this weapon, the minister began walking out among the jeering, shouting rioters, quickly turning the tide: "Right and left the undaunted Quinn swept his ponderous weapon, and right and left ruffians both cursing and crying for mercy as they fell like wheat before the reaper's scythe." The preacher continued on through the pack of men "as though he was threshing corn." Garnet says the attackers were astonished by the boldness and force of one man.[3]

As the thrashed mob fled, the camp meeting returned to its holy business. Garnet had one final comment about the matter: "During the entire transaction . . . the Rev. gentleman did not speak a single word, and when the work was finished, he calmly took his seat on the stand."[4] This was the last disturbance of the Methodist camp meetings in Allegheny County. Quinn's actions greatly contributed to his notoriety, especially the rough-and-tumble reputation that marked his ministry. In the minds of many, his actions were necessary and suitable for a pioneering minister who would face the physical requirements of opening the West to the church. Eastern clergy, however, would not hold his actions in the same high regard.

Intellectual as well as physical stamina were necessary for a successful ministry. That year's conference leadership encouraged every member to do all in their power to promote and establish common schools, Sunday schools, and temperance societies among the people. At conference after conference, each minister in charge of a circuit or station was urged to use "every exertion to establish schools wherever convenient, and to insist upon parents sending their children to school; and to preach occasionally a sermon on the subject of education."[5] Ministers failing to do so would be censured by the conference. The state of Ohio enacted Black Codes that denied African Americans access to public schools. The state was not alone in attempting to control access to literacy and education for African Americans. Because the codes restricted movement, advancement, and education for Blacks, schools instituted by the AME Connection were a lifeline. Quinn was dedicated to education, as a necessity for the clergy and a path to citizenship for congregants.[6]

In his journeys the missionary went to some lengths to portray himself as a moderate, making few public references to the Underground Railroad or slavery, except in the context of his preaching. His clandestine activities constantly kept him on the edge of caution. Between 1834 and 1836, Quinn was active in "the dangerous business of assisting fugitive slaves to northern territory, winning the reputation among abolitionists as one of the most skillful slave smugglers," according to reports in the WPA Papers.[7] There is little doubt of his passionate involvement in the abolitionists' intellectual as well as physical confrontation with slavery. Through his vigilance he took every opportunity to quietly assist the work of the Underground Railroad. Wherever Quinn visited or established an AME station, it acquired a deep and documented reputation for Underground Railroad activism. Quinn's close friends and the majority of his associates across his life can be linked to involvement in the movement or, at the very least, the radical arm of the activist abolitionist movement.

Interactions between Quinn and his friends, associates, and religious followers bring the minister's actions to the forefront. One such associate, White abolitionist Augustus Wattles, wove in and out of Quinn's life, as did Henry Highland Garnet and Lewis Woodson. With the encouragement of activist Theodore Weld, Wattles moved to Cincinnati, Ohio, in 1833 to attend Lyman Beecher's Lane Theological Seminary. Beecher, Harriet Beecher Stowe's father, ranked among the best-known clergymen of the first half of the nineteenth century. His presence at Lane brought national prominence, attracting the nation's top students to the newly formed Presbyterian school. For many of the students, the institution became the center of the abolitionist movement. Students pushed to open classes to Black students. To the great consternation of Cincinnati Whites, the students dined and socialized with African Americans, visited their homes, walked openly with Black women, and advocated for equality on all levels.[8]

Quinn's constant push for education placed him at the heart of one of the country's most famous abolitionist controversies, centered at Lane Seminary. Weld, who was turning into a fiery abolitionist, Wattles, and a number of other Lane students began holding open debates on slavery. Beecher, as Lane's president and a foremost evangelical leader of the day, from one of the foremost abolitionist families of the time, feared such debates would provoke dissention within the student ranks and incite local townspeople.

With slavery devouring the moral core of America, Cincinnati operated as both pro-Southern and anti-Black. There a withering riot by White citizens had decimated the Black population in 1829. Many African Americans fled and helped to establish the Wilberforce community in Canada West. To add to the furor, the Presbyterian Church was beginning its own descent into schism and disunion, cleaving into Old School and New School Presbyterians over slavery. The religious climate was tense, divisive, distrustful, and brimming with animosity. All of this contributed to the Lane trustees' decision to restrict the antislavery activities of the students, who kept pushing for an immediate end to slavery—a cause known as *immediatism*. One author offers this assessment of the impact of the Lane debates: "A remarkable series of debates at an upstart Presbyterian theological seminary near Cincinnati . . . helped shape the course of a region—and a nation."[9]

As a result of the debates, on the abolitionist front, antislavery activism put the spotlight on slavery as a national issue rather than narrowly defining it as a Southern practice. David Walker, a Black radical and an activist pamphleteer, began contributing to this shift with the publication of his *Appeal to the Colored Citizens of the World* in 1829. Sending shock waves across the growing nation, the pamphlet confirmed Southerners' worst nightmares about sanctioning literacy for the people they enslaved in addition to access to literacy on the part of free Blacks, such as David Walker.

William Lloyd Garrison's antislavery newspaper, *The Liberator*, first published in 1831, continued the antislavery salvo first fired in print by Walker's *Appeal*. Walker's blistering condemnation of slavery and Garrison's constant bombardment began public confrontation with the hidden side of slavery—in particular, the cruel, violent, and inhumane treatment of the enslaved. The appalling and unjust practices were making their way into public consciousness.

As Walker and Garrison led the abolitionist charge in the press, those establishing schools for Blacks galvanized literacy's battleground. Access to education honed Quinn's work in Cincinnati in the 1830s, when he was active with the Lane rebels, though his participation in the midst of the fight was barely acknowledged.

The preacher had first come to Cincinnati a decade earlier, when he'd helped establish Allen Temple, the city's venerable AME Bethel Church. Initially, the prayer group met in an old lime shed and other buildings, and from the beginning, they helped freedom seekers. This activism led gangs to burn down the early churches three times between 1812 and 1815. In 1824, soon after hearing about the formation of the new AME denomination, the congregation joined the AME Connection.[10]

By 1834 the fourth Ohio Annual Conference had assigned Quinn to the Cincinnati Station; there he pastored Old Bethel Church, which he had helped establish a decade earlier.[11] The church was known by several names: the little red church on the green, Father King's Church, Old Bethel, and, finally, Allen Temple (its present name). It would grow into one of the fortresses of the AME denomination. From its earliest days, the church earned a reputation as an antislavery church. Its ministers openly preached against slavery. AME historian Benjamin Arnett observes that as a result, the church found itself the object of hatred from Cincinnati's pro-slavery masses, who often labeled them Black abolitionists. "As fast as fugitives from the south came across the river, the members of the church would hide them away, and convey them to places of safety on the underground railway to Canada. . . . When a free man or woman came from the South, he or she found an asylum in the little red church on the green."[12] Local accounts affirm that "it had been a first stop on the Underground Railroad for many escapees running from Kentucky several generations earlier." The writer describes how men and women had "crouched shivering in dark cellars, hoping not to be discovered and forced back into enslavement." Husbands and wives, sometimes entire families, waited in closets big enough for only two people, while "free Blacks concealed their presence by singing fervently as they worshiped on the floors above." Allen Temple continued its work helping freedom seekers until the end of the Civil War.[13]

Lane seminarians began their work in education with a Sabbath School that opened for Blacks in Cincinnati in September 1832. Building on a foundation of Black community-directed efforts that extended back at least a decade, Wattles and Weld, part of the "rebels" from the seminary, and especially the antislavery women who'd traveled from New York gave valuable assistance. Building on the already-existing Sabbath Schools in Cincinnati, Bro. Quinn and Baptist minister David Nickens, among other Black leaders and Lane seminarians, opened their first school in March 1834. The coalition of Black and White teachers established circulating libraries and twice-weekly lectures "in Father King's church"—Quinn's church—as well as in an area of Cincinnati known as the Bottom. Father King's church refers to the congregation that first met in the home of Rev. James King before the members had officially joined the AME Connection, and it is the forerunner to Allen Temple, the first AME church in Cincinnati. Together the ministers, with the White dissenters from Lane, organized an evening school and an extensive, uplifting program of instruction. "Schools for blacks were usually physically located within the black community—either in or near the black churches or in private homes," relates one Cincinnati historian. Nickens' school operated in Quinn's Bethel AME Church on Sixth Street.[14]

This marked the second time Quinn and Nickens had teamed up. They had been together in Chillicothe, on the banks of the Scioto River. Nickens had been setting up the first Baptist church at roughly the same time Quinn was establishing the first AME church in the Ohio town. Nickens is remembered in Chillicothe for establishing an antislavery Baptist church committed to ending slavery. Church members actively assisted freedom seekers along the Underground Railroad. Before he and his family moved on from Chillicothe to Cincinnati, Nickens participated directly by hiding fugitives in his home. Simultaneously, on the AME side of the ledger, the same can be said of Quinn's good friends, the Woodson family, who were deeply entwined with the Underground Railroad in Chillicothe.

In Cincinnati Samuel Wells, one of the activist seminarians, wrote to Theodore Weld to let him know that "Bro. Quin the new Minister in our coloured church, takes hold with us and is . . . doing well. He attends all our Lectures and does what he can both publicly and privately to increase the attendance. . . . Our lectures twice a week in Father Kings Church and on the bottom are pretty well attended."[15]

Both Quinn and Nickens opened their churches to the Lane seminarians.[16] Wells boasts that all the students are taught by "whole souled" abolitionists, saying, "We want no other. . . . Bro. Quinn who preaches there now is heartily with us in all our operations, and so is Br. Nickens who preaches on the Bottom."[17] Bible classes, plus a day school for the children and a night school for adults of all sexes and ages, soon had a marked impact.[18] Students began to understand the need for spending more than three or six months in school to obtain the blessings of a quality education and a depth of knowledge. Scholars feasted on an intellectual diet covering moral, secular, and practical topics, including abolitionism.[19] One author has speculated that they also had a hidden agenda and "may have aided fugitive slaves."[20]

Lane Seminary leaders' dissatisfaction and discomfort with such efforts stoked tensions. Rather than capitulate to the tightened regulations laid down by Lane Seminary's Board of Trustees, on December 15, 1834, nearly all the students chose to leave for Oberlin, the newly founded coeducational college in Ohio. The students marched into history, forever known as the Lane rebels. As a result of their dismissal from Lane Seminary, Oberlin College became nationally known as a hotbed of abolitionism and a busy Underground Railroad station, where at least five lines converged. J. M. Brown, a later bishop of the AME Church, may have earned his Underground Railroad pedigree there.

Quinn's involvement was short-lived; other assignments increased his responsibilities elsewhere for greater segments of the church. The Lane students stayed on to teach the night classes, and young women, including the Grimké sisters, came from northern Ohio and central New York to teach the day school. All, however, suffered from acts of mob violence and endured public ridicule and scorn. Augustus Wattles withdrew from Lane and stayed behind in Cincinnati to serve as one of the teachers and a superintendent of instruction at the Bottom. He lived among the African Americans he taught, causing an enormous breach in the social and racial dictates that kept the races almost completely separate.[21]

Each indignity or betrayal by the White Christian church, every law passed in support of slavery or against literacy, propelled African Americans toward Canada beginning in the 1820s, within Baptist as well as Methodist churches. Every Black community in Canada of any significance established a church of one denomination or the other. Growth of the church burst forward with the abolition of slavery in Canada in 1834. Three years later, the New York Conference received a petition from St. Catharines asking for pastoral care. Two decades later, Harriet Tubman would find refuge there when she escaped slavery.

Wherever Deacon Quinn went, he had an outsized impact on the world around him. The influence of his words and actions radiated beyond the pulpit. The minister left few printed texts, but he did leave enduring pieces of writing. Quinn penned a tract that contained a section paying tribute to radical Black pamphleteer David Walker and his *Appeal*. The mutual admiration between Walker and the AME Church was palpable. Walker heaped effusive praise on Richard Allen and the denomination.[22] The denomination, in the form of William Paul Quinn, responded and elaborated from Pittsburgh in 1834.

Quinn followed Walker's radical Black intellectual tradition when the minister wrote his own treatise against slavery. The twenty-four-page pamphlet *The Origin, Horrors and Results of Slavery, Faithfully and Minutely Described in a Series of Facts, and Its Advocates Pathetically Addressed* endures as a passionate attack on slavery, slave owners, and Congress. Quinn opens by quoting Psalm 15: "Thine arrows are sharp in the heart of the king's enemies, whereby the people fall under thee." Addressing his readers as "My dearly beloved fellow countrymen, and courteous reader," he expounds on "the unbounded diffusion of civil and religious liberty," urging the reader to "stir from our lethargy, embark in the cause of freedom" and "fight the good fight of faith." He beseeches his esteemed readers to acquire "the spirit of unfeigned patriotism" and begs slaveholders to find "a spirit of equity and sympathy respecting . . . our fellow Brethren in bondage." Borrowing from Isiah 52:2–3, Quinn lets the Lord speak for him: "May God Almighty soon address the captive sons and daughters of Africa. . . . Shake thyself from the dust, arise, and sit down O Jerusalem: loose thyself from the bonds of thy neck, O captive daughter of Africa . . . ye have been sold for naught to your profit, but ye shall be redeemed without money."[23]

The minister was directly confronting the evil and degradation of slavery, meeting the enslaver head-on in print—something that he often could not do in person. All his words were bathed in God's love and the promise of redemption. But only the introduction, which he signs W. Quinn, and the conclusion appear to be entirely in his own words.

Quinn added to the intellectual framework of the pamphlet by appending unattributed portions from two major works. As Marcy Dinius observes, the majority of the text was taken from Thomas Branagan's "A Preliminary Essay on the Oppression of the Exiled Sons of Africa," as well as the last four pages of the third article of David Walker's widely distributed *Appeal*. Dorothy Porter, compiler of Quinn's essay, suggests that he may have been provoked to include Branagan's "An Address to the Legislators of South Carolina." The state had enacted laws in 1834 preventing the education of Blacks, as well as advocating for the destruction of their schools.

Dinius speculates that Quinn himself wrote, assembled, had printed, and possibly personally circulated and distributed his pamphlet, thereby entwining his own thinking with the radical works of Branagan and Walker as he preached and founded churches in the West. Through Quinn's churches and travels, he maintained a broad base of supporters who, by his efforts, were attaining an appreciation of and a capacity for literacy, giving him a ready audience.[24]

Quinn closes the pamphlet by explaining that his intent for addressing the reader in print "is to excite [them] to watch and pray daily at God's throne, until the spirit of light, love and liberty shall be poured down on every soul. . . . May you have the spirit of God, for where it is there is liberty." Leaving his "little book to God and his blessing," he signs his treatise, "The Rev. W. Paul Quinn, of African Descent."[25] Porter describes "the gathering thunder of abolition" resounding through Quinn's forceful attack on slavery and slaveholders. His use of Branagan's and Walker's words to harpoon legislators give some sense of the fire that emerged from his lips during his sermons.[26] Religious historian Milton Sernett emphasizes that men like Quinn felt that, as with all sins, slavery also had to be denounced from the pulpit. Such itinerant preachers moved freely along the frontier and "could lash out at slavery and then, when threatened, simply shake off the dust of that locality." This may have been true for many itinerant preachers, but Quinn's reputation provoked his attackers to be on the lookout.[27]

The AME Church remained mindful of the plight of its enslaved members while it pushed against the institution of slavery. The Baltimore Conference members resolved to use their "influence and energies against all systems that rudely [trampled] underfoot the claims of justice and the sacred principles of revelation."[28] Slavery, they observed, "pollutes the character of the church of God" and puts the Bible out of reach for "thousands of immortal beings." The conference affirmed education as the path to elevating captives above "the condition of brute" and recommended that all preachers devote "undeviating attention" to its promotion. Education, along with the moderation of temperance, or upholding the principles of total abstinence of all intoxicating drinks, set the course for the moral and intellectual direction of the denomination.[29]

Quinn's disdain for drunkenness brought out his combative qualities, which were important for survival on the frontier. The travel demands of his itinerancy and sparse accommodations forced him to stop at inns that doubled as saloons. Feeling "cold and miserable" after a long, cold winter's ride through a blinding Michigan snowstorm, Quinn, according to Welch, "stalked into the bar and sprawled out in a chair before the great fireplace," attracting the attention of a local souse. Quinn's reputation may have preceded him. The man yelled, "Well if it ain't the fighting parson. Come on parson, and have a drink. It will warm you up." Quinn's refusal and hopes of avoiding a confrontation did not defuse the situation.[30]

The man called for "eight or ten fellows lolling around the place" to come and make Quinn not only drink but also "sing and dance" for them. Welch maintains that "some one bought a quart of whiskey, and the taunter took the bottle and started towards Quinn. The parson rushed to the fellow, seized the bottle, and, with a quick whack, broke the bottle over his head, before the astonished fellow knew what had happened." After that incident the attitude of the crowd changed. "No one cared to fight Quinn, for he had a reputation throughout the lake region for fisticuffs."[31]

Quinn's authoritarian attitude and confidence seemed to attract ruffians and brawlers. His six-foot, two-inch frame and brawn drew admiration—and abuse. An Irish blacksmith, "who had heard a great deal of Quinn and was anxious to make a reputation for himself" by beating him, challenged the minister. Running down the road after Quinn, the smith yelled, "Are you the 'Big Negro' of Lake Michigan?" To this Quinn responded, "Yes." The blacksmith had been told that "Quinn never refused to fight anyone."[32] Quinn got off his horse, which "some obliging fellow held," while a boxing, wrestling, and kicking fight broke out. The pair rolled about in the deep sand. It was, Welch recounts, "the same old story, the parson had licked the blacksmith to a frazzle. Admiring hands brushed the sand from the parson's well known broadcloth suit. They handed him his hat. He mounted his horse and off he raced."[33] Quinn straddled a jagged line between religious responsibility and practicality, between respectability and self-defense. His ruggedness and endurance, combined with his willingness and ability to defend himself, were integral to his success as a church leader, particularly in the West.

By 1834 Quinn was emerging as a national spokesperson, and African Americans were gathering strength through their continued organizing. Few Black newspapers reported such activities, however. *Freedom's Journal* and *The Rights for All* had folded, and *The Christian Recorder*, AME's official newspaper, would not be published until years later. Quinn's activities were noted in scattered newspaper references. After the fact, perhaps in commemoration of Andrew Jackson's death in June 1845, for example, Martin Delany, Quinn's friend from Pittsburgh and editor of *The Mystery*, reported a major event in Quinn's life.[34]

As AME expanded, the state of Maryland stepped up its attempts to control and regulate the freedom and movement of African Americans coming into the state, beyond those already living there. A delegation of clergymen of color visited President Andrew Jackson at the White House in Washington, seeking his advice about the possibility of holding the 1834 Baltimore Annual Conference in Washington, DC. Paul Quinn headed the delegation (see fig. 5.1).[35]

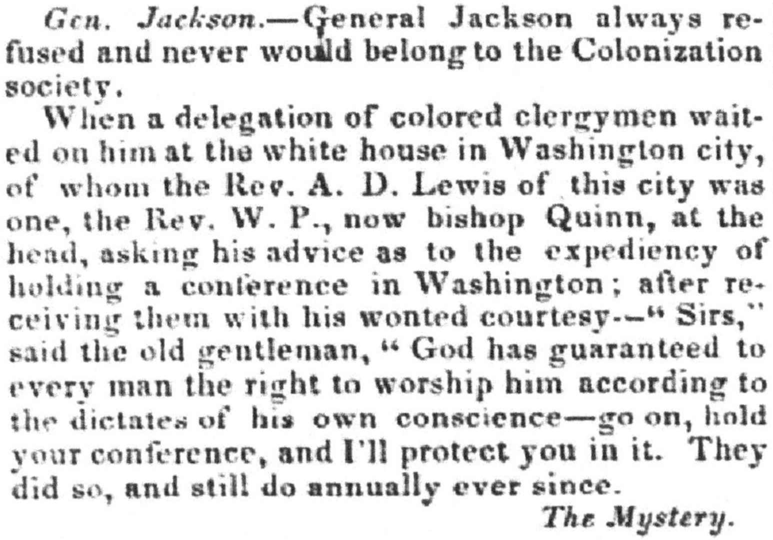

> *Gen. Jackson.*—General Jackson always refused and never would belong to the Colonization society.
> When a delegation of colored clergymen waited on him at the white house in Washington city, of whom the Rev. A. D. Lewis of this city was one, the Rev. W. P., now bishop Quinn, at the head, asking his advice as to the expediency of holding a conference in Washington; after receiving them with his wonted courtesy.—" Sirs," said the old gentleman, " God has guaranteed to every man the right to worship him according to the dictates of his own conscience—go on, hold your conference, and I'll protect you in it. They did so, and still do annually ever since.
> *The Mystery.*

Figure 5.1 Quinn Meets with President Andrew Jackson. "Gen. Jackson" is a republication of an article that was originally printed in Martin Delany's *The Mystery*. From the *Emancipator and Republican*, published as *Emancipator and Weekly Chronicle* (Boston), July 9, 1845. President Andrew Jackson had died a month earlier, June 8, 1845.

Baltimore held the distinction of being a foremost city in the AME Connection. In 1832 Maryland had passed a law forbidding unaccompanied free Blacks from entering the state or assembling for religious purposes, which continued to wreak havoc on the denomination. The Quinn-led delegation turned to Jackson for approval and assurance of protection after settling on Washington, DC, as their alternative conference site. The Baltimore Conference was forced to hold its annual conference in the District of Columbia to ensure all members who wished to attend the conference could do so.[36]

Andrew Jackson's biographer refers to the president as an "ecumenical unionist in religion, at least among Christians."[37] The president bestowed his blessings on the endeavor, stating that every man had the right to worship God "according to the dictates of his own conscience." He then said, "Go on, hold your conference, and I'll protect you in it."[38] In mid-April, the AME Connection reported that the Third Annual Baltimore Conference, held in Washington, DC, caused general excitement and quite a stir among the Washington public. It was "the first colored body" ever convened in the capital of the United States. "Many hundreds, both Black and white assembled at the preaching hours, especially on the Lord's day and listened with delight to the ambassadors of the cross."[39] The first-of-its-kind convention catapulted the denomination's influence beyond all other Black churches. As President Jackson had promised, city authorities did offer their "protection should any evil designed persons attempt any interruption." President Jackson's "warmest commendation of the proceedings of the Conference" and his wish for "a hearty success" were fully accomplished.[40]

By the summer of 1835, Quinn was back in the western mission field, where he encountered an aspiring Methodist Episcopal minister, Rev. Dandridge Davis, from Kentucky, at an AME camp meeting near the Kentucky–Ohio border of the Ohio River. Davis left a vivid account. The young man of color was "astonished" to learn that the meeting would be "conducted entirely by their own Ministers, and their Bishop would be present also!"[41] He moved slowly through the meeting, witnessing what he called "one of the wonders of his day." After he arrived at the grove, "the sound of the gospel trumpet; the cry of mourners; and shout of believers vibrated through every avenue of his soul! . . . the trumpet waxing louder and louder, till the place appeared filled with the glory of God." The young aspirant met Bishop Brown and Rev. Quinn and was warmly received by all. Seeing ministers of his own color awed Davis, offering him a new concept of and a new possibility for his own ministry.[42]

The following day, Rev. Quinn preached the sermon. When Quinn ended, "the Ministers came down and prepared to march around the encampment with singing, and now and then the trumpet would sound as they moved along slowly and sinners crying out for mercy. . . . With tears of joy and wonder, the convert fell to the ground as souls found their way home."[43]

Davis remained at the camp meeting for several days, then told Bishop Brown he was ready to join the denomination. After returning to his studies at Augusta College in Kentucky, Davis told his White professors and friends, "Never did I see the like before . . . such preaching, praying, and singing, it was like heaven on earth!"[44] Such was the power and forceful effect of camp meetings and of the denomination he was determined to join.

The preceptors at the Methodist Episcopal school considered this an unsound direction for Davis, explaining to him that the work of the AME Church would prove "deleterious" to enslaved brethren in the South. Rather than doing them good, the church would inflict harm by creating dissatisfaction, instilling a desire to "follow his example" in this choice and in other matters.[45] His White instructors summed up their intense apprehension that free Blacks would set a lasting example among the enslaved for possibilities of their own freedom. Three years later, however, when Quinn was "seeking his brethren in the States of Indiana and Illinois" and was looking for good assistance, he either remembered or was reminded of Rev.

Davis. To Davis's great joy, he was offered an appointment to the Richmond circuit in Indiana. Quinn continually honed his abilities for recognizing and exploiting talent and spiritual gifts in service of the church.[46]

As part of his religious duties, Quinn ministered to, baptized, and served church members. Hannah Dickson, for example, had all nine of her children baptized by Quinn before she died. Among those anointed was Hannah's son, Moses Dickson, born in April 1824. In choosing to name him Moses, his mother "dedicated her boy to the cause of freedom . . . and predicted that he would, like Moses of old, lead his people from bondage to freedom."[47] Perhaps in a reflection of his own radical stand, Quinn blessed the man who became one of the most radical Black organizers of his time.[48] As an adult, Moses Dickson served in several capacities: he cofounded Lincoln Institute, the predecessor to Lincoln University; he served as Grand Master of Missouri Masons; and he headed the Knights Liberty, an organization dedicated to liberating the enslaved via the Underground Railroad. Later in his life, Dickson became an ordained AME minister who preached at several churches in the St. Louis area.

A biographical sketch of Dickson written after his death in 1901 in the *St. Louis Star* lamented the loss of "one of the world's greatest Negro organizers and fraternal society leaders of the nineteenth century."[49] The newspaper went on to note that Dickson had "founded and perfected the largest secret Negro organization in the world."[50] Before the Civil War, Dickson organized the Order of Twelve of the Knights and Daughters of Tabor, later known as the Knights of Liberty. Booker T. Washington asserts that its purpose was nothing less "than the overthrow of slavery in the United States."[51] As conditions shifted and the country appeared likely to take up that cause, the Knights "became actively connected with the Underground Railroad."[52] Quinn's life constantly transected the lives of radical abolitionists dedicated to securing freedom for the enslaved.

Quinn was soon to be appointed missionary to the northwestern states. The preacher would set about, with his customary effectiveness, bringing souls to the Lord and members to the AME Church. Initiating a string of African Methodist churches about a one-day wagon ride apart—from Louisville, Kentucky, to Detroit, Michigan, and from St. Louis, Missouri, to Chicago, Illinois—became part of a recognizable pattern. These churches, in addition to their sacred and secular functions, would become shelters for freedom seekers during the coming years. At the same time, Quinn "became the best known man throughout the connection" by attending all the annual conferences and meetings of the church. It would serve him well.[53]

CHAPTER 6

Local Circuits to an International Conference 1836–1844

West to Indiana and Missouri—South to Kentucky and Louisiana—North to Canada

Astride his horse, with saddlebags and hymn book at the ready and his Bible tucked under his arm, Quinn began his long and fruitful relationship with Indiana. In 1836 he was appointed general missionary and sent to the western states beyond Ohio, particularly Indiana, Illinois, and Michigan. In September Quinn earned the gratitude of the African American community of Richmond, Indiana, when he organized sixteen believers into a Methodist society. They grew into an established congregation, adopting the name Bethel AME Church, "for God was with them," signaling that they were the first AME church in Indiana.

Within a little more than thirty years, the congregation would amass $4,000, the *Richmond Palladium* reports. Quinn would use the funds to purchase a brick church on the corner of Market and Marion. The church still occupies that corner.[1]

Quinn liked Richmond well enough to stay. When he chose to make the village his home, less than fifty of its twelve hundred residents formed his spiritual community. Finally, he'd found home ground—the first since his days in New York City, although he had settled in Pittsburgh for a time. Most of the African Americans in Richmond had come from Virginia and North Carolina to escape the Black Laws enacted in those states mainly against free people of color. Slaveholding states had enacted antiliteracy laws between 1740 and 1834, and Northern states, such as Ohio, Indiana, and Illinois, enacted Black Codes that limited access to education.[2] Richmond's substantial community of free Blacks, one of the strongest in the Midwest, was not permitted to attend schools at that time. Quinn quickly realized that one of his principal tasks would be to provide for the educational and social needs of his congregants. The circuit rider had come a long way from New York in both physical distance and sacred mission, when Quakers first provided him with letters of introduction.

Quinn would live a few doors down from the church on Marion Street. Similar to Philadelphia, the town had a strong Quaker presence, which appealed to him. The early influence of Elizabeth Walker permeated his life and "made him love the Friends." Richmond was a Quaker town, and there existed "a kindred spirit between them and Quinn," confirms Welch. They shared three strong convictions: a hatred of war, slavery, and drunkenness.[3]

Over a twenty-year period, Quinn would become a substantial landowner in the state, eventually acquiring twenty parcels amounting to three hundred acres and approximately seventeen lots. Much of the land was located primarily in Wayne County as well as in nearby New Garden Township, the home of famed Quaker abolitionist Levi Coffin and his wife, Catherine.[4] Quinn owned a seventeen-acre horse farm outside Newport and a lot in Dublin.[5]

In his rare moments of respite, Quinn gave over his time to breeding horses for market. The cultivation of horses also guaranteed he would have a ready supply of steeds to ride along his circuits whenever needed. Welch learned from those who had known Quinn that he fed a special diet to the chestnut horses he preferred so their dark brown coats would "sheen like satin." The heavy, wavy black manes and tails revealed the level of care and grooming the horses received. Adding a fine bridle, a handsome saddle, and an expert rider left an unforgettable impression.[6]

At the time, nearby Newport was known as Fountain City. For eight years William Paul Quinn and Levi Coffin lived less than ten miles from one another. Coffin and his wife, Catharine, Indiana's most notable Quakers and Underground Railroad workers, had arrived in Fountain City in 1826. The Underground Railroad would have been running there for at least ten years before Quinn decided to settle eight miles away, in Richmond. Coffin suggested that it had been in operation before he had arrived as well.

Quinn's responsibility for initiating AME churches across at least seven states was well understood by then. Their consistent operation as stations on the Underground Railroad, however, was not. Quinn established an AME church in Fountain City so the likelihood that he and Coffin at least knew of one another is extremely high. Brian Dolinar reports that "along with the Quakers of the neighborhood, Quinn took an active part in the work of the Underground Railroad and on several occasions risked his life directing runaway slaves to Canada."⁷

Levi Coffin ran what has been called the "Grand Central Station" of the Underground Railroad, which was in close proximity to the AME church in Fountain City and literally down the road from Bethel AME in Richmond. Routes fed into small local towns and stations, such as Dublin, the location of one of the local AME churches (see fig. 6.1). Under the Coffins' leadership, more than two thousand freedom seekers passed through during the twenty years the couple lived in Newport, before they decided to relocate to Cincinnati.

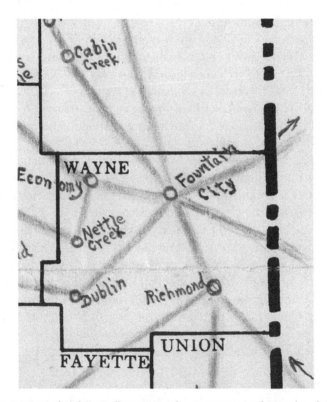

Figure 6.1 Excerpt of Siebert Indiana Map. This is an excerpt from a hand-drawn map by Wilbur Siebert that lays out the Underground Railroad routes in Indiana. His final published printed map eliminated some of the smaller stops, such as Dublin. Note that Quinn's hometown of Richmond and Dublin (lower arrow) are routes feeding into Fountain City (also known as Newport), an important hub and the home of Levi Coffin (upper arrow). "Underground Routes of Indiana by Prof. W. H. Siebert," ca. 1888?, Wilbur H. Siebert Underground Railroad Collection, Ohio History Center, courtesy of Ohio History Connection. https://ohiomemory.org/digital/collection/siebert/id/9123

A hand-drawn map by Underground Railroad historian Wilbur Siebert brings these geographic relationships into focus (see fig. 6.1). Fountain City was a hub fed by escapees from Richmond and Dublin. Quinn established AME churches there and had personal ties to both towns. A merging of Underground Railroad maps with a map of the AME churches of the period indicates how the two pathways of escape from slavery converged for the length of the state (see fig. 6.2).

Bounty hunters tracking down freedom seekers complained that after they followed escapees to Newport, all trails disappeared. Three escape routes across the Ohio River converged into Newport's heavy Underground Railroad traffic. A trio of crossing points at Cincinnati, Ohio, and Madison and Jeffersonville in Indiana ultimately led north to Canada.[8]

Abolitionists such as Quinn and Coffin were driven by religious motivations in their quest for justice. Untenable tensions between godly actions and legal dictates left some religious leaders with only one choice: obey higher law. Nowhere was this more evident than in Richmond. Confronted by this conundrum, religious-minded men and women often took a moral stand within both a Black and White interdenominational fight against the vile practices that perpetuated slavery.

Prince Hall Masons also acted as agents of the Underground Railroad in the area. While living in New York City, Quinn had been invested with Masonic rites and remained committed to their cause. However solidly Quakers supported the Underground Railroad, they were generally opposed to secret societies, such as the Free and Accepted Masons. When the Masons attempted to rent space for a Masonic hall in Richmond, they had trouble finding willing renters. Quinn came to their aid and allowed them to use one of his houses. Because of his generosity and support, the Masons "respect the memory of Paul Quinn, who is their patron saint," Welch explains after her study of the Quinn Lodge records. In his honor they designated their order, Quinn Lodge No. 28, which remains in existence today. The minister could prove himself a Mason, although he did not enroll as a member in the Richmond lodge.[9]

Quinn's continuing success helped him reach another milestone: his election as an AME elder in 1838.[10] Elders were the eyes and ears as well as the conduits that kept small local or rural churches connected to one another and to the mother church. Quinn holds the distinction of having established the greatest number of churches in Indiana. In 1837 he had organized Allen Chapel, the oldest Black church in the western part of the state, in Terre Haute, Indiana, before working both sides of the Ohio River.

Local Circuits to an International Conference ~ 75

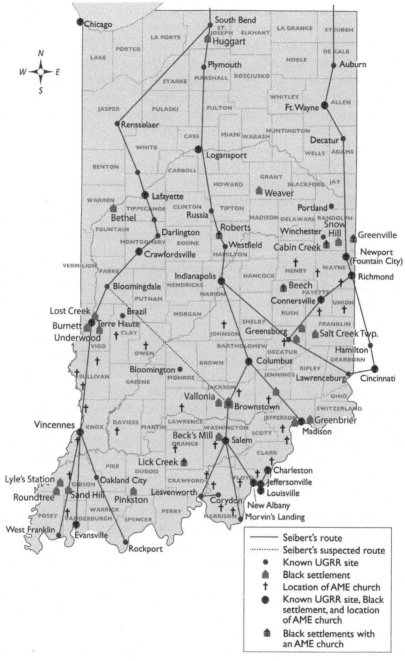

Figure 6.2 AME and Underground Railroad Map. Map showing AME churches and overlapping known Underground Railroad routes. Courtesy of the author.

Quinn was always out among the people; he first organized the New Albany AME Church on the Indiana side of the Mississippi River in the spring of 1838. The church was essential to his efforts in cultivating the growth of AME in nearby Louisville, on the south side of the riverfront. Quinn had tilled the soil by first planting churches in Indiana, particularly in New Albany in Floyd County. During his first trip to Indiana, he'd apparently also worshipped with Louisville's African American Methodist community. For Kentucky bondsmen and women, "he sowed the seed of mind, soul and body *freedom*," acknowledges Bishop Arnett.[11]

Louisville's growing free Black population came together as a viable community around 1830. According to historian Blaine Hudson, "it became the largest free black population in the Upper South, west of Baltimore, and the only meaningful concentration of free people of color in Kentucky."[12] Paul Quinn would want to bring this substantial and viable community under the banner of the growing AME Church. The preacher had given twenty years of his life in service to the Lord through the AME Church and had steadily planted the seeds of African Methodism in the West years earlier. Now he was evangelizing in forbidden Southern territory.

David Smith helped ease the minds of those worried about the "abolition church" when he came to Louisville around the time the church was being established in Kentucky. He spoke of a White Methodist Episcopal preacher who had charge of both the Black and the White Methodists of Louisville and was acquainted with "the nature and object" of the AME Church. The minister had persuaded Smith "not to say anything about the AME Church, as it was very dangerous at that time for anyone to advocate the principles of Christian manhood which the AME church held and taught her adherents."[13] Other critics incited discontent toward the church by labeling it (with good cause) as abolitionist. Increasing numbers of escapes accompanied the rise of abolitionism. More stringent laws soon followed.[14]

Southern Indiana lay across the Ohio River from Kentucky. Geography plus the presence of thriving free African Americans communities on both sides of the river made Louisville an important gateway in the quest for freedom. Slave catchers kept a sharp eye on the city. They understood the importance of its strategic location at the Falls of the Ohio. A two-mile-long series of white-water rapids offered the only navigational barrier for the 981-mile length of the Ohio River. Louisville on the Kentucky side and New Albany and Jeffersonville on the Indiana side—all can trace their existence as communities to the geography of the Falls. As obstacles to navigation, the Falls required local expertise for navigating river traffic. At that point the river also could be crossed on foot during a drought or when it was solid ice. The Louisville vicinity experienced an extended drought in 1838, the year Quinn came to the area. In addition to the Falls, the city was a crucial location for potential water escapes from slavery as well. To combat this, Kentucky enacted several laws regulating the mobility of Blacks, particularly on steamships and other riverboats. The fight extended to the ownership of the waters of the Ohio River—was the river slavery territory or free?[15]

For anyone escaping enslavement, Louisville's geography presented both an impediment and a benefit. The Falls of the Ohio turned the city into a transportation hub, served by steamboats, trains, and several active ferries. Enslaved Black watermen often piloted riverboats on the Ohio. Simultaneously, free African Americans were required to present documentation of their status before taking passage. Laws specifically targeting ferrymen who aided freedom seekers carried steep yet ineffective fines. At times, however, escapees would slip through because the ferrymen had a business to run, but it was always a risky undertaking.

Historian Pen Bogart found hundreds of advertisements in Louisville newspapers offering rewards for the capture and return of fugitives. New Albany–based Pam Peters also found that working-class African Americans were the true engine of the Underground Railroad in the Louisville area. In the process of scrutinizing census records, Peters found that nearly a quarter of the working African American population was "employed in river-related occupations, crewing and loading the steamboats and ferries." Another large percentage was involved in land-based transportation, driving wagons and carts that carried goods to and from the ferries—"sometimes carrying fugitives hidden under hay or straw (or, Peters notes, 'sewn up in feather beds')."[16]

Quinn's reputation as a powerful and effective abolitionist preacher meant that he was safer in Indiana and would have been arrested had officials known he had entered Kentucky. Undaunted, he exhorted Louisville Blacks from Corn Island, at the bend in the river, just beyond the Louisville riverfront at the Falls, a short distance off the Kentucky coast. At low water extremes, rocky Corn Island could be reached from the Kentucky bank (see fig. 6.3).[17] Quinn's potent voice carried and allowed him to sing, pray, and preach for extended periods.

Louisville's early African American Methodists first met in a livery stable near Second and Main Streets, across from the old Galt House. This location became the birthplace of the Bethel House of God, renamed Bethel AME Church, then later, Quinn Chapel. When Quinn finally entered Louisville, he was arrested on the second floor of the livery stable for holding a

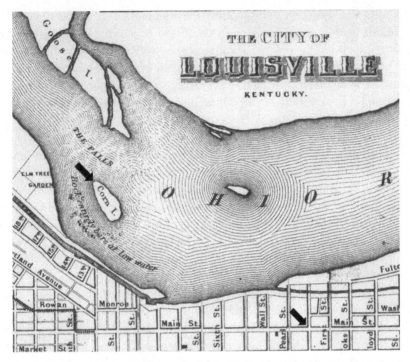

Figure 6.3 The City of Louisville Map. Originally the Bethel Church, now known as Quinn Chapel, Louisville, was strategically located at the corner of Second and Main Streets, across from the Galt House, one block from the river (center arrow). Quinn was arrested there, on the second floor of the livery stable, which was used for the first religious gathering. By custom, a Bethel church would usually be the first church established in a city. The first location of an AME church, along the river, held a strategic advantage for freedom seekers. (The church has since moved). The *upper left* arrow indicates Corn Island, near the falls where Quinn was said to have preached before he entered Kentucky. The map indicates, "Rocks entirely bare at low water." J. H. Colton & Co., "City of Louisville," created 1855, courtesy of Ball State University Digital Media Repository, https://dmr.bsu.edu/digital/collection/AmrcnCtyHis/id/31/rec/3.

religious meeting. Fortunately, after finding that all the missionary's papers were in proper order for conducting the gatherings, the arresting officer was forced to release him. At the end of Quinn's preaching, his Methodist listeners organized an AME congregation in Louisville and, later, a school. The Louisville church was renamed Quinn Chapel in his honor in 1841. As the reputation of Quinn Chapel spread, it became known as "the abolition church," with reputed ties to the Underground Railroad.[18]

Louisville is an example of a phenomenon rarely understood today: the development of independent Black churches consisting of free and enslaved congregants in slaveholding states before the Civil War. By the 1840s such developments took place in the southern cities of Baltimore, New Orleans, and St. Louis. In Louisville, slaveholders could not abide the idea of the abolition church operating among an enslaved population, so they barred them, when they could, from attending. Authorities had less control over the lives of the city's free Black worshippers.

Risking his safety, Quinn preached equality of men before God. He battled injustice wherever and whenever he found it, and he was never afraid to use his fists if pushed in that direction. Welch suggests that perhaps he carried "a ready gun strapped to his side." Hotels were unsafe, travel was treacherous, and trouble lurked for travelers on the highway. "One sometimes feared to remove his boots, should he drop off to sleep," and upon waking, he might find himself barefoot, Welch explains.[19]

Whether through scripture, escape, or education, Elder Quinn offered spiritual nourishment, seeking constant relief for his enslaved and beleaguered brethren as his work expanded the reach of the church. In addition to the Indiana and Kentucky churches, he had established churches in Alton and Rocky Fork in southern Illinois by late 1839.

By the end of the decade, Quinn was spending time in the Wisconsin–Iowa region in a quest for more favorable conditions for his African American worshippers. He consulted with agents in Iowa "to form a colony of colored people who may settle in some part of the West." The southern part of Iowa Territory appeared the most favorable. Unlike in Wisconsin, the land had yet to be surveyed, and speculators had not grabbed the "first quality" parcels. The conditions led Quinn to observe that "nearly all the emigration is going to Iowa."[20] Such untapped regions could be fertile ground for the continued growth of the church.

Quinn had a business side as well. Welch claims he could have been a captain of industry. His reliable fiscal stewardship instilled the same financial responsibility in the laity that he demanded of himself. He taught them to follow the practices first espoused by Richard Allen: owning the ground on which the church stood and securing church premises firmly by deed, binding them permanently to the AME Church. This allowed his followers to amass the funds necessary to build their houses of worship. Quinn is remembered for building more churches than any other man in the AME Connection.[21]

Churchgoers applied these same sound financial principles to their personal lives. The *Indianapolis Journal* reports that Quinn "not only preached the gospel, but he studied how to look out for the body, and advised the people to get homes and make themselves comfortable in life. And all through Indiana and Illinois there are men and families who are prosperous today because they followed his advice."[22]

As his reputation grew, churches filled whenever Quinn was expected to deliver a sermon, but travel by horseback could be unpredictable. If he was delayed in reaching his destination, a crowd often gathered outside the church, "waiting to see him make his dramatic arrival," Welch declares. "Finally he came surrounded by clouds of dust, riding his horse in full heat," dismounting as "the horse was either galloping at full speed" or as the animal was standing on his front hooves "or perhaps [rearing] on his hind legs, the more perilous the more excitement." After a daring dismount, Quinn loudly greeted bystanders, shaking hands all around, sometimes jovially greeting an acquaintance. It was hard to determine who enjoyed these acrobatic feats more, his admiring audience and onlookers or Quinn himself, who seemed to be electrified by the energetic performances and delivering a rousing sermon. He would join with the church faithful as they launched into a hymn—Quinn enthusiastically lending his voice with his off-key singing.[23]

Upon returning to Indiana, Quinn found the faithful eager to join the denomination. An Indianapolis coworker gave organizer Augustus Turner a copy of the AME discipline. In 1836 he used it to gather together a small study group with the intention of affiliating with the AME Church. They petitioned to be annexed to the western circuit. The Philadelphia conference accepted Turner's petition and sent Quinn to Indianapolis to help the small society achieve membership in the AME Church in Indiana.[24]

When Elder Quinn visited the city late in the summer of 1838, the pastor carried the credentials of a traveling missionary and organizer of the AME Church as well as letters of introduction from prominent members of the Society of Friends in Philadelphia, New York, and far-off England. Such letters vouched for his character and intention and helped shield this man "of singular gifts" and high esteem from meddling constables and sheriffs.[25]

Augustus Turner, Elder Quinn, and the small congregation met in Turner's barbershop home. Quinn became the first AME minister to serve Indianapolis Station, as the church was known at the time. The little frame building stood on the north side of Georgia Street, between Capitol and Senate Avenues—near the canal. Nothing, neither houses nor fences, stood between the church and the river.[26] Following Quinn's decades-old formula, the congregation became active in the antislavery movement, often harboring fugitives headed for Canada. To the consternation of some among the local White community, church members' activism in promoting the abolitionist movement and their activities with the Underground Railroad persisted. Proslavery supporters are believed to have set the fire that destroyed the church in 1862. AME Church history says more directly that "the church was burned by revolutionaries in rebellion against [an] abolition gospel" preached by its pastor, Rev. Willis Revels, "brother of the illustrious Black [future] Georgia Senator." The church again suffered destruction by fire in 1868. In a continual battle against Indiana's antiliteracy laws, Bethel "sponsored and initiated . . . the first black high school in Indianapolis in 1867."[27]

Churches established in Terra Haute and Dublin, as well as Cambridge City and Newport (now Fountain City), attest to Quinn's long and fruitful relationship with Indiana. Most of the AME churches in Ohio and Indiana point to Quinn's organizing influence. As Quinn moved across the country, he owed much of his success not only to the vast network of intertwined congregations and churches he'd helped establish but also to the friendships he'd developed. Among his friends in faith, he counted the influential Revels brothers, Willis and Hiram, who were both AME ministers. Elder Quinn relied on extended-family relationships, such as the Woodsons of Ohio. Each of the faithful in Quinn's life filled roles important for the development of the church and the political evolution of the nation. Internationally, Quinn's friend Willis Nazrey, the "able young giant," would later lead the Canadian branch of AME.[28] The New York conference accepted Nazrey's application for admission in June 1840. Quinn, Daniel Payne, and Nazrey became the rising leaders of the church who would guide it through the great yet tumultuous period of change that lay ahead.

In the 1830s and 1840s, Quinn's major preoccupation had been to advance the AME Church. The rapidly growing membership that resulted led Bishop Brown to organize two new conferences, the first in Toronto, Upper Canada, and the second in Blue River, Indiana. Morris Brown presided over the Indiana meeting, placing Quinn in charge of the Indiana Circuit and its forty-five congregations. The denomination had grown to a total of six conferences.

In a short four years, the two conferences—one, international; the other, in the West—crowned Quinn's successful labors.[29] Elder Quinn had rendered such good service through his western missions that the members of the 1840 General Conference in Baltimore expressed their pleasure by officially designating him general missionary to the West. The conference expected him to "plant the A.M.E. Church in the far West," beyond Ohio. Illinois and Indiana in particular benefited from his ministry. He had been mining souls in the West for the church for at least seven years before his official appointment.[30]

With the extension of the AME Church into Canada, the denomination faced a different hurdle. Church members were required to travel across the border back into the United States on a regular basis to attend conferences and official church functions, some of which involved slaveholding states.

For Canadian members attempting to cross the border into the United States, the threat of kidnapping loomed constantly. The majority of AME's Canadian members had escaped slavery in the United States and had found freedom and safety in the Canadian provinces. Looking across the border, Canadian congregants and ministers faced an American environment increasingly hostile to both free Blacks and freedom seekers in the North as well as the South. The very real fear of Black Canadian Methodists of being captured, transported, and forced into slavery in the South prompted the church to act. Canadian members introduced a resolution requesting the Methodist churches in British North America (Canada) separate from the American association and form their own independent church. A decade and a half later, the church acted on the request.

Elder Quinn's new assignment as general missionary included overseeing the Brooklyn circuit. In his new capacity, he made his way back to Mother Baltimore in East St. Louis, Illinois. With her help, he had established the Brooklyn church there earlier, in the 1830s. On this second trip, Quinn again operated from her home, which she always made available to him and to his horse, supplying whatever was needed. Pushing to extend African Methodism across the Mississippi River into St. Louis, Missouri, the missionary asked Mother Baltimore if he might preach the Word of Christ. She went about spreading the good news. Fifty people attended his first meeting.[31]

Quinn repeated the same effective strategy for Missouri that he had used in Kentucky, preaching from a safe distance, as his abolitionist activities placed him in danger of arrest. Missouri also enforced restrictions on Black ministers preaching to the enslaved. Abolitionists often fell victim to violence in proslavery Missouri; antislavery advocates were scarcely more successful. Prayer groups were forbidden to hold night meetings unless a White preacher conducted the prayers.[32]

Once more Quinn preached from a safe distance, beyond danger of arrest. Standing on the Illinois side of the Mississippi River, he preached across the waters to the men and women, many of them enslaved on the Missouri side, in St. Louis. Cha-Jua says Quinn found numerous ways to get behind "the Cotton Curtain. When he could not smuggle himself into the belly of the beast, he shouted his message across the river." At Alton, north of Brooklyn, he managed to get his message to the enslaved gathered on the Missouri side, perhaps from Ellis Island or a sandbar. A Brooklyn legend claims that after the river had frozen over, Quinn would simply walk over "and preach the gospel of freedom to those still shackled in slavery on the Missouri side."[33]

The intrepid minister had to pursue his objectives at night. Priscilla Baltimore, a dedicated Underground Railroad conductor, ferried the evangelist in the late hours to keep him beyond the reach of municipal authorities. Renowned for its treacherous snags and bars, the Mississippi River made crossing in darkness in a small boat no easy task. To first attract the attention of the gathered crowd on the Missouri side, according to Brooklyn legend, Quinn would amplify his hymns using a black kettle to throw his voice across the waters to the faithful.[34]

Although not mentioned in the historical record, Quinn may have been able to accomplish this feat from one of two islands that were present off the St. Louis shore in 1836 but have since disappeared. Bloody Island lay between Brooklyn and St. Louis. A second island, Duncan Island, existed farther south and was much closer to the St. Louis shore (see fig. 6.4). Rather than row Quinn over the entire expanse of the Mississippi River, Priscilla Baltimore may have deposited him on Bloody Island or Duncan Island, and perhaps from there, he used this closer yet still safe distance to preach the word to the enslaved in Missouri. But we may never know for sure.

In a newspaper article, Rev. Henderson went on to say that the next day, Sunday, Mother Baltimore crossed the Mississippi River and gathered together three hundred people of color to come to her meeting across the river, on the Illinois side. The aspirants were eager, but the ferryboat captain was worried about transporting so many enslaved people across the river. He asked, "What security shall I have that you will return to your masters?" At that point, Mother Baltimore offered herself, claiming, "I'll be their security." The captain, "knowing the soundness of her reputation, . . . transported the '300 souls' across the river to attend that meeting. That night one of the vanguard African Methodist Churches in the west was organized in Priscilla Baltimore's bedroom."[35] Homes such as Baltimore's were a powerful site of institution building throughout the early church years. In 1841 St. Paul's Chapel in St. Louis would be an outgrowth of Baltimore's efforts.

Quinn befriended another of his lifelong allies, Jordan Winston Early, in St. Louis. A decade before, Early had left the Methodist Episcopal Church to come over to the AME Church under Quinn's influence as he was organizing the church in the city. Early helped cajole the White authorities in St. Louis, obtaining their respect and their favor. He worked to ease the way in for the church.[36] Early gave a clear picture of how the AME Church was viewed in slaveholding states such as Missouri. Carrying the radical label of "abolition church," the AME Church racked slaveholders with suspicion and "sometimes the members and local preachers were brought before the courts of justice to answer for the absence of some slave who had made his escape."

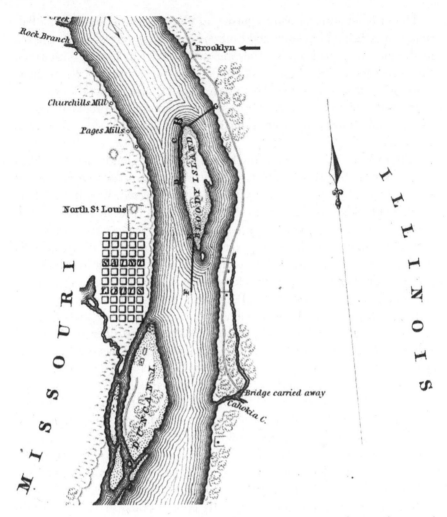

Figure 6.4 St. Louis Harbor Sketch Reduced from Capt. Lee's Map of 1837. This period map clarifies how Quinn could have preached across the Mississippi River. Two islands existed off the St. Louis banks in the 1840s: Bloody Island, which is closer to Brooklyn, and Duncan Island, which is immediately off the Missouri coast. It is unclear from where Quinn preached, but it could have been Bloody Island. The arrow indicates the location of Brooklyn, in what is now known as East St. Louis, Illinois. Courtesy of National Archives.

One writer states that "when Quinn returned to Illinois, he often brought fugitive slaves with him."[37]

Baptist minister John Berry Meachum, pastor of First Baptist Church, also defied and bedeviled St. Louis authorities. Meachum, like Quinn, pushed for educational reform. St. Louis lawmakers considered Meachum's efforts to teach enslaved and free children to read subversive. Punishment for violations of an 1825 law that banned education of free African Americans ranged from twenty lashes to imprisonment and fines. After Meachum's school was shut down, he circumvented the law by establishing the quietly inconspicuous Floating Freedom School on a riverboat in the middle of the Mississippi River, complete with desks, chairs, and a library. Reflecting the ambiguous jurisdictions around river ownership, Meachum's decision navigated around the law, as the Mississippi River was considered federal space and a marginal area separating slavery in Missouri from freedom in Illinois. Therefore, Meachum's Floating School was not in violation of the law. Like Quinn, Meachum transported freedom seekers across the Mississippi River to Illinois. A local newspaper stated that his church, First Baptist, was the leader of the "mischief" in their midst, operating as "headquarters of the underground railroad."[38]

The slaveholding state of Missouri was uninterested in the radical proselytizing of independent preachers of color, including Quinn and Meachum, so St. Louis authorities would not allow Quinn to stay overnight. When he did ultimately enter the state, Missouri officials detained him until the missionary sent for his ministerial papers in which he claimed that he was a British subject. He persuaded authorities that American laws did not apply to him, which effected his release.[39]

According to Missouri law, "meetings, religious or otherwise, conducted by other African Americans, were prohibited unless some sheriff, constable, marshal, police officer, etc., was present. Violations could receive a $500 fine, six months in jail, or both."[40] Authorities were right to worry about the vehemence of Quinn's antislavery stand. He had developed into an "expert in smuggling slaves, and could on the spur of the moment form a ruse, by which the slave owner could be misled," Welch reveals. The city of St. Louis took Quinn before the grand jury three times for his supposed offenses.[41] Nonetheless, in 1841, Quinn, with the help of Baltimore, established St. Paul Church, the first AME church west of the Mississippi River and one of the leading churches in the state of Missouri. As with all AME churches, it was freestanding and self-governing.

Lay members such as Mother Baltimore offered crucial help at several stages of the denomination's development. Seamstresses, rivermen, and teamsters joined teachers, fishermen, and laborers to form the lay congregation of this "self-consciously abolitionist" denomination, remarks a local historian.[42] They formed the backbone of the small congregations Quinn used as the first step in developing a church in each location. For her indispensable role in establishing African Methodism in Illinois and Missouri, Priscilla Baltimore is considered the mother of African Methodism in the West.[43]

In 1841 Elder Quinn marked another achievement with his appointment as presiding elder of Illinois, Indiana, and Missouri. Increasing responsibilities accompanied Quinn's new duties. Morris Brown, as senior bishop, officiated at the August opening of the new Indiana conference in 1841. Since Bishop Waters, the third bishop, played a minimal role, Elder Quinn was voted assistant to Brown for the eight days of the conference.[44]

Quinn's journey from excoriation to honor was almost complete. A preamble and resolution passed two years after Quinn was appointed to lead the western Christian mission validated the esteem and affection the denomination held for the elder. He was accorded the high honor "to sit and counsel with the Bishop during this Conference."[45] The ecclesiastical body recognized Quinn's efforts as being "largely responsible for this 'new age' in African Methodist missionary history."[46] The 1842 Ohio Annual Conference called the work "the greatest Christian enterprise ever undertaken by the African Methodist Episcopal connection, since its rise and progress in our country."[47] The church's "wide-spreading influence, and future prospect of good to the present and rising generations in the western States" entitled brother Quinn to that "honor and esteem . . . paid to all men of great minds and enterprising habits."[48] Through his untiring zeal, the western mission, within a mere two years, could boast of eight circuits with a membership of eight or nine hundred that encompassed Black communities of twelve to fourteen thousand, all of which were under the superintendency of Elder Quinn.

With Quinn in the West and Nazrey destined for Canada, the pious and studious Daniel Payne was assuming increasing responsibility for the eastern churches. Like Allen, Brown, and Quinn before him, Payne was involved in offering both indirect and direct aid to escapees. His work can be seen best with his membership in the vigilance committee in Philadelphia, which he joined in the 1840s. The *Minute Book of the Vigilant Committee of Philadelphia* lists Daniel A. Payne, AME minister. The first Philadelphia committee he served became a model for the later, more famous one. Both iterations of the vigilant committee assisted freedom seekers entering the city of Philadelphia, rescuing them from kidnappers and facilitating the flow of escapes to Canada.[49]

Payne wielded scripture to reinforce his argument that slavery was wrong. From 1842 to 1843, "Payne was a leader of the Vigilance Committee which was organized for the purpose of hiding runaway slaves from state, local, and federal authorities who sought to take the slaves back to their masters," according to one historian.[50] Payne worked on behalf of this important vigilant-committee arm of the Underground Railroad. The committees in

Philadelphia, New York, and Boston could boast of having some of the most important Underground Railroad activists among their members.

In 1841 Payne worked directly with Robert Purvis, who lived up to his title as president of the Underground Railroad, and with wealthy sailmaker James Forten, raising money for the committee. Payne served on the acting committee for a portion of the year, working on behalf of escapees. By early 1842, however, his name disappears from the membership list; his responsibilities to the AME Church had expanded, and his movements increased.

In a quiet but equally effective manner, Payne is reported to have assisted White Underground Railroad activists after his assignment to Union Bethel AME in Washington, DC. Under the Black Codes of the District of Columbia, Payne had to secure a bond of $1,000 before he could remain in the nation's capital and officiate as a minister.[51] Quinn then assigned Payne to Baltimore, where he had the exhausting duties of overseeing five churches in addition to his more clandestine activities; Payne understood and contributed to the work of the Underground Railroad throughout the pre–Civil War period, when Quinn was his senior bishop.[52]

This circle of activism constantly surrounding Quinn expanded in word and deed. Henry Highland Garnet, Quinn's old friend from his New York days, publicly crossed a line that Quinn and other AME ministers challenged by acting in a different way, largely from the pulpit and through their unseen actions in helping with escapes from slavery. Black Presbyterian pastor Garnet had lost his leg to amputation, but none of his fire. Reflecting his growing Black radicalism, Garnet delivered one of the most provocative speeches of the time, "An Address to the Slaves of the United States," to the 1843 Colored Convention held in Buffalo, New York. Echoes of David Walker could be heard in this speech in which Garnet called for the enslaved to rebel.

Steadily, Quinn's reputation spread. "It appeared as though the genius of persuasion had possession of his lips," one observer explained. Thousands gathered to hear his words of truth. Fearless in denouncing enslavers during his sermons, Quinn generally climaxed his remarks with his favorite expression, "May God have mercy on him; I never will."[53]

With ministers Payne and Nazrey assuming increasing leadership roles, Quinn, armed with his missionary dedication, continued building the church. Writing from Indianapolis on January 5, 1844, Elder William Paul Quinn reports,

> I was sent by the General Conference on a mission to the state of Indiana, and, in the providence of God, I am happy to inform you that I have succeeded in laying out eight circuits in the state of Indiana, and three in the state of

Illinois, and have succeeded in laying out two circuits in the state of Missouri. I have just returned from the states of Kentucky and Tennessee, and have obtained authority from the city council, and from Judge Brown of Louisville, Ky., to establish the A.M.E. Church in the state of Kentucky. After having obtained this authority in Louisville, I procured a fine house, and forty-nine joined on the first invitation, among whom was one ordained minister. I then left my carriage and took steamboat, and went to Tennessee, and obtained permission to establish the A.M.E. connection in that state." . . . We have 17 in the itinerancy, and 27 local for a total of 44 preachers. . . . To accomplish this great enterprise, I have been compelled to lie out in the wilderness more than two hundred nights, and have been brought before the grand jury in St. Louis three different times, and honorably acquitted—thanks be to God.[54]

He thought it needless to go on about his "privations."[55]

CHAPTER 7

Bishop Quinn

1844–1849

In 1844, for the first time in church history, Pittsburgh hosted the General Conference. Delegates traveled by railcar and packet boat to reach the city. Daniel Payne was enthralled by the view from the train, remarking on the indescribable beauty of the scenery. The well-cultivated gardens, flowers, "crystal springs gushing out of the rocky hills, rivulets, creeks and rivers," captivated him. Julia Foote, an AME preacher and one of the women also traveling to the conference, was filled "with adoration and praise to the great Creator of all things" by the grand, romantic scenery" she beheld "while crossing the Allegheny mountains." Their fascination and descriptions give some idea of what Quinn treasured about the West. The sounds of the birds combined with the breathtaking views inspired "emotions of wonder, love and praise; causing the soul to look through Nature, up to Nature's God."[1]

As the conference began, Bishop Brown, knowing he was "sinking down to the grave," urged the convention to elect and ordain a bishop before he succumbed. Much of the conference's work preceded the election. Many of the sixty-eight delegates arriving at the conference had come with the intention of electing a different man to lead them as their fourth bishop. Quinn's friend and disciple, Richard Robinson, was their choice. Robinson had returned from his successful mission to Haiti, where Quinn had encouraged him to go twenty years earlier. Quinn and Robinson had traveled their respective circuits in the 1830s. While Quinn focused on the western states, Robinson had filled posts in New York, Baltimore, Boston, and Philadelphia stations, emerging as a formidable contender for the bishopric.

The air was charged with excitement as the two aspirants vied for the episcopal office. By 1844 Robinson stood out as a very prominent candidate. He revealed to one writer that had he been more anxious for the office, he

90 Chapter 7

BISHOP WILLIAM PAUL QUINN

Figure 7.1 Bishop Quinn. Arnett, ed. *Proceedings of the Quarto-Centennial Conference of the AME Church of South Carolina, at Charleston, South Carolina, on May 5, 16, and 17, 1889*. African Methodist Episcopal Church, South Carolina Conference, courtesy of Duke University Libraries / Internet Archives.

could have been elected. But he also admitted "that a bishop ought to be able to defend his Church and doctrine with his pen," and he knew he could not.[2] Robinson's remarks highlight the general illiteracy of the itinerant ministry before 1844. Quinn had not received a traditional or formal education "but was well versed in men and things," explains his longtime secretary, J. M. Brown.[3]

As Robinson hesitated, Quinn aggressively sought nomination and election as their spiritual leader. Before the Civil War, the bishopric in the Black church was one of few, if not the highest, attainable offices for men of color in the United States. Historiographer Daniel Payne later reports that Quinn's supporters overwhelmed the "eastern men who had been prejudiced against him as a man, but more particularly as a candidate for the Episcopal office." The easterners considered him a ruffian and resented him for being crude. The aspiring bishop had a reputation as a man who would not back away from a fight.[4] Furthermore, his opponents may not have forgotten Quinn's five-year separation from the denomination.

During the previous decades, Quinn had started most of the AME churches in Western Pennsylvania, as well as Ohio, Michigan, Illinois, and Indiana. He had visited all the annual conferences and meetings of the church. In this way, Welch explains, "he became the best known man throughout the connection."[5] The devotion of supporters, friends, and colleagues during Quinn's missionary travels across the country propelled him toward the role that would define his life.

Quinn gave the conference "a brief outline of the rise and progress of [their] mission in the west." He reported his travels from Pittsburgh to three hundred miles beyond the Missouri line. The indefatigable preacher stressed his labors on behalf of the church. He had organized 47 churches and 72 congregations, as well as established 40 schools and 50 Sabbath Schools, with 200 teachers instructing 2,000 scholars. He had held seventeen camp meetings and established forty temperance societies. All were set up in the Northwest Ordinance states of Ohio, Indiana, Illinois, and Michigan, as well as in the slaveholding states of Maryland, Louisiana, Kentucky, and Missouri. He had been effective in New York, New Jersey, and Pennsylvania before he'd left his mark on the western states.[6]

The acclaim swirling around the candidate and his astonishing report convinced the delegates that he was the right minister to lead the church. Quinn's longtime secretary insists, "Few men had a clearer insight into the duties of life, and few accomplished so well the requirements of their chosen profession."[7] Quinn's strong faith in God matched his "uncommon love for the souls of men."[8] He was plainspoken and able, with a high sense of justice, of punctuality, and promptness. Nothing escaped his notice. Both agreeable and pleasant, he was also strong-minded, resolute, and lighthearted—qualities that endeared him to his followers.

Quinn's emotional report to the convention on the state of the faith in the West was one of the factors leading to the establishment of a separate Indiana conference. He described the two thousand AME members living west of Ohio as able farmers and craftsmen. Seven circuit-riding elders served these faithful, along with twenty traveling and twenty-seven local preachers, all under his guidance. The classes Quinn mentioned in his report were intended for new and aspiring church leaders. The Methodist Episcopal Church had established study classes, frequently found in the West, in response to a lack of ordained deacons and elders. The AME Church found this system most helpful in ministering to African Americans scattered across the western settlements.

Although not specifically acknowledged, women's efforts contributed to the impressive statistics. Women, such as Quinn's ally Priscilla Baltimore, among many others, "steadfastly led the formation of new congregations in these territories and continued to count for the majority of their members." Preaching women as well as other church women had been consistently and "exceptionally successful in bringing new members to African Methodism," according to religious studies professor Jualynne Dodson.[9]

Quinn concluded his report by telling of the more than eighteen thousand Black settlers in Indiana and Illinois: "There is an immense mine of mind, talent and social qualities, all lying measurably in embryo, but by a proper direction of the missionary hammer and chisel, they can be shaped to fit in the new spiritual building of God."[10] Despite obstacles and misgivings, when the vote came on the thirteenth day of the conference, Bishop Morris Brown elevated William Paul Quinn to the position of bishop on Sunday morning, May 19, 1844, unleashing a force that would continue to alter the course and direction of the AME denomination for thirty more years. Tanner observes that "it is not too much to say" Quinn's report "won for him, and deservedly too, the Episcopacy."[11]

With his consecration, Quinn was the first person ordained bishop after Allen's death, and the torch passed from Allen to Brown to Quinn. He served as senior bishop for nearly twenty-five of his twenty-nine years of service—the only individual in the history of the church to be elevated to the episcopacy directly from the mission field. His election and ordination also marked the first time a bishop was not elected and consecrated in Philadelphia. Thirdly, the fact that the seventh General Conference of 1844 was held in Pittsburgh, Pennsylvania, rather than in Philadelphia or Baltimore, signaled the church's blessing to the importance of the West. Pittsburgh and Quinn were rewarded for the explosive westward growth of the church.

Quinn's vigor infused a new spirit over the conference. The delegates made provisions "for organizing missionary societies in every church and in every conference." The newly organized Home and Foreign Missionary Departments took general charge of the missionary activities of the church.[12] Daniel Payne maintains, "Never before had there been such an amount of talent and general information concentrated in any ecclesiastical [meeting] since the memorable convention of 1816." The eastern churches and membership united with the new western missions. Payne prayed that they be kept as "one till the church militant shall be assembled with the church triumphant in the paradise of God."[13]

Garnet claimed Quinn was made for the work. His "large stock of common sense" was widely recognized as one of "his extraordinary natural gifts." The bishop's "marvelously interesting" manner of narrating his trials and colorful experiences captivated his friends, followers, and congregants. "The quiet dignity, and the ease, and beauty of his language that characterize his conversations, are seldom surpassed or equaled. His words seem literally to flow in eloquent streams from his mouth," extols Garnet.[14]

Two men dominated the conference: Paul Quinn and Daniel Alexander Payne. The general enthusiasm and exuberance over Quinn's election only heightened the inevitable conflicts. The General Conference contended with major divisions over the role of education, the call for an educated ministry, and the licensing of women preachers. Payne, a former schoolteacher and a young seminary graduate, emerged as the leader in the movement to increase the competency of the ministry through literacy and education. Thirty-three years old at the time of the General Conference, Payne, the first college-educated, seminary-trained clergyman, began his ascent in the leadership of the AME denomination. He had attended Oberlin College and received a scholarship to Lutheran Theological Seminary at Gettysburg. He studied there for two years and is recognized as the first African American admitted to the school. Payne had changed his religious affiliation to AME in 1841 and dedicated himself to increasing both the professionalization and credentialing of the AME clergy.[15]

Two years prior to the conference, Payne had recommended a full program of study for ministers, including English grammar, geography, arithmetic, ancient history, modern history, ecclesiastical history, and theology. When both the latest course of studies and the resolution were presented at the outset of the conference, immediate "pandemonium broke loose." The session was thrown into so much confusion that it was forced to adjourn. A schism loomed between those who felt the education requirement was high-minded and exclusionary and those who understood the necessity of a literate leadership.[16]

New ideas often crash on the craggy shores of convention, where they meet defeat. To Payne's dismay, his plan for educational reform was initially vetoed, voted down by the General Conference. With little clout or persuasiveness to present the resolution with success, Payne lost his battle on the first round. He and the education resolution were to be saved by an older, perhaps more politically able and persuasive, allied clergyman, who argued Payne's case for a formally educated ministry. They found an ally in

Quinn, who had been on the frontlines, promoting education of congregants through Sabbath Schools. Bishop Brown also gave an impassioned, eloquent address in favor of the proposal, which melted the hearts of the opposition. When reintroduced a few days later, the proposal met with acceptance after a heated discussion. A detailed four-year curriculum and course of study was adopted, and the AME leadership began their tradition of educational ideals.

A year or so later, Payne tried to establish a short-lived AME seminary and succeeded in gradually raising the level of educational preparation required for ministers. This was a monumental achievement on Payne's part, "for the course of studies has influenced more men than anything else Payne ever did," one writer recognizes. This remarkable achievement is set against the fact that it was illegal to teach Blacks to read or write in many of the states in the nation in 1844. Payne's native state of South Carolina had passed antiliteracy laws beginning in 1739. By 1835 several state laws called for fines, punishment, whippings, and imprisonment for anyone caught fostering literacy for enslaved or free Blacks.[17]

Not only were there souls to save but also minds to train and cultivate. This commitment to an educated, well-trained ministry marked Payne's lasting legacy, which reshaped the direction and development of the AME Church. Thus began Quinn's leadership as the denomination's fourth bishop and his emerging partnership with Daniel Payne. Under Payne's guidance, a committee went on to draft a course of study with a mandatory requirement for all ministerial candidates.[18]

The same General Conference that elected Quinn bishop was equally excited about creating educational opportunities for their members. The governing body placed great emphasis toward establishing a college "for the education of our children and young men, as one of the most powerful and successful means of attaining the rights and dignity of American citizens."[19] From that pivotal conference forward, the AME Church progressed steadily toward an educated ministry and laity.

Other petitions had been put forward forward at the conference prior to Quinn's elevation as bishop. One, on the question of suppressing Freemasonry and other secret societies among the ministry, received heated discussion but was tabled. Another, a major point of contention, met with almost immediate dismissal. The question of licensing women to preach occupied the attention and also aroused the opposition of the Pittsburgh General Conference. Up on hearing the motion, many members rose to their feet at once. The petition to amend the discipline so as "to admit females to receive a license to preach in the connexion" was also tabled.[20]

Although a few women, such as Jarena Lee, had been exhorting and preaching since 1809, women carried no official authority or recognition within the denomination. One of the great leaders of the movement for women preachers, Lee had begun preaching before the official organization of the church. Allen had given her verbal authorization to exhort, allowed her to hold prayer meetings in her "hired house," and encouraged to exhort as she found opportunities. Exhorters were not sanctioned to preach in an official capacity, nor were they ordained ministers. They were expected to "exhort the people to righteous living."[21] However, Lee's bold preaching style had impressed Richard Allen, who gave his public endorsement. Although Bishop Allen had denied female ordination and preaching, Lee became the first woman preacher in the AME Church and one of two women given permission to preach at the founding of the denomination. She had hoped to expand the role of women in the new church. She had submitted her autobiography to the AME Book Concern for publication. Both the General and the New York Annual Conference considered its' publication in 1844. No action was taken.[22]

According to Julia Foote, who preached as an itinerant minister and evangelist, the ministers at the 1844 General Conference were so "incensed" at the brother who offered a "motion to allow all the women preachers to become members of the conference" that they "threatened to take action against him. . . . All talked and screamed to the bishop, who could scarcely keep order."[23] Bishop Brown could not command the power or amass the authority to change their vociferous perspective. Although minimally successful, the women's quest for recognition, spiritual legitimacy, and access to the pulpit would continue for decades. Their progress toward the ministry was agonizingly slow.

On Monday, May 20, the General Conference closed its seventh session with "an impressive benediction" that expressed Bishop Brown's warmest wishes for the future prospects and happiness of the church. The hospitality and graciousness of their Pittsburgh hosts received high praise and commendation. With grateful hearts, the conference expressed its appreciation for the brotherly kindness lavished upon them.[24]

At the close of the General Conference, Quinn stepped into his new responsibilities with zeal, but one month beyond his election, disaster descended. The hazards and harrowing experiences of the life of a traveling minister struck shortly after he'd attended the Philadelphia Annual Conference. Quinn was planning a return to Terre Haute's Allen Chapel in August to hold his first official meeting there after his election. It would be his first responsibility as new bishop.

Traveling in his own private carriage, about twenty miles from his destination, some part of the carriage harness broke. The "naturally fiery" horse Quinn preferred took fright and bolted. The bishop held on until the reins gave way. With the front of the carriage already broken, Quinn fell out, clinging to the broken rein. The horse dragged him another two hundred yards. The animal finally freed itself from Quinn's grasp and fled, breaking what was left of the carriage to pieces. Severely bruised on the left side and breast, Quinn also suffered a fractured arm. Battered, wounded, and broken-boned, he remained undaunted. "Though almost insensible when raised from the ground," shares one church historian, "his powerful and vigorous constitution, as an auxiliary to the best medical skill, enabled him to open the Conference two days later."[25]

Quinn sent agents to introduce the AME denomination to Chicago that year. Seven original charter members, five of whom were women, of an independent Methodist prayer band had been meeting at State and Lake Streets in a member's home, not far from Lake Michigan. Taking the initial steps toward establishing a church, the prayer band formally organized into a society. Quinn, after hearing of the society's desire to establish a formal church, sent a missionary from the New York conference to lead the aspirants. The church, which later became Quinn Chapel, ranked among the most influential churches in the abolitionist movement.

Chicago's Quinn Chapel emerged as a well-known Underground Railroad haven, operating as one of the northernmost stops and one of the last refuges in the United States for escapees before crossing into Canada. Here, too, women were among the most important supporters. Four female members of Quinn Chapel actively worked for the Underground Railroad. Known as the Big Four, the group included Mary Richardson Jones, the wife of well-known Chicago activist John Jones. Richardson Jones provided freedom seekers food, shelter, and other necessities for their journey through or their respite in Chicago. The Jones's home became an Underground Railway station.[26] Quinn would establish a lifelong association with the church and a lasting friendship with its members, particularly John Jones and Mary Richardson Jones.

Bishop Quinn pressed on to his duties in the West as the Canadian conference assembled in Toronto, with Bishop Brown presiding. Freedom seekers from the United States had pushed for AME's first international conference. Using the Underground Railroad, escapees such as Josiah Henson had found refuge in Canada and were actively working to bring others considered fugitives to safety. Fame would envelop Henson's life once Harriet Beecher Stowe revealed the influence of his narrative as part of her inspiration for writing *Uncle Tom's Cabin*.

Henson had been ordained a deacon in July 1842 at the third session of the Canadian conference, at Hamilton. The AME Church in Canada had set up a church and a school a short distance from Colchester, where Henson was living at the time. Henson served as the AME minister for a brief period, and by 1842, he'd organized the Colchester circuit before moving on to establish the Dawn settlement. Bishop Brown ordained Josiah Henson an elder at the 1844 Canadian conference.[27]

The urgency in advocating for the ordination of another bishop became clear at the close of the Canadian conference. Bishop Brown suffered an incapacitating paralytic stroke during the conference in Toronto, Canada West, just two months after he had ordained Quinn. Brown was taken home to Philadelphia and was largely debilitated for the remainder of his life. The 1844 conference marked the last Canadian conference that Bishop Brown was able to attend.[28]

The rugged Quinn, the sole acting head of ecclesiastical affairs, managed not only his own responsibilities but Brown's as well. With this tragic health crisis, Brown's active episcopal service began to collapse. Impaired speech and mental faculties compounded the bishop's physical struggles, yet he continued to press on like a good soldier and "lift high the cross for Christ."[29] By June, though frail and worn from the demanding travels of ministry, Bishop Brown presided over the New York conference for the six days before Quinn was able to arrive in New York City to relieve him.[30] When the Ohio churches assembled at Columbus on September 17, 1844, Bishop Quinn presided alone; Bishop Brown was too ill to participate, and Bishop Waters had confined his ministerial duties to a limited local sphere around Baltimore.

Quinn came to power and led the church, largely alone, during turbulent times. He was at the head of a unified and strengthened AME denomination at the moment of the great division—the Methodist Schism and the formation of the Southern Methodist branch. The most uncompromising of the Methodist abolitionists had seceded, withdrawing from the church in 1842 to organize the Wesleyan Methodist Church with nonslaveholding as a condition of membership.[31] Until 1844 Episcopal Methodism in the South had been an integral part of a unified American Methodism for the White churches. The rift now divided the Methodist Episcopal Church in two. Southerners, defining slavery as a political problem recognized in the Bible rather than as a moral wrong, framed the practice of slavery as a question with which the church should not engage nor meddle. The function of the church was divinely appointed, argued one religious historian.[32]

Although Methodist founder John Wesley "had stigmatized slavery as a great evil" and the early Methodist preachers all seemed to have agreed on the subject, ultimately, the schism hinged on the question of the relationship between the church to the institution of slavery. According to Cone, the white Methodist Church's vacillation on slavery, "is consistent with Wesley's less than passionate approach to the issues."[33] With the growing economic advantages attained through slaveholding, "the Church ceased to maintain an absolute condemnation of slavery on moral grounds," according to one social historian.[34] White Baptists would follow when they formed the Southern Baptist Convention, a precursor to their own split over slavery a year later. The northern group became the Northern Baptist Convention, known today as the American Baptist Churches USA. The southern branch, the Southern Baptist Convention, separated in order to support slavery.

Secular rather than sacred intervention tackled the Christian church's abdication to slavery. Harriet Beecher Stowe began her influential work *Uncle Tom's Cabin* in 1851, which is based in part on the narrative of AME minister Josiah Henson. Stowe believed in John Wesley's summation of slavery as "the sum of all human villainy" and fulfilled her intention to produce a book that would "show the wickedness and horrors of the slave-trade, and thus promote its overthrow."[35] Such was the religious and racial climate that greeted newly ordained Bishop Quinn in 1844.

Morris Brown felt well enough to open the Baltimore Annual Conference the following year, although he referred to his own afflicted condition by expressing that he might not be with the body again. The aging bishop's powers of speech and locomotion continued to fail. Quinn arrived to preside over the last days of the conference. Bishops Quinn, Ed Waters, and Brown were there. Quinn delivered the annual address to the Philadelphia Annual Conference that followed. Observing the state of Bishop Brown's faltering health, the Philadelphia district felt compelled, for Brown's "own ease and comfort as well as for the general interest of the Connection, to declare him incompetent to travel and exercise his episcopal office in the Church," and they retired him.[36]

Quinn's election to the bishopric, largely through the urgings of Morris Brown, allowed the business of the church to progress. Time and again, "the sacred cause of education" proved vitally important to the interests of the Church. The push toward education consumed the conferences in 1845. The Ohio Annual Conference, expressing a deep interest in the moral and literary improvement of both male and female youth, reported that they had met to select a tract of land with the intention of building a seminary of learning. Youth were to receive instruction in the various branches of literature, science, agriculture, and mechanic arts. Of course, instruction would be available for young men who desired to prepare for the ministry.[37]

In 1846 Bishops Brown, Waters, and Quinn again were forced to hold the Baltimore Annual Conference, in the District of Columbia. Paralysis had reduced Brown's mobility, but he was able to walk with assistance. This marked the last moment the three bishops would assemble together.

Despite the state's ambiguous, loosely adhered-to policies, Maryland was a slaveholding state. Baltimore churned as a transit hub for freedom seekers, who both came and went. Some, such as Frederick Douglass, had escaped the city by train, and the law reflected the caution as well as the frustration of local authorities who attempted to control outbound movement of people of color.

Although the ministers, bishops, and prelates were of the highest rank, Maryland law required that free people of color wishing to leave Baltimore by train present bonds given by White men willing to vouch for them. Maryland law notwithstanding, Baltimore maintained its position of prominence in the AME church in the East, and the bishops continued to push the boundaries of their autonomy. Quinn pressed on. He traveled familiar ground as the fourth bishop, presiding over the Ohio conference upon his return to Cincinnati. An 1846 eyewitness account describes the impact of the first AME conference held in Cincinnati, when the congregation was worshipping in the old Bethel church. "There was great curiosity to see a colored bishop; such a person had never been in the city, and every person was on the lookout for the conference; for months you could have seen new carpets, chairs, beds, knives and forks, etc., going to the homes of the members of Bethel," describes one local newspaper. The visiting ministers were well entertained and left an outstanding impression for African Methodism in a city that had been torn apart by deep racial strife a decade earlier.[38]

In Cincinnati Quinn ordained his lifelong friend and colleague, J. M. Brown, as a deacon. J. M. Brown also served as Quinn's private secretary until 1855, which gave him "ample opportunity to learn something of the inner life of the man." The intimate nature of their relationship, which continued throughout Quinn's life, gave J. M. Brown the opportunity to study the peripatetic minister. Brown preserved his insights in a sharp-eyed essay on Quinn.[39]

Despite the danger, Bishop Quinn continued to travel great distances in his capacity as AME's newest bishop. In 1846 he led the standard range of conferences in the United States, as well as the Canada conference, which began his long association with the AME Church across the northern border. After setting up their own Canadian churches as early as 1826, freedom seekers petitioned the New York conference for help in organizing the Canada missions.

Continuing the twenty-year religious relationship between AME and the Canadian branch of the church, Quinn presided over the seventh conference, at Queen's Bush, Peel County, Canada West.[40] Thereafter, he made yearly visits to Canada West between 1846 and 1853. Quinn, largely associated with the westward and southern spread of AME, also facilitated the internationalization of the church at the time the expanding Underground Railroad was moving refugees from slavery in the United States to freedom in Canada.

By 1847 Bishop Morris Brown's health declined to the extent that he was no longer able to leave his home in Philadelphia. Compounding the problem, Bishop Edward Waters died suddenly and tragically of injuries he'd sustained after a carriage ran over him in late spring. Bishop Quinn alone presided over the Baltimore conference when it met at Bethel Church.[41]

Quinn traveled east to preside over the eighth General Conference, in Philadelphia. Morris Brown remained at home, too ill to preside. On May 1, 1848, four years into leading the church, Quinn gave his first written address at the General Conference. It was known at the time as the bishop's address, but it was later changed to the Episcopal Address at the General Conference of 1852. At previous conferences the secretary merely referred to the address in the records. The Quadrennial Address (every four years) was read by one of the conference secretaries. A written address gave the conference access to the full text. This was but one of several important recommendations and changes to the bishopric presented by Bishop Quinn. He understood the hardships and demands of the mission field. He recommended that conferences or the Connection elect presiding elders to reduce the many difficulties occurring on circuits and in stations, which could not be satisfactorily resolved without the authority of the presiding elders. After a spirited debate, however, the proposition was defeated.[42]

In his Bishop's message, Quinn encouraged the conference delegates to uphold their duty "to promote, by wise and sound legislation, the temporal and spiritual interests over the many thousands over whom we exercise ecclesiastical jurisdiction." The recent death of Bishop Waters and the protracted illness of Bishop Brown led Quinn to remind the conference of the deficiency in the episcopal office. Despite Quinn's repeated requests, the conference postponed indefinitely a recommendation of the episcopal committee to elect another bishop.[43]

Always looking ahead, Quinn sought an official written history during this 1848 conference. Early church men—most notably, Revs. David Smith and Thomas Henry—had written autobiographies that provided a partial history of the young church, but these men were not historians. Sarah Jane Early's useful biography of her husband, Rev. Jordon Early, came decades later. The question of having a written history was put to a vote. Rev. Daniel

Payne received a great majority of votes and was "invested with the power and work of Historiographer of the African Methodist Episcopal Church."⁴⁴ When Quinn requested that Payne write the official history of the Church, Payne begged the bishop to release him from his pastoral work so that he could search for historical documents. Payne especially wanted to speak with the contemporaries of Bishop Allen, his intimate friends and advisers, many of whom were still living but rapidly dying. "But," Payne tells us, "the Bishop refused," saying, "I will give you a small appointment which you can manage, and at the same time go on in search of what you need."⁴⁵ This Payne thought impossible. But the earnest clergyman persisted.

The explosive growth of the church meant greater numbers of members, circuits, and stations, all of which increased Quinn's duties and his workload. Recognizing the demands on the bishop, the committee on episcopacy expressed a strong desire for the election of another bishop. Although the General Conference reached an agreement and designated the time for the election, it did not happen. Quinn had taken Daniel Payne into the basement of Philadelphia's Bethel Church and urged him to allow his name to be put forth as a candidate for the bishopric, a mere seven years after Payne had joined the denomination. Payne respectfully but flatly declined in part because, as the newly appointed historiographer, he wanted to focus on his latest assignment, which required extensive travel and time to write. Payne had four years to pray over his decision before the next General Conference.⁴⁶

Throughout Quinn's life he had led across multiple institutions. At the Philadelphia General Conference, however, he faced opposition on the issue of Freemasonry. As a master Mason who had been deeply involved in Prince Hall activities since his New York City days, Quinn served as chaplain of the National Compact Prince Hall Organization in Chicago.⁴⁷ Some among the AME membership found this type of involvement with the Masons objectionable and introduced an anti-Masonic resolution stating that "no preacher [will] be allowed to graduate into ministerial functions who is and continues to be a member of any Free Mason lodge." The resolution was tabled. Similar resolutions had met the same fate at the 1836 and 1844 General Conferences. Part of the issue centered on a struggle for control between pastors and boards of trustees, who fought over who would be supreme in local churches.⁴⁸

Women attending the General Conference of 1848 again asked for ministerial privileges paralleling those of men. The women also challenged "the long-standing taboos against women speaking in public," asserts one historian.⁴⁹ The motion, presented by a local Philadelphia delegate, passed. Daniel Payne led the minority protest against the favorable majority vote to license women to preach. Not only did Payne see this affirmation of women preachers as a distraction, he thought it "calculated to break up the sacred relations which women bear to their husbands and children, by sending them forth as itinerant preachers, wandering from place to place, to the utter neglect of their household duties and obligations"; he went on to point out that "the whole history of the Church does not furnish a single instance where the legislative body of a Church has ever licensed women to preach."[50] His supporters entered "their solemn protest in the presence of the Church against this movement of the majority of the General Conference."[51] Payne concluded by calling the measure "anti-Scriptural, anti-domestic and revolutionary."[52] Although Quinn led the conference, he did not sign the protest.[53] The women-led Daughters of Zion had managed to push forward the resolution in 1848 and again in 1852; however, the male leadership overwhelmingly voted against them each time. The backlash against female preachers had been so strong that these women were deliberately excluded from several official denominational histories, largely written by Payne.[54]

Quinn was responsible for the oversight of one international and four national conferences. His distinguished position as the only functioning AME bishop in America did not protect him from tragedy, however. Danger routinely encircled the bishop's life. He was stabbed at a camp meeting and nearly killed in 1848.[55] Nevertheless, he managed to attend the consecration of a new place of worship on Saratoga Street in Baltimore. Insufficiently recovered from the aftereffects of the attack, he was too wounded to officiate. Rev. Daniel Payne, pastor of the church, assumed Quinn's duties and led the dedication.[56] Upon his recovery Quinn continued to ensure the growth and spread of the church. In 1849 he ordained as an elder Thomas Marcus Decatur Ward, another trailblazer of African Methodism (in California), as the first ordained minister to labor on the Pacific coast.[57] Ward would persist in his work on the Pacific coast for fourteen years.

Less than a year later, at the dawn of a clear and pleasant Wednesday, Bishop Morris Brown succumbed. Payne says they literally watched this great man fade away hour by hour as a result of the stroke. He had been incapacitated for five years. Due to Bishop Brown's reduced financial circumstances and the lack of funds from the Connection, Brown had both pastored Mother Bethel and fulfilled his duties as bishop during his decline.[58] His death on May 9, 1849, left a mournful church, a grieving widow, six children, and numerous friends in faith—and one bishop. A sense of loss engulfed the Connection.

At the appointed time, the funeral procession left the late bishop's Philadelphia residence on Bainbridge Street and moved above Eighth, up Ninth to

Spruce, and then down Spruce to Sixth, to Bethel Church. The AME Zion conference, in session in Philadelphia at that time, adjourned to attend the funeral. The casket was borne by a number of ministers. Bishop Quinn; his old friend, AME Zion bishop Christopher Rush from New York City; and Bishop George Galbreath, also of Zion Church, led the procession. "The members of the two Annual Conferences followed, then came the Daughters of Conference."[59] Daniel Payne preached the funeral sermon. The remains of Bishop Brown were placed in a vault in front of Mother Bethel Church, with those of Richard Allen, "to await the resurrection morning."[60]

Following Richard Allen's stand against slavery, Brown made sure that "if the slave solicited means to obtain liberty, the fetters soon fell from his limbs." Brown had not wavered from his radical views against slavery since his days as pastor of Denmark Vesey's church in South Carolina. "As a minister of the Gospel," Morris Brown was, as Daniel Payne recalls, "zealous, devout, irreproachable. As a Bishop in the AME Church, he had endured much hardship, privation and suffering in the discharge of his itinerant duties over thirteen states in the union."[61]

Two months later, Sarah Allen, widow of founder Richard Allen, passed away. She had lived to see eighty-five years after much good service to her husband and to the church. Quinn officiated at her funeral and remembered her work on behalf of freedom seekers in an obituary notice. Quinn knew her as "a staff to her husband, and a counselor and the encourager of the pioneers," as the bishop once had been. Sister Allen took her place among the most dedicated in the cause of liberty. "The poor flying slave, trembling and panting in his flight, has lost a friend not easily replaced," Quinn lamented. Her purse "was ever open" to them. The fire in her eyes "kindled with peculiar brightness as she wished them Godspeed to the land of liberty, when the slave is free from his master, and the voice of the oppressor is no longer heard."[62] Mother Allen's death severed one of Quinn's final bonds with the founders of the denomination. Quinn alone would lead the church as its senior bishop over the next four years. The faithful laborer of the church militant was about to guide the denomination through the country's most tumultuous political crises.

CHAPTER 8

The Tumultuous Years
1850–1858

The AME Church kept pace with the westward incursions of the country. Gold had been discovered in the Sacramento area of California in 1848. By 1849 Quinn dispatched Thomas Marcus Decatur Ward, another trailblazer of African Methodism, to labor on the Pacific coast. The nation was coming to the end of a largely silent balancing act between the advancement of slavery across the country and demands for its abolishment. California found itself at the center of political wrenching around slavery when the state joined the AME family.

On June 10, 1850, three months before California was admitted to the Union, St. Andrews (originally Bethel AME) in Sacramento petitioned for admission to the Indiana Conference as the first AME church to be established on the Pacific coast. More than likely, the church was led by the laity, perhaps under the class system, until Ward arrived.[1] He would continue his work in California for another fourteen years. Quinn alone presided over the AME denomination, which extended across the United States, from the East Coast to the West and from Canada to New Orleans, with missions in Haiti and Africa.[2]

The state of California had a troublesome birth in 1850. It came into the Union as a free state—forbidding slavery in its constitution—as part of five components that made up the Compromise of 1850.[3] The congressional trade-off for that admission to the Union was the Fugitive Slave Act, and it changed everything. The law reinforced the US Constitution's guarantee to enslavers that the government would help in the retrieval and return of their enslaved property. The act compelled citizens anywhere in the country to cooperate with law enforcement authorities in all states and territories to aid in efforts to recapture fugitives.[4]

Northerners were indignant that they, too, were expected to turn in suspected fugitives and help apprehend runaways. Fines and imprisonment loomed as the consequences if they did not comply. As part of a compromise made between Northern and Southern legislatures, the act was a desperate attempt to both preserve slavery and douse the firestorm over the question of its expansion. After most of the nation's churches had already fractured over the practice of slavery, the compromise represented one of the last legislative attempts to prevent the nation from sinking into war.

The 1850 law was a "shocking capitulation of the government to slaveholders."[5] Quinn thought the law more sinister than slavery itself. He understood the greed and self-interest of slaveholders, but the actions of the federal government, Welch says, "left him choking with rage."[6] In anticipation of the law, Pittsburgh's Wylie Avenue congregation held a mass meeting of local Blacks three months before the law took effect. The time had come, they resolved, "when [they] must stand by [their] own rights, or fall still deeper into degradation, the mangled victims of treachery and despotism."[7]

A few days after the passage of the Fugitive Slave Act, over three hundred Black and White residents of Chicago met at Quinn Chapel. To respond to the outrageous law, John Jones, a longtime supporter of Quinn, helped form a vigilance committee with regular watch patrols that were able to quickly confront slave catchers.[8] In response to the law, Quinn Chapel lost nearly half its membership in October and November 1850—the vast majority fled to Canada. The mass defection exposed their tenuous lives as escapees as well as the composition of the AME Church. As a member of Quinn Chapel, John Jones was instrumental in sending hundreds of freedom seekers to the northern province. One day after President Millard Fillmore had signed the act, ten carloads left Illinois bound for Canada to prevent those on board, who had escaped captivity years earlier, from being returned to slavery. Within two weeks of the law's passing, one hundred freedom seekers left Pittsburgh for Canada. All the Black waiters in one hotel in the city did the same. Nearly three hundred in total left.[9]

AME conferences that year rose up and took a public stand against slavery and set aside the last Friday in June as a day of fasting and prayer for its abolition. Churches in the Philadelphia district looked upon the Fugitive Slave Act of 1850 with unmistakable abhorrence. The Annual Conference dutifully expressed its gratitude to the British government's Canadian subjects and expressed its concerns as its members witnessed and experienced "the peril and danger to the liberty of the colored race of these United States."[10] The law would haunt the country ever after.

By 1851 Indiana had adopted a new state constitution. Article 13 stated, "No negro or mulatto shall come into or settle in the State, after the adoption of this Constitution." Fines and fees were imposed for anyone who violated the provision. Article 1, the Bill of Rights, declared, "That all men are created equal; that they are endowed by their Creator with certain unalienable rights." The Indiana constitution helped perpetuate the conflict between race and liberty, between equality and the myth of White supremacy.[11]

Five months later, Reverend M. M. Clarke, Quinn's secretary at the time, executed an affidavit in Pittsburg, Indiana, attesting to Quinn's Honduran birth. Rev. Clarke's sworn testimony supported the motive for the affidavit, which was to protect the bishop against being detained or kidnapped in the unsafe political and racial climate generated by the Fugitive Slave Act. Clarke swore Quinn had been born in Honduras of an Egyptian mother and a Spanish father and had "no Negro blood," implying that his birth and racial lineage put him beyond the clutches of the law.[12]

Across the early years of the second half of the nineteenth century, the United States trained its eyes more intently on Canada, which had been one outlet for the AME Church and the focus of escapes from slavery since at least the War of 1812. After 1850 people of color found it equally dangerous in free states such as Pennsylvania, New Jersey, Ohio, and even Massachusetts as it was in Mississippi, Georgia, or South Carolina. Thousands of free, escaped, and formerly enslaved African Americans left the no-longer-safe free states and looked to Canada for security, safety, and freedom. The Fugitive Slave Act did not apply to Canada, where refusal to acquiesce or to extradite escapees was seemingly universal. Canada became a lifeline of hope, a place where the AME Church had long ago established its presence—perhaps in preparation for and anticipation of the drastic congressional and legal support slavery would receive for its perpetuation.

The shock of the new law put everyone on edge. This law required citizens to help with arrests if ordered to do so. Yet the latest attempts by the federal government to thwart escapes from slavery through the Fugitive Slave Act did not deter the bishop. Through all the turmoil, Quinn's focus on the church and on education as spaces of refuge never faltered.

Quinn presided over the Baltimore conference, which met in Israel Church in Washington, DC, that fateful year. The fugitive slave legislation added to his worries about the laws of the country that were further impacting large swaths of church membership on both sides of the border of the United States and Canada. Quinn appointed (future bishop) Jabez Campbell to Buffalo, New York, to oversee Western New York; this occurred while Harriet Tubman was operating in the region. After escaping slavery on the Eastern Shore of Maryland in 1849, Tubman made her first trip to St. Catharines, Ontario, with eleven freedom seekers in December 1851. As Tubman saw it, "there was no safety except 'under the paw of the British Lion.'"[13] The Canadian town just over the bridge from Buffalo and Niagara Falls, New York, was a well-known safe haven for African Americans fleeing slavery. Tubman, a devoutly religious woman of unwavering faith, joined Salem Chapel in St. Catharines, an AME Church in the Annual Conference of the New York district. Later Salem Chapel joined the British Methodist Episcopal (BME) Church, when most AME churches in Canada would convert to BME five years later.

Over a ten-year period, Tubman used the "colored village," the African Canadian community in the Niagara, Ontario, town, to start and end many of her legendary Underground Railroad rescue missions. The influx of so many freedom-minded people arriving via the Underground Railroad made building a larger AME church in St. Catharines a necessity. According to church history, "as a Methodist meeting house, the church provided aid, assisted with temporary shelter for the newly arrived African Americans and hosted many anti-slavery lectures."[14] The third and current Salem Chapel was built by African American freedom seekers, beginning in October 1853.

After the passage of the Fugitive Slave Act, travel to the annual conferences of the AME Church in the United States became increasingly dangerous for African Canadian church officials. Desiring a more accessible church government closer to home and anxious to underscore allegiance to their new homeland, members of the AME Church in Canada began lobbying for self-governance of their local churches.

Payne observed that passage of the law "forced many of the best families of color to seek asylum in Western Canada, where they were safe from bounty hunters and 'bloodhounds.'" Payne began to explore Canada more carefully and visited the Dawn Settlement, where at least five hundred African American expatriates had settled, looking for "a safe asylum for [his] people" fleeing the consequences of the Fugitive Slave Act. Josiah Henson, after his escape from Kentucky, chose to settle among the Canadians in the Dawn Settlement before his ordination as an AME minister.[15]

Quinn had a massive amount of territory to oversee. He presided over the Meeting for the Promotion of Education in Philadelphia in May 1851 at Bethel Church. Richard Robinson, an earlier contender for the episcopal office, served as vice president. The meeting was held for the people; the poor and the oppressed were its primary concern. The Allegheny Institute in Pittsburgh represented one of the institutions anxious to promote education among the people. The school, which was fully prepared to impart a collegiate education for youth of color of both sexes, had been open for more than a year. However, misinformation, concerns about meeting tuition costs, and the belief that it was a secular institute all hampered the recruitment process. Once the problems were laid before the ministers in attendance, they resolved to take an active part in recruiting students, promoting education, and the institution.[16]

During the snowy winter of late 1851 or early 1852, Quinn continued to lead by example. He attended a meeting in Newport, Indiana, on behalf of Methodist minister Calvin Fairbank, a defiant Underground Railroad conductor. The noted White abolitionist harbored an intense hatred of slavery and everything that upheld it. Arrested for the second time in Kentucky, authorities had jailed Fairbank under the Fugitive Slave Act. Noted White female Underground Railroad conductor Laura Haviland visited Fairbank in the Louisville jail. He had been aiding fugitive slaves—notably, Lewis Hayden and his wife, helping them escape to Boston. In freedom the couple became celebrated Underground Railroad agents in their new home.[17]

Abolitionists rallied to the cause. Haviland, one of the few known female conductors, Black or White, read a letter from Fairbank's lawyer to assembled supporters, Quinn among them. Haviland reported that the bishop had generously contributed a third of the money raised that night to help free Fairbank from a fifteen-year prison sentence.[18] The law could not shake Quinn, and he continued to associate with the most radical abolitionists, supporting their efforts however he could.

Despite the devastating laws extending and supporting slavery in the United States, Quinn struck a conciliatory tone in his remarks at the close of the 1851 New York conference. The agenda was full of references to the Fugitive Slave Act. He rose to speak and exhorted his listeners: "See the difficulties we encounter from prejudice and persecution—the Devil and the Fugitive Law. . . . We should work together. Nine out of ten when we look in the face of a white man we see the enemy. A great many like to see us in the kitchen but few in the parlor." He continued, "[We seek] God's blessing on our own wise, strong, and well-directed efforts."[19]

The committee on Canadian churches gave their report in relation to slavery to the bishop and to the conference: Slavery, they stressed, "is a most gross outrage against humanity, and a positive violation of every one of the ten commandments of God, and destructive of all political, moral and religious rights." The report continues, "Slavery is in itself theft, murder, robbery, licentiousness, concubinage, adultery, and everything else that is sinful and devilish between heaven and earth." The committee reminded ministers of their duty and obligation to "lift up their voices against the monstrous iniquity, and more especially American slavery . . . it being the vilest upon which the sun ever shone, and in defiance of the laws of God, the claims of humanity, and the rights of our poor, outcast, downtrodden brethren."[20] Canadian members resolved that they would "not open the doors of our houses of worship to any slaveholding preacher or lecturer, or their aiders and abettors, under any circumstances whatsoever." The committee reaffirmed "that the African Methodist Episcopal Church has been, theoretically and practically, anti-slavery from its commencement until the present, and was never otherwise known."[21]

Although Quinn served as the sole bishop leading the church during these turbulent years, he depended heavily on two upcoming and promising ministers, Willis Nazrey and Daniel Payne. Quinn appointed Nazrey as his assistant at the 1851 Baltimore Annual Conference. Although Daniel Payne had declined consideration for the bishopric at the 1848 General Conference, he thrived as the denomination's newly appointed historiographer. Frantically, Payne sought original material relating to the origins of the church while the resources were still available and some living founders could inform him of the early history. Between the 1848 General Conference and the upcoming General Conference of 1852, Payne visited every church in the Connection in the eastern and western states, in the South as far as New Orleans, and in the north into Canada in search of relevant historical material.

In New York City on the first Monday in May 1852, the ninth General Conference consolidated the leadership, setting the future course of the church. This was an important year for the bishopric. For the first time, Quinn delivered the bishop's address (now known as the Episcopal Address) from a written transcript. The impact set a tradition in the Church that has resounded across the ages.

Quinn began his address by first remembering "[their] esteemed Father in the Gospel, the Rt. Rev. Morris Brown." In reflecting on Brown's "piety, labors, talents, and exemplary life," Quinn hoped "some able hand may hand down to posterity his name, with all his usefulness" and his major contributions to the church. Quinn singled out several other important matters requiring deliberation and the attention of the meeting.[22] The conference was reluctant to establish the office of presiding elder as Quinn had requested. The question of licensing women also required the attention of the delegates.

Quinn drew their attention to the election of another bishop, one of the pressing issues of the conference. Bishop Allen had served the church alone for the first sixteen years of the Connection. From Allen's death, in 1832, to 1836, Morris Brown had also acted as the sole bishop serving the church.

Edward Waters, the third-elected bishop, died in 1848, leaving an ailing Morris Brown and Bishop Quinn to preside. With Morris Brown's end-of life incapacitation and then his death in 1849, Quinn alone had presided for the previous five years. Bishop Quinn would be the last bishop to preside alone at the head of the denomination.[23]

All of the leaders of the church were assembled. Within two hours of Payne's arrival at the beginning of the New York General Conference, Quinn ordered the very tattered minister to preach the opening sermon. Payne lamented, "My clothing was almost threadbare. I was the shabbiest member of the General Conference of 1852."[24]

Six conferences were represented: Philadelphia, Baltimore, New York, Ohio, Indiana, and Canada. For the fourth time in the history of the AME Church, female members of the conference pushed the leadership and fellow members to address the question of licensing women to preach. Bishop Allen had denied female ordination and preaching, yet Jerena Lee, one of two women given permission to preach at the founding of the denomination, had hoped to expand the role of women in the new church. With "a fire shut up in my bones" (Jeremiah 20:9), as Lee shares, she fervently evangelized from New York to Ohio.[25]

Quinn, saving his bombshell for last, proposed an up-or-down vote on licensing women to preach. It left little room for maneuvering or debate. Distancing himself from this persistent and controversial issue, Quinn admitted that he had "given the subject some thought, but not enough to warrant . . . expressing an opinion as to its merits." Quinn continued, urging, "All that I ask is that something distinct may be done that will be satisfactory to all, and the question be put to rest."[26] With that, Quinn postponed the vote until Friday evening. The question was brought before the General Conference, where it was discussed at length and a motion, presented by a male ally who moved that a license be granted. Though Quinn supported the motion to license women preachers, it was voted down by a large majority of the membership and immediately dismissed. The outcome failed to accomplish Quinn's request to find an answer "satisfactory to all."[27]

Daniel Payne, a strong believer that men and women should inhabit separate spheres, sought to resolve the question of the rights of churchwomen in order to further the orderly administration of church business. Payne believed that "man, strong in body and mind, is fitted by nature to execute what the weaker sex is incapacitated for, both physically and mentally. This view carried the day," according to one historian.[28] Julius Bailey explains, "As women in the church fought to gain access to the pulpit, male AME Church leaders guardedly protected their places in the church structure, not only to uphold tradition, but because their manhood depended on it."[29] Bishop Payne would later publish a manual on domesticity that upheld many of the cardinal gendered opinions of the mid-to-late nineteenth century. The process of allowing women to preach did not begin until 1948.[30]

The conference moved on to the election of new bishops as set forth in Quinn's masterly bishop's address, according to Handy. Singing and prayerful guidance of the great head of the church was sought prior to selecting the men who would fill the holy office.[31] Though Payne is celebrated as the first AME minister to receive formal theological training, he felt unfit for this high level of ministry. Mercifully, he could no longer refuse God's calling. Daniel Payne and Willis Nazrey, both Quinn's loyal supporters, were elected and ordained bishops on May 13 at the General Conference.

Nazrey and Payne were elected at the same time, although Nazrey received more votes than Payne. Payne, however, was the first upon whom ordination was confirmed. This, rather than the number of votes received, established the right of seniority. The first ordained is always established as the senior among those elected by the same ballot. Bishop Quinn and five elders laid hands on the heads of the newly elected bishops. For the first time in four years, Quinn would have assistance in governing the church. Payne was poised to become the educational leader of the denomination; Nazrey, destined to lead in Canada. As Quinn brought the General Conference to a conclusion, Payne thought his "pithy" closing address "so full of sound advice that it may be safely presented as a matter of history." He considered it "one of the literary efforts of the year."[32]

The 1852 conference had attracted a number of notable attendees. Presbyterian minister J. W. C. Pennington, a famed freedom seeker and former Underground Railroad stalwart, was present and introduced to the conference. Charles Avery, founder of Avery College, spoke to the conference about the institute as a place of learning. Avery hoped the "great aim of the church should be, first, to educate the young men for the ministry, and second, to educate the entire community for usefulness in society."[33] His goals aligned with the education mission of the church.

With the election of new bishops, the work of the growing denomination could be divided into districts: Bishop Payne assumed oversight of the first district, the Philadelphia and New England conferences. Bishop Nazrey was given oversight of the second district, Baltimore and New York. Quinn maintained responsibility for the third district, in Indiana, to which the Canadian conferences and their territories were added.[34] The church had grown to forty thousand members and expanded to five hundred traveling and local preachers. The three serving bishops covered staggering distances while caring for church members.

As part of his circuit, Quinn traveled to Toronto, Canada, in July 1853, where he presided with the assistance of Bishop Nazrey. By September Payne was visiting Quinn's diocese in Terre Haute, Indiana. The visit was part of the plan for the bishops to alternate in each other's districts following the reorganization laid out at the 1852 General Conference. Payne, moved by the visit, provides a glimpse of what Quinn found endearing about Indiana: "Never did I leave a place with such keen regret as I did Terre Haute. All the company seemed affected." Bishop Quinn was moved to tears. For Payne, "it seemed strange to see a man of such gigantic proportions and so heroic a heart with such tender feelings."[35] As they parted, Quinn headed home to Richmond; Payne went on to Louisville.

A few years later, during the bitter winter of 1856, Bishop Payne learned the same lesson that Quinn had learned in Missouri, and they both resorted to the same solution. Although Payne had sought and secured written protection from the mayor of St. Louis, authorities accused Payne of failing to provide the proper authorization before visiting [presumably] St. Paul's AME. Religious meetings and other gatherings conducted by African Americans were prohibited in Missouri unless some sheriff, constable, marshal, police officer, or other authority was present. Violations could be subject to a $500 fine, six months in jail, or both. Jordan Early describes the problem: "The enemies of African Methodism, who were always on the alert, had [Payne] arrested and brought before a magistrate" for violating the laws of the state by coming into it to preach the gospel.[36] Negotiating these types of arrests required good legal minds, quick thinking, and a bit of timely blessing. Church leaders hired a shrewd lawyer, who found enough of a procedural error in the arrest record to warrant Payne's release. The lawyer advised Early to get Payne out of town immediately. Heeding the recommendation, Early hurried Payne out of court. Payne describes the scene in his *Recollections*: "I was scarcely outside the door of the magistrate's office when a new warrant was issued. But my dear friend, Rev. [Jordan] Early, was waiting for me with a swift horse and a wagon, into which I stepped."[37] They could hear the constable cry, "Stop that horse! Stop that horse!" "If ever a horse was made to travel," Early remembers, "my horse did that day. We crossed the ice on the Mississippi" and landed Payne "safely in the State of Illinois, in the house of Mrs. Priscilla Baltimore, where he was out of danger." Always a shelter in the storm, the home of Mother Baltimore in the waterfront community of Brooklyn, Illinois, provided protection to AME ministers of the gospel as they evaded St. Louis authorities.[38]

The newest bishop continued his dedication to spreading the gospel and to improving education for all AME members. The White-led Methodist Episcopal church also understood the problems African Americans encountered in their quest to obtain an education. The church met to consider and report on a plan "for the improvement of the intellectual and moral condition of the thirty thousand people of color of Ohio, and those of other free States."[39] Promoting education for African Americans was the primary motivation. Sabbath schools originally set up in most churches focused on teaching reading through Bible study.

The Methodist Episcopal Church had purchased Tawawa Springs in Ohio for $13,000, which included fifty-four timbered acres, a resort hotel, and cottages, in order to establish a university for African Americans. The AME Church would ultimately gain full ownership of Wilberforce University at Tawawa Springs. The campus occupied ten of the acres. Tawawa House, the remodeled resort hotel, was transformed into recitation rooms and other activity areas; the cottages readily served as dormitories. Bishop Payne moved to the campus and, by the magnitude of his willpower, helped guide it to success. Many Hoosier AME members and clergy gained a superior education there.[40]

The church saw education as vital. In his early years as a circuit rider, Quinn met the problem head-on, with his customary vigor. He was sure to establish schools everywhere he presided. Withholding of and general lack of access to education, particularly literacy, cut off access to meaningful employment. Poverty combined with slavery and the inability to read or write plagued nineteenth-century Blacks. Such were the triple forces that confronted and challenged Black ministers and their congregants.

AME leaders, stressing the importance of education, formally established Wilberforce University in 1856 to train Black teachers. One of the nation's oldest private, historically Black universities was named on behalf of the great British abolitionist William Wilberforce. This early institution of higher learning for Blacks in the United States reflects Payne's lofty vision, his tremendous influence on the modern church, and the church's resulting dedication to education. Payne's most significant achievement during the Civil War would be the purchase of Wilberforce University. His dedication led the church to distinguish him as "the Apostle of Education," one of the "Four Horsemen of the AME Church."[41]

Local, domestic, and educational concerns did not crowd out broader interests. Black migration to Canada represented one solution to American racism and to the broad question of emigration and African colonization. African Americans viewed voluntary relocation across the Black Atlantic (through the Underground Railroad) and the emigration movement as migratory solutions to slavery and the racism it spawned in the United States. Forced colonization to Liberia or Sierra Leone on the west coast of Africa was essentially a deportation scheme of the American Colonization Society.

At the 1853 Philadelphia Annual Conference, presided by Bishop Nazrey, a document condemning African Colonization "advised those of our people who intended to migrate to go to Canada, Haiti, or the British West Indies rather than Liberia as advocated by the Colonization Society." For decades the American Colonization Society had attempted to persuade Blacks to leave the United States and resettle on African soil. To meet needs closer to home, Bishop Quinn presided over the Canadian church at the 1853 Annual Conference while Bishop Nazrey stressed the duty of the AME Church to look after its foreign missions in Africa and the West India Islands.[42]

Quinn's old friend from Pittsburgh, Martin Delany, opposed the African Colonization Society and emigration to Liberia. Quinn associated himself with the increasingly strident views of emigrationists, such as Martin Delany, Henry Highland Garnet, and Henry and Mary Bibb. These activists were determined to find a better, more accepting world beyond the punishing blows of American slavery. The Fugitive Slave Act and religious schisms over slavery confirmed for many African Americans that citizens, institutions, and leadership in the United States could not or would not view them as social and political equals.[43]

Quinn served as one of the vice presidents of Delany's 1854 First National Emigration Convention, held in Cleveland.[44] More than 150 attendees gathered to consider the possibility of leaving the United States, the hatred-filled country of their birth, for the more welcoming realms of the Black Atlantic world. As first vice president of the conference, Quinn represented Wayne County, Indiana. Perhaps as a result of Quinn's influence and knowledge of his birthplace, organizers and delegates met to "devise a practical plan of emigration to Central or South America, of the colored people of the United States." There they could "establish an independent and free Republic of colored men [and women] which could set an example to the world of civilization, progress and self-government."[45] The organizers proffered projected destinations other than Africa or Haiti.

Convention attendees hailed from a dozen or more states, in addition to Canada. The gathering, held in the Universalist Church in Cleveland, reflected, perhaps, the unpopularity among many African Americans at the time of the idea of leaving one's homeland. One reporter remarks, "Colonization to Africa was not broached. We are surprised to learn that the objects of the Convention meet with but little favor from our colored citizens."[46]

Quinn's consistent search for relief and escape from oppression knew no geographic or national boundaries—whether through emigration or through escape from slavery. In Quinn's worldview, Canada, Central and South America, Haiti, or even Africa, if necessary, stood as effective alternative spaces of liberation and freedom from oppression.

Quinn served along with Vice President Mary Bibb, widow of infamous freedom seeker Henry Bibb. Bibb was a devout believer in the work of "self-emancipation." After escaping from Kentucky to Canada, the Bibbs launched and edited an influential newspaper in Canada, *Voice of the Fugitive*. Delaney delivered an impassioned eulogy of Henry Bibb, extolling his virtues, merits, and accomplishments.

The Black abolitionists who served with Quinn at the emigration convention were either pillars of the Underground Railroad, such as W. C. Munroe and William Lambert, or known activists, such as Richard De Baptiste, who, among several others, represented Detroit. Theodore Holly and J. M. Whitfield represented New York. Future congressman John Mercer Langston, ever a friend to the fugitive, presented a lengthy eloquent speech. William C. Nell and Charles Remond were on the national board of commissioners, representing Massachusetts.[47]

Quinn's broad geographic reach enabled him to leave no avenue, no possibility, unexplored in his attack of slavery. Later in the year, he was back in Chicago. Curiously, the bishop's name appeared in an entirely different venue. He was listed as a reference for numerous ads that ran in *Frederick Douglass' Paper*, which stated that Agents Jones and Bonner's general intelligence office would procure "situations for servants."[48] Several later ads also included Quinn's name as a vouching reference, as well as Philadelphia's M. M. Clarke, Quinn's longtime secretary. Bonner, the author of the ads, offered the following: "Situations procured for Stewards, Cooks, Waiters Seamstresses, Chambermaids, and girls to do general housework both for the city and Country. Persons wanting situations, male or female, would do well to call at my office before going elsewhere. We have lived in Chicago for the last ten years, and being generally known, families and those that need help will find it to their advantage to apply at my office for their supplies." Bonner and Jones let it be known that "persons in the Country or Eastern States" wishing for further information could contact them directly. In the same ad, the businessmen offered money loaned in small sums: "Loans of Money procured on the best of terms. Houses to Rent, and Rents Collected, Taxes Paid, and all this done on Reasonable Terms (see fig. 8.1)."[49]

The advertisements were placed by Chicago's noted Black abolitionists, John Jones and James Bonner, both members of Quinn Chapel and both

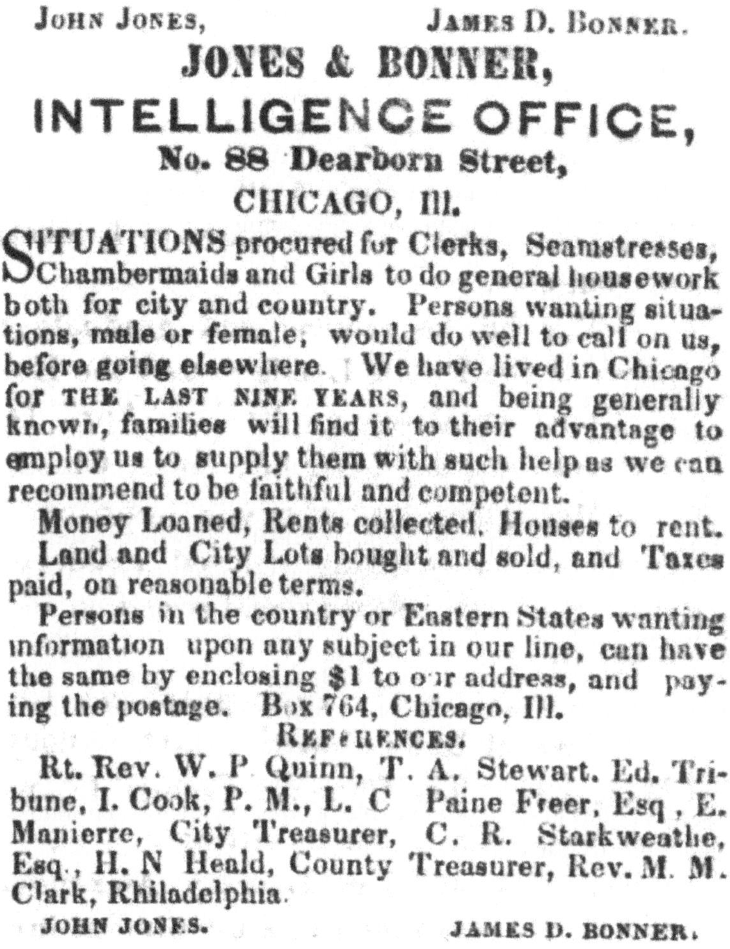

JOHN JONES, JAMES D. BONNER.
JONES & BONNER,
INTELLIGENCE OFFICE,
No. 88 Dearborn Street,
CHICAGO, Ill.

SITUATIONS procured for Clerks, Seamstresses, Chambermaids and Girls to do general housework both for city and country. Persons wanting situations, male or female, would do well to call on us, before going elsewhere. We have lived in Chicago for THE LAST NINE YEARS, and being generally known, families will find it to their advantage to employ us to supply them with such help as we can recommend to be faithful and competent.

Money Loaned, Rents collected. Houses to rent.

Land and City Lots bought and sold, and Taxes paid, on reasonable terms.

Persons in the country or Eastern States wanting information upon any subject in our line, can have the same by enclosing $1 to our address, and paying the postage. Box 764, Chicago, Ill.

REFERENCES.

Rt. Rev. W. P. Quinn, T. A. Stewart, Ed. Tribune, I. Cook, P. M., L. C Paine Freer, Esq , E. Manierre, City Treasurer, C. R. Starkweathe, Esq., H. N Heald, County Treasurer, Rev. M. M. Clark, Rhiladelphia.

JOHN JONES. JAMES D. BONNER.

Figure 8.1 John Jones and James D. Bonner Advertisement. Newspaper advertisement by avowed abolitionists and Underground Railroad activists, John Jones and James D. Bonner. Quinn's name appears on the first line of the References. *Frederick Douglass' Paper*, April 21, 1854, 4.

involved with the Underground Railroad. Jones ran his own tailoring business and eventually became one of the wealthiest African Americans in the pre–Civil War United States. After moving to Chicago in 1845, Jones used his house and his office, located on Dearborn Street, as stops on the Underground Railroad through Chicago. His home was known as a meeting place for local and national abolitionist leaders, including Frederick Douglass and John Brown. He also authored a number of influential antislavery pamphlets.[50] Jones provided John Brown direct aid by sheltering him during his most famous rescue of freedom seekers. Bonner, too, was directly involved with facilitating escapes from slavery.

It is reasonable to suspect the situations offered by the advertising agents—domestic service, chambermaids, cooks, servants, and so forth—offered quick, no-questions-asked employment for freedom seekers looking for work to support themselves in their new but precarious post-1850s freedom. The offer of small sum loans, favorable terms, and houses for rent could help relieve the immediate uncertainty and tenuousness of escape from slavery. Quinn's roots ran deep in Chicago, and his association with Jones and Bonner would have formed a protective shield if they were, indeed, running an Underground Railroad operation.

Frederick Douglass' Paper frequently reported on Bishop Quinn's activities across the years the newspaper was in print, from 1851 to 1860. For example, during one of Quinn's return trips to Canada, also in 1854, *Frederick Douglass' Paper* quoted a disturbing story about the bishop that was taken from *The Provincial Freeman*, an abolitionist Canadian newspaper run by Mary Ann Shadd. Racism respected no geographic boundaries, even in Canada.

Although Canada, St. Catharines in particular, enjoyed a reputation as a legal and political haven for people of color escaping slavery, the country was by no means without prejudice, which the article exposed. Public transportation had been a chronic site of racial contention on both sides of the border. The article pointed out that for several weeks, Canadian drivers of omnibuses belonging to the St. Catharine's House and the American Hotel adhered to a policy of excluding people of color or, "by special indulgence," allowing them "to ride outside."[51]

"The Rt. Rev. Paul Quinn, of Philadelphia, Bishop of the African Methodist Episcopal Church of the United States and Canada," arrived at the St. Catharine's Depot "in a feeble state of health" about a month ago. "This fine old gentleman, whose presence would honour any board of Bishops, was compelled to climb up and take his seat outside to ride into town." The Rev. Dr. Payne, "Bishop of the same Church, a man of superior intelligence and refinement of manners, who would pass as an accomplished gentleman among all civilized and enlightened people, [along] with his wife, an accomplished lady-like person," met the same harsh treatment. They had come to St. Catharines from Toronto aboard the new steamer *Welland* with no complaints. When the couple reached Port Dalhousie, they were excluded from the two omnibuses "upon the false pretence [sic]" that the buses had been reserved by other clients. "Being a mild, amiable man, richly imbued with the spirit of gentleness," Payne did not argue with the drivers, "who first took advantage of him by lying." Like Quinn, Payne was also "in a poor state of health, not having fully recovered from a severe turn of illness experienced in Toronto." Payne and his wife were forced to remain at the Port "till a late hour in the night, when a conveyance was sent down for them by the Rev. Mr. Copeland, who was permitted to ride up outside."[52]

Like Quinn, newspaper editors such as Frederick Douglass and Mary Ann Shadd in Canada maintained a commitment to exposing and confronting injustice and hypocrisy wherever it revealed itself. It is possible that over the years, the paths of these three great freedom fighters may have crossed.

Quinn's ministry was having an effect from St. Catharines to New Orleans. Under the bishop's leadership, the AME Church penetrated deeper into the South. Although Quinn had set up churches in New Orleans earlier, in 1848, the Indiana AME conference received an official petition from New Orleans, Louisiana, asking to join the conference and establish an independent AME church in that city. Their petition was approved.

In 1854, an antislavery newspaper, *The National Era*, published a story that focused on Bishop Quinn, "The South Again in Peril," compiled from several newspaper accounts. The South was "excited by the fact that the African Methodist Episcopal Conference had a church or two under its care in New Orleans, and . . . there [was] some talk of establishing one in Mobile." The newspaper observed that for four or five years, a branch of the church had been in operation there, "numbering a half dozen preachers and several hundred members." The AME Church had been "quietly operating, and now has two or three posts in the city; the main one being a large brick chapel, built by themselves."[53]

In the middle of 1853, Quinn had written a letter to the *Recorder*. The boldness, authority, and independence that Quinn displayed by apparently ordaining deacons and elders "on the spot" in New Orleans set off alarm bells in the press. He may have ventured 140 miles to Mobile, Alabama, and spoken "encouragingly of the cause of the South." The anxious writer warned that this independent Black church "breeds discontent, impracticability of wholesome discipline, and a restlessness for ministerial orders." The Methodist Episcopal Church South felt "periled by having this questionable organization." The writer continued, saying that an independent Black church organization of free people of color, "with its own bishops, elders, and deacons, its own property and discipline, may nurture feelings of self-respect and habits of self-reliance" in the Black population—enslaved and free—"and the example may be mischievous by quickening in the slaves the latent idea of manhood. Therefore, it is questionable, in fact, dangerous, and must be put down." The writer claimed "local authorities" had been alerted to this "grave subject." The newspaper then assured readers that the

"Methodist Episcopal Church South . . . doubtless is anxious to exclude the black Bishop Quinn from the South, and gather his colored flock into its own sheepfold, under white shepherds. . . . Would Bishop Quinn, with his four or five hundred harmless disciples, worshipping God in their own . . . way, throw any community into a panic, not conscious of maintaining an institution at war with human nature and the laws of God!"[54]

Ever on the move regardless of how authorities viewed his presence, Quinn opened the tenth General Conference of the AME Church in Cincinnati, Ohio, on May 5, 1856. Calling the conference to order, Quinn led, singing, "Come let us use the Grace Divine," before the opening prayer. Bishop Payne took the scripture lesson from John. In comparison to the organizational and institutional turmoil of the previous quadrennial, one AME historian thought the convention productive but not earth shattering.[55]

Rev. Payne's presentation of a gold episcopal seal to Bishop Quinn marked the highlight of this conference. At the previous General Conference, Quinn had assigned Payne to supervise the procurement of the seal. The face of the seal, embellished with an open Bible with divine light radiating forth and a heavenly cross resting on the book, bore an inscription on its border: "God our Father, Christ our Redeemer, Man our Brother." The bishop received a gold-headed cane, or episcopal staff, which was given with the understanding that it was to be forever handed down to successors. The gold seal, contributed by Baltimore, and the staff, a gift of Philadelphia, were presented before a large concourse of spectators at Bethel Church. The gifts were matched by Quinn's inspired eloquence. The symbols of office honored Quinn and marked the denomination's growing stature.[56]

The upheaval that year came from Canada. Bishops Payne and Quinn came to Chatham in 1856 to begin the process of establishing a new denomination. The Canadian conference in Chatham, held two years earlier, had openly determined to sever connections with the American church. The AME leadership agreed. In September that year, the British Methodist Episcopal Church (BME) was born. Quinn's former assistant, the newly elected bishop Willis Nazrey, was chosen to lead the church. Nazrey, as the first bishop of the BME, moved to Canada and withdrew entirely from AME. The BME flourished under his guidance and leadership. At the close of the conference, Quinn, consistently noted for his powerful singing voice, rose and lifted up the hymn "Come, Let Us Join Our Cheerful Songs." Payne offered the benediction, declaring that after seventeen years, "the Annual Conference of the A.M.E. Church in Canada is extinct."[57]

The BME Church continued the growth originally nurtured under the AME denomination, establishing congregations not only in Upper Canada but also in Nova Scotia and Bermuda.[58] Disagreements erupted over delegates, representation, and the elevation of an American, Bishop Nazrey, to lead the British Church. Quinn's reputation among the people, as Payne observed, "[was as] honorable and upright as any of [their] Bishops," which helped quell the dissension. Quinn did remind the separatists, "My dear brethren, be careful, for you are now going to make a breach in our connexion, that forty years can never mend."[59] The bishop admitted "he had much in his mind to say, but that he would not say all." Among the earliest lessons he'd taught his itinerants, "Speak evil of none, because your words eat as a canker" calmed the tensions. "Keep your thoughts within your breast," Quinn continued, "till you come to the persons concerned." The senior bishop used his own British roots to win over the dissidents, but the turmoil of discontent persisted for nearly a decade. Payne understood the Canadians held themselves as distinct from the AME Church and were free to govern themselves while continuing "a reciprocity of feeling and interest."[60]

Echoing Salem Chapel in St. Catharines, the new BME Church operated as a refuge from American slavery in British North America. Most of its members had escaped slavery in the United States and were anxious, as British citizens, to show their loyalty to an exclusively Canadian organization that would protect them from American oppression.

Flight to Canada relieved one danger faced by church leaders and their members—namely, crossing the US/Canadian border to attend conferences and official church functions. However, back in the United States, danger from bandits and physical assaults stalked the dark side of evangelizing. Being a man of God did not shield ministers from violence. In the winter of 1858, Quinn experienced this firsthand. The bishop was attacked in Cincinnati "by some desperadoes" on Sixth Street, near Stone, as he fulfilled his duties as bishop, presiding over the rapidly growing church. He was on his way to the Cincinnati, Hamilton, and Dayton Railroad depot on an early February morning. Quinn was knocked to the ground and robbed of a pocketbook containing $112, of which $50 had been in gold.[61]

One newspaper account calls the 6:00 a.m. robbery an "attack on his life." He was set upon by two villains. Quinn reported one was armed with a slingshot and the other, with a bludgeon. When they were at first unsuccessful in knocking him down, Quinn loudly cried out, "Murder!" which was heard at the depot.[62] A nearby grocery merchant also heard his cry of alarm, rose from his bed, and looked out his window in time to see the robbers beating a prostrate Quinn. The merchant fired two barrels of a revolver at them, with little effect, before the robbers finally fled.

A number of people at the depot also rushed to Quinn's aid, but he was already lying, badly injured, on the ground. The newspapers noted, "The robbers performed their bloody work speedily and surely, for even after his outcry they beat him until he was insensible, and rifled all of his pockets before they abandoned their bleeding victim." He withstood several heavy blows to the back of his head, and his forehead was badly cut; his nose, smashed. The newspaper speculated that "his face will be disfigured for life."[63]

The "highway robbery" left him insensible. Quinn's wounds were dressed after he was taken to the Ninth Street stationhouse. He was moved to a friend's home on Sixth Street to recuperate. So severe were Quinn's injuries that he "did not obtain full possession of his reason for a day or two," the newspaper reported.[64] It was a shockingly bold and outrageous attack in a busy area of town although, at 6:00 a.m., the thieves had been operating under the darkness of a winter's morning. Quinn often mentioned the dangers of evangelizing but rarely delved into specifics.

It may not be surprising that Quinn was carrying fifty dollars in gold. Perhaps the robbers learned of and believed the rumors about Quinn that would make their way into print after his death—that he literally had found a very rich gold mine of untold wealth right around this time. The rumor attracted considerable attention and fueled much speculation. The newspaper offered supporting evidence:

> About that time he returned home after being out on a long circuit as a missionary, and prefacing his remarks by stating he was a miner before coming to this country, said, in a secluded spot, the location of which he would never define, he saw signs of gold. Hitching his horse he followed a little stream in its windings through a ravine lined on either side with jagged rock until he came to a kind of precipice. . . . Here he found the rock studded with a precious metal and broke off several large pieces. These he wrapped in an old horse blanket and threw in the bottom of his buggy, where he carried them over a hundred miles, until he finished his circuit, when he took them to Philadelphia and had a part of the gold that was then converted into coin. To Mayor Poe he showed about $500 in new bright gold pieces, and a certificate, purporting to be from the master of the mint, certifying that they had been coined from quartz or stone [that] he still had a piece of and exhibited, which was interspersed with a yellow shining substance, whether gold or not. He also said he bought the land the gold was on, and Samuel Bundy, an intimate friend, says he has often seen lumps of the same kind, one of which weighed seven pounds. Mayor Poe, who attended to considerable of his business for several years, further says that Mr. Quinn certainly had some lucrative source that he could never learn anything about, for he often saw, in their money transactions,

express packages marked from one to eight thousand dollars, which he was, it seemed, in regular receipt of.⁶⁵

The newspaper article was written after Quinn's death in 1873 and states that he had found the mine about twelve or fifteen years before, which would be right around 1858, the time of the robbery. The presence of gold in Indiana had been known since about 1848 and was reported in several of Indiana's midstate counties, primarily in Morgan and Brown but also in some streams.

Quinn purchased property from both James Poe and Samuel Bundy, the two men mentioned in the news article. Landholdings in Henry and Orange Counties, in addition to Wayne County, were among the twenty or so pieces of property Quinn owned. The presence of gold was also recorded in Henry County. Quinn easily could have passed through these areas on his way to Terre Haute or from Indianapolis, heading south. Quinn's birthplace of Honduras had a long tradition of gold mining, which conceivably allowed him to recognize signs of its presence, particularly since he'd stated that he had been a miner before coming to this country, presumably in Belize. Similar to the robbery in New York City decades earlier, the robbers may have targeted Quinn as a man of wealth. According to Welch, he certainly dressed well.⁶⁶

Severely beaten, stabbed, and incapacitated in the assault and robbery, Quinn was unable to function for several months. These latest injuries left him incapable of fulfilling his ecclesiastical duties. Quinn had been expected to assist Bishop Payne at the May 1858 Baltimore Annual Conference. In the midst of the conference, Payne received a letter from the West, informing him that Bishop Quinn was at home in Richmond, Indiana, too ill to travel, and would not be able to attend. Perhaps the strains of the previous years were beginning to accumulate. His life of near-constant travel and numerous physical assaults was beginning to take its toll. Quinn arrived late, after the Philadelphia conference had been in session a few days, and could not participate actively due to the seriousness of his injuries.⁶⁷ Wayman, disturbed by Quinn's appearance, reported, "He looked very bad."⁶⁸

Bishop Payne took the senior bishop's place, presiding over both the Baltimore and Philadelphia conferences, to the detriment of his own health. Between 1856 and 1860, Quinn was to assume responsibility for the Philadelphia, New York, and New England conferences. During the same period, in keeping with the strategy of alternating regions and conferences, Bishop Payne assumed responsibility for the Missouri and Indiana regions, which strained his health due to Quinn's incapacitation. Payne was quite ill from

February to March, unable to speak in public for more than twenty minutes—and only weakly when at his best.[69]

AME bishops suffered from physical attacks, but legislative setbacks driven by Congress and the Supreme Court were equally withering. The decade of the 1850s was bookended by two of the worst congressional and legal decisions ever handed down: the Compromise of 1850 opened the decade, and the Dred Scott decision brought it to a close. Adding to the burden wrought by the lack of education, slavery, and the hardships of racial discrimination, judicial disasters threatened with each advancing day. Seven years after passage of the Fugitive Slave Act, widely viewed as the most disastrous law ever enacted by Congress, the Supreme Court was responsible for its own devastating landmark ruling in *Dred Scott v. Sanford*. As noted historian Benjamin Quarles observes, the militant spirit among Blacks was "fanned full sail in 1857 by the Dred Scott decision in which the Supreme Court opened the territories to slavery." The Supreme Court declared no slave or descendant of a slave could be a US citizen—or ever had been. As a noncitizen, the court stated, Dred Scott had no rights and could not sue in a federal court and must remain a slave. Notoriously, Chief Justice Roger Taney ruled that Blacks "had no rights which the white man was bound to respect; and that the Negro might justly and lawfully be reduced to slavery for his benefit." Blacks could be "bought and sold and treated as an ordinary article of merchandise and traffic, whenever profit could be made by it."[70]

The decision further outraged African Americans and their allies as it simultaneously reassured the nation of the court's position, sounding one more drumbeat in the death march toward the Civil War. For African Americans, the decision radically eroded whatever inadequate legal rights they'd possessed. The country was fracturing, not just along racial and religious fault lines but along political, geographic, and economic fissures as well. That "juridical monstrosity," as one writer has demonized the decision, pushed abolitionists to open aboveboard warfare against the government. The highest court in the nation had stepped in to defend slavery and stripped all African Americans—not restricted to the enslaved population—of their rights as citizens or even to consider themselves as citizens.[71] The Dred Scott decision further radicalized many free Blacks. Churches regularly held indignation meetings. This ruling convinced Black abolitionists that slavery would not end by legislative or court action.[72] It would require much more. The path to rupture and war had been set.

CHAPTER 9

Quinn, the Underground Railroad, and the Civil War

1859–1865

Quinn disappeared from public sight for months after the robbery and bludgeoning, his injuries and incapacitation apparently much deeper than he'd revealed to his church family. There is no public mention of him during this period other than a sole 1859 newspaper notice in Dawson's *Fort Wayne Daily Times*, which respectfully alerted readers that the bishop would preach a candlelight service on Wednesday evening, March 30, at the Wayne Avenue Church and invited them to join. It may have been a candlelight vigil for the country.

Historic times, such as the Civil War period, are marked by definitive dates. However, the long, descending years of the pre–Civil War era are littered with signs and markers. Some historians point to the Fugitive Slave Act and the Dred Scott decisions as radicalizing factors. Congress and the South made escaping slavery a national problem from beginning to end. Others credit (or blame) Harriet Beecher Stowe's 1851 publication of *Uncle Tom's Cabin* for its widespread exposé of slavery. The Kansas–Nebraska Act allowed settlers in Kansas to determine the state's position on slavery. John Brown's bloody fight to save the Kansas territory from slavery and his subsequent raid on Harpers Ferry share near universal responsibility. The "states' rights" argument, shorthand for a states' right to preserve and spread slavery, was a clear catalyst. If the admission of California to the Union disrupted Congress's balancing scheme around slavery, then the entry of Kansas as a free state toppled it. The admission of Kansas into the Union in March–April 1861 knocked a nation already staggering over slavery into civil war. By December 1860, when Quinn had recovered enough from his wounds to resume public duties, South Carolina had seceded from the

Union. By February 1861, the Confederate States of America had formed and elected their provisional president.

Despite grinding national tensions at the onset of the war in April, Quinn and the denomination dared to follow the normal schedule. One month after the outbreak of the war, as the effects of the hostilities began to strengthen their grip locally, a disturbing incident rattled the AME Church in Baltimore. Maryland, designated as one of five slaveholding border states, had often cast a wary eye on the activities of free Blacks living within the state.

With the start of the war, Baltimore authorities clamped down on free people of color. Meddling directly in the affairs of the Black church, city officials again denied the Baltimore Annual Conference permission to hold its yearly gathering. The police commission refused Bishop Payne entry into the city, arguing that he lived in Ohio and was not a Baltimore resident. City officials permitted the conference to meet only after the AME Connection had agreed to hold its Annual Conference without the presence or guidance of its bishop.[1]

In the face of increasing harassment, AME ministers conferred about the wisdom and safety of continuing to hold all of their conferences and questioned whether it would be prudent to change to a wartime mode of operation. Considering all the perils and uncertainties they were facing, the AME bishops decided to guide the church with a steady hand and meet the needs of the faithful following the traditional schedule, in the traditional manner.

Quinn attended a quarterly meeting for the first time in quite a while. He crossed over to Brooklyn, Illinois, where he visited with his old friend Priscilla Baltimore. By Saturday, August 31, Quinn had moved on from Illinois to Missouri, where he opened the Missouri Annual Conference. In St. Louis at St. Paul's Chapel, another of the Bethel churches he had consecrated, Quinn was back to preaching, singing, and praying, reading from Isaiah 12.

At the close of the conference, Quinn appointed one of his disciples, Jordan Early, to the St. Louis circuit. From his new post, Early would carry the AME banner through the war and into the future. Rev. Early reported that in "perilous times of the civil war, it was both dangerous and difficult to travel in the Southern and Western states."[2] Missouri, a border state like Maryland, fought for the Union but kept slavery fully legal. AME—its churches, preachers, and beliefs—stood as contradictions to arguments in support of the practice. The state's proslavery laws presented a constant challenge to the denomination and its ministers. W. E. B. Du Bois explains the church's position: an open forum on abolition proved "the most important issue" for the Black church. "In many ways the early African American church can be seen as an extension of the resistance so evidenced in the Underground Railroad."³

As senior bishop, Quinn set the stage for the denomination's future as an enduring contribution to his congregants. At the same time, he continued a whirlwind of preaching and overseeing his conferences. Henry McNeal Turner, an up-and-coming young intellectual force, entered the ranks of the church in 1860. Rev. Turner, a native of South Carolina, converted at the hands of Methodist evangelists at the age of fourteen and became a licensed preacher in the Methodist Episcopal Church by nineteen. The broad-shouldered, powerfully built Turner accepted a position as an itinerant preacher with the Methodist Episcopal Church South, traveling widely throughout the Southern states. Turner then decided to leave the church and the South with his new bride, Eliza, in the wake of the Dred Scott decision.

In Turner's early years of development, during his rigid examination and his trial by fire at the hands of the senior AME ministry, Quinn came to the neophyte's aid. "My young brother, you need not be discouraged because these older men went for you as they did, everybody who is admitted into the Conference has experienced the same thing, and a number of applicants have gone out of the door and have never been seen since. They treat everybody that way," Quinn reassured Turner.⁴

Turner's turbulent beginning gave way to a swift reception into the ranks of the AME Church. Well versed in Greek, Latin, Hebrew, and theology, Turner was sent to pastor Union Bethel Church in Washington, DC. Bishop Payne transferred him to the Baltimore conference, where he received a series of increasingly important ministerial assignments, including Baltimore's Tessier Street mission.

Bishop Payne happened to visit Turner's home and remarked on the vastness of the new preacher's library. Turner reports that Payne was "dum[b]founded at our books and the various subjects which they treated."⁵ In addition to Turner's spiritual and religious power, the knowledge he had derived from years of study would also benefit the denomination politically. One historian remarked that "his intelligence, erudition, and high flights of oratory achieved wide acclaim throughout the AME Church, and his bishop and presiding elder saw to it that his rough edges[,] including an uncertain grasp of English grammar," had been smoothed by careful study. Turner's captivating oratory left no trace of his earlier struggles.⁶

By July 1861 Congress decreed that the war would be fought to preserve the Union but not to end slavery, leaving much work for the Church militant. AME's senior bishop pushed on, making his way farther west. Quinn's legacy is most visible in the circuits and stations of the Ohio, Indiana, and Missouri Annual Conferences. In February 1862, ten months after the firing on Fort Sumter, Quinn reported visiting many of the places that comprised his circuits—stations, conferences, and a great many others he chose not to mention. The following list provides a window into the strenuous, demanding pace of Quinn's life during the Civil War (see fig. 9.1.)[7]

Figure 9.1 Annual Conferences Visited by Bishop Quinn, 1862

Chicago	IL (and established the second station of the AME Church in that city)
Freeport and Galena cities on Severn River	IL
St. Paul	Minnesota Territory
Berea	IL
Urbana	IL
St. Louis	MO
Brooklyn	IL
Alton	IL
Decatur	IL
Terre Haute	IN
Indianapolis	IN
Dublin	IN
Richmond	IN
Oxford	OH
Hamilton	OH
Cincinnati	OH
Dayton	OH
Xenia	OH
Columbus	OH
Zanesville	OH
Cambridge	OH
Wheeling	VA
Washington	PA
Brownsville	PA
Monongahela city	PA
Pittsburgh	PA
Cleveland	OH
Toledo	OH
Detroit	MI
Windsor	Canada
Chatham	Canada
Bellefontaine and Urbana	OH

A partial list of the Annual Conferences visited by Quinn during the Civil War reveals the great distances the missionary traveled for the church despite the conflict. He mentioned that this was not a complete list. "Meetings of Annual Conferences," *The Christian Recorder*, February 1, 1862.

Bishop Payne had oversight of the eastern conferences. A year later, Payne assigned Turner to Israel AME on Capitol Hill in Washington, DC, in July 1862. The war was on full blast, according to Turner. The AME denomination used Israel Church to maximize its influence in Washington. The church welcomed its indefatigable twenty-eight-year-old pastor to the pulpit and to the nation's capital just as Congress was acting finally to abolish slavery in Washington, DC (but not in the nation). Turner's fine preaching style ensured that every seat was filled until, he reports, eventually "hundreds had to stand outdoors," listening as best they could "to the words that came through the windows."[8]

Daring, eloquent, and distinctive, Turner was a conspicuous preacher, an intellectual genius. His biographer describes him as a "fiery pulpit orator" who emerged as a preeminent national figure. During these challenging times, all eyes were on Washington, and Turner's church was playing a leading part in the drama. Although it no longer exists, Israel AME stood within walking distance of the Capitol, "a couple hundred yards" according to Turner. Often, the young preacher could be found in the galleries of the United States House of Representatives, listening attentively to the speeches in favor of enlisting Black men into the Union Army. He befriended prominent members of Congress, such as Charles Sumner, Thaddeus Stevens, and Henry Wilson. The minister invited his new friends to speak to the Black citizens of the city on the dominant issues of the day, seeking to encourage them in the height of the warring nation's most troubled hour. Turner, for his part, spent hours in the Capitol, absorbing the political debates and arguments taking place on the floor of the House of Representatives and in the Senate chamber. As he listened, he learned about the Declaration of Independence, the Constitution, and politics in general. There the rising young AME minister honed the art of deliberative oratory that would contribute to his renown.[9]

While Turner applied political pressure from his church in the District of Columbia, Quinn confronted slavery head-on by taking physical action in the West, contending with his own Civil War challenges. Quinn "went from place to place, urging [AME's] people to educate and secure homes for themselves," as Rev. Arnett remembered. The freedom fighter was seventy-four years old. Nonetheless, "he was always on the go; he could not remain still; he wanted to be on the march, or in the fight, in the camp was not his place."[10]

Three quite different accounts converge to describe Quinn's exploits and time spent in Kansas during the Civil War. Uncharacteristically, Quinn provided an 1862 report of his western tour to *The Christian Recorder*: "I left Richmond, Ind., on the 11th of July, stopped at Indianapolis, and arrived at Terre Haute on the 12th. I attended Quarterly Meeting and preached twice on Sabbath." On July 12 Willis Revels reported the following to *The Christian Recorder* from Indianapolis: "Right Rev. Bishop Quinn, on his tour west," passed through Indianapolis last week "en route for Kansas" and visited "many intermediate points in his district. The Bishop [was] looking well . . . and . . . in good spirits." His stay was short, but it cheered all "to see the veteran pioneer again travelling over and surveying the ground where he [had] bestowed so much labor in planting our beloved Zion in early days."[11]

In Terre Haute the bishop ministered to the faithful for several days. On Sunday he preached from Psalm 84, verses 10 and 11.[12] In the middle of the war, Quinn continued his advance, moving across Missouri, a border state supporting both the Union and slavery. "I left Terre Haute on the 15th, and arrived in St. Louis on the 16th, and preached three times on the Sabbath, the 20th, to a crowded house," he recounts in his report. He was gratified to find "the church in this city in a prosperous condition," with a flourishing Sabbath School.[13]

Quinn left no explanation describing how he had maneuvered across Missouri or entered Kansas, both states that were heavily involved in the fighting along the Missouri–Kansas border. Train travel was the most likely option. "I left St. Louis on the 24th . . . for Leavenworth city, Kansas—a travel of some five hundred miles. I arrived at this point on the 25th, and found . . . [the] flock doing well." Two days later, he chaired the quarterly conference in Leavenworth, where he preached an "awakening sermon from Revelation—third chapter and twentieth verse."[14]

The congregation in Leavenworth had been in existence two years prior to Quinn's arrival in 1862. Quinn observed substantial progress. Under the able direction of their minister, worshippers in Leavenworth had "built a neat frame church edifice, which [Quinn] had the pleasure of dedicating."[15] A large assembly came to witness Quinn's dedication of the church to God. The bishop was satisfied with the successful visit and commended its pastor and congregation on their progress over the previous two years.

The city of Leavenworth stood on the bluffs of the Missouri River, and Bethel Church was strategically situated on Kiowa Street, only blocks from the river. As with so many churches associated with Quinn, for some time prior to 1861 until the close of the Civil War in 1865, the church served as a vital link in the Underground Railroad. It operated as one of the first stops for freedom seekers escaping from Missouri heading west.[16] Unsurprisingly, *The Christian Recorder*, the official organ of the AME Church, never mentioned or acknowledged such clandestine activities.

Yet in Kansas, which offered the possibilities of a new state with wide-open prospects, virulent racist violence routinely plagued Blacks who sought refuge in this misperceived "racial nirvana," the dominant description of Kansas at that time, as identified by historian Brent Campney. The lure of Kansas to freedom seekers was balanced by intimidation and confrontation: aggravated assaults and battery were intended to push African Americans out of the state. The new churches established in Leavenworth and Lawrence needed to take extra precautions. Campney reported that Whites targeted Blacks through property damage or destruction, generally by clandestine acts of arson aimed not only at churches but at homes, schools, and businesses.[17] St. Luke AME in Lawrence, for example, known as the old stone church, was fortified against arson.

The *Leavenworth Daily Times* reported on the exodus from Missouri, which was "almost denuded" of African Americans, to Kansas.[18] Freedom seekers "were leaving by day and by night. Very few owners pretend to stay the exodus"; many escapees would "pack up their 'duds' and walk boldly off in broad day, while others [would] quietly retire in the night."[19] If would-be freedom seekers fleeing Missouri did not know where to find refuge in Kansas, the haranguing of proslavery newspapers clearly laid out the road to peril and the path to relative safety. Proslavery forces had found abolitionist activity such a problem in Leavenworth before the war that they would forcibly stop steamboats from ascending the Missouri River in an effort to block passengers and freight intended to aid antislavery activists and to prevent "abolitionist immigration" to Kansas.

Blacks escaping slavery risked recapture, death, and lynching once they reached the Kansas River. Freedom seekers who came close enough to the Missouri River swam or rafted across, or they escaped by boat if they had access. If temperatures dropped severely enough, they crossed on the ice, but the greatest numbers crossed over the land border to the south of the Missouri River. "Undeterred in their pursuit of freedom, some of the enslaved people boldly walked across the Missouri River to freedom in Kansas during the unusually cold winter of 1862 when the ice formed a solid sheet" reports one historian of the era. By March, the ice was still strong enough to hold up teams of horses and mules.[20]

In early summer 1862, the Civil War had begun in earnest on the Missouri–Kansas border. Railroads, bridges, and river-crossing points were particularly vulnerable and volatile. Confederates initiated a well-devised scheme to bring reinforcements into Missouri and to ultimately gain possession of the Union state. Much of the work was covert. Marauding bands of rebels known as bushwhackers secretly passed Union lines and evaded arrest.²¹ Several guerrilla bands sprang into existence and attempted to surprise and capture small detachments of Union forces, meeting with limited success.

As the army reported, the desperate and bloody guerrilla war, begun about July 20, 1862, raged for nearly two months almost without cessation. No official report was filed for the skirmish in Lawrence on the twenty-seventh, so the details are lacking. This is the environment into which Quinn inserted himself during his July western tour to visit churches. At one point Union commanders ordered "all boats and other means of crossing the Missouri River" not under guard of Union troops "to be destroyed or securely guarded, and stopped all navigation of the river, except by strongly guarded boats."²² Gunboats patrolled the river. Presumably, Quinn knew of the general enrollment of Missouri men called to active Civil War service on July 22, 1862, which may have affected the timing of his western tour.

Arnett states that Quinn gathered freedom seekers as they came across Union lines. In Arnett's version, Quinn was captured several times by rebel forces and managed to escape once by swimming "the river while there was ice in it."²³ The Missouri River, which had become a frozen solid sheet of ice during the brutally cold preceding winter, may not have fully thawed, even in July. Although *The Christian Recorder* account derived from Quinn's report and letters from other observers depicts Quinn's presence in Kansas less graphically, danger clearly surrounded the bishop in July 1862. It is likely that Quinn, in orally recounting his adventures to Arnett and other listeners, elaborated beyond the spare, official details he provided *The Christian Recorder*. Arnett may have wanted to further dramatize an already dramatic life, or legend may have crept into the hero's story. Undoubtedly, Arnett listened to and captured Quinn's narration of his thrilling adventures, which have been mentioned by so many authors who knew him.

Quinn and his traveling companions stayed a total of four days in this "nest of abolitionism," as the proslavery newspapers defamed Leavenworth. "I left Leavenworth on the 29th," Quinn reported. By then the bishop had taken quite ill on the road; his war efforts may have aggravated the effects of the beating and stab wounds from the earlier robbery in Cincinnati. He arrived safely in Lawrence, a flourishing town on the Kansas River, thirty-five miles south of Leavenworth city. Quinn, however, was unable to preach or get to the place of worship in Lawrence because of his illness, much to the disappointment of the church family. Writers to *The Christian Recorder* thought "the appearance of our worthy old chieftain in the West" would hearten and encourage the people of Kansas.²⁴

The Kansas River cuts through northeastern Lawrence, home of St. Luke AME Church, founded in 1862. The city is the county seat of Douglas County, on the south bank of the Kaw (Kansas) River, about forty miles west of the Missouri border. St. Luke AME sat two blocks from the river. Quinn was pleased to find the faithful in Lawrence "upright, industrious and enterprising." The bishop, ever devoted to temperance, complimented the sober nature of the congregants. "The population of our people in Lawrence was between four and six hundred, and of the entire population not one can be said to bear the character of a drunkard. This is something worthy of note," he stressed to *The Christian Recorder*.[25]

"The Civil War came early to Missouri and Kansas, and stayed late," denotes one historian. AME's ability to arrange conferences during wartime and Quinn's ability to travel with impunity to congregations in proslavery Leavenworth and abolitionist Lawrence were significant. Visits to newly established AME churches in Kansas provided the rationale for Quinn's western trip. The tour placed the bishop in the heart of early Civil War skirmishes at a time when Black men were not officially sanctioned to take up arms and fight in the brewing Slaveholder's Rebellion, as it was called at the time.[26] US troops regularly passed through the town or stopped and camped on the way to battlefields in Missouri and the South.

The onslaught of African Americans seeking freedom from slavery and oppression represented the most significant movement of civilians along the Kansas border at that time. In Rev. Arnett's remembrances, he reports that Quinn spent part of the war years providing relief to freedmen in the West, particularly Kansas, the leading edge of the armed conflict for Black soldiers, some of whom had joined the First Kansas Colored Infantry in the Union Army at Fort Scott as early as 1862.[27]

One African American man did not know specific routes into Kansas but had heard that if he could just get "to the Yankees" in Lawrence, approximately forty miles from the Missouri border, he could find freedom. According to another reporter, "an (unnamed) 19th century minister once claimed that the number of escaped slaves who passed through his town of Lawrence, Kansas, amounted to $100,000 worth of property during the territorial period. Depots in Kansas proved to be especially important to fugitive slaves from Missouri en route to Nebraska, Iowa, and even Canada."[28]

The Jim Lane Trail, a major passageway for escapees moving north and east, ran through Kansas and other western states into Canada. The trail had developed as an overland solution to the closing of the Missouri River route to Kansas by steamboat. Freedom remained precarious in Kansas for conductors and freedom seekers alike. Federal and territorial fugitive slave laws were strictly enforced. The proslavery legislature in Kansas meted out excessively harsh punishment for violation of these laws. Kidnappers, freedom seekers, and bounty hunters made Lawrence a dangerous, risky crossroads. Proslavery activists from Missouri and abolitionists from New England converged with local Underground Railroad operatives, all fighting either for or against slavery. Proslavery fighters from Missouri were determined to control Lawrence's political and economic life.

Less than a week after Quinn's departure, First Kansas, recruited by Jim Lane, recruiting commissioner for Kansas territory, was organized without federal authorization and against the position of Secretary of War Edwin M. Stanton. By August 4, 1862, Lane had authorized raising the regiment, which became the "first African American regiment to fight in combat with white soldiers during the Civil War."[29] Many of the early Black war recruits had escaped to Kansas, fleeing slavery in Missouri and Arkansas. Jim Lane was out ahead of federal efforts and began recruiting Black soldiers to join his Kansas forces.[30] Quinn's Kansas trek put him in the middle of the fight. Quinn's activities in helping freedom seekers escape were illegal at the time of their occurrence, particularly for AME's senior bishop, the most distinguished member of the church at the time.

Quinn and his accompanying travelers left Lawrence by railroad on their return trip to St. Louis. At the end of the tour, the bishop reported seeing evidence of recent fighting and Confederate troops assembling. He sent his observations to *The Christian Recorder*:

> We found the country in great excitement. Guerilla bands are formed in large numbers and are robbing, killing and plundering the Union men. We passed hundreds of them along the road, near Hudson—a station on the road. They hung three rebels the day before we arrived there and buried them with the ropes around their necks. They had two more on hand, to be hung.
>
> As we came on, at another station, the rebels were drawn up in line of battle and marching on the town, some five or six hundred strong. Had we been five or ten minutes later, they would have had us all; but thanks be to God, we were delivered, and arrived safe in St. Louis. Since writing, we have received information that the Union men met them promptly at the place alluded to above, and killed one hundred and seventy-three of them; but finally had to surrender, being inferior in numbers.[31]

Miraculously, the train passed through shortly before the Confederate attack on the unspecified location. Relieved to escape the danger, Quinn and his traveling party made their way home via the Hannibal and St. Joseph Railroad.[32]

It took weeks for Quinn to regain his strength following his Kansas forays. He resumed oversight of the conferences, traveling by train and carriage more often. He headed for a camp meeting near Alton, Illinois, on Thursday, August 7, then presided over the twenty-third session of the Indiana Annual Conference, held at Indianapolis on August 15, 1862.[33] Two weeks later, he returned to St. Paul's Chapel in St. Louis to open the Missouri Annual Conference. Displaying his powerful voice, the bishop sang the verse of the old Methodist hymn "Waiting at the Cross," which began "Father, I dare believe thee merciful and true."[34]

Civil War activism stretched across Quinn's conferences. In Indiana, Willis Revels, pastor of Bethel Indianapolis, was deeply entwined with the Freedmen's Aid Society, which helped freedom seekers and free Black migrants. Revels's religious, political, and social commitment defined his life and his work in the church. He was quick to assist escapees who passed through Indianapolis, sheltering them in his home if necessary. Following a pattern Quinn found effective, Revels helped others find much-needed local work. The activism of Bethel Indianapolis in promoting the abolitionist movement and its activities in support of the Underground Railroad were not well received by some members of the local community. Proslavery supporters are believed to have set the fire that destroyed the church in 1862.[35]

About a month after Quinn's return, President Lincoln issued the preliminary Emancipation Proclamation on September 22, 1862, which stated that if the rebels did not end the fighting and rejoin the Union by January 1, 1863, all those enslaved in the rebellious states would be free. On January 1, 1863, the Emancipation Proclamation went into effect.[36]

When the day of deliverance finally arrived, Rev. Henry McNeal Turner rushed to the printers in Washington, DC, to obtain a newspaper copy. Winded from the mile run to return to Israel Bethel Church, Turner was unable to read the proclamation aloud to the throngs gathered in the church yard. His assistant bestowed the precious words on the listeners: "All persons held as slaves within any State or designated part of a State . . . in rebellion against the United States, shall be . . . forever free."[37] So jubilantly was the news of emancipation received, Turner observed that

> men squealed[,] women fainted, dogs barked, white and colored people shook hands, songs were sung. . . . Every face had a smile, and even the dumb animals seemed to realize that some extraordinary event had taken place. . . . Rumor said that in several instances the very thought of being set at liberty and having no more auction blocks, no more separation of parents and children, no more

horrors of slavery, was so elative and heart gladdening that scores of colored people literally fell dead with joy.[38]

Turner predicted that "Richmond, the headquarters of the southern Confederacy, would never fall till black men led the army against this great slave-mart."[39] The president had been resistant to the push to enlist African Americans into the Union Army to fight for their own freedom. The thought of arming Black men for the purpose of killing their White enemy caused general alarm.

Demonstrating his own radicalism, Jabez Campbell, *The Christian Recorder* editor who would be consecrated bishop the following year, openly questioned President Lincoln's commitment to the abolition of slavery and spoke out about the discriminatory practices toward Black soldiers. One Lincoln scholar points out, "When black leaders asked that regiments of black soldiers be enrolled under the flag of freedom, Lincoln and his advisors refused."[40]

Contained within the Emancipation Proclamation, however, was a call for the enrollment of Black soldiers in the Union Army and Navy. Bishop Payne thought the proclamation "was the greatest event in the history of the nation since the adoption of the Declaration of American Independence."[41] The entire AME Church withstood the avalanche of joy that followed. Quinn celebrated a day of jubilee to commemorate the historic moment with the African American citizens of Chicago. The bishop blessed the gathering, offering benediction at the close of the celebration. Emancipation celebrations would continue for years. Wayman noted that excitement spread throughout the conference: "There was nothing heard and seen but the rattling of the drum, and the boys in blue."[42]

The Emancipation Proclamation offered only partial freedom to those enslaved in the rebelling Southern states. Missouri was not among them, nor was Maryland, Delaware, or Kentucky, all of which remained loyal to the Union while continuing the practice of enslavement. With the exception of Delaware, Quinn had been heavily involved in the establishment of AME churches in each of those border states. This may have compelled Quinn to help with the escape of enslaved persons from Missouri to Kansas; the proclamation did not include freedom for the enslaved there. Anyone not freed by the proclamation had to gain their freedom on their own by fleeing into states where free status would be granted. In Kansas Quinn had seen the power and determination of freedom seekers as they streamed out of Missouri, the neighboring state.

Rev. Turner attributed to Senator Charles Sumner much of the relentless pressure that had induced Lincoln finally to consider the actual, direct end of slavery. Both Daniel Payne and Henry McNeal Turner led the AME lobbying efforts to convince President Lincoln of the wisdom of enlisting the new freedmen into the Union Army.[43] In 1863 Lincoln finally agreed, and the North opened its armed forces to Black enlistment. Quinn Chapel in Chicago, one of the dozens of churches named for Quinn, hosted the first Black recruitment rally in the city.

Turner organized the First Regiment of US Colored Troops in the same church yard where the reading of the Emancipation Proclamation had stirred so many to the heights of jubilation. Turner entered into the service as one of the first Black chaplains in the US Army. The minister was attentive to governmental procedures, and so the vibrant young preacher was of interest to some members of Congress. Charles Sumner regularly visited Turner's nearby church on Sundays.[44] "Slavery dies hard," lamented Sumner after hearing complaints from fellow senators. "It died hard in the Senate chamber. It dies hard on the field of battle. The body of the beast was killed in the District of Columbia, but the tail was alive yet. The Senate of the United States was helping to hold on to that tail."[45]

Wilberforce University also suffered the debilitating impact of the war, which caused a decline in student enrollment. The original university failed, and Wilberforce closed its doors in June 1862. The pressures of war forced the trustees to suspend operations, abandon the school entirely by March 1863, and sell off the property to the Methodist Episcopal Church. Bishop Payne, however, would not relinquish his dream of an institution of higher learning where African Americans could gain a sacred and secular education.

A month later, Quinn opened the religious services of the Ohio Annual Conference in Springfield, Ohio, in April 1863. The bishop, "looking very well" and never appearing "to get much older," greeted conference delegates with his rapid style and hearty handshakes.[46] Bishop Payne, along with Nazrey, assisted Quinn. Payne came to the conference with a plan for reclaiming Wilberforce, requesting that the AME Church approve his course of action and commit $3,000 to Wilberforce University. The plan was adopted without dissent, and a committee formed to take up the important question. The committee recommended that cost be equally divided among the seven Annual Conferences at $2,000 each.[47] Thus, in the midst of the Civil War, Bishop Payne managed to raise the funds to repurchase the property from the Cincinnati conference of the Methodist Episcopal Church on behalf of the AME Church. Under Bishop Payne's direction, AME would regain full ownership of Wilberforce University. Quinn had encouraged and supported Payne throughout his quest for an educated ministry. The reclamation of Wilberforce returned Payne and AME to the central mission of education.

Bishop Payne realized his most significant achievement with the purchase of Wilberforce University. By early July 1863, Wilberforce was reincorporated.

Quinn and most of the church's senior leadership were on the board of trustees—Quinn, from 1863 to 1867. Payne served as the school's president from 1863 to 1876, the first Black man in America to lead a college in this position. President Payne moved his residence to the campus and guided its success. According to the history of Wilberforce, the school had been founded as a "refuge from slavery's first rule: ignorance"; many AME members and clergy would gain a superior education at this "intellectual Mecca."[48] Given Payne's stand for an educated ministry and his overall dedication to education in general, Payne has been called perhaps the most dynamic intellectual of the earliest leaders. His championing of education led him to advocate at several General Conferences that the clergy of the AME Church be required to obtain an education. Bishop Quinn always allied with the idea of an educated ministry. He had pushed education in all his churches, on all of his circuits, and at the Annual and General Conferences. Sabbath Schools flourished alongside the churches Quinn had started.

The church's unwavering stand for education ensured that Black learners were intellectually equipped to meet the challenges before them and to overcome the struggles that lay ahead. Quinn and Payne's support for education positioned the church as an effective agent for creating and preserving not only the spiritual and intellectual well-being but also the morale of African American churchwomen and -men. Payne's lifelong efforts brought him the well-deserved title the Apostle of Education. Allen's ministers had risen to become powerful leaders in spiritual and political affairs. They stood at the forefront in the moral, social, and civic realms, beyond educational spheres. Rev. Arnett understood that "no institution has been so vital to the struggle for black liberation as the black church."[49]

As the country roiled over the war and the abolition of slavery, Quinn adhered to his hectic schedule of overseeing conferences. By mid-1863 he was again listed in the city directory of his hometown, Richmond, Indiana. He continued the relentless pace of his life, presiding over the Indiana Annual Conference in Chicago in August. By spring the following year, *The Christian Recorder* observed that the old members of the General Conference looked healthy and cheerful and "wear" well in the gospel work; "the Bishops are all in good health, and Bishop Quinn, the senior Bishop, looks unusually well, and truly venerable, and impresses the Conference with the idea of gravity and wisdom, and carries one's mind back to days of yore."[50]

Noted poet Frances Watkins Harper lectured twice on "The Mission of the War" at the Bethel AME Church in Indianapolis. It is possible that she met Quinn at that time. Unfortunately, by summer, arsonists had burned the church to the ground. "It was the work of an incendiary-one," Rev. Willis R. Revel reported in *The Christian Recorder*.[51] Burning churches and other buildings important to Black accomplishments reassured antagonists that the success they were witnessing would not be sustained.

The Civil War dragged on, although the Confederacy was approaching collapse. Emancipation had taken hold, and once-enslaved self-liberators and freedom seekers surged toward the Union Army. Many AME congregants returned from Canada to serve. The eventful May 1864 General Conference of the AME Church took place in Philadelphia, assembling in old Bethel Church on the ground where Allen once preached and the denomination had realized its beginnings. Quinn conducted the opening exercises along with Bishops Payne and Nazrey. The important work of the church also continued. Jabez Campbell and Alexander Wayman were elected and ordained as bishops who would help bring the church into the twentieth century.

Captain Robert Smalls, a famed Civil War hero, visited this conference. Smalls had commandeered the Confederate gunboat *Planter* during the Civil War, sailed it out of Charleston Harbor and through the Union blockade under the noses of the Confederate watch, and delivered this war prize to the Union Army. It was the most valuable war vessel the Confederates had in Charleston.[52]

The General Conference of 1864 showed particular interest in Lawrence, Kansas, a subject of concern for Quinn. Two important emerging AME congregations thrived in Kansas, a part of Quinn's district. The news of Quantrill's massacre in Lawrence, Kansas, a year earlier had captivated and troubled the conference: Missouri and Kansas had been racked by border tensions before, during, and after Quinn's encounters with the Confederate guerrilla fighters known as bushwhackers. On August 21, 1863, William Quantrill led a guerrilla attack against citizens of Lawrence that killed more than 150 boys and men. He burned much of the town.

According to AME Church history of Lawrence, "[the] old stone church was a secure hiding place for many citizens, both black and white during Quantrill's raid."[53] Freedom seekers combined with newly freed men, women, and their children to constitute the membership of the early church. "Many came here through the underground railroad system."[54] The vital presence of the AME Church in Lawrence left the presiding clergy across the country understandably anxious to learn of the welfare of church members. Most Blacks in Lawrence had managed to flee, but "the old and decrepit men," unable to escape the carnage, suffered the most.[55] Quantrill had roamed the

Missouri and Kansas countryside with a group of bandits, looking for escapees from slavery. Quantrill's raid, also known as the Lawrence Massacre, brought the tension between local abolitionists and proslavery partisans along the Missouri–Kansas border to a bloody conclusion and kept the war at the forefront of the conference.

Quinn moved on to Kentucky. By August 27 the indefatigable bishop presided over the Missouri Annual Conference in Louisville, Kentucky. He opened the conference with Hymn 142: "Lord, all I am is known to Thee." The conference began provisions for the ordination of a bishop for Africa to be elected by the Liberia conference.[56] The triumvirate of Quinn, Payne, and Nazrey, bishops in the 1852–1864 period, led AME in this vitally important twelve-year period that led up to and encompassed the war.

These long years of service by senior leadership lent stability to the developing church throughout the war and into a new era. Experienced guidance and steady governance enabled the AME trailblazers to advance the institution under the Lord's blessed assurance while impressing Allen's legacy on the denomination. By September 1864 a large number of African American itinerants from the Southern Methodist Episcopal Church in Tennessee, Arkansas, and Missouri, in addition to Kentucky and Kansas, flooded the AME denomination, seeking ordination, perhaps in anticipation of the promise of freedom.[57] When the end of the war came with the Confederate surrender in April 1865, these new converts saw the vast opportunities ahead and were eager to lead the missionary work in the South under the AME banner.

CHAPTER 10

Passing the Torch

1865–1872

Good Friday, April 14, 1865, five days after General Lee had surrendered to Ulysses Grant at Appomattox Courthouse largely ended the Civil War, was an ominous day for both the AME Church and for the country. That night, as John Wilkes Booth fatally shot Abraham Lincoln at Ford's Theater in Washington, DC, unknown arsonists set a fire that burned Wilberforce University to the ground. The main classroom building, the dining hall, and chapel all were torched. Within half an hour, the beautiful edifice was reduced to smoldering embers. Fortunately, the headmaster and almost all the students were away from the campus.

All the artifacts donated to the school by Martin Delany and the souvenirs given by Elizabeth Keckley from Mary Todd and President Lincoln for the nascent museum collection were destroyed. Keckley's son had attended Wilberforce before losing his life in the Civil War, which gave her a particular fondness for the school, where she would later become the director of domestic art.

But resolve reigned. According to Payne, the trustees vowed that "out of the ashes of the beautiful frame building a nobler one shall rise." They transformed one of the unburned cottages into a schoolroom, and classes continued. Bishop Payne would not let anything break his determination that Blacks shake off all residue of slavery. Quinn attended the Wilberforce commencement exercises that year, as did all other bishops. New construction was already under way. Quinn led the conference with his $150 pledge for the rebuilding effort, which Reverend Shorter hoped would inspire other contributors to follow the example of his generous subscription.[1]

The second tragedy left a shocked country to mourn the death of President Lincoln. The entire Baltimore conference traveled to Washington,

DC, to attend the president's funeral. Bishop Daniel Payne had met with Lincoln in 1862, when Payne observed, "Washington looked then more like a great military encampment than the seat of national legislation and judicial action." On this day the federal city was consumed by grief as it prepared for the funeral. The proud Twenty-Second US Colored Troops had been chosen to head the funeral procession. The AME ministers may have marched with the "clergy in attendance" of the various denominations for the opening of the civic procession. Citizens and strangers were listed at the end of the procession, and *The Christian Recorder* indicates that men of color closed out the march. The man who had done so much to preserve the Union and bring about the end of slavery was dead.[2]

Slowly, relentlessly, the work of the church resumed. Rev. Arnett, who knew Quinn and listened to his many stories, called him "the main stay in the great conflict which culminated in the emancipation and enfranchisement of the race." Bishop Allen had infused the denomination with a liberatory ethos that passed to succeeding leaders. The church consistently took a vanguard position on important questions that affected its membership and their ability to lead purposeful lives, particularly in its publications and instruction. Education, financial literacy, and acquiring property were the instruments of racial uplift.[3]

The church recognized the new horizons available to AME ministers. This anticipation of extending preparation for productive citizenship into the South met with mixed results. Of the twenty thousand members the church could claim in 1858, few had been in the Southern states, and of those few, most were in churches organized by Quinn or formed under his influence.[4] Despite the racial prejudice that continued to plague people of color, with the end of slavery and the Civil War, Southern membership increased dramatically. Newly freed men and women reached for long-withheld opportunities—homes, paid work, and education for themselves but especially for their children. Family reunification and marriage offered the hope of stability. Senior Bishop Quinn had fought for, prepared for, and dreamed of this moment of freedom from the outset of his ministry.

Quinn could focus on overt political advocacy beyond the covert strategies of escape from slavery. He was prepared to lead the faithful forward in the direction of those aspirations as he concentrated on his ecclesiastical duties. He opened the Philadelphia conference, held at Union Church.[5] With a hearty handshake and his customary "rapid style," Quinn visited the quarterly conference in Delaware, Ohio.[6] Bishop Campbell presided over a joyous Annual Conference held in St. James Chapel in New Orleans. With the end of the war and the dawning of freedom, Jordan Early reported that education, along with temperance, commanded the church's refocused attention. Ministers were "required to do all in their power to enlighten their own minds and to encourage the building up of schools."[7]

The Emancipation Proclamation and the Thirteenth Amendment, proposed by Lincoln before his death and ratified December 6, 1865, brought an uneven patchwork of freedom across the country. African Americans had rights that they could expect to be protected. At last, as historian Eric Foner declared, the "irrevocable abolition of slavery throughout the reunited nation" came with the ratification of the Thirteenth Amendment.[8] However, some Confederate strongholds, such as Texas and Delaware, withheld freedom or the news of freedom for the enslaved. Freedom for all finally came on June 19, 1865.

M. M. Clarke, Quinn's devoted disciple and secretary, carried the pioneer bishop's legacy into Texas. Clark had organized the first Texas AME church in Galveston, which grew as radical Republicans—those who had insisted on the "ultimate extinction" of slavery—gained strength during the Reconstruction era. Clarke's efforts led to the establishment of Reedy Chapel AME Church, "the Mother AME Church in Texas." General Order No. 3, announcing the end of slavery in Texas, was read aloud in Galveston at Reedy Chapel, which launched the church's reputation as the home of the original Juneteenth celebrations. Similar to the reading of the Emancipation Proclamation in the churchyard of Turner's church in Washington, DC, years earlier, the AME Church helped spread the news of the ultimate end of slavery in the United States.[9]

The process of adopting the Thirteenth Amendment, which abolished slavery throughout the country except for convicted criminals, encompassed all of 1865. Passed by United States Congress in January, the amendment was not ratified until December. Radical abolitionist and Presbyterian minister Henry Highland Garnet, Quinn's longtime friend from the early days in New York City, delivered an address from the desk of the Speaker of the House of Representatives heralding the amendment. Garnet became the first African American to speak in the House chamber. Since the late 1820s, prior to Garnet's speech, African Americans had been banned from both congressional chambers.[10]

The AME Church emerged nationwide as the second-largest Reconstruction-era Black denomination, second only to the Baptists. African American churches actively helped the newly freed men and women lead independent lives. The end of the Civil War brought new opportunities to the denomination once constrained by slavery and barred from extensive organizing in Southern states. Lifting of restrictions opened vistas in the

South and far West, presenting new opportunities for the denomination.¹¹ Bishop Jabez Pitt Campbell organized the California conference at Sacramento as early as April 5, 1865, as the war was still winding down.

Norfolk, Virginia, and Wilmington, North Carolina, as well as Georgetown, Raleigh, Charleston, Beaufort, Newbern, and Hilton Head, from the South Carolina coast to Savannah, became the new frontier for the AME Church. AME evangelists and missionaries covered the northern and western parts of Georgia, including Augusta, Macon, Atlanta, and Columbus.¹² On November 1, 1865, the Louisiana conference was formed in St. James Chapel in New Orleans, with Bishop Campbell again presiding. This church had been a part of the Missouri Annual Conference, which had been organized by Bishop Quinn in Louisville in 1855. The new Louisiana Annual Conference included the states of Louisiana, Mississippi, Arkansas, and Texas.¹³

With so much change happening, Bishop Quinn called an episcopal meeting in January 1866 to consider the status of the several districts of the expanding church and the educational work ahead. They met in Pittsburgh's Wylie Street AME church. Bishops Quinn, Payne, Wayman, and Campbell were present. As senior bishop, Quinn set the stage for the future of the denomination as his final contribution to his congregants while, at the same time, he continued a whirlwind of preaching. He was looking ahead, planning for the commemoration of the semicentenary of African Methodism during the year. He appointed Bishop Campbell to write an address to the Black people in the United States.¹⁴

For the celebration of the church's fiftieth anniversary, Bishop Payne praised the unceasing work of Paul Quinn as its pioneer bishop. Quinn had sustained the church through its founding, through its growing influence, and across difficult and dangerous times. Payne lauded Quinn's achievements as the greatest "crowning glory that ever attended the splendor of the highest royalty."¹⁵ In a few days, Payne observed, the Connection would be a half century old. Quinn, by this time, had been a bishop of the AME Church for nearly a quarter of a century. He had led the church as its presiding bishop for not quite half of its time. Payne concluded, saying the following:

> Nature eminently fitted him for a leader. Who can think of him without being reminded of his commanding presence, his complacent countenance, so indicative of moral strength, his penetrating wit, his never sleeping sagacity, his short cuts to sound conclusions; and above all his forbearance, implicit trust in the Divine agency, and love of the Connection? Increasing years have not bent his stature: his step is still elastic, and his usual flow of wit and humor breaks the monotony of any circle he may chance to be in. . . . We love to

study the history of Bishop Quinn's career, exhibiting as it does a model of Christian heroism, untiring energy, and human sagacity, as well as devotion to the church of Christ.[16]

In April Quinn, who all agreed was looking well, especially for a man who had spent much of his life on the frontiers of both his young country and his young church, briefly visited the forty-ninth session of the Baltimore Annual Conference, held at Israel Church in Washington, DC. In May he arrived in Philadelphia for the Annual Conference. In June Quinn delivered a rousing sermon in New Haven, which was part of the New England Annual Conference (which he held again in 1867).[17] Political efforts were yielding the long-desired rewards of his dreams. With the war's end, Quinn's disciples continued to bear fruit for the church. He then headed for New York City and Philadelphia before heading home to Richmond, Indiana. Upon his departure local congregants regretted that he could not stay longer. Quinn may have cut his stay short to attend to more pressing business.

After nearly forty years of riding his circuit and spreading the word of God and the AME Church across the Midwest, Quinn decided to marry! *The Christian Recorder* noted that Mrs. Mary Simms of Hamilton, Ohio, "long known as a useful member of our church," left Philadelphia for her home at the same time Quinn departed from there. Perhaps she had attended the conference. Hamilton had been part of Quinn's circuit in Ohio, so he must have seen his future wife often through the years, although he did not mention her. On June 28 Bishop Daniel Payne officiated at the marriage of Bishop William Paul Quinn to Mrs. Mary J. Simms at her residence in Hamilton, Ohio (see fig. 10.1).[18]

After decades of devotion to the church and thirty-six years after the death of his first wife, Margaretta, Quinn had found a companion in Mrs. Simms, a widow and mother of four children. Quinn had remained unmarried throughout his energetic missionary career in Western Pennsylvania, Ohio, Indiana, Illinois, and Missouri. Now, at the age of seventy-eight, he had chosen a thirty-seven-year-old companion.

Quinn brought his new wife to Indiana, and the couple settled in Newport. They made the most of married life. Welch affirms that "his home life was beautiful."[19] He took time to rest and enjoy his new family and admiring old friends. Quinn loved children. Welch portrays him as a kindly father to his wife's four children, his new charges.[20] The family's days were filled with music. Welch characterizes Quinn's time at home as "one long love feast." Their home became a place for large dinner parties. Famous men and women of the day journeyed to visit. The Quinns made sure their guests were well

MRS. MARY JANE QUINN
Born, June 29th, 1829. Died, Febuary 18th, 1889.

Figure 10.1 Mary Jane Simms Quinn. Proceedings of the quarto-centennial conference of the AME Church of South Carolina, at Charleston, South Carolina, May 5, 16, and 17, 1889, African Methodist Episcopal Church, South Carolina Conference, courtesy of Duke University Libraries / Internet Archives.

entertained, and visitors often stayed on as houseguests. Quinn mentored several young men who aspired to the ministry and lived with the family. They studied Quinn's library and looked after his farm and the livestock while the bishop rode his circuits and visited his districts.[21]

In November Quinn was away from home, giving a retrospective lecture in Danville, Kentucky, discussing his travels, the hardship of imprisonment, and the organization of the many churches he had helped to establish. He reminisced about the rise and progress of the Bethel Church from a blacksmith shop to seven hundred churches, schools, and colleges.[22] The following year, *The Urbana Union* reported in April that the enduringly powerful evangelist had baptized twenty-nine colored men by immersing them at the factory pond late on a Sunday afternoon. Between five hundred and a thousand people were on hand to witness the occasion, which was punctuated by frequent and hearty applause.[23] Quinn's imprint on the church continued. He ordained future bishop Benjamin William Arnett a deacon on April 30, 1868, in Columbus, Ohio.

In May Quinn presided over the 1868 General Conference, the first post–Civil War General Conference, held at Israel Bethel AME in Washington, DC. Quinn led the religious exercises. By now Henry McNeal Turner, the rising giant of the denomination, observed that the conference had grown to such an extent that it had begun to "monopolize more attention in Washington than the impeachment trial of the president," Andrew Johnson. "Such an array of corpulent . . . preachers and black Bishops" had never before been seen in Washington, DC. The fact that many were "D.D.'s and M.D.'s and professors of languages, theology and a variety of scientific branches only added to the curiosity."[24] A communication read from an old and faithful antislavery society in England set forth their "eager desire for the civil and political elevation of the colored people in North America," although Turner found the tone of the communication condescending.[25]

During a highlight of the conference, Quinn, along with the bishops, ministers and delegates to the General Conference, called on Pennsylvania's Hon. Thaddeus Stevens. He had been elected to the United States House of Representatives from 1849 to 1853 and again from 1859 until his death in August 1868. As chairman of the House Ways and Means Committee and also of the Appropriations Committee, Stevens was responsible for funding both the Civil War effort and, later, Reconstruction. They came to thank Stevens for all he had done "for the race, as well as the Conference." In his reply, Stevens said that he "rejoiced that the day had at last arrived when he could call them his fellow-citizens." He thought that "the nation owed them, as a race, a heavy debt" and that the affliction of "grievances and innumerable wrongs" had spanned the ages.[26] Rev. H. M. Turner, who had helped organize the Georgia Republican Party and been elected both as a delegate from Georgia and a member of the Georgia State legislature, replied to Mr. Stevens, only asking that "now . . . they be treated as freemen, freedom having been established." The conference delegation, led by Rev. John (Mifflin) Brown, expressed its appreciation and "unfeigned thanks" for Stevens's interest and efforts, particularly around suffrage and on behalf of freedom.[27]

That small phrase, "on behalf of freedom," may have had a deeper meaning for the conference members of 1868. Their tribute and expressions of gratitude came from a place of deep understanding of Stevens as a principled man of conviction. Thaddeus Stevens had taken an active part in the Underground Railroad before the war. In 1848 he'd personally escorted freedom seekers from his law office in Lancaster to their next destination. He'd used his Caledonia Iron Works in Franklin County, Pennsylvania—a conduit for the Underground Railroad—to provide work and refuge for freedom seekers. The conference members took the time to offer their "unfeigned thanks" perhaps because they recognized the full dimensions of Stevens's commitment to freedom.[28]

Quinn was at the center of concern as the conference returned its attention to the needs of the church. There was much talk of superannuating, or retiring, "[their] infirmed Bishops" and electing "young, educated men in their stead—and thus lay Bishop Quinn on the shelf." They estimated he was near "a hundred years old."[29] The conference admitted, "Whether we can so dispose of Bishop Quinn or not is doubtful, owing to his long career of usefulness, and his whole-souledness yet, and his utter abhorrence to being superannuated. All revere him for past services, and there will hardly be pluck enough to override the old man's pleasure." Quinn moved forward, the only direction he knew or understood.[30]

New bishops continued to fulfill the enormous legacy that Quinn and the founding bishops had established before the Civil War. On May 25 the elderly Quinn, surrounded by Bishops Payne, Wayman, and Campbell, ordained to the bishopric James Alexander Shorter and Thomas Myers Decatur Ward, the first preacher to have brought AME to California twenty years earlier. He was elected the tenth bishop of the AME Church. Quinn's old friend from New Orleans, Louisville, and Baltimore, the steadfast John Mifflin (J. M.) Brown rose to become the eleventh bishop of the AME Church that year (see fig. 10.2).[31]

Quinn's friendship with Brown followed the usual pattern of his association with known Underground Railroad agents. John Mifflin Brown was one of Ohio's most important activists in the Underground Railroad movement. Quinn must have been gratified to ordain his longtime acolyte, but he also continued to lift up younger preachers.[32]

Bishop Quinn lived to see the fulfillment of another of his long-cherished aspirations with the ratification of the Fourteenth Amendment. Passed in June 1866 and ratified in July 1868, the Fourteenth Amendment established citizenship for all persons "born or naturalized in the United States," which included African Americans. For the first time, the nation's newly freed population of Black Americans could expect "equal protection under the laws." The amendment fostered new ideas that some rights went beyond national identity and authorized the government to punish states that infringed on

Figure 10.2 Bishops at the 1868 General Conference, Washington, DC. Every bishop shown had been ordained by William Paul Quinn. From left to right, there is Willis Nazrey, James A. Shorter, J. M. Brown, Jabez Campbell, William Paul Quinn, Alexander Wayman, Daniel Payne, and T. M. D. Ward. At eighty years old, Quinn sits in the center, holding the "sombrero" he was known for wearing late in his life. "Thirteenth General Conference of the AME Church," (the conferences were renumbered), courtesy of Payne Theological Seminary. https://archive.org/details/thirteenthgenera00unse/mode/2up.

citizens' right to vote. The Fourteenth Amendment extended the provisions of the Bill of Rights to the states; no state could deprive any person of life, liberty, or property.[33]

Growing freedom, new rights, and the promise of government protection energized the expansion that constantly preoccupied the church. Around January 6, 1869, a group in Wisconsin requested that Quinn send a minister to help organize a church in Milwaukee. At the outset the church had its humble beginnings in one room at the corner of Plankinton and Wisconsin Avenues. It is the oldest church body to be established by Blacks in the state of Wisconsin: St. Mark AME (Church of the Anvil). Quinn had been in Wisconsin decades earlier in his quest for suitable settlements for people of color.[34]

At the August 12, 1869, Annual Conference in Leavenworth, Kansas, Bishop Quinn retained stamina enough to travel the long distance to preside. Two weeks later, he was in Springfield, Illinois, presiding over the Indiana Conference. From the beginning of Quinn's life as a circuit rider, his itinerancy had been filled with the trials and hazards associated with open-air travel across the rugged terrain of the United States and Canada. Under the assurance of relative safety and freedom, Bishop Quinn and his new wife took a return train to Leavenworth a year later, in August 1870, for the Annual Conference.

At the end of their stay, the couple could ride in comfort, so they left for St. Joseph, Missouri. Unfortunately, quite a scuffle erupted on the train; the brakeman objected to the attempts to board the ladies' car of the train made by the party of African Americans scheduled to join the Quinns. The arriving minister and his wife were ordered to the smoking car, from all accounts, a smelly, vile section of the train. The newly arrived passenger persisted in his efforts to enter the ladies' car, and a scuffle followed, with the minister getting the best of the brakeman. The minister managed to open the door and hold it open until his wife was able to board. Although the Civil War had ended, the deeply ingrained effects of racism remained imprinted on much of the country. The issue was resolved without fully coming to blows, but "not without resentment and seething anger," according to the newspaper account of the incident.[35]

Although Quinn's steps began to falter between 1869 and 1871, the senior bishop was in the chair for the sixteenth session of the Missouri Annual Conference at Ebenezer Chapel in St. Joseph, Missouri. Later that month, Quinn returned to preside over the thirty-first session of the Indiana Annual Conference, held in the Vernon Street church. His wife most likely accompanied him.

The year 1870 began with two political milestones. Quinn had lived to see the ratification of the Fifteenth Amendment (February 1869 to February 1870), which dictates that a (male) citizen's right to vote "shall not be denied or abridged on account of race color or previous condition of servitude." He must have been overjoyed, although the amendment does not guarantee access to the vote. In places such as Louisville, where Quinn had long labored, Whites threatened violence and harm to Blacks if they voted. The amendment notwithstanding, the rocky path to the ballot box remained unsafe and thwarted.[36]

One can imagine that the election of Hiram Rhodes Revels, the first African American lawmaker to serve in the United States Congress beginning in 1870, occurred as a personal triumph for Quinn and a political victory for the AME Church. Hiram Revels and his brother Willis Revels were both AME ministers who followed in Quinn's footsteps, pastoring churches the bishop had established in Indianapolis, Richmond, and Terre Haute. Hiram moved to central Indiana and settled in Richmond, near Quinn, in 1844, the same year Quinn had been ordained bishop. Quinn, quick to recognize potential, ordained Hiram Revels into the ministry at the 1845 Indiana conference, held at Allen Chapel in Terre Haute, where Revels along with his brother Willis eventually settled in the 1850s.[37]

Repeatedly—and by now, predictably—Quinn's spiritual disciples shared Allen's determination and Quinn's battle against slavery. According to the *Tribune Star*, Hiram Revels "was a pastor in the Allen Chapel of the local

African Methodist Episcopal Church while being active with the local Underground Railroad helping runaway slaves make their way to freedom in Canada." Terre Haute's Allen chapel celebrated its activism of providing food and shelter to escapees from North Carolina, the Revels brothers' original home before they'd moved to Indiana. By Hiram Revels's own terse admission, he "sedulously refrained from doing anything that would incite slaves to run away from their masters. It being understood that my object was to preach the gospel to them, and improve their moral and spiritual condition; even slave holders were tolerant toward me. But when in free states I always assisted the fugitive to make his escape."[38]

Hiram Revels had been ordained an elder at the Indiana Conference in 1849, the year Quinn became senior bishop, and he served as secretary to Quinn, who was the presiding officer of the 1853 Ohio Annual Conference. Revels's older brother, Dr. Willis Revels, MD, had pastored Indianapolis's Bethel church during Quinn's nascent years as bishop and ministered to AME churches in Indianapolis, Richmond, and Louisville, Kentucky. Willis Revels came to Bethel AME in Indianapolis in 1845 and remained there throughout the Civil War.[39]

Hiram Revels was the pastor of St. Paul's in St. Louis from 1854 to 1855, when a dispute erupted between him and church officers. Men with strong ideals and bedrock convictions often clashed. Hiram Revels withdrew from the denomination after the dispute, which has led to conflicting and confusing assessments of his denominational affiliations. His later war efforts included the recruitment of two Black regiments from Maryland and Missouri, and he fought at the Battle of Vicksburg in Vicksburg, Mississippi. By the end of the war, Revels had reunited with the AME Church. Quinn's billowing influence extended from Canada to New Orleans, across the Black Atlantic, from the AME Church to Civil War regiments to the halls of Congress. After the war Hiram Revels filled the Mississippi Senate seat formerly held by Jefferson Davis, president of the Confederacy.[40]

The AME Church continued to offer gestures of appreciation for Quinn's praiseworthy life. The bishop was honored by the merit and esteem shown him at the 1871 Illinois Annual Conference, held in Chicago. The ministers made a gift of a "splendid suit of clothing" to the venerable preacher. Bishop Campbell presented him with a valuable gold medal, a gift from the Philadelphia conference. A Latin inscription commemorating Quinn's life of preaching the gospel adorned one side. An evocative engraving of a preacher on horseback carrying a light adorned the reverse. The medal perfectly captured Quinn's life, and he appeared deeply affected by this mark of respect and appreciation. Following the presentation, Bishop Campbell gave the conference a brief history of Quinn's fifty years of dedication to the church. At the conclusion of the tribute, Quinn offered a few well-timed remarks, concluding with "God bless the Philadelphia Conference and the brethren in the East."[41]

The health of the legendary bishop began failing as he aged, forcing him to reduce his activities. He continued, nonetheless, to bring new light to the AME Church.[42] To the end of his life, Quinn "clung to the habits of his early days, riding horseback to Conferences and meetings, preaching and ministering to churches, large and small, with that personal oversight that brought him great reputation and fame."[43] One newspaper declared that "his name had become a household word throughout the land among the people of his race."[44] Displaying an indomitable spirit, he found the strength to lead and preside over the religious exercises at the Nashville General Conference. The fifteenth General Conference opened at St. Paul's Chapel on Cherry Street in May 1872. The largest conference held to date was called to order by Senior Bishop Quinn, although his age compromised his strength. He was so infirmed that he could not effectively preside over the proceedings. The Committee on the episcopacy resolved that "Bishop Quinn, [their] senior Bishop be allowed to take the general oversight of all the work, to go where he feels disposed, and that his traveling expenses be paid, and that each Episcopal District be taxed an amount sufficient to give him reasonable support."[45]

In August Quinn continued his political involvement with the upcoming 1872 presidential elections, held in Indiana in November. The Hon. Henry C. Wilson of Massachusetts, U. S. Grant's running mate, visited Richmond to an "almost unprecedented outpouring of the Republican masses" from Wayne and the surrounding counties. City streets were overrun by ten in the morning, although the event wasn't scheduled to begin until the afternoon at the county fairgrounds. Quinn had been selected as one of the vice presidents of the meeting who would formally organize the events. After the campaign speeches, amid "boundless enthusiasm," a torchlit parade closed out the festivities. Quinn's final political efforts contributed to a decisive victory for Grant and Wilson.[46]

Undaunted, Quinn managed to attend several other conferences during the remainder of 1872, after his retirement but before the final onset of stomach cancer that had afflicted him in later years. Rev. Jordan Early observed the decline of God's servant: "This was the last General Conference attended by the venerable senior Bishop, Rt. Rev. William Paul Quinn, who after a life of the most arduous toil and wonderful endurance expressed himself as ready to lay down his armor and receive the crown." The old "soldier of the cross" was ready to go home. Jordan Early recalled Quinn's commitment during the "days of the poverty and weakness of the infant church," which had advanced by now "beyond his utmost expectation."[47]

The AME Church was an institution that promised the religious freedom so many desired and which Quinn helped fulfill. The esteemed bishop expressed his satisfaction with the advancement made by the church in gaining favor with the world and was astonished at its rapid growth. Starting with comparatively a handful at the beginning of Quinn's labors, the church grew in the course of his lifetime to number in the hundreds of thousands. He recalled the days when he had forded rivers, climbed mountains, crossed forests, encountered wild beasts, and faced and fought vindictive mobs, assaults and robbers, as well as when he was called before courts of justice to establish the church he so loved.

Despite "hunger and thirst and peril," he had traveled thousands of miles "to plant the Church in the West." His labors on earth were coming to an end. Early continues, saying that Quinn reminded his worthy colleagues, "who had labored and suffered with him, and whose heads were whitening with age, to be of good cheer and finish the fight of faith with unshaken confidence in God and soon they would meet and lay their trophies at the Savior's feet."[48]

He was strong enough to introduce Bishop Wayman at the Indiana conference when it met in Alexander Chapel in Evansville in August that year before he moved on in September to the Illinois conference in Bloomington (Illinois). There he again introduced Bishop Wayman to the conference and preached the Sunday sermon.[49] Still, the AME Committee on Church Union concluded, "The physical condition of Bishop Quinn was such that he could no longer do effective work." Accordingly, the commission on the episcopacy recommended that he be retired; he was relieved of active work.[50]

Bishop Wayman provided insight into the last few appearances of Bishop Quinn, who preached in Bloomington on Sunday morning, September 8. Wayman remembered that when he asked Quinn to preach, the bishop "said he had been to the General and several Conferences, and he had not been asked to sing or pray." Wayman prevailed on him, and he consented. Wayman "saw that his strength had begun to fail him." Where he had once moved with majesty and strength, "his frame is weak, his steps are slow." What hair remained was peppered with grey.[51]

Nonetheless, Quinn pressed on to assist Bishop Wayman at the eighteenth session of the Missouri Annual Conference, held in Hannibal from late September to early October. It would be his last. He must have been deeply gratified as Wayman ordained Moses Dickson an elder at this conference. Quinn had baptized Dickson thirty years earlier, in Chillicothe, during his early circuit-riding days in Ohio. Dickson, one of the Underground Railroad's most mysterious and highly effective operatives, had been under Quinn's influence from baptism to ordination.[52]

In his remarks, the retired bishop spoke of his struggles in Missouri and across his long efforts on behalf of the AME Church. He then began to weep as he extended his hand to the members of the conference: "The Lord bless you all."[53] After he narrated "in his inimitable way" a few incidents from his early experiences as a pioneer preacher in the valley, he closed by urging his brothers and sisters, "Go on! Go on!"[54] Wayman lamented that "it was inferred from his appearance, that he came to visit his brethren for the last time."[55] Quinn's condition worsened in December. Fatal cancer of the stomach that troubled him in later years would bring an end to his days.[56]

In 1872 in honor of Bishop Quinn, "Apostle of Liberation," the AME Church in Texas founded Paul Quinn College, intended to educate a generation of new freedmen and women. The school began as a high school in Austin, Texas, under the initiative of a small group of AME preachers at Metropolitan AME Church in the city. The forerunner to Paul Quinn College began enlightening minds on April 4, 1872, before moving to Waco, Texas, in 1877 (see fig. 10.3).

PAUL QUINN COLLEGE, WACO, TEXAS.

Figure 10.3 Paul Quinn College, Waco, Texas, ca. 1898. The Paul Quinn College was founded on April 4, 1872, by a group of African Methodist Episcopal Church preachers in Austin, Texas. The school's original purpose was focused on the education of those newly freed from slavery and their children. The college moved to southeast Dallas in 1990. *The Educator*, John R. Hawkins, Kittrell, NC: Educational Department of the A.M.E. Church, 1898, p. 11, courtesy of Monroe C. Gutman Library, Harvard Graduate School of Education, Harvard University, https://iiif.lib.harvard.edu/manifests/view/drs:444725848$.

Figure 10.4 Paul Quinn Art Class. Coed art class at Paul Quinn College, ca. 1914. Courtesy of Baylor University.

Bishop Quinn had envisioned an expanded campus and broader curriculum for its students that included liberal arts and trades. Grammar and languages, literature, math, and science formed the core curriculum. Carpentry, agriculture, art, printing, sewing, and dressmaking fulfilled Quinn's vision for a broad education.[57] Classic scientific, theological, and music courses rounded out the field of study (see fig. 10.4).[58]

Ten years of fund-raising preceded the first building, which was constructed on twenty acres of land after the school was moved to a more central location in Waco. The college was chartered by the state of Texas in 1881, when it was officially named for William Paul Quinn. The college produced several of the teachers who would work in the Texas public schools—some as principals in city schools, others as high school faculty members.

Paul Quinn College endures today as a historically Black college that pays fitting tribute to the minister who had done so much to promote education across the country and throughout the denomination. In 1990 the school moved to southeast Dallas.[59] It serves as the oldest liberal arts institution of higher learning for African Americans west of the Mississippi River.

The church Quinn had first encountered as a young man leaning against a tree in Pennsylvania was on solid footing, resting on the divine guidance of Daniel A. Payne and the six other bishops Quinn had ordained. Henry McNeal Turner, the young rising star, was fully prepared to operate and meet the demands of America during Reconstruction. He would be the bridge to the modern church.

In Quinn's years of service to AME, his contributions helped spark the growth of the membership from 3,000 to 250,000 and the ministry, from seven itinerant preachers to 1,260 pastors. Quinn, as "the great expansionist" and the apostle of liberation, has been described as the "St. Paul of African Methodism, a tough, spirited itinerant preacher."[60]

Later that fall, Bishop Wayman reported that he "found Bishop Quinn very ill" upon his arrival at Richmond, Indiana: "I spent one or two days with him."[61] By December 1872 Quinn told his neighbor and friend that he had settled his affairs and had made "peace with God and man." He told his brethren in faith, "The bridge I have been building these years I am not afraid to cross." He could see "a light brighter than the fire, along my path to heaven!"[62] He selected his own hymn, "A Solemn March We Make, Toward the Silent Grave," and let Bishop Shorter know that he wanted to be buried in a plain manner in keeping with how he had conducted his life: "I want no fuss over me . . . but if people want to sing and shout they can do so."[63]

CHAPTER 11

Receiving His Crown

Stubbornly, Quinn fought stomach cancer "on his feet" for more than a year, explains Arnett. By the first Sunday in December 1872, his expansive world had shrunk to home confinement. A telegram went out to Quinn's brethren announcing the urgency: "Come and see the last of him," and many did hasten to his side. He rallied from the crisis and appeared to be gathering strength. Toward the end, however, he could not speak, but he waved and waved, according to Arnett, "like friends parting." On Friday night, February 21, 1873, as Bishop Wayman tells us, all could see "the dying sweat gathered upon his brow . . . and William Paul Quinn was no more."[1]

At the age of eighty-five, the grand man laid down the banner of the AME Church, which he had carried faithfully for more than a half century. The bishop had left final instructions: "When I am dead let me be buried in a quiet manner, without music, and the parading of societies, but they can sing and pray as much as they please." He wanted to be buried as simply as he had lived.[2]

Late in the month, as Bishop Payne was en route to Pittsburgh, he received a telegram announcing Bishop Quinn's death. Two days later, Payne and Bishop Shorter left to make their way to the funeral, only to learn upon arrival that the service had been postponed to allow time for all the bishops to attend. Quinn had ordained them all.

Obituaries and eulogies across the country charted the astonishing breadth of Quinn's spiritual and physical journey in the name of AME. Turner estimated Quinn had traveled over three thousand miles and preached over thirteen thousand sermons. No longer would the bishop's brilliant life in Christ illuminate the way. One of the most productive, long-serving evangelists of the AME Church, the bishop had been a traveling preacher for sixty-six years after entering the ministry at nineteen.[3]

The leaders of the church spoke of the mightiness and power of William Paul Quinn. Long after his death, he was remembered for "the faith and daring of Paul, the intrepidity of Francis Asbury, and the blood and iron of Bismarck." Churchmen lionized the "militant soldier of the cross for his matchless heroism, superb courage," and relentless "attacks on the foes of the people." These qualities bound the bishop to the hearts of the faithful everywhere he'd traveled in the name of the Lord.[4]

Citizens found their way to the home of the late senior bishop to pay final respects. Bishops Campbell and Shorter greeted them. Fittingly, Quinn was laid to rest in the parlor in a beautiful mahogany casket. A wreath of silver flowers rested on top. A large, inscribed plate, also on top of the casket, read, "Right Reverend *William Paul Quinn*, Fourth Bishop of the A.M.E. Church, died February 21, 1873." Quinn's wishes to be "buried in a plain manner" and "with no fuss" were overruled by the desires of the mournful church to show the utmost respect and appreciation for its bishop.[5]

Arnett left a vivid account of the funeral in Richmond, Indiana. The day was very cold but bright. Richmond's Bethel AME was not large enough to receive the throngs. The Pearl Street Methodist Episcopal Church hosted Quinn's funeral on March 4. Mourners braved cold, sharp winds; tramped through snow; and filled even this larger church to capacity to grieve the passing of their fallen bishop. Funeral goers from near and far could be seen wending their way from the depot, satchels in hand.

The funeral procession began at 1:00 p.m. with Bishops Payne and Campbell in the lead carriage. Pallbearers walked alongside the hearse, drawn by two black horses. A carriage with Quinn's widow and family, along with Bishop Shorter, followed. The procession of friends, carriages, and buggies moved slowly toward the Pearl Street church. The sidewalks were filled with people; signs of sorrow were visible along the route. When the mourners neared the church, all sides of the streets were filled with people of all ages and colors—the rich and poor, merchants and farmers, mechanics and preachers—who had come to honor the great man of God. All came to pay tribute to his moral worth. The church was filled to standing. Quakers were there. Businessmen left their businesses farmers, their farms; and merchants, their shops.

Quinn's final hymn request, "A Solemn March We Make Toward the Silent Grave," was honored. The congregation sang the hymn with a haunting solemnity and depth that Arnett had never heard. In their grief it "felt as though they were making long steps toward the silent grave." Bishop Payne read the fifteenth chapter of 1 Corinthians as the scripture lesson. Bishop Campbell's sermon was from 2 Timothy 4:7: "I have fought the good fight, I have finished my course, I have kept the faith."[6]

As congregation members gazed at their bishop for the last time, tears of sorrow could be seen stealing down their cheeks. On and on they came to say goodbye to the man who had been a husband, friend, and shepherd. The most painful farewell was from his widow. She wailed in sorrow. "All hearts felt for our sister in distress of mind and heart."[7] She would live another sixteen years without her cherished partner.

The long and imposing procession accompanying the remains to the cemetery of the Society of Friends grew larger than the first that led to the church.[8] As evidence of his lifelong association with the Quaker sect, Bishop Quinn was buried in the elegant cemetery at Earlham College, a Quaker institution in Richmond. Bishop Shorter committed the body, and Payne delivered the benediction.

The original grave marker erected by his widow fell into decay after several years. Future bishop Levi Coppin later reported the following:

> At our last Presiding Elders' Council, arrangements were made to properly mark his grave. He is buried in one of the public cemeteries, at a prominent place along a main drive; and since Richmond has been sufficiently civilized to make no discrimination as to his resting place, it seems but our bounden duty to place at the grave a stone that will be in keeping with the prevailing monuments there.[9]

That headstone marks his grave. Most sources agree that Quinn was born in 1788. But his gravestone bears the inscription 1800–1873, the same years his widow had inscribed on the original headstone. This 1800 birthdate is incorrect. Mary Jane Simms probably thought she had married a man twelve years younger than he was in actuality. Quinn's wife was forty-one years his junior. Ambiguity marked the seasons of Quinn's life from birth to death.[10]

Extensive press coverage of his passing and funeral informed friends, family, and the nation of the death of the beloved pastor. Newspaper articles leave a lasting impression of the man: "In complexion, he was simply a shade darker than some of the Anglo Saxon race"; "in appearance, Bishop Quinn was commanding, and in character bold, fearless, and energetic"; "he had evidently had the advantage of a collegiate education, and his grammar, elocution and arguments in all his discourses are above the ordinary standard of preachers." Bishop J. M. Brown, one of Quinn's closest associates, remembered him as stern, tender, and fatherly: "no one was more cheerful than he—a real Methodist preacher for jokes." Others knew that "no one could be dull about him," as "he was very pious and loved Christ with all his heart" and had an "uncommon love for the souls of men."[11]

A second funeral and several memorials followed, a testament to the breadth of his influence. A week after the Richmond funeral, ministers at Warren Chapel in Toledo, Ohio, hosted one of the largest, best-documented, and most notable of the funeral rites. By March 9 the universal grief of the AME's members over the loss of their bishop found great expression at the chapel. On that mournful, gusty Sunday morning, a violent snowstorm bore down on Toledo an hour before the services. A fierce north wind greeted Baptists and AME members alike as they came to pay their final respects to the sturdy preacher.

Scores of his scattered flock gathered on that gloomy March day to sing the favorite hymns he'd been so fond of singing. As they raised their voices in praise, the words rang throughout Toledo's Warren Chapel, delivering a soothing balm that softened the painful loss.[12] About to be memorialized was the man who had inherited Allen's philosophy and helped spread the radical idea of a free and independent Black church from the Atlantic to the Pacific, from the Great Lakes to the Gulf, and from the Caribbean to the shores of Africa.

Mourners arrived to find black festoons gracing the small chapel in preparation for the homegoing celebration. A large crepe-wreathed photograph of the pioneer bishop was suspended over the pulpit; portraits of Bishops Campbell, J. M. Brown, Payne, Wayman, and Shorter, all of whom had been ordained by Quinn, hung at intervals on either side of the chapel.

Reflecting Quinn's ecumenical appeal, Baptist ministers were invited to participate on behalf of Third Baptist Church, and they urged the congregation to heed Quinn's example by making their lives as his had been: "a blessing and benefit to all around them."[13] The eloquent Bishop Wayman preached an hour-long funeral sermon, referencing Isaiah 64:6.[14] Opening with John, verse 35, Benjamin Arnett delivered one of the most enduring and notable eulogies of Quinn. Arnett said the following of this humble servant of God: he was "eminent in his day and useful to his generation. . . . He crossed the Allegheny mountains, and all along the Monongahela valley the voice of this pioneer was heard encouraging his people to arise and call upon their God." Perhaps referring to Quinn's potent preaching at camp meetings, Arnett described the "thousands gathered to hear the word of truth that fell from his lips, and the multitudes listened with rapture and delight to his message of salvation." One funeral attendee noted how much they missed "many of those pleasing anecdotes" that Bishop Quinn told as "incidents in his religious experience."[15]

At the Toledo memorial at Warren Chapel were the ministers that Quinn had mentored; Moses Dickson, the man Quinn had baptized years before in Ohio, and Jordan Early, from Quinn's early days as an itinerant preacher in St. Louis, paid honor and tribute to the man. Willis Revels and the poet J. Madison Bell served among the stewards. Bell wrote an extended poem in Quinn's honor. Bishop J. M. Brown was there. He had worked as Quinn's secretary for nearly ten years and had been arrested five times in New Orleans for offering the support of his church to freedom seekers. Quinn's old friend John Jones, his long-standing and famed Underground Railroad ally known for sheltering John Brown and his men in Chicago, came to honor the pioneer bishop.

Toledo's newspaper editor, public servant, and Underground Railroad pillar, Clark Waggoner, offered insight into Quinn's effectiveness: "Bishop Quinn's eminent success was due, not to the fact that he was a noble specimen of human organism, standing over six feet in height, well proportioned, and uniformly vigorous, but to the indwelling principle of the grace of God in his soul, whereby he was qualified for the great heart-work of his valuable life."[16] Waggoner wanted Quinn's dedication to the church to move others to action. "The same blessed power must inspire and direct human actions to all truly noble ends."[17] One funeral goer spoke of tracing Quinn's footsteps from Portland, Maine, to New Orleans, Louisiana; another traced Quinn's beginnings in Carthage, Ohio, in 1836, where he preached from Exodus 3:7: "I have heard the groans of my people."[18] At the end of the year, Bishop Wayman delivered a eulogy in St. Louis, where Quinn, Priscilla Baltimore, and Jordan Early had first brought the denomination west of the Mississippi.

Quinn's was the first death in the bishopric in twenty-five years. For the first time since 1849, when Bishop Morris Brown passed away, the number of bishops was broken by the hand of death. Daniel Payne rose to senior bishop. Every bishop then living as well as most of the elders had received ordination from the hands of Paul Quinn.

After Quinn's passing, his widow approached Payne, asking that a biography be written of her husband. Had it been undertaken when first proposed, clarity rather than confusion would have defined his legacy. Perhaps his widow merely wanted the sweep of Quinn's accomplishments remembered. Her attorney was willing to undertake the task for $500 and the endorsement of the bishops; they refused the offer.[19]

Quinn's home in Richmond is one of the Indiana properties listed in the National Register of Historic Places in recognition of his significant role in organizing Bethel AME in Richmond and his efforts in connection with the Underground Railroad.[20] The National Park Service has also recognized

Quinn and his home for their association with the Underground Railroad. Of the more than 3,500 AME churches in the United States, at least forty-two are named in honor of him.[21] Benjamin Tanner captured Quinn's contributions to the Church: "The sum of his fruits were not a few individuals, nor yet Churches, but he lay whole conferences at the feet of the King."[22]

At the beginning of Quinn's life's work as an itinerant preacher, two Annual Conferences existed—one in Philadelphia; the other, in Baltimore. By the time Quinn was called home, his impressive contribution to the growth of the church included six episcopal districts and twenty-three Annual Conferences. When Quinn entered the ministry, there had been seven itinerant preachers; nearly two thousand were in place to carry on the work of the Lord at the time of his death. AME ministers and preachers had planted churches in virtually every town and village where any number of African Americans had settled. In hindsight, one writer affirms, these churches were "what the pillar of cloud and fire was to Israel—the sign of God's presence."[23]

During the emerging years of the denomination, there were two meeting houses worth less than $4,000. At the time of Quinn's passing, the church, parsonage, and school properties were valued at no less than $10,000,000. And while most of these accomplishments are normally ascribed to Daniel A. Payne, Quinn was the senior bishop whose approval and direction set much of the work in motion, particularly in the West. Under Paul Quinn's leadership, the membership had grown from 1,500. Between 1866 and 1876 alone, AME national membership, including probationers and preachers, climbed from 70,000 to 207,000.[24]

For several years beyond the bishop's passing, colleagues at all of the conferences and many of the pastors of various churches throughout the country held memorial services. The New Jersey conference presented a tribute in memory of the departed worthy of the Right Rev. William Paul Quinn, late senior bishop of the African Methodist Episcopal Church. In the providence of God's tender mercies, he departed this life on the twenty-first day of February 1873 in hope of a blest immortality in heaven. For decades following his death, commemorations continued. In 1920 delegates attending the annual convention of the AME Church of Indiana made a pilgrimage to Earlham Cemetery, where they held a graveside service to honor Indiana's great missionary.[25]

The independent Black church and its ministers are important parts of the American spiritual tradition. The AME Church uplifted the faith, morale, and spiritual aspirations of its members. The church ably addressed their educational needs and navigated their political and social concerns. As one of

Black America's major religious, civic, social, and educational institutions, it provided needed inspiration for the people during the terrorizing times then and the challenging times now.[26]

Quinn's "extensive travels during his long ministry made his name a household word throughout the land and among the people of his race; and his death will cause sorrow in thousands of hearts," proclaimed one newspaper.[27] "Bishop Quinn is not dead and as long as American Methodism lives, he will live," forecast Moses Dickson. "The path, the hope, the trust that he manifested in opening up the Western country, still lives in the church."[28] Bishop Arnett eulogized him as *"one of the greatest men of this age. . . . He was a burning and shining light—a torch—yea, a fire brand in dry stubble; the star to the mariner—a bright and morning star."*[29] Like the light of day visible long after the sun has disappeared from the horizon, Quinn's light lingers still.

Afterword

In July 2016 I joined Pamela Tilley, historiographer of the Connectional Lay Organization of the AME church (2009–2017), for the two hundredth anniversary of the denomination. I was in Philadelphia, receiving spiritual nourishment and witnessing the pageantry at the Fiftieth Quadrennial Session. My mind drifted to Bishop William Paul Quinn, to Allen (of course!), and to the Four Horsemen of the Liberation Church: Bishops Allen, Quinn, Payne, and Turner. I always include Morris Brown too.[1]

Had they foreseen this day would lie ahead, in the future of the church? The swirling liturgical dancers twirling their colorful flags, the formalities, the inspiration and preaching of the bishops, the soaring voices of the choir, and the strength of the membership all strove to give thanks for the blessings and majesty of this accomplishment. They came together to praise God and honor the remarkable survival and growth of the church in the face of incalculable odds. The African Methodist Episcopal Church, formed as one of the first major Black religious denominations in the Western world, developed out of racial rather than theological differences.

Bishop Vashti McKenzie was the host bishop for the 2016 General Conference. In 2000 McKenzie realized the dreams of Jerena Lee and the women who had preceded her. McKenzie became the first woman to be elected as a bishop in the denomination's history. It took 213 years for Bishop Vashti McKenzie, who was serving as chief pastor of the Eighteenth Episcopal District in southeast Africa, to be consecrated the 117th bishop of the church.

At this General Conference hosted by McKenzie, Anne Henning-Byfield was ordained the 135th bishop of the church—the fourth woman elected to the episcopal office. As Bishop Henning-Byfield reflected on what it meant to be elected to the highest office of the AME Church in its bicentennial year, her thoughts also turned to Quinn. When an interviewer listed the two places of distinction she held, Byfield added a third. Yes, she was the sister of Bishop Cornal Garnett Henning Sr., as well as the fourth woman elected to the episcopal office, but she reminded her interviewer that she held a third achievement. "William Paul Quinn, one of our first bishops, was elected while serving in Indiana in 1844. There's been no person elected from Indiana who was serving Indiana since 1844." She was proud of that honor too.[2] The consecration of women as bishops fulfilled the dream of Jerena Lee, who is now recognized for her pioneering role. The church posthumously recognizes Lee's groundbreaking efforts as its first female preacher.

From the denomination's inspirited founding in 1787, when members broke free of domination of the White-led Methodist Episcopal Church by forming the African Methodist Episcopal denomination in 1816, to its two hundredth anniversary, the church consistently has served the spiritual strivings of its followers worldwide. Ministering to their spiritual and emotional needs, intellectual sustenance, and political demands continues to scaffold the AME mission.

In 1986 the church celebrated the bicentennial of the founding of the Free African Society, the precursor to the AME denomination. As the church entered its third century, the theme set by Bishop Vinton R. Anderson, the head of the church's ecumenical relations and development, continues to resonate. Stressing the theme "Retooling for the third century," he noted that the pioneers we honor gave their lives and their strength to the Liberation Church. They not only fought for religious freedom but they brought the blessings and enlightenment of education to their grateful followers.[3]

The Black church is the alpha and the omega; it has been the center, the cement, and the soul of African American community and religious life. There is no stronger continued advocacy for Black people than that of the church. It embraces all of life and is concerned about body, mind, and spirit. The church gives its people the strength and substance to confront the everyday as well as the religious challenges of life. Bishop Anderson said, "The issues of self-determination, self-esteem, self-respect are still major agenda items for the black community. . . . We may be in a different kind of society but the issues haven't really changed. We must develop a resurrection of confidence in black institutional life."[4]

Today the African Methodist Episcopal Church has membership in twenty episcopal districts in thirty-nine countries on five continents. The work of the church is administered by twenty-one active bishops and nine general officers, who manage the departments of the church. Membership stretches from Philadelphia to South Africa and India. The World Council of Churches estimates membership in the AME Church at around 2,510,000, with 3,817 pastors and 7,000 congregations. Evidence of the church's commitment to education endures in the nine colleges and seminaries founded and sustained by the denomination. The nineteenth-century foundation laid by these men and women of God positioned the church for its bold advance into the twenty-first century. Bishop Anderson reminds us that the Black church must dwell in its responsibility to the future.

The Four Horsemen of the Liberation Church

The vision of Bishops Richard Allen (1760–1831), William Paul Quinn (1788–1873), Daniel Alexander Payne (1811–1893), and Henry McNeal Turner (1834–1915) carried the denomination forward into a new century— an era of renewal. Known as the "four horsemen" of the Liberation Church, their commitment to AME ordered their steps. The four horsemen earned this recognition while being among the first twelve bishops: Allen, the first; Quinn, the fourth; Payne, the sixth; and Turner, the twelfth. The four bishops led the way and set the course that AME has followed over the last two hundred plus years. Richard Newman, one of Richard Allen's biographers, describes the inspiration "the impressive phalanx of black Itinerants" evoked as they moved across the country "in seemingly free fashion[,] even as white citizens everywhere" attempted to restrict their migration, rights, education, and opportunity.[5]

Allen is revered as the apostle of freedom; Quinn is honored as the apostle of liberation; Payne, as the apostle of education; and Turner, as the apostle of expansion. Together these men, their wives, and the women who supported the church have symbolized the conquest of the church over adversity and evil and, above all, over the pestilence of slavery. All four men arrived at AME after first joining or being ordained in the Methodist Episcopal Church. These stellar men and unsung women fearlessly and tirelessly advanced the mission of the church. If they faltered, they recommitted themselves.

Responsibility for the formation and organization of the AME Church is attributed to Allen and the progress of the Western work of the church, to Quinn. Payne is recognized as AME's first historian, as well as for the educational and intellectual advancement of the denomination, particularly its ministers, and Turner, for its missionary work and international expansion. These four apostles successfully upheld the gospel at home and spread the Word into new lands and foreign territories.

Richard Allen had traveled an improbable path, from once being enslaved to his unanimous election as AME's founding denominational bishop. Reflecting Allen's earliest concerns, church doctrines explicitly call upon ministers to "Preach expressly on education . . . and use every other means to attain it."[6]

Bro. Quinn was among the young church's original clergy in 1816. Quinn's journey started with him as a youthful immigrant; then, in 1818, as a deacon; and finally, as an elder and a senior bishop in 1844. Allen would have been the sole authorized AME prelate to ordain Quinn as a deacon when he joined the Connection. The episcopal office has sustained an unbroken line of succession in the AME Church for more than two hundred years because of Allen's ordination of Quinn and Morris Brown and Morris Brown's subsequent ordination of Quinn as the denomination's fourth bishop.

Operating during a time when slavery was legal, Quinn strode and rode across the land sometimes defying and always daring racial conventions. These men and women did not veer away from their cause. Building on Allen's guiding principles, Quinn was dedicated not only to the sacred mission of the church but also to its secular obligation—the special purpose of assisting in "relieving the African race from their physical, mental and moral bondage. As the Apostle of Liberation, he was determined to do all in his power to weaken the strong hold of the oppressor."[7] The Lord had sent him to "bind up the broken hearted, to proclaim liberty to the captive, and the opening of the prison to those who were in bonds."[8] Quinn found within the doctrine of the church a marriage between his love of Christ and his commitment to freedom, as well as love of the bondsmen and -women.

Two of AME's schools pay tribute to Paul Quinn and Daniel Payne. Paul Quinn College in Dallas, Texas, honors the memory of its namesake. The school embodies his dedication to the uplifting power of education. And Daniel Payne was almost singlehandedly responsible for the survival of Wilberforce University. The school cherishes the revered memory of Bishop Daniel A. Payne, its first president, and his commitment to an educated ministry. Neither fire nor hardship nor doubters nor resisters deterred his mission. Payne led two major institutions, serving as a bishop in the AME Church and as president of Wilberforce University. Payne's long tenure—serving forty-one years—remains the longest number of years served by a bishop of the AME Church. Payne Theological Seminary at Wilberforce was named in his honor.

Bishop Henry McNeal Turner's religious, political, and international influence positioned him as one of the nation's most influential leaders in post–Civil War, Reconstruction-era America. He accepted a chaplaincy in the Union Army during the Civil War. After the conflict Turner helped organize the Georgia Republican Party in 1868. His advocacy for emigration to Liberia and the international expansion of the church into Africa inspired his title: the apostle of expansion.

The four horsemen set the foundation for this church that has praised the name of God unceasingly for nearly two hundred and ten years. The theology and guidance of Allen, the master spirit, has borne fruit since its inception, leaving a remarkable legacy of endurance. Horace Talbert says this of the ministry, particularly of the four horsemen:

> Each and all have served the cause of Methodism as founder, evangelist, preacher, pioneer, historian, orator and missionary. It is impossible to estimate the value and magnitude of their work. The church never can know what it owes to the labor, zeal, devotion, and saintly character of its bishops. Many of them rest from their labors, but their work for the church so dear to their hearts wreathes their names with flowers immortal. They have heard the glad "Well done" in the glorious splendor of the Church Triumphant, but eternity holds for them the joyous gratitude of myriads of saved souls who will rise up to call them blessed.[9]

We in the twenty-first century hold them and their blessed memory in our hearts and minds as we strive to fulfill their vision.

Churches, Chapels, and Institutions Named for William Paul Quinn across the United States

Churches

AL

1. Quinn Chapel, 100 Williams Ave., Uniontown, AL 36786

AR

2. Quinn Chapel, 4200 Young St., Fort Smith, AR 72904
3. Quinn Chapel, 8520 Colonel Miller Rd., Little Rock, AR 72210
4. Quinn Chapel, 1935 AR-133, Crossett, AR 71635

CA

5. Quinn AME Church, 16130 Lasselle St., Moreno Valley, CA 92551

CO

6. Paul Quinn AME Church, 1218 Twenty-Third Street., Denver, CO 80205

IL

7. Quinn Chapel, 108 N Fifth St., Brooklyn, IL 62059

8. Quinn Chapel, 2401 South Wabash Ave., Chicago, IL 60616
9. Quinn Chapel, 108 N. Fifth St., Lovejoy, IL 62059
10. Quinn Mission, 401 Mary St., Eagle Park Acres, Madison, IL 62060

KS

11. William Paul Quinn Church, Kansas City, KS
12. Quinn Chapel AME, 416 E. Main St., Independence, KS 67301

KY

13. Quinn Chapel, 744 Charles Ave., Lexington, KY 40508
14. Quinn Chapel, 1901 W Muhammad Ali Blvd., Louisville, KY 40203

LA

15. Quinn Chapel, 70198 Martin Luther King Dr., Tangipahoa, LA 70465

MD

16. Quinn Chapel, 106 East Third St., Frederick, MD 21701

MI

17. Greater Quinn AME Church, 13501 Rosa Parks Blvd., Detroit, MI 48238
18. Quinn Chapel, 2101 Lippincott Blvd., Flint, MI 48503
19. Quinn Chapel, 408 Harding St., Cassopolis, MI 49031

MS

20. Quinn Chapel, 419 Dr. Martin L. King Jr Dr., Lexington, MS 39095

MO

21. Quinn Chapel, 529 Lafayette St., Jefferson City, MO 65101
22. Quinn Chapel, 512 W Johnson St., Sedalia, MO 65301
23. Quinn Chapel, 227 Bowen St. (Carondelet Section), St. Louis, MO 63111

NE

24. Quinn Chapel, 1225 South Ninth St., Lincoln, NE 68502

NJ

25. Quinn Chapel, 107 Prospect Ave., Atlantic Highlands, NJ 07716

NC

26. Quinn Chapel, 824 Durham Rd., Roxboro, NC 27573

OH

27. Quinn Chapel, 181 W Main St., Chillicothe, OH 45601
28. Quinn Chapel, 10998 Southland Rd., Cincinnati, OH 45240
29. Quinn Chapel, 3241 E 130th St., Cleveland, OH 44120
30. Quinn Chapel, 514 S Eighth St., Ironton, OH 45638
31. Quinn Chapel, 437 N Park St., Marion, OH 43302
32. Quinn Chapel, 50 N Lincoln St., Wilmington, OH 45177
33. Quinn Memorial Church, 515 North St., Steubenville, OH 43952
34. Quinn Chapel, 10998 Southland Blvd., Forest Park, OH 45240

PA

35. Quinn Chapel, 317 First St., Donora, PA 15033
36. Quinn Chapel, Fourth Ave., West Elizabeth, PA 15088
37. Wayman–Quinn AME Church, 318 McKee Way, Monessen, PA 15062

SC

38. Quinn Chapel, 2400 Queen Chapel Rd, Sumter, SC 29153

TN

39. Quinn Chapel, 4228 Quinn Adams St., Chattanooga, TN 37410
40. Quinn Chapel, 218 Church St., Paris, TN 38242

TX

41. Quinn Chapel, 710 W Elm St., Denison, TX 75020
42. Paul Quinn AME Church, 1108 Walnut St., Bastrop, TX 78602

Educational Institutions

Paul Quinn College, 3837 Simpson Stuart Rd., Dallas, TX 75241 (formerly in Waco, TX)

Fraternal Lodges

Quinn Lodge No. 28, Free and Accepted Mason Prince Hall Grand Lodge Jurisdiction of Indiana, 1750 S Fifth St., Richmond, IN 47374

William Paul Quinn Lodge No. 1539 of the Grand United Order of Odd Fellows in Toledo, Ohio, was closed in 1882.

Statistics

In total, the following forty-five institutions have been named for the bishop across twenty states:

Forty-two churches
One college
Two fraternal lodges
Numerous societies

Acknowledgments

Quinn's life sprawled across two continents, Central America, and at least fifteen states. His influence extended internationally, reaching Canada, Haiti, Jamaica, and Africa. I am grateful for all the assistance and support I received in hunting down the disparate pieces of his expansive story. Quinn's name repeatedly surfaced as I moved across the Midwestern United States. When I came home to Maryland, I found a Quinn chapel there in Frederick.

I met Ambassador Ronald D. Palmer while conducting early research on free Black communities and the Underground Railroad. He had been researching Quinn for years, primarily in Pennsylvania. A mutual acquaintance in Kentucky had given him my name and number. We would spend hours disentangling the conflicting facts of Quinn's life and became research and writing partners until Ambassador Palmer's death in 2014. Before he passed, he urged me to go on.

Several people made substantive contributions to this book. I pray that my expression of gratitude adequately reflects my deep appreciation. Dona Stokes Lucas in Indiana has been my stalwart partner. She acted as my eyes and ears in Indiana and as a sounding board whenever I hit the rocky cliffs and shores of Quinn's confusing life. She once drove halfway across the state to research Quinn's Indiana landholdings when that research became unwieldy. After years of dedication to researching Quinn in Indiana, she, like Ambassador Palmer, gave over her extensive research files to me in the hopes that I would fit Indiana into Quinn's national and international story and carry this biography over the finish line.

Pamela Tilley, former historiographer of the Connectional Lay Organization of the AME church (from 2009–2017), brought me inside the denomination. She introduced me to bishops and ministers, took me to relevant churches and research sites, and invited me to the seminal General Conference of 2016, held in Philadelphia, which celebrated the two hundredth anniversary of the AME church. She has been a champion of this work, and I am grateful for her support.

Likewise, Deanda Johnson of the National Park Service graced me with her amazing research skill, often finding facts, images, or articles that had eluded me. I think of her as a magician, able to produce the most elusive information. For the majority of the time I spent writing this book, she served as the Midwest regional coordinator for the National Park Service Network to Freedom program. She has since moved to a different position. Diane Miller has retired from her role as national program manager for the National Underground Railroad Network to Freedom program. Diane; Sheri Jackson, the Southeast regional coordinator (also now retired); and most recently, Robin Krawitz, the new program manager, were never too busy to help or to answer my requests. Under the National Park Service, the Network to Freedom program solicited and vetted applications for Underground Railroad sites across the country to become a part of the network. African Methodist Episcopal (AME) churches often were among the sites nominated. Frequently, the information in the applications confirmed a church's involvement with the Underground Railroad. Since I knew Quinn to have been the originator of many of the churches, the applications formed a bridge linking Quinn, AME, and the Underground Railroad.

A word about electronic sources. I am grateful to Eric Nils Lindquist, the librarian for history, American studies, classics, and religion at the University of Maryland libraries, for helping me navigate the African American Historical Serials Collection. Ric Murphy and Bob Burns alerted me to FamilySearch's new land-records database. With Bob's help and with assistance from Emily Kathrine Bakly of FamilySearch, I accessed original deeds and the transcripts for all nineteen of Quinn's Indiana land transactions. The land records, which I had been able to access but not fully read, contained important clarifying details. Major websites, including Documenting the American South, HathiTrust, Internet Archives, the Colored Conventions Project, the Library of Congress, and particularly Chronicling America, as well as the various sites that digitize newspapers, books, and scholarly articles, have enabled my access to obscure information that otherwise would have taken me years, if not a lifetime, to uncover.

Visual culture is a vital and constant avenue of research for my work. Cherise Wilson's willingness to share her graphic design and technological expertise has enabled me to augment the written material with graphic expression and illustration. The Bethesda Writers Group has read and reread every word of this book. Their insights, edits, and critiques, their encouragement and support, buoyed me over the rough patches and sharpened the manuscript. Thank you to Kenneth Ackerman, Nancy Derr, Michael Kirkland, Judi Moore Latta, Tara McKelvey, Bonny Miller, Diana Parcel, Michael Scadron, and Sonja Williams.

And finally, my family patiently listened to Quinn stories over the past twenty years, particularly while Ambassador Palmer lived. I am sure they wondered if I would ever bring this story to light. Thank you, one and all. To my sister, Vicki Wilson, I appreciate the multiple ways that you have championed this project over the years. To my daughters, Gina LaRoche, Renee LaRoche Morris, and Danielle LaRoche, as well as to their husbands and to my grandchildren, thank you for your continuing support and love. Thank you, too, to Harold Freeman, who sustained my efforts through his kindness and belief in the project. To all who suggested or found source material, listened, read parts of the manuscript, hosted or attended lectures, helped me decipher legal material, and cheered me on, thank you.

Notes

Preface: Pages xi–xx

1. William Paul Quinn Certificate, Affidavit by M. M. Clarke, February 12, 1851, Pittsburgh, PA, DR 14-312, Wayne Co., IN.

AME historian Dennis Dickerson pinpoints Quinn's birth year as 1784 and location as either Central America or the Caribbean; Quinn's second wife, Mary Simms, had a birth date of 1800 inscribed on his tombstone (FamilySearch says 1788). The Richmond City directory lists 1813 as his date of birth. See Dennis Dickerson, *The African Methodist Episcopal Church: A History* (New York: Cambridge University Press, 2020).

2. George N. Lamb, ed. *The Mahogany Book* (Chicago: Mahogany Association, 1947); Melissa A. Johnson, "The Making of Race and Place in Nineteenth-Century British Honduras," *Environmental History* 8, no. 4 (October 2003): 598–617.

3. Johnson, "The Making of Race and Place," 598–617; Dickerson, *The African Methodist Episcopal Church*, 84.

4. Invisible Black, "Pen And Ink Sketches of The African General Conference. As Viewed from the Gallery of Bethel Church," *The Christian Recorder*, May 7, 1864; Benjamin Arnett, *In Memoriam: Funeral Services for Rev. William Paul Quinn; Late Senior Bishop of the African M.E. Church, Held at, Warren Chapel, Toledo, Ohio, March 9th, 1873* (Toledo: Warren Chapel, 1873), 21.

5. Julius H. Bailey, *Around the Family Altar: Domesticity in the African Methodist Episcopal Church 1865–1900* (Gainesville: University of Florida Press, 2005); H. J. Jackson, "AME Celebrates 200th Year by Honoring Heroes," *St. Louis Post-Dispatch*, May 29, 1988, https://www.newspapers.com/article/the-courier-4-horseman-29may1988-200th-a/137599275/.

6. Brent M. S. Campney, "The Antebellum Old Northwest: 'For the White Man, and the White Man Only.'" In *Hostile Heartland: Racism, Repression, and Resistance in the Midwest*, edited by Brent Campney, 13–34 (Urbana–Champaign: University of Illinois Press, 2019).

7. Daniel A. Payne, *History of the African Methodist Episcopal Church*, ed. C. S. Smith (Nashville: Publishing House of the A. M. E. Sunday School Union, 1891), 374.

As early as 1995, efforts by descendants and historic community activists helped spark the creation of an Underground Railroad Advisory Committee. Out of those efforts, Congress passed the National Underground Railroad Network to Freedom Act of 1998 within the National Park Service (NPS). See "National Underground Railroad Network to Freedom Act of 1998. PUBLIC LAW 105–203—JULY 21, 1998," https://www.congress.gov/105/plaws/publ203/PLAW-105publ203.pdf.

The intra- and interstate nature of the Underground Railroad coupled with the transnational, transracial, multireligious, and sociopolitical acts of resistance also pushed the National Park Service to bring national stewardship to the movement. The legislation named it one of the most significant expressions of the American civil rights movement. The Network to Freedom brought together local stories, sites, and people scattered across the United States (and now internationally) to share knowledge and help bring segments of escapees' journeys into a cohesive whole. By challenging a centuries-old description, NPS broadened the definition of the Underground Railroad to simply "the resistance to enslavement through escape and flight, through the end of the Civil War." It refers to the "efforts of enslaved African Americans to gain their freedom by escaping bondage." "What is the Underground Railroad?" Underground Railroad, National Park Service, https://www.nps.gov/subjects/undergroundrailroad/what-is-the-underground-railroad.htm.

8. Elaine Welch, *William Paul Quinn, A Militant Churchman: A Biographical Sketch* (Chicago: n.p., 1933), 14. This is decades before the term came into popular use.

9. Welch, *William Paul Quinn, A Militant Churchman*, 6. Welch claims he moved to Indiana in 1838, but more recent scholarship cites the date as 1836. Her biographical sketch was drawn from interviews and oral accounts of people from Chicago's Quinn chapel as well as from friends who had known Quinn. Many of the dates associated with specific incidents are inaccurate; Payne, *History of the African Methodist*, 374.

10. Richard R. Wright, *Centennial Encyclopaedia of the African Methodist Episcopal Church. Containing Principally the Biographies of the Men and Women, Both Ministers and Laymen, Whose Labors during a Hundred Years, Helped Make the A.M.E. Church What It Is; Also Short Historical Sketches of Annual Conferences, Educational Institutions, General Departments, Missionary Societies of the A.M.E. Church, and General Information about African Methodism and the Christian Church in General; Being a Literary Contribution to the Celebration of the One Hundredth Anniversary of the Formation of the African Methodist Episcopal Church Denomination by Richard Allen and Others,*

at Philadelphia, Penna., in 1816 (Philadelphia: Book Concern of the A.M.E. Church, 1916) https://docsouth.unc.edu/church/wright/wright.html.

11. The National Park Service has documented escapes to thirty-nine states and the United States Virgin Islands.

12. Henry Highland Garnet, "Rev. William Paul Quinn, Third Bishop, Pioneers of the A.M.E. Church. No III," *The Christian Recorder*, March 13, 1869.

13. Welch, *William Paul Quinn*.

14. Payne, *History of the African Methodist*, vii.

15. Handwriting being what it was in those days, his name was sometimes written as "Guin."

16. Garnet, "Rev. William Paul Quinn."

17. "Daniel A. Payne, to Dr. Garnett. Rev. H.H. Garnet, D.D," *The Christian Recorder*, April 10, 1873.

18. L. L. Berry, *Century of Missions of the African Methodist Episcopal Church, 1840–1940* (New York: Gutenberg Printing, 1942), 54.

19. George A. Singleton, *The Romance of African Methodism: A Study of the African Methodist Episcopal Church* (New York: Exposition Press, 1952), 35.

20. "Payne, Daniel A., to Dr. Garnett. Rev. H. H. Garnet, D. D.," *The Christian Recorder*, April 10, 1873.

21. "Quinn Memorial Services," *The Christian Recorder*, May 18, 1876.

22. Benjamin T. Tanner, *An Apology for African Methodism* (Baltimore, 1867), 146.

23. Singleton, *Romance*, 25.

24. Benjamin Arnett, *In Memoriam: Funeral Services for Rev. William Paul Quinn; Late Senior Bishop of the African M.E. Church, Held at Warren Chapel, Toledo, Ohio, March 9th, 1873* (Toledo: Warren Chapel, 1973), https://babel.hathitrust.org/cgi/pt?id=wu.89097214688&view=1up&seq=24&q1=Kansas.

25. Arnett, *In Memoriam*.

26. See the appendix for the complete listing.

27. "Bishop William Paul Quinn," *The Christian Recorder*, April 7, 1866.

28. Jackson, "AME Celebrates 200th Year."

Chapter 1: Pages 1–15

1. Elizabeth Holand Walker was born in 1761 and died in 1827; see Memorial of Elizabeth H. Walker, *Memorials Concerning Deceased Friends, Published by Direction of the Yearly Meeting of New York* (New York: James Egbert, 1859), 116.

2. Daniel A. Payne, *Recollections of Seventy Years* (Nashville: A.M.E. Sunday School Union, 1888; New York: Arno Press, 1969), 101–2.

3. Memorial of Walker, *Memorials Concerning Deceased Friends*, 116; Payne, *Recollections of Seventy Years*, 101–2; United States Federal Census of 1810, Westtown, Chester, Pennsylvania. A Samuel Collins is listed in the 1810 census, along with eight free people of color living with him. We cannot be certain of Quinn's exact age.

4. "Richmond City Directory 1865," FamilySearch, accessed March 14, 2024, 164–65, https://www.familysearch.org/ark:/61903/3:1:3Q9M-CSZK-72NV?cc =3754697&personaUrl=%2Fark%3A%2F61903%2F1%3A1%3A6ZBY-YL54.

5. Brycchan Carey and Geoffrey Gilbert Plank, eds, *The Essential Elias Hicks: Quakers and Abolition* (Nerberg, OR: Inner Light Books, 2013), 83.

6. Carey and Plank, eds. *The Essential Elias Hicks*, 83; Elias Hicks, *Journal of the Life and Religious Labours of Elias Hicks* (New York: Published by Elias Hopper, 1832).

7. Milt Diggins, *Stealing Freedom along the Mason Dixon Line* (Baltimore: The Maryland Center for History and Culture, 2016); Bishop John M. Brown, "William Paul Quinn," in *Lives of Methodist Bishops*, eds. Theodore L. Flood and John W. Hamilton (New York: Phillips & Hunt, 1882), 659–66, https://archive.org/details / livesofmethodist0000floo/page/n7/mode/2up?q=%22Lives+of+Methodist+Bishops%22.

8. Wright, *Centennial Encyclopaedia of the African Methodist Episcopal Church*, 280–81.

9. Jualynne E. Dodson, *Engendering Church: Women, Power, and the AME Church* (Lanham, MD: Rowman & Littlefield Publishers, 2002).

10. Abel Stevens, *History of the Methodist Episcopal Church in the United States of America*, vol. 4, bk. 5 (Ann Arbor: University of Michigan Library, 1866), 174, https://archive.org/details/historyofmethodi04instev/mode/2up.

11. Gordon Melton, comp., "African American Methodists in the Antebellum and Reconstruction Periods: A Timetable, 1760–1876," African American Methodists, Historic St. George's United Methodist Church, published 2013, https://www.historicstgeorges.org/s/AFRICAN-AMERICAN-METHODISTS.doc; Stevens, *History of the Methodist Episcopal Church*, 174.

12. Richard Allen, *The Life Experience and Gospel Labors of the Rt. Rev. Richard Allen. To Which Is Annexed the Rise and Progress of the African Methodist Episcopal Church in the United States of America. Containing a Narrative of the Yellow Fever in the Year of Our Lord 1793: With an Address to the People of Colour in the United States* (Philadelphia: Martin & Boden, 1793; New York: Abingdon Press, 1960), 21.

13. Allen, *The Life Experience and Gospel Labors*, 21.

14. William Douglass, *Annals of the First African Church, in the United States of America, Now Styled the African Episcopal Church of St. Thomas, Philadelphia, in Its Connection with the Early Struggles of the Colored People to Improve Their Conditions, with the Co-operation Of Friends, and Other Philanthropists; Partly Derived from the Minutes of a Beneficial Society, Established by Absalom Jones, Richard Allen and Others in 1787, and Partly from the Minutes of the Aforesaid Church* (Philadelphia: King & Baird, 1862); Howard D. Gregg, *History of the African Methodist Episcopal Church (The Black Church in Action)* (Nashville: The African Methodist Episcopal Church, 1980), quoted in J. T. Jenifer, *Centennial Retrospect History of the African Methodist Episcopal Church* (Philadelphia: Sunday School Union Press, 1916), 10.

15. Douglass, *Annals of the First African Church*; Gregg, *History of the African Methodist Episcopal Church*.

16. Gregg, *History of the African Methodist Episcopal Church*.

17. Douglass, *Annals of the First African Church*, 15–17; George F. Bragg, *The First Negro Organization: The Free African Society, Established on April 12th, 1787* (Baltimore: G. F. Bragg, 1924), 7; Benjamin T. Tanner, *An Outline of Our History and Government for African Methodist Churchmen, Ministerial and Lay: In Catechetical Form: Two Parts with Appendix* (Philadelphia: Grant, Faires & Rodgers, 1884), 140.

18. Allen, *The Life Experience and Gospel Labors*, 18.

19. Douglass, *Annals of the First African Church*, 10–11; Richard Allen and Jacob Tapsico, *The Doctrines and Discipline of The African Methodist Episcopal Church*, 1st ed. (Philadelphia: The African Methodist Connection in the United States, 1817), 10–11; Allen, *The Life Experience and Gospel Labors*, 22, 29.

20. William Smith, *The Works of William Smith, D.D. Late Provost of The College and Academy of Philadelphia, Vol. II* (Philadelphia: Hugh Maxwell and William Fry, 1803), 271.

21. Gary B. Nash, "Reverberations of Haiti in the American North: Black Saint Dominguans in Philadelphia," *Pennsylvania History: A Journal of Mid-Atlantic Studies* 65 (1998): 44–73, https://www.jstor.org/stable/27774161.

22. Smith, *The Works of William Smith*, 271; Nash, "Reverberations of Haiti," 44.

23. "People & Ideas: Richard Allen," WETA, PBS, published October 11, 2010, https://www.pbs.org/wgbh/pages/frontline/godinamerica/people/richard-allen.html.

24. George F. Bragg, *Richard Allen and Absalom Jones* (Baltimore: Church Advocate Press, 1915).

25. Brown, "William Paul Quinn, 659."

26. Payne, *Recollections of Seventy Years*, 300.

27. Payne, *Recollections of Seventy Years*, 300.

28. Manisha Sinha, *The Slave's Cause: A History of Abolition* (New Haven: Yale University Press, 2016).

29. Mary F. Corey, "Daniel Coker," in *African American Lives*, eds. Henry Louis Gates Jr. and Evelyn Brooks Higginbotham (New York: Oxford University Press, 2004), 177–78; Christopher Phillips, *Freedom's Port: The African American Community of Baltimore, 17901860* (Urbana: The University of Illinois Press, 1997).

30. Payne, *Recollections of Seventy Years*, 101.

The names from Baltimore are Rev. Daniel Coker, Rev. Richard Williams, Rev. Henry Harden, Mr. Edward Williamson, Mr. Stephen Hill, and Mr. Nicholas Gilliard; from Philadelphia, Rev. Richard Allen, Rev. Clayton Durham, Rev. Jacob Tapsico, Rev. James Champion, and Mr. Thomas Webster; from Wilmington, Delaware, Rev. Peter Spencer; from Attleborough, Pennsylvania, Rev. Jacob Marsh, Rev. William Anderson, and Rev. Edward Jackson; and from Salem, New Jersey, Reuben Cuff.

31. Jualynne E. Dodson, "Jarena Lee," in *African American Lives*, eds. Henry Louis Gates Jr. and Evelyn Brooks Higginbotham (New York: Oxford University Press, 2004), 522–24.

32. Payne, *Recollections of Seventy Years*, 107.

33. J. W. Hood, *Sketch of the Early History of the African Methodist Episcopal Zion Church with Jubilee Souvenir and Appendix* (Charlotte, NC: A.M.E. Zion Publishing House 1914), http://docsouth.unc.edu/church/hood/hood.html.

34. Bensalem African Methodist Episcopal Church, 1200 Bridgewater Road (Bensalem), Bridgewater, Bucks County, PA, photograph, Library of Congress, accessed January 24, 2024, https://www.loc.gov/resource/hhh.pa1729.photos/?sp=1&st=image.

35. Payne, *Recollections of Seventy Years*, 102.

36. Maurice Newell, "This Is Bethel—Reading. Come Ride the Underground Railroad, Where Culture and History Come to Life." Central Pennsylvania African American Museum, Museum Exhibit, Reading, PA; Mary Blakinger, "'It's Going to Get Done' Perseverance, Faith and Dollars Help Minister Restore Black Church," *Preservation News* (Cornell University), February 1, 1987. The physical church was not built until 1832.

37. Richard Allen, ed., *A Collection of Spiritual Songs and Hymns* (Philadelphia: John Ormrod, 1801), https://hymnary.org/hymnal/CSSH1801; Payne, *Recollections of Seventy Years*, 102; Bensalem African Methodist Episcopal Church, Historic American Building Survey, Department of the Interior, 1982, accessed August 6, 2023. https://tile.loc.gov/storage-services/master/pnp/habshaer/pa/pa1700/pa1729/data/pa1729data.pdf.

38. Earl E. Kerstetter, "The Glorious Camp Meetings of the Nineteenth Century," Lycoming College, accessed March 11, 2024, https://umarch.lycoming.edu/chronicles/1993/4.%20KERSTET.pdf.

39. Lewis V. Baldwin, *The Mark of a Man: Peter Spencer and the African Union Methodist Tradition: The Man, the Movement, the Message, and the Legacy* (Lanham, MD: University Press of America, 1987), 11.

40. Larry Gara, *Liberty Line: The Legend of the Underground Railroad* (Lexington: University Press of Kentucky, 1961), 45; Benjamin Drew, *The Refugee: Narratives of Fugitive Slaves in Canada* (Boston: John P. Jewett, 1856), 299–301.

41. *American and Commercial Daily Advertiser*, August 25, 1842.

42. *Daily National Intelligencer*, August 8, 1831; *Cambridge Chronicle*, August 16, 1824; *Cambridge Chronicle*, August 27, 1825; *Washington DC National Intelligencer*, November 13, 1809; *Newbern Gazette*, August 15, 1800.

43. "History of the Negro in Hoosier State," *Indianapolis Recorder*, April 15, 1916.

44. Benjamin Arnett, *Proceedings of the African Methodist Episcopal Church of Cincinnati, Held in Allen Temple, February 8th, 9th, and 10th, 1874, with an Account of the Rise and Progress of the Colored Schools; Also a List of the Charitable and Benevolent Societies of the City* (Cincinnati: H. Watkin, 1874); Fergus Bordewich, *Bound for Canaan: The Underground Railroad and the War for the Soul of America* (Amistad/HarperCollins, 2005), 87.

45. Dickerson, *The African Methodist Episcopal Church*; Baldwin, *The Mark of a Man*, 11.

46. Horace Talbert, *The Sons of Allen: Together with a Sketch of the Rise and Progress of Wilberforce University, Wilberforce, Ohio* (Xenia, OH: Aldine Press, 1906), 38, https://docsouth.unc.edu/church/talbert/talbert.html.

47. Graham Russell Hodges, ed., *Black Itinerants of the Gospel: The Narratives of John Jea and George White* (Madison: Madison House Publishers, 1993), 6.

48. "Salem Chapel BME Church Harriet Tubman Underground Railroad National Historic Sites," Salem Church, National Park Service, published September 27, 2023, https://www.salemchapelbmechurch.ca/index.html.

49. Allen and Tapsico, *The Doctrines and Discipline*.

50. Sylvia Frey and Thomas E. Carney, "African Methodist Episcopal Church," Oxford African American Studies Center, published December 1, 2006, https://doi-org.proxy-um.researchport.umd.edu/10.1093/acref/9780195301731.013.44522.

51. Singleton, *The Romance of African Methodism*, 4.

52. Douglas R. Egerton, *He Shall Go Out Free: The Lives of Denmark Vesey*, rev. ed. (Lanham, MD: Rowman & Littlefield, 2004), 110.

53. James H. Cone, *A Black Theology of Liberation: 50th Anniversary Edition* (Maryknoll, NY: ORBIS, 2020), 36.

54. Brown, "William Paul Quinn," 661.

55. Standard English Version, Isaiah 61:1.

Chapter 2: Pages 17–31

1. David Smith and Daniel Payne, *A Biography of Rev. David Smith of the A.M.E. Church; Being a Complete History, Embracing over Sixty Years' Labor in the Advancement of the Redeemer's Kingdom on Earth. Including "The History of the Origin and Development of Wilberforce University"* (Xenia, OH, 1881), 65.

2. Benjamin Arnett, ed., *The Budget: Containing the Annual Reports of the General Officers of the African M.E. Church of the United States of America* (Xenia, OH: Torchlight Publishing, 1881), vi.

3. Benjamin T. Tanner, *An Apology for African Methodism* (Baltimore, 1867), 145; B. W. Arnett, *Proceedings of the African Methodist Episcopal Church*; "African American Perspectives: Pamphlets from the Daniel A. Murray Collection, 1818–1907," Library of Congress, accessed December 4, 2022, https://www.loc.gov/resource/lcrbmrp.t0d02/?sp=24&st=image&r=0.162,0.922,0.755,0.371,0; Welch, *William Paul Quinn*.

The seven original itinerants were Daniel Coker, Richard Williams, Charles Pierce, Richard Allen, William Paul Quinn, Jacob Tapsico, and Clayton Durham.

4. Cooper H. Wingert, *Slavery & the Underground Railroad in South Central Pennsylvania* (Charleston, SC: The History Press, 2016), 113; Payne, *Recollections of Seventy Years*, 61; "History of Quinn Chapel African Methodist Episcopal Church, Frederick Maryland, 1800–Present," Quinn Chapel AME, accessed August 16, 2022, https://www.quinnamefrederick.org/history/.

5. Howard Wallace, *Historical Sketch of the Underground Railroad from Uniontown to Pittsburgh* (n.p., 1903).

6. Payne, *History of the African Methodist*, 262.

7. Payne, *History of the African Methodist*; J. Gordon Melton, *A Will to Choose: The Origins of African American Methodism* (Lanham, MD: Rowman & Littlefield, 2007).

8. Payne, *History of the African Methodist*.

9. Daniel A. Payne, *Semi-centenary and the Retrospection of the African Methodist Episcopal Church in America* (Baltimore: Sherwood, 1866), 23, https://babel.hathitrust.org/cgi/pt?id=emu.010002588604&seq=1.

10. Robert L. Paquette and Manisha Sinha, "Revisiting Denmark Vesey's Church," in *Fugitive Movements: Commemorating the Denmark Vesey Affair and Black Radical Antislavery in the Atlantic World*, ed. James O'Neil Spady, 179–96, 182 (Columbia: University of South Carolina Press, 2022), https://doi.org/10.2307/j.ctv1n35799.15

11. Paquette and Sinha. "Revisiting Denmark Vesey's Church; Stanley Harrold and Randall M. Miller, eds., "Forward," in *The Denmark Vesey Affair: A Documentary History*, eds. Douglas R. Egerton and Robert L. Paquette (Gainesville: University Press of Florida, 2017); Jeremy Schipper, "On Such Texts Comment Is Unnecessary," *Journal of the American Academy of Religion* 85, no. 4 (December 2017): 1032–49, https://www.jstor.org/stable/10.2307/48556266.

12. Douglas R. Egerton, *He Shall Go Out Free: The Lives of Denmark Vesey* (Madison, WI: Madison House Publishers, 1999; rev. ed., Lanham, MD: Rowman & Littlefield, 2004), 146. The church is now known as Emanuel African Methodist Episcopal Church, or Mother Emanuel.

13. Dickerson, *The African Methodist Episcopal Church*.

14. Harrold and Miller, *The Denmark Vesey Affair*, 178.

15. "Denmark Vesey," *This Far by Faith*, PBS, accessed January 24, 2024, http://www.pbs.org/thisfarbyfaith/people/denmark_vesey.html.

16. Payne, *History of the African Methodist*, 262.

17. Richard R. Wright, *Centennial Encyclopaedia of the African Methodist*, 281; Arnett, *In Memoriam*; Payne, *History of the African Methodist*, 262; Smith and Payne, *A Biography of Rev. David Smith*.

18. J. P. Q. Wallace, "Unique Biographical Sketch of a Pioneer Missionary," in *A Century of Missions, 1840–1940*, ed. L. L. Berry, 54 (New York: Gutenberg Printing, 1942).

19. Wallace's full name is Jessie Paul Quinn Wallace and appears to have been named for the bishop. See Wallace, "Unique Biographical Sketch," 54; Brown "William Paul Quinn," 662.

20. Brown, "William Paul Quinn," 661.

21. Arnett, *In Memoriam*, 17.

22. Allen and Tapsico, *The Doctrines and Discipline*, 84–85.

23. Brown, "William Paul Quinn," 662.

24. James A. Handy, *Scraps of African Methodist Episcopal History* (Philadelphia: AME Book Concern, 1902), 343–44; Richard S. Newman, *Freedom's Prophet: Bishop Richard Allen, the AME Church, and the Black Founding Fathers* (New York: New York University Press, 2008).

25. Welch, *William Paul Quinn*, 21.
26. Berry, *Century of Missions of the African Methodist*, 33
27. Brown, "William Paul Quinn," 662.
28. Arnett, *In Memoriam*, 17.
29. Welch, *William Paul Quinn*.
30. Welch, *William Paul Quinn*, 8.
31. By 1827 four AME missions had already been established in Canada. For the Missouri Compromise, see "Missouri Compromise: Date, Definition & 1820," History, accessed March 13, 2024, https://www.history.com/topics/slavery/missouri-compromise.
32. Joseph H. Morgan, *Morgan's History of the New Jersey Conference of the A.M.E. Church, from 1872 to 1887: And of the Several Churches, as Far as Possible, from Date of Organization, with Biographical Sketches of Members of the Conference* (Camden, NJ: S. Chew, 1887), 89, 92.
33. Smith and Payne, *A Biography of Rev. David Smith*, 63–64.
34. See Cheryl Janifer LaRoche, *Free Black Communities and the Underground Railroad: The Geography of Resistance* (Urbana: University of Illinois Press, 2014), 142–44.
35. See LaRoche, *Free Black Communities*, xi–xiii.
36. Samuel Ringgold Ward, *Autobiography of a Fugitive Negro: His Anti-slavery Labours in the United States, Canada, & England* (London: John Snow, 1855).
37. William J. Switala, *Underground Railroad in New York and New Jersey* (Mechanicsburg, PA: Stackpole Books, 2006), 49.
38. Switala, *Underground Railroad in New York*, 49–50; Wilbur Siebert also identifies the Greenwich line as an escape route in New Jersey.
39. Switala, *Underground Railroad in New York*, 50.
40. Dorothy Porter, ed., "Minutes of the Four Last Annual Conferences of the African Methodist Episcopal Church Held at Pittsburg, Pa., Washington, D.C., Philadelphia, and New York 1833–4," in *Early Negro Writing, 1760–1837*, edited by Dorothy Porter (Philadelphia: Joseph M. Corr, 1834; Baltimore: Black Classic Press, 1995), 189.
41. Edward W. Lampton, *Digest of the Rulings and Decisions of the Bishops of the African Methodist Episcopal Church from 1847 to 1907* (Washington, DC: The Record Publishing Company, 1907), 41.
42. Payne, *History of the African Methodist*, 123. He organized churches in Mount Pleasant, Belmont, Zanesville, Lancaster, Chillicothe, and Steubenville. Bryan W. Woodson Sr., *A President in the Family: Thomas Jefferson, Sally Hemmings, and Thomas Woodson* (Westport, CT: Praeger, 2001).
43. "The Underground Railroad in Chillicothe/Ross County, Historic Underground Railroad Site," The Historical Marker Database, https://www.hmdb.org/m.asp?m=118737; "Quinn Chapel African Methodist Episcopal Church," *Underground Ohio* (blog), https://undergroundoh.com/churches/.
44. "Obituary," *Pittsburgh Commercial Gazette*, January 15, 1878; LaRoche, *Free Black Communities*.

45. *Steubenville Herald-Star*, May 8, 1908.
46. Welch, *William Paul Quinn*, 10.
47. Stephen W. Angell, "'The Shadows of the Evening Stretched Out': Richard Robinson and the Shaping of African Methodist Identity, 1823–1862," *Journal of Africana Religions* 3, no. 3 (2015): 227–50.
48. Angell, "The Shadows of the Evening," 227–50.
49. Welch, *William Paul Quinn*, 9.
50. Alexander Walker Wayman, *Cyclopaedia of African Methodism* (Baltimore: Methodist Episcopal Book Depository, 1882), 138.
51. Angell, "The Shadows of the Evening," 229. See Stephen W. Angell, "Black Methodist Preachers in the South Carolina Upcounty, 1840–1866: Isaac (Counts) Cook, James Porter, and Henry McNeal Turner," in *Ain't Gonna Lay My 'Ligion Down: African American Roots in Southern Religion*, ed. Alonzo Johnson and Paul Jersild (Columbia: University of South Carolina Press, 1996), 98.
52. Angell, "The Shadows of the Evening"; Charles Spicer was sent to New Bedford in 1822.
53. Chris Hedlin, "How Did Pittsburgh's Oldest Black Church Form? What Was Its Role in the Underground Railroad and Fighting Slavery?" PublicSource, published January 31, 2022, https://www.publicsource.org/pittsburgh-faith-race-place-oldest-black-church-underground-railroad-anti-slavery/.
54. Laurence A. Glasco, ed., *The WPA History of the Negro in Pittsburgh* (Pittsburgh: University of Pittsburgh Press, 2004).

In the 1950s, Bethel AME Church on Wylie Avenue and Elm Street in the Lower Hill District, encompassing almost the entire block, was taken and destroyed through eminent domain to create the Civic Arena. In 2023, in a move reminiscent of Richard Allen's fight to regain Mother Bethel, Pittsburgh's Bethel AME won back the land and has restorative development plans for Pittsburgh. See Talia Kirkland, "Members of Bethel AME Church Continue Working on Deal to Recover Land," WPXI-TV, published November 18, 2022, https://www.wpxi.com/news/local/members-bethel-ame-church-continue-working-deal-recover-land/3SMTBIGJNFDQDPBE4O4DSPFF4I/; and Nora Davenport, "Bethel AME Wins Back Land and Has Exciting Restorative Development Plans for Pittsburgh," RHLS (Regional Housing Legal Services), published May 24, 2023, https://www.rhls.org/2023/05/bethel-ame-wins-back-land-and-has-exciting-restorative-development-plans-for-pittsburgh/.

55. Brown, "William Paul Quinn," 663.
56. The report stated that "he traveled more than . . . 300,000 miles[,] established about 13,000 places of worship and nearly a thousand churches." These numbers are well out of line with what can be proven. *Steubenville Herald-Star*, May 8, 1908.
57. *Steubenville Herald-Star*, April 23, 1960.
58. "Allen Temple A.M.E. Church," *Underground Ohio* (blog), https://undergroundoh.com/churches/.
59. Michelle Alfini, Cincinnati's Historic AME Church Keeps Community Connected During Pandemic, Spectrum News 1, published February 8, 2021,

https://spectrumnews1.com/oh/columbus/news/2021/02/08/cincinnati-s-historic-ame-church-keeps-community-connected-during-pandemic.

60. Brown, "William Paul Quinn," 663.

61. Handy, *Scraps of African Methodist Episcopal History*, 31; Effie Lee Newsome, "Early Figures in Haitian Methodism," *Phylon* 5, no. 1 (Quarter 1, 1944): 51–61; Angell, "The Shadows of the Evening," 230; Wright, *Centennial Encyclopaedia of the African Methodist*, 319.

62. Angell, "The Shadows of the Evening," 228.

63. Donald George Simpson, "Negroes in Ontario from Early Times to 1870," PhD diss., University of Western Ontario, 1971; Daniel Payne, *Semi-centenary and the Retrospection*, 28.

64. Handy, *Scraps of African Methodist Episcopal History*, 6.

Chapter 3: Pages 33–42

1. Welch, *William Paul Quinn*, 24.

2. William J. Walls, *The African Methodist Episcopal Zion Church: Reality of the Black Church* (Charlotte, NC: A.M.E. Zion Publishing House, 1974); Elmer T. Clark, J. Manning Potts, and Jacob S. Payton, *The Journal and Letters of Francis Asbury In Three Volumes, Vol. II The Journal 1794–1816* (Epworth Press: London: Epworth Press; Nashville: Abingdon Press, 1958), 598, https://media.sabda.org/alkitab-6/wh3-ref/aj-v2.pdf.

3. Handy, *Scraps of African Methodist Episcopal History*, 60.

4. Christopher Rush, *A Short Account of the Rise and Progress of the African M. E. Church in America, Written by Christopher Rush, Superintendent of the Connexion, with the Aid of George Collins. Also, a Concise View of Church Order or Government, from Scripture, and from Some of the Best Authors on the Subject of Church Government, Relative to Episcopacy* (New York: Published by the author, 1843), 34–5.

5. Rush, *A Short Account*.

6. Smith and Payne, *A Biography of Rev. David Smith*, 67–68.

7. Howard D. Gregg, *History of the African Methodist Episcopal Church (The Black Church in Action)* (Nashville: The African Methodist Episcopal Church, 1980); Howard D. Gregg, *The African Methodist Episcopal Church, One Hundred Eighty-Eight Years of Progress, Our Beginning*, https://centerforurbanstudies.ap.buffalo.edu/wp-content/uploads/sites/16/2020/02/BAME_1976-01-01_Books_The_African_Methodist_Episcopal_Church_Our_Beginning.pdf. Records for the New York Conference were not well kept during this period. I believe six of the eight churches are as follows: (1) Macedonia, Flushing, 1811; (2) Bethel AME, Setauket, Brookhaven, Long Island, 1815; (3) Bethel AME Copiague, Long Island; (4) Bethel AME on Mott Street, 1819; (5) Bridge Street, Brooklyn, 1820; and (6) Bethel AME on Elizabeth Street. Two may have been part of the White Plains circuit.

The following is the New York District, as reported in 1822: New York, Bethel Church, Brooklyn, Long Island; White Plains, subsequently called Huntingdon circuit; Cove, now called Glen Cove; Harlem; Jamaica, Long Island; Flushing; and New Bedford, Massachusetts.

8. Judith Wellman, *Brooklyn's Promised Land: The Free Black Community of Weeksville, New York* (New York: New York University Press, 2014); "Bridge Street AWME Church," MAAP, Mapping the African American Past, accessed August 26, 2022, https://maap.columbia.edu/place/11.html; Wright, *Centennial Encyclopaedia of the African Methodist*, 71. Weeksville was south of Fulton Street, north of East New York Avenue, east of Troy Avenue, and west of Ralph Avenue. Hunterfly Road is the centerpiece of the Weeksville Heritage Center, found between Troy Avenue, Pacific Street, Schenectady Avenue, and Dean Street.

9. AWME Church was originally located on the east side of High Street, Brooklyn, and was known by its location. Lee states, on June 6, 1823, "[I] Spoke in the Church in High Street, Brooklyn, from Jer. ix, 1." Jarena Lee, *Religious Experience and Journal of Mrs. Jarena Lee Giving an Account of Her Call to Preach the Gospel*, Project Gutenberg, released December 16, 2021, https://www.gutenberg.org/files/66953/66953-h/66953-h.htm; *248th Anniversary Souvenir Journal* (Brooklyn: Bridge Street AWME Church, 2014), 15–20; Payne, *History of the African Methodist*, 36.

10. Amos M. Jordan, comp., *Compiled History of the African Wesleyan Methodist Episcopal Church, Inc.* (Brooklyn: Board of Trustees, 1973); *The Long Island Star*, October 4, 1817. Weeksville was bound to the north by Fulton Street, to the east by Ralph Avenue, to the south by Eastern Parkway, and to the west by Troy Avenue.

11. "Macedonia A.M.E. Church," *Flushing Daily Times*, June 6, 1903; Smith and Payne, *A Biography of Rev. David Smith*; Henry D. Walker, *History of the Town of Flushing, Long Island, New York* (Flushing, NY: J. H. Ridenour, 1899); "Worthy of Attention," *The Evening Star* (New York), January 7, 1826.

12. *Freedom's Journal* (New York), May 4, 1827.

13. Charles H. Wesley, *Richard Allen: An Apostle of Freedom* (Washington, DC: Associated Publishers, 1935), 163; Newman, *Freedom's Prophet*, 7.

14. *The Long Island Star*, August 23, 1826.

15. Bear in mind that African churches are often dated to the founding of the congregation rather than the building of the church. "Mortuary Notice," *The Elevator* (San Francisco), March 15, 1873.

16. Karl Bernhard (Duke of Saxe Weimar-Eisenach), *Travels Through North America, Vol. I*, (London: Carey, Lea, & Carey, 1826), 126.

17. Bernhard, *Travels Through North America*, 126; The Brooklyn Benevolent African Association was incorporated in 1831.

18. *Freedom's Journal*, April 27, 1827; *Freedom's Journal*, July 6, 1827; *Freedom's Journal*, October 12, 1827.

19. *Genius of Universal Emancipation*, July 14, 1827. See also Henry H. Garnet and James M. Smith, *A Memorial Discourse by Henry Highland Garnet Delivered in the House of Representatives, Washington, DC.* (Philadelphia: Joseph M. Wilson, 1865), 24–25.

20. Benjamin Quarles, *Black Abolitionists* (New York: Oxford University Press, 1969), 119.

21. New York Probate Records, 1659–1999, for Margaret Quinn, box 8-28694, vol. 0027-0028, 1830–1836. Margaret Quinn, February 15, 1830. She, formerly Margaret (Margaretta) Potts, died February 11, 1830. Bishop Tanner reports that a Mrs. Quinn is "mentioned in some old Bucks County African Methodist records bearing a date of 10th February 1824 but this cannot be verified." Some reports say that Quinn had two children, but this cannot be verified.

22. "Golden Achievements of the Women's Missionary Society," *The Baltimore Afro-American*, June 13, 1987.

23. "Golden Achievements of the Women," *The Baltimore Afro-American*.

24. "Notice," *Freedom's Journal*, February 1, 1828; Leslie M. Alexander, *African or American? Black Identity and Political Activism in New York City, 1784–1861* (Urbana: University of Illinois Press, 2012).

25. *Colored American*, March 17, 1838.

26. "Annual Report of the African Dorcas Association," In *History of the New York African Free Schools, from Their Establishment in 1787, to the Present Time: Embracing A Period of More than Forty Years Also a Brief Account of the Successful Labors of the New-York Manumission Society: With an Appendix*, ed. Charles C. Andrews (New York: Mahlon Day, 1830), 105.

The African Clarkson Association was incorporated in 1829.

27. William J. Simmons, *Men of Mark: Eminent, Progressive and Rising* (Cleveland: Geo. Rewell, 1887), 1004.

28. Henry Highland Garnet, "'The Secret of His Success and Popularity,' Rev. William Paul Quinn, Third Bishop, Pioneers of the A.M.E. Church, No. III," *The Christian Recorder*, March 13, 1869.

29. The Masonic lodges in New York at that time were Celestial No. 2 and Hiram No. 4, as well as Boyer. Rising Sun No. 2, which was in Brooklyn.

30. *Freedom's Journal*, December 31, 1827.

31. *Freedom's Journal*, December 31, 1827.

32. *Freedom's Journal*, December 31, 1827.

33. Daniel A. Payne, "Morris Brown," in *Lives of Methodist Bishops*, eds. Theodore L. Flood and John W. Hamilton (New York: Phillips & Hunt, 1882), 670.

34. Smith and Payne, *A Biography of Rev. David Smith*. There is no official mention of Quinn's removal in the various histories of the AME Church. In the minutes, disciplines, and proceedings available and consulted, there is little discussion of Quinn's expulsion, only his readmission.

35. Berry, *Century of Missions of the African Methodist*, 53.

36. Smith and Payne, *A Biography of Rev. David Smith*, 64.

37. "New-York African Free School records, 1817–1832, Vol. 2," New-York Historical Society, accessed August 20, 2022, https://digitalcollections.nyhistory.org/islandora/object/islandora%3A139453#page/36/mode/1up.

38. "New York City Directory," 1831–32, 722, New York Public Library Digital Collections, Irma and Paul Milstein Division of United States History, Local History

and Genealogy, The New York Public Library, accessed December 27, 2021, https://digitalcollections.nypl.org/items/f58e2a30-2b8c-0136-d580-0f70555aba17.

39. Tanner, An Outline of Our History and Government, 23.

Chapter 4: Pages 43–56

1. Payne, *History of the African Methodist*, 96.
2. Payne, *History of the African Methodist*, 96.
3. Smith and Payne, *A Biography of Rev. David Smith*, 67–68.
4. Peg Quann, "Bensalem AME Church to Honor Founder Richard Allen," *Bucks County Courier Times*, February 11, 2016, buckscountycouriertimes.com/article/20160211/news/302119907; Baldwin, *The Mark of a Man*, 11, quoted in Richard Allen, *The Life Experience and Gospel Labors*, 29; Lewis V. Baldwin, *"Invisible" Strands in African Methodism: A History of the African Union Methodist Protestant and Union American Methodist Episcopal Churches, 1805–1980* (Metuchen, NJ: Scarecrow Press, 1983), 22–23, 47–50; *The Morning News*, August 26, 1889. Episcopacy is government of the church by bishops—a church government in which there are three distinct orders of ministers; namely bishops, priests or presbyters, and deacons.
5. Smith and Payne, *A Biography of Rev. David Smith*, 64; "African Camp Meeting," *Long Island Star*, August 7, 1828.
6. "The Executions," *Vermont Stateman*, May 20, 1829.
7. "The Executions," *Vermont Stateman*, May 20, 1829.
8. "The Executions," *Vermont Stateman*, May 20, 1829.
9. "The Executions," *Vermont Stateman*, May 20, 1829. Richard Johnson and Catharine Cashiere were the last public hangings in New York City. Headsman, "1829: Richard Johnson and Catherine Cashiere, the Last Public Hangings in New York City," ExecutedToday, published May 7, 2015, http://www.executedtoday.com/2015/05/07/1829-richard-johnson-and-catharine-cashiere/.
10. Don Papson and Tom Calarco, *Secret Lives of the Underground Railroad in New York City: Sydney Howard Gay, Louis Napoleon and the "Record of Fugitives"* (Jefferson, NC: McFarland, 2015), 205.
11. Eric Foner, *Gateway to Freedom: The Hidden History of the Underground Railroad* (New York: W. W. Norton, 2015); Bella Gross, "Life and Times of Theodore S. Wright, 1797–1847," *Negro History Bulletin* 3, no. 9 (June 1940): 133–38.
12. Lisa Bowens, "A Biographical Reflection of Theodore Sedgwick Wright," Princeton Theological Seminary, published October 14, 2021, https://www.ptsem.edu/news/biographical-reflection.
13. "Land of Liberty," *Freedom's Journal*, December 5, 1828.
14. Henry Highland Garnet, "'He Fights for Liberty and Wins; His Fidelity to Liberty and Justice,' Rev. William Paul Quinn, Third Bishop, Pioneers of the A.M.E. Church. No. III," *Christian Recorder*, March 13, 1869. Noted abolitionist Isaac Hopper, disowned by his Pennsylvania Quaker meeting for public antislavery agitation, relocated to NYC in 1829. There is no way of knowing whether the two

knew one another, but the likelihood seems high. Henry Highland Garnet, *Garnet's Memorial Discourse* (Philadelphia: Joseph M. Wilson, 1865), 25.

15. Garnet, "He Fights for Liberty and Wins."

16. Kwame Anthony Appiah and Henry Louis Gates Jr., eds., "Henry Highland Garnet," in *Africana: The Encyclopedia of the African and African American Experience* (New York: Basic Books, 1999); Joel Schor, *Henry Highland Garnet: A Voice of Black Radicalism in the Nineteenth Century* (Westport, CT: Greenwood Press, 1944), 4.

17. Garnet, "He Fights for Liberty and Wins."

18. Foner, *Gateway to Freedom*, 52. See also Leslie M. Harris, *In the Shadow of Slavery: African Americans in New York City, 1626–1863* (Chicago: University of Chicago Press, 2003), 7–9; C. Peter Ripley, ed., *Black Abolitionist Papers 3* (Chapel Hill: University of North Carolina Press, 2015), 180; *Mirror of Liberty*, January 1839; *Weekly Advocate*, January 14, 1837.

19. Garnet, "He Fights for Liberty and Wins."

20. Maurice Newell, "This Is Bethel—Reading. Come Ride the Underground Railroad, Where Culture and History Come to Life." Central Pennsylvania African American Museum, Reading, PA; Wilbur H. Siebert, *The Underground Railroad from Slavery to Freedom* (New York: The Macmillan Company, 1898); Charles Blockson, *The Underground Railroad in Pennsylvania* (Jacksonville, NC: Flame International, 1981).

21. Alexander Crummell, *Eulogium on Henry Highland Garnet, D.D. Presbyterian Minister, Late Minister Resident of the US to the Republic of Liberia, Delivered under the Auspices of the Union Bethel Literary and Historical Association in the Nineteenth Street Baptist Church, Mar 4, 1882* (United States, 1882); "Let Your Motto Be Resistance," The Legacy of Henry Highland Garnet, accessed December 2, 2023, https://kentcountyhistory.org/wp-content/uploads/2018/08/Henry-Highland-Garnet.pdf.

George Trusty gave new names to the family. His wife, Henny, became Elizabeth; his daughter, Mary, Eliza. Although the original first names of George and Henry are unknown, the family abandoned the Trusty name and took the surname Garnet.

22. "Henry Highland Garnet," Examination Days, The New York African Free School Collection, accessed February 16, 2024, https://www.nyhistory.org/web/africanfreeschool/bios/henry-highland-garnet.html; Ripley, ed., *Black Abolitionist Papers 3*.

23. Garnet and Smith, *A Memorial Discourse*.

24. Joseph A. Boromé et al., "The Vigilant Committee of Philadelphia." *The Pennsylvania Magazine of History and Biography* 92, no. 3 (July 1968): 320.

25. Rev. Alfred L. Thompson, *The History of St. Paul AME* (1999). The church is located in Uniontown, Pennsylvania. The Quin spelling (sometimes spelled Guin) was also in the historical records in New York City and is close enough to Quinn's name to surmise that they are one and the same.

26. *Indianapolis World*, February 23, 1893.

27. *Indianapolis World*, February 23, 1893.

28. *Indianapolis World*, February 23, 1893.

29. Sundiata Keita Cha-Jua, *America's First Black Town: Brooklyn, Illinois 1830–1915* (Urbana: University of Illinois Press, 2000), 37.

30. Sarah J. W. Early, *Life and Labors of Rev. Jordan W. Early: One of the Pioneers of African Methodism in the West and South* (A.M.E. Church Sunday School Union, 1894; Freeport, NY: Books for Libraries Press, 1971) , 21–22; Cha-Jua, *America' First Black Town*, 53.

31. "St. John African Methodist Episcopal (AME) Church," Encyclopedia of Cleveland History, Case Western Reserve University, https://case.edu/ech/articles/s/st-johns-african-methodist-episcopal-ame-church; "1,200 at St. John's A. M. E. Mark 100th Anniversary," ClevelandMemory.org, accessed August 21, 2022, https://clevelandmemory.contentdm.oclc.org/digital/collection/press/id/2477.

32. "First Negro Church Was St. John's AME," *Cleveland Call and Post*, June 24, 1961; William Ganson Rose, *Cleveland: The Making of a City* (Kent, OH: Kent State University Press, 1990), 124. The church does not appear in the city records until 1848, when the members purchased a lot for $300 on Bolivar Street, east of Erie Street, on the site of the Pick Carter Hotel (Carter Apartments). At the time, this location was considered the outskirts of the city.

33. Carter Goodwin Woodson, *Free Negro Heads of Families in the United States in 1830* (Washington, DC: The Association for the Study of Negro Life and History, 1925), 100.

34. Margaret Quinn died February 11, 1830. New York Probate Records, 1659–1999, for Margaret Quinn, box 8-28694, vol. 0027-0028, 1830–1836.

35. Tyler Anbinder, *Five Points: The 19th-Century New York City Neighborhood That Invented Tap Dance, Stole Elections, and Became the World's Most Notorious Slum* (New York: Plume, 2002).

36. Payne, *History of the African Methodist*, 97-98.

37. Payne, *History of the African Methodist*, 68.

38. Payne, *History of the African Methodist*, 68; Newman, *Freedom's Prophet*, 1, 289.

39. Berry, *Century of Missions of the African Methodist*, 53.

40. Smith and Payne, *A Biography of Rev. David Smith*. The New York Annual Conference met in the city of Brooklyn on June 9, 1832. Benjamin Croger and George Hogarth were its secretaries.

41. Payne, *History of the African Methodist*, 95.

42. "Session Laws, 1831, Vol. 213, 447–48," Archives of Maryland Online, last updated October 6, 2023, https://msa.maryland.gov/megafile/msa/speccol/sc2900/sc2908/000001/000213/html/am213--447.html.

43. Handy, *Scraps of African Methodist Episcopal History*; Herbert Brewer, "Chesapeake Free Blacks and the Origins of the Liberian State, 1776–1848," PhD diss., University of Maryland, 2017, https://api.drum.lib.umd.edu/server/api/core/bitstreams/6d014c7f-eb02-4f93-8ca5-f8db93c07414/content.

44. Transcribed from New York City (Manhattan) Directories by Tom Gregory. Quinn's name is misspelled in the records as either Quin or Guin.

45. *The Liberator*, January 1833

46. Ward, *Autobiography of a Fugitive Negro*, 6, 139.

47. Imani Vieira, "Separate but Equal": From the African Free Schools to the New York City Public School System," Arts, Culture, Community, Lower East Side, accessed February 27, 2024, https://www.fabnyc.org/2022/02/03/4481/; Leslie. M. Alexander, *African or American? Black Identity and Political Activism in New York City, 1784–1861* (Urbana: University of Illinois Press, 2012).

48. Lewis Tappan, *The Life of Arthur Tappan* (New York: Hurd & Houghton, 1870), 158–59; LaRoche, *Free Black Communities*, 2004; John W. Cromwell, *The Negro in American History* (Washington, DC: The American Negro Academy, 1914), 34; John W. Cromwell, *The Early Negro Convention Movement* (Washington, DC: The American Negro Academy, 1904), 10, https://www.gutenberg.org/files/31328/31328-h/31328-h.htm; Bella Gross, "Freedom's Journal and the Rights of All," *The Journal of Negro History* 17, no. 3 (July 1932): 241–86, https://doi.org/10.2307/2714274; Dorothy B. Porter, "The Organized Educational Activities of Negro Literary Societies, 1828–1846," *The Journal of Negro Education* 5, no. 4 (1936): 555–78, https://doi.org/10.2307/2292029; Joseph Wilson, *Sketches of the Higher Classes of Colored Society in Philadelphia* (Philadelphia: Merrihew and Thompson, 1841), 9; *First Annual Report of the American Anti-Slavery Society with the Speeches Delivered at the Anniversary Meeting, Held in Chatham-Street Chapel, in the City of New York, on the Sixth of May, 1834* (New York: Dorr and Butterfield, 1834).

49. Smith and Payne, *A Biography of Rev. David Smith*, 68.

50. Payne, *History of the African Methodist*, 97; Tanner, *An Outline of Our History and Government*, 82.

Chapter 5: Pages 57–69

1. Berry, *Century of Missions of the African Methodist*, 51.

2. Henry Highland Garnet, "Pioneers of the A.M.E. Church. No. III," *The Christian Recorder*, March 13, 1869.

3. Henry Highland Garnet, "The Lives of Methodist Pioneers," *The Christian Recorder*, March 13, 1869.

4. Garnet, "The Lives of Methodist Pioneers."

5. Benjamin T. Tanner, *An Outline of Our History and Government for African Methodist Churchmen, Ministerial and Lay: In Catechetical Form: Two Parts with Appendix* (Philadelphia: Grant, Faires & Rodgers, 1884), 157.

6. At least seven slaveholding states in the South enacted antiliteracy laws. In addition to these, Indiana restricted access to education in an 1847 act. "Being Black in Indiana," Indiana Historical Bureau, https://www.in.gov/history/for-educators/download-issues-of-the-indiana-historian/indiana-emigrants-to-liberia/being-black-in-indiana/.

In 1847 the legislature of Missouri passed an act prohibiting "Negroes and mulattoes" from learning to read and write and from assembling. See "Missouri Prohibits Education of Black People," Equal Justice Initiative, https://calendar.eji.org/racial-injustice/feb/16.

Ohio did not allow African American children access to public schools until 1849. See Arlette Ingram Willis, *Anti-Black Literacy Laws and Policies* (New York: Routledge, 2023).

7. Brian Dolinar, ed., *The Negro in Illinois: The WPA Papers* (Champaign: University of Illinois Press, 2015), 70; "AME Churches in Rural Area Meet Community Challenges," *Pittsburgh Courier*, August 8, 1953; *The Liberator*, October 12, 1833. WPA is the Work Projects Administration project of the 1930s.

8. "Throwback Thursday: Lane Theological Seminary," Walnut Hills Redevelopment Foundation, published February 7, 2013, https://walnuthillsrf.org/throwback-thursday-lane-theological-seminary/.

9. Kenneth Griffler, *Front Line of Freedom: African Americans and the Forging of the Underground Railroad in the Ohio Valley* (Lexington: University Press of Kentucky, 2004), 67.

10. Richard Cooper and Dr. Eric R. Jackson, *Cincinnati's Underground Railroad*, (Charleston, SC: Arcadia Publishing, 2014), 59.

11. *The Liberator*, December 20, 1834, 4.

12. Arnett, *Proceedings of the African Methodist Episcopal Church*, 19.

13. Excerpted by permission, Judi Moore Latta, "Dancing," August 24, 2022, unpublished manuscript with the author.

14. Nikki Marie Taylor, *Frontiers of Freedom: Cincinnati's Black Community, 1802–1868* (Athens: Ohio University Press, 2005), 95.

15. "ASL Samuel Wells to Theodore Weld, December 15, 1834," in *Letters of Theodore Dwight Weld, Angelina Grimké Weld and Sarah Grimké 1822–1844*, eds. Gilbert H. Barnes and Dwight L. Dumond (New York: D. Appleton-Century, 1934), 178.

16. "ASL Samuel Wells to Theodore Weld, December 15, 1834," 178.

17. "ASL Samuel Wells to Theodore Weld, December 15, 1834," 191–92.

18. Ohio Anti-slavery Society, *Report on the Condition of the People of Color in the State of Ohio, with Interesting Anecdotes* (Boston: Isaac Knapp, 1839), https://www.loc.gov/resource/gdclccn.12002909/?sp=5&st=image.

19. William F. Cheek and Aimee Cheek, *John Mercer Langston and the Fight for Black Freedom, 1829–65* (Champaign: University of Illinois Press, 1996).

20. Lawrence Thomas Lesick, *The Lane Rebels: Evangelicalism and Antislavery in Antebellum America* (Metuchen, NJ: The Scarecrow Press, 1980), 232.

21. Lynne Marie Getz, "Partners in Motion: Gender, Migration, and Reform in Antebellum Ohio and Kansas," *Frontiers: A Journal of Women Studies* 27, no. 2 (2006): 102–35.

22. David Walker, *Walker's Appeal, in Four Articles; Together with a Preamble, to the Coloured Citizens of the World, but in Particular, and Very Expressly, to Those of the United States of America, Written in Boston, State of Massachusetts, September 28, 1829* (Boston: printed by the author, 1830).

23. William Paul Quinn, "The Origin, Horrors and Results of Slavery, Faithfully and Minutely Described in a Series of Facts, and Its Advocates Pathetically Addressed," in *Early Negro Writing 1760–1837*, ed. Dorothy Porter (Baltimore: Black Classic Press, 1995), 614–36.

24. Marcy J. Dinius, "Notes," in *The Textual Effects of David Walker's "Appeal": Print-Based Activism against Slavery, Racism, and Discrimination, 1829–1851* (Philadelphia: University of Pennsylvania Press, 2022), 241–84, https://doi.org/10.2307/j.ctv1q6bn79.11; Thomas Branagan, "A Preliminary Essay on the Oppression of the Exiled Sons of Africa. Consisting of Animadversions of the Impolicy and Barbarity of the Deleterious Commerce and Subsequent Slavery of the Human Species: To Which Is Added, A Desultory Letter Written to Napoleon Bonaparte, Anno Domini, 1801" (Philadelphia: John W. Scott, 1804), 87–88, 220–23, https://www.google.com/books/edition/A_Preliminary_Essay_on_the_Oppression_of/U5QSAAAAIAAJ?hl=en&gbpv=1&bsq=hint%20to%20congress; Dorothy Porter, ed., *Early Negro Writing 1760–1837* (Baltimore: The Black Classic Press, 1995), 518; John Belton O'Neall, "The Status of the Negro, His Rights and Disabilities, Chap. 2, Sec. 41," in *The Negro Law of South Carolina Collected and Digested*, ed. O'Neall (London: Forgotten Books, 2016), http://genealogytrails.com/scar/negro_law2.htm. According to the act of 1834, slaves are prohibited to be taught to read or write under a penalty (if a White person may offend) not exceeding a one hundred-dollar fine and six months imprisonment. If a free person of color offended, the penalty would not exceed fifty lashes or a fine of fifty dollars.

25. Quinn, "The Origin, Horrors and Results of Slavery," 628–30; Peter Hinks, *To Awaken My Afflicted Brethren: David Walker and the Problem of Antebellum Slave Resistance* (University Park: Pennsylvania State University Press, 1997).

26. Porter, ed., "Introduction" in *Early Negro Writing*, 2.

27. Milton C. Sernett, *Black Religion and American Evangelicalism: White Protestants, Plantation Missions, and the Flowering of Negro Christianity, 1787–1865* (Metuchen, New Jersey: Scarecrow Press, 1975), 154.

28. "African Methodist Episcopal Church Conference, 1840," *A.M.E. Church Magazine* (Brooklyn), September 1, 1841, 7–8, as quoted in Herbert Aptheker, ed., *A Documentary History of the Negro People in the United States*, Vol. I (New York: Citadel Press, 1990), 205–6.

29. "African Methodist Episcopal Church Conference, 1840," *A.M.E. Church Magazine*.

30. Welch, *William Paul Quinn*.

31. Welch, *William Paul Quinn*, 15.

32. Welch, *William Paul Quinn*, 14–16.

33. Welch, *William Paul Quinn*, 16.

34. "Legislative Acts / Legal Proceedings," *Emancipator and Republican* no. 11 (July 9, 1845): 44.

35. H. W. Brands, *Andrew Jackson: A Life and Times* (New York: Doubleday, 2006), 423; "Gen. Jackson," *The Mystery*, quoted in *Emancipator and Weekly Chronicle*, July 9, 1845, 44.

36. "Session Laws 1831, Vol. 213, 448," Archives of Maryland Online.

37. H. W. Brands, *Andrew Jackson: A Life and Times* (New York: Doubleday, 2006), 423.

38. "Gen. Jackson," *The Mystery*, quoted in *Emancipator and Weekly Chronicle*, July 9, 1845.

39. "Nineteenth Baltimore Annual Conference of the African Methodist Episcopal Church, Washington, D.C., April 10, 1834, in Dorothy Porter, ed., "Minutes of the Four Last Annual Conferences of the African Methodist Episcopal Church Held at Pittsburg, Pa., Washington, D.C., Philadelphia, and New York 1833–4," in *Early Negro Writing, 1760–1837*, ed. Dorothy Porter (Jospeh M. Corr, 1834; Baltimore: Black Classic Press, 1995), 187–88.

40. John W. Cromwell, "First Negro Churches in the District of Columbia," *Journal of Negro History* 7, no. 1 (January 1922): 64–106; Porter, ed., "Minutes of the Four Last Annual," 188.

41. Augustus R. Green, *The Life of the Rev. Dandridge F. Davis, of the African M.E. Church, with a Brief Account of His Conversion and Ministerial Labors, from August 1834, Till March 1847. Also, a Brief Sketch of the Life of the Rev. David Conyou, of the A.M.E.C. and His Ministerial Labors. To Which Is Annexed the Funeral Discourse Delivered at the Ohio Conference, in Zanesville, on the Decease of the Rev. D. F. Davis, by the Author* (Pittsburgh: Ohio Conference, 1850), 27, https://docsouth.unc.edu/neh/greena/greena.html.

42. Green, *Life of the Rev. Dandridge F. Davis*, 27.

43. Green, *Life of the Rev. Dandridge F. Davis*, 28.

44. Green, *Life of the Rev. Dandridge F. Davis*, 28.

45. Green, *Life of the Rev. Dandridge F. Davis*, 28–29.

46. Green, *Life of the Rev. Dandridge F. Davis*, 39.

47. "The Underground Railway—Review of the System by Which Many Thousands of Slaves Were Liberated," *The Freeman*, February 24, 1900.

48. Moses Dickson, *Manual of the International Order of Twelve Knights and Daughters of Tabor* (St. Louis: A. R. Fleming, 1891), 7.

49. "Moses Dickson: The Great Negro Organizer and Fraternal Society Leader," *St. Louis Star*, April 1902.

50. "Moses Dickson," *St. Louis Star*, April 1902.

51. Booker T. Washington, *The Story of the Negro: The Rise of the Race from Slavery* (New York: Doubleday, 1909; New York: Barnes and Noble, 2009), 286–87.

52. Washington, *The Story of the Negro*, 286–87. Washington gives no citation, but Herbert Aptheker says that Booker T. Washington seems to have known Dickson; Herbert Aptheker, "Militant Abolitionism," *The Journal of Negro History* 26, no. 4 (October 1941): 438–84.

53. Bethel A.M.E. Church, National Register of Historic Places Inventory—Nomination Form, United States Department of the Interior, National Park Service, September 1975, https://www.iowa-city.org/WebLink/0/edoc/1887924/Bethel%20AME%20form.pdf.; Welch, *William Paul Quinn*, 12.

Chapter 6: Pages 71–88

1. *Richmond Palladium*, June 8, 1869.

2. Payne, *History of the African Methodist*; Article XIII of the 1851 Indiana Constitution contributed to the restricted education, employment, and social

progress of Black communities in Indiana for decades. See "Article XIII of the 1851 Indiana Constitution," IndianaHistory.org, accessed December 7, 2022, https://indianahistory.org/wp-content/uploads/NHD Exhibit - 1851 IN Constitution.pdf.

3. Welch, *William Paul Quinn*, 13.

4. Wayne County Deed Books, Wayne County Recorder of Deeds, Richmond, Indiana, 11–56, 11–87 (1848); 12–231 (1849); 14–312, 14–314 (1851); 14–618 (1852); 19–148 (1854); 20–351, 20–470 (1855); 21–265 (1856); 26–304 (1859); 37–209 (1865); 42–359 (1866); 44–531, 44–532, 44–535 (1867); 52–249 (1868), 52–250, 52–251 (1869), 59–312 1874 (1859); *Richmond Palladium*, February 21, 1867; *Richmond Palladium*, September 9, 1974.

5. *Richmond Palladium*, February 21, 1867; LaRoche, *Free Black Communities*. Dublin is twenty-five miles southwest of Fountain City and twenty miles due west of Richmond, about the distance one could travel in a night between Underground Railroad stations.

6. Welch, *William Paul Quinn*, 22.

7. Brian Dolinar, ed., *The Negro in Illinois*, 70.

8. Levi Coffin, *Reminiscences of Levi Coffin, the Reputed President of the Underground Railroad; Being a Brief History of the Labors of a Lifetime in Behalf of the Slave, with the Stories of Numerous Fugitives, Who Gained Their Freedom through His Instrumentality, and Many Other Incidents* (Cincinnati: Western Tract Society, 1879); Dolinar, ed., *The Negro in Illinois*, 70; Wilbur H. Siebert, "Underground Routes of Indiana by Prof. W. H. Siebert," Ohio History Center, Wilbur H. Siebert Underground Railroad Collection, ca. 1888, https://ohiomemory.org/digital/collection/siebert/id/9123; "Bishop William Paul Quinn (1806?–1873)," Morrisson-Reeves Library, Richmond, IN, accessed October 10, 2023, https://mrlinfo.org/history/biography/quinn.htm; Levi & Catharine Coffin State Historic Site & Interpretive Center," Visit. Discover. Explore. Richmond, Accessed March 2, 2024, https://visitrichmond.org/listing/levi-catharine-coffin-state-historic-site-interpretive-center#:~:text=The%20Underground%20Railroad%20safety.

9. Welch, *William Paul Quinn*, 11; On June 16, 2018, the Masons honored Quinn's memory at the Bishop William Paul Quinn State Historical marker dedication in Richmond, Indiana.

10. It was the same year Underground Railroad operatives Louis Hayden and John M. Brown reportedly assisted in organizing a Colored Methodist Society in Detroit, Michigan, which evolved into the Bethel AME Church by 1844.

11. Howard Gregg, *The African Methodist Episcopal Church, One Hundred Eighty-Eight Years of Progress, Our Beginning*, accessed July 11, 2024, https://centerforurbanstudies.ap.buffalo.edu/wp-content/uploads/sites/16/2020/02/BAME_1976-01-01_Books_The_African_Methodist_Episcopal_Church_Our_Beginning.pdf; Pamela R. Peters, *The Underground Railroad in Floyd County, Indiana* (Jefferson, NC: McFarland, 2001), 69; Arnett, *In Memoriam*, 19.

12. J. Blaine Hudson, "'Upon This Rock'—The Free African American Community of Antebellum Louisville, Kentucky," *The Register of the Kentucky Historical*

Society 109, no. 3/4 (2011): 295–326, http://www.jstor.org.proxy-um.researchport.umd.edu/stable/23388023.

13. Smith and Payne, *A Biography of Rev. David Smith*, 82–83.

14. Ivan E. McDougle, "The Legal Status of Slavery," *The Journal of Negro History* 3, no. 3 (July 1918): 211–328.

15. Leland R. Johnson and Charles E. Parrish, *Triumph of the Falls: The Louisville and Portland Canal* (Louisville, KY: Louisville District U.S. Army Corps of Engineers, 2007), 70, https://www.lrl.usace.army.mil/Portals/64/docs/Ops/Navigation/TriumphAtTheFalls.pdf.

16. Marty Rosen, "Gateway to Freedom," *Louisville Magazine* 63, no. 10 (October 2012): 42–45.

17. Peters, *The Underground Railroad in Floyd*, 69.

18. H. C. Weeden, ed. and comp., *Weeden's History of The Colored People of Louisville* (Louisville, KY, 1897), 18; Diane P. Coon, Early African-American Congregations North Central Kentucky," Academia, published April 12, 2024, https://www.academia.edu/14439494 /Early_African_American_Congregations_North_Central_Kentucky; Hudson, "Upon This Rock," 311; Ronald D. Palmer, "AME Bishop William Paul Quinn—Notes toward A Biographical Chronology of an American Original, *The A.M.E. Church Review* 120, no. 395: (July–September 2004): 40–61.

19. For more on churches in southern Illinois, see LaRoche, *Free Black Communities*; Cha-Jua, *America's First Black Town*; Early, *Life and Labors of Rev. Jordan*; and Welch, *William Paul Quinn Quinn*.

20. *Colored American*, August 31, 1839.

21. Welch, *William Paul Quinn*, 28.

22. *Indianapolis Journal*, September 28, 1891.

23. Welch, *William Paul Quinn*, 26-27.

24. Stanley Warren, "The Bethel African Methodist Episcopal Church," *Traces of Indiana and Midwestern History* 19, no. 3 (Summer 2007): 32, https://images.indianahistory.org/digital/collection/p16797coll39/id/3306.

25. Wallace, "Unique Biographical Sketch," 52; "Negroes Start Church," *Indianapolis Times*, October 1, 1936.

26. Wallace, "Unique Biographical Sketch."

27. Bethel AME Church, "Aboard the Underground Railroad," National Park Service, accessed October 9, 2023, https://www.nps.gov/nr/travel/underground/in1.htm.

28. Robin W. Winks, *The Blacks in Canada: A History*, 2nd ed. (Montreal: McGill-Queen's University Press, 1997), 356; Wright, *Centennial Encyclopaedia of the African Methodist*, 43.

29. Handy, *Scraps of African Methodist Episcopal History*, 138.

30. Wright, *Centennial Encyclopaedia of the African Methodist*, 9.

31. "Mother' Baltimore's Burial," *St. Louis Daily Globe-Democrat*, December 4, 1882.

32. "Missouri State Law Banning the Teaching of Reading and Writing to Black Missourians," accessed July 11, 2024, 103–4, https://www.sos.mo.gov/CMSImages

/MDH/AnActRespectingSlaves,1847.pdf; Missouri Secretary of State, Missouri's Early Slave Laws: A History in Documents, Missouri Digital Heritage, accessed February 13, 2023, https://www.sos.mo.gov/archives/education/aahi/earlyslavelaws/slavelaws.asp.

33. "New Sectional Map of the State of Illinois: Compiled from the United States Surveys," Historical Maps Online, Illinois Library Digital Collections, accessed March 16, 2024, https://digital.library.illinois.edu/items/a6ade740-994e-0134-2096-0050569601ca-6; Cha-Jua, *America's First Black Town*, 38.

34. Dolinar, ed., *The Negro in Illinois*, 70; Cha-Jua, *America's First Black Town*, 38.

35. "'Mother' Baltimore's Burial," *St. Louis Daily Globe-Democrat*, December 4, 1882, 10; "The Cathedral at St. Paul AME Church Annual Report 2021," St. Paul AME Church, accessed October 9, 2023, https://stpaulamestl.net/church-history.

36. Dolinar, ed., *The Negro in Illinois*, 70; Christina Dickerson-Cousin, *Black Indians & Freedmen: The African Methodist Episcopal Church & Indigenous Americans, 1816–1916* (Urbana: University of Illinois Press, 2021).

37. Early, *Life and Labors of Rev. Jordan*, 37; John J. Dunphy, *From Christmas to Twelfth Night in Southern Illinois* (Charleston, SC: The History Press, 2010), 108–09.

38. Dennis L. Durst, "The Reverend John Berry Meachum (1789–1854) of St. Louis: Prophet and Entrepreneurial Black Educator in Historiographical Perspective," *The North Star* 7, no. 2 (Spring 2004), https://www.princeton.edu/~jweisenf/northstar/volume7/durst.html; R. J. M. Blackett, *The Captive's Quest for Freedom: Fugitive Slaves, the 1850 Fugitive Slave Law, and the Politics of Slavery* (New York: Cambridge University Press, 2018), 143.

39. William Paul Quinn Certificate, Affidavit by M. M. Clarke, February 12, 1851, Pittsburgh, Pennsylvania, DR 14-312, Wayne Co., Indiana.

40. Missouri Secretary of State, Missouri's Early Slave Laws; "Missouri State Law Banning the Teaching of Reading and Writing," 103–04.

41. Welch, *William Paul Quinn*, 6; Benjamin T. Tanner, *An Outline of Our History and Government for African Methodist Churchmen, Ministerial and Lay: In Catechetical Form: Two Parts with Appendix* (Philadelphia: Grant, Faires & Rodgers, 1884).

This work is taken from interviews and oral accounts of people from Chicago's Quinn Chapel, friends who had known Quinn.

42. Tim Fox, ed., *Where We Live: A Guide to St. Louis Communities* (St. Louis: Missouri Historical Society Press, 1995).

43. *Harper's Bazaar*, January 6, 1883; Sundiata Keita Cha-Jua, "Founded by Chance / Sustained by Courage: Black Power, Class, and Dependency in Brooklyn, Illinois, 1830–1915," PhD diss., University of Illinois at Urbana–Champaign, 1993.

44. Handy, *Scraps of African Methodist Episcopal History*, 144.

45. Berry, *Century of Missions of Missions of the African Methodist*, 51.

46. Berry, *Century of Missions of Missions of the African Methodist*, 51.

47. Tanner, *An Outline of Our History*, 165.

48. Tanner, *An Apology for African Methodism*, 146.

49. Joseph A. Boromé et al., "The Vigilant Committee of Philadelphia," *The Pennsylvania Magazine of History and Biography* 92, no. 3 (July 1968): 320–51; Sinha, *The Slave's Clause*.

50. Henry J. Young, *Major Black Religious Leaders: 1755–1940* (Nashville: Parthenon Press, 1977), 72–73. See Charles D. Killian, "Bishop Daniel A. Payne: Black Spokesman for Reform," PhD diss., Indiana University, 1971; Nelson T. Strobert, "Education for Liberation: Daniel Alexander Payne," in *Critical Voices of Black Liberation: Resistance and Representations in the Americas*, eds. Kimberley L. Phillips, Hermine D. Pinson, Lorenzo Thomas, and Hanna Wallinger (New Brunswick, Canada: Transaction Publishers, 2003), 115–25.

51. *Indianapolis Indiana State Sentinel*, March 7, 1843; Worthington G. Snethen, "Terms upon Which Free Colored Persons Are Permitted to Reside in the City of Washington," chap. 64 in *The Black Code of the District of Columbia in Force September 1st, 1848* (New York: A & F Anti-slavery Society, 1948), 39, https://archive.org/details/0823eecd-d5d9-4017-99b9-2d4a01141fbb/page/n3/mode/2up?view=theater; Snethen, "Secret, Private and Religious Meetings of Colored Persons beyond the Hour of Ten at Night, Prohibited," chap. 82 in *The Black Code of the District of Columbia*, 46; Cromwell, "First Negro Churches," 69.

52. Stanley Harrold, *Subversives: The Anti-slavery Community in Washington, D.C., 1828–1865* (Baton Rouge: Louisiana State University, 2003), 41.

53. Arnett, *In Memoriam*, 18; Brown, "William Paul Quinn," 663; "Bishop Paul Quinn, Death of a Distinguished Colored Divine—A Brief Sketch of His Eventful Career," *Richmond Telegram*, February 28, 1873; Berry, *Century of Missions of the African Methodist*, 54.

54. Tanner, *An Outline of Our History*.

55. Tanner, *An Outline of Our History*.

Chapter 7: Pages 89–103

1. "Seventh General Conference," *African Methodist Episcopal Church Magazine*, June 1844, 2; Handy, *Scraps of African Methodist Episcopal History*, 154; Julia A. J. Foote, *A Brand Plucked from the Fire: An Autobiographical Sketch* (New York: George Hughes, 1879), 92.

2. Wayman, *Cyclopedia of African Methodism*, 139.

3. Brown, "William Paul Quinn," 664.

4. Payne, *History of the African Methodist*, 170–71.

5. Welch, *William Paul Quinn*, 12.

6. Tanner, *An Outline of Our History*, 170.

7. Brown, "William Paul Quinn," 664.

8. Arnett, *In Memoriam*, 24.

9. Dodson, *Engendering Church*, 31.

10. Tanner, *An Outline of Our History*, 176.

11. African Methodist Episcopal Church, *General Conference Journal* (Philadelphia: A.M.E. Book Concern, 1900), 297; Tanner, *An Outline of Our History*, 173–75.

12. Bishops of the AME Church, *The Quadrennial Address of the Bishops of the A.M.E. Church to the General Conference* (Wilmington, NC, 1896), 28.

13. Payne, *History of the African Methodist*, 173.

14. Henry Highland Garnet, "The Lives of Methodist Pioneers," *Christian Recorder*, March 13, 1869.

15. Ralph Craig Watkins, "The Institutionalization of the African Methodist Episcopal Church," PhD diss., University of Pittsburgh, 1997, 148.

16. Singleton, *The Romance of African Methodism*, 90.

17. James T. Campbell, *Songs of Zion: The African Methodist Episcopal Church in the United States and South Africa* (New York: Oxford University Press, 1995), 38; Dorothy E. Hoover, *A Layman Looks with Love at Her Church* (Philadelphia: Dorrance, 1970), 44; "Slave Codes 1690–1865," South Carolina Encyclopedia, last updated August 23, 2022, https://www.scencyclopedia.org/sce/entries/slave-codes/. Blacks were first prohibited from learning to read and write in South Carolina in 1739, following the Stono Rebellion.

18. Watkins, "The Institutionalization of the African Methodist," 152; Katherine E. Stovall, "The Development of an Educated Clergy within the African Methodist Episcopal Church," Master's thesis, Trinity International University, 86.

19. Payne, *History of the African Methodist*, 175.

20. C. S. Smith, ed., *History of the African Methodist Episcopal Church: Being a Volume Supplemental to a History of the African Methodist Episcopal Church, by Daniel Alexander Payne, D. D., LL. D., Late One of Its Bishops: Chronicling the Principal Events in the Advance of the African Methodist Episcopal Church from 1856 to 1922* (Philadelphia: Book Concern of the AME Church, 1922), 415.

21. Tanner, *An Outline of Our History*, 134.

22. "Seventh General Conference," *African Methodist Episcopal Church Magazine*, June 1844, 2; Frederick Knight, "The Many Names for Jarena Lee," *The Pennsylvania Magazine of History and Biography* 141, no. 1 (January 2017), 59–68; Payne, *History of the African Methodist*; Lee, *Religious Experience and Journal*; "Journal of Jarena Lee," *African Methodist Episcopal Church Magazine* (Brooklyn), September/October 1841.

23. Foote, *A Brand Plucked*, 93.

24. "Seventh General Conference," *African Methodist Episcopal Church Magazine*, June 1844, 2, 4, 6, 9.

25. Handy, *Scraps of African Methodist Episcopal History*, 166; Payne, *History of the African Methodist*, 179.

26. Wallace D. Best, "Passionately Human. No Less Divine: Racial Ideology and Religious Culture in the Black Churches of Chicago, 1915–1963," PhD diss, Northwestern University, 2000, footnotes 13, 47; Earl Calloway, "Historic South Side Church Celebrates 160 Years of Ministry," *Chicago Defender*, July 2007, 13; Earl Calloway, "Quinn AME Church Presents Its Historic 'June Rose Concert' Sunday," *Chicago Defender*, June 12, 2004, 27.

Mary Jones, wife of Underground Railroad activist, John Jones is consistently named as one of the four. "Death of John Jones," *The Inter Ocean*, May 22, 1879; Jennifer Harbour, "Mary Jane Richardson Jones, Emancipation and Women's Suffrage Activist," National Park Service, Department of the Interior, accessed January 23, 2024, https://www.nps.gov/articles/000/mary-jane-richardson-jones.htm#:~:text=Mary%20.

27. Wright, *Centennial Encyclopaedia of the African Methodist*, 296; Payne, *History of the African Methodist*, 178. Donald George Simpson, "Negroes in Ontario From Early Times to 1870," PhD diss, University of Western Ontario, 1971. Henson's autobiography has been credited among the inspirations for Harriet Beecher Stowe's *Uncle Tom's Cabin*. She directly cites the influence of Josiah Henson's narrative in *A Key to Uncle Tom's Cabin*, 19, 26–27.

28. Payne, *History of the African Methodist*, 179.

29. Ernest L. Gordon, "The Legacy and Contributions of Bishop Morris Brown," *The A.M.E. Church Review* 119, no. 391 (July–September 2003): 27–32; Payne, *Semi-centenary and the Retrospection*, 76, 184.

30. Gordon, "The Legacy and Contributions," 27–32; Payne, *Semi-centenary and the Retrospection*, 76, 184.

31. Hunter Dickinson Farish, *The Circuit Rider Dismounts: A Social History of Southern Methodism 1865–1900* (Richmond, VA: The Deitz Press, 1938), 5–8.

32. Farish, *The Circuit Rider Dismounts*.

33. Bordewich, *Bound for Canaan*, 87. For discussion of the schism, see John Wesley Slider, *Essays on American History: Historical Studies* (Scotts Valley, CA: CreateSpace Independent Publishing Platform, 2013); Cone, *A Black Theology of Liberation*, 36.

34. Farish, *The Circuit Rider Dismounts*, 5.

35. John Lobb, ed. "Editorial Note in Uncle Tom's Story of His Life," in *An Autobiography of the Rev. Josiah Henson (Mrs. Harriet Beecher Stowe's "Uncle Tom"). From 1789 to 1876*, ed. John Lobb (London: Christian Age Office, 1877) 5–11.

36. Payne, *History of the African Methodist*, 183.

37. Tanner, *An Outline of Our History*, 186.

38. Arnett, *Proceedings of the African Methodist Episcopal Church of Cincinnati*.

39. Brown, "William Paul Quinn," 659.

40. Eunice Griffin, *The Rise of American Missions The African Methodist Episcopal Church* (New York: Coker Books, 1960), 22.

41. Alexander Walker Wayman, *My Recollection of African M. E. Ministers, or Forty Years' Experience in the African Methodist Episcopal Church* (Philadelphia: A.M.E. Book Rooms, 1881), 32.

42. "Paul Quinn, Bishop's Address," in Payne, *History of the African Methodist*, 272.

43. Smith, ed., *History of the African Methodist Episcopal Church*, 19.

44. Payne, *History of the African Methodist*, iii

45. Payne, *History of the African Methodist*, iii.

46. Payne, *Recollections of Seventy Years*, 109.

47. Joseph A. Walkes Jr., *Black Square and Compass: 200 Years of Prince Hall Freemasonry* (Richmond, VA: Macoy, 1979), 64.

48. Clarence E. Walker, *A Rock in a Weary Land: The African Methodist Episcopal Church during the Civil War and Reconstruction* (Baton Rouge: Louisiana State University Press, 1982). See Singleton, *The Romance of African Methodism*, 74.

49. Catherine Anne Brekus, "'Let Your Women Keep Silence in the Churches': Female Preaching and Evangelical Religion in America, 1740–1845." PhD diss., Yale University, 1993.

50. Tanner, *An Outline of Our History*, 186.

51. Tanner, *An Outline of Our History*, 186.

52. Tanner, *An Outline of Our History*, 186.

53. Tanner, *An Outline of Our History*, 185.

54. See Julia Foote, *A Brand Plucked*, 216, 348.

55. Wayman, *My Recollection of African M. E. Ministers*, 39.

56. *The Baltimore Sun*, July 11, 1848; *National Era*, July 13, 1848.

57. Payne, *History of the African Methodist*.

58. Daniel A. Payne, "Morris Brown," in *Lives of Methodist Bishops*, ed. Theodore L. Flood and John W. Hamilton (New York: Phillips & Hunt, 1882), 668–74.

59. Wayman, *My Recollection of African M. E. Ministers*, 41.

60. Payne, *Recollections of Seventy Years*, 94–95.

61. Payne, *History of the African Methodist*, 261.

62. Payne, *History of the African Methodist*, 86–88; George A. Singleton, "Sarah Allen: A Portrait of a Heroine Mother of African Methodism," *The African M. E. Church Review*, written 1960, accessed March 20, 2023, https://archive.org/details/sarahallenportra00sing /page/n1/mode/2up?q=Quinn.

Chapter 8: Pages 105–124

1. It would be two years before Ward could succeed in reaching his destination at the close of 1852.

2. Established by Barney Fletcher in the home of Daniel Blue.

3. Enacted on February 12, 1851.

4. "The Fugitive Slave Bill," *The Liberator*, September 27, 1850.

5. Welch, *William Paul Quinn*, 23.

6. Welch, *William Paul Quinn*, 23.

7. "Mass Meeting of Colored Citizens," *North Star*, July 11, 1850.

8. *Chicago Daily Journal*, October 3, 1850; "The Railroad to Freedom," WPA Papers, Vivian Harsh Collection, Chicago Public Library, Box 7, Folder 2; *Milwaukee Daily Free Democrat*, October 12, 1850; Gara, *Liberty Line*, 102; Alfred Theodore Andreas, *The History of Chicago from the Earliest Period to the Present Time in Three Volumes. Volume I—Ending with the Year 1857* (Chicago: A. T. Andraes, 1884), 333.

9. Richard R. Guzman, ed., "John Jones (1816–1879)," in *Black Writing from Chicago: In the World, Not of It?* (Carbondale: Southern Illinois University, 2006), 3; Andreas, *The History of Chicago*, 333; Rufus Blanchard, *Discovery and Conquests of the North-West, with the History of Chicago in Two Volumes, Vol. II* (Chicago: R. Blanchard, 1900), 298; Weston A. Goodspeed and Daniel D. Healy, *History of Cook*

County, Illinois—Being a General Survey of Cook Country History, Including a Condensed History of Chicago and Special Account of Districts Outside the City Limits; from the Earliest Settlement to the Present Time. Volume I* (Chicago: Goodspeed Historical Association, 1909), 408; R. J. M. Blackett, *The Captive's Quest for Freedom: Fugitive Slaves, the 1850 Fugitive Slave Law, and the Politics of Slavery* (New York: Cambridge University Press, 2018), 165; "Affairs in Pittsburg—Fugitive Slaves," *The Liberator*, October 4, 1840.

10. Payne, *History of the African Methodist*, 251.

11. "Constitution of 1851 as Originally Written," Indiana Historical Bureau, accessed March 2, 2024, https://www.in.gov/history/about-indiana-history-and-trivia/explore-indiana-history-by-topic/indiana-documents-leading-to-statehood/constitution-of-1851/https://www.in.

12. William Paul Quinn Certificate, Affidavit by M. M. Clarke in Respect of Reverend William Paul Quinn's Parentage and National Origin, February 12, 1851. Pittsburgh, PA, DR 14-312, deposited at Wayne County, Indiana, Courthouse on October 28, 1851. The affidavit was executed in Pittsburg and is on file in the Wayne County Courthouse in Richmond, Indiana. There are two major errors in the affidavit. First, Reverend Clarke contends that Quinn was forty-six in 1851, suggesting he was born in 1805, which is incorrect. By 1805 it appears Quinn had come to North America and was residing with Quaker leader Elias Hicks. By 1808 Quinn was a member of the Methodist Episcopal Church in Bucks County, Pennsylvania. Second, Reverend Clarke maintains Quinn had been in the United States for at least twenty-four years, presumably meaning since 1827. Most evidence indicates Quinn may have arrived as early as 1800. These errors have cast doubt over Reverend Clarke's assertion that Quinn was born in Honduras. Payne was not the only contemporary of Quinn to write this different assertion about Quinn's birth (see C. S. Smith, ed., *History of the African Methodist Episcopal Church*).

13. Sarah H. Bradford, *Scenes in the Life of Harriet Tubman* (Auburn, NY: W. J. Moses, 1869), 77, https://docsouth.unc.edu/neh/bradford/bradford.html.

14. "Salem Chapel BME Church Harriet Tubman Underground Railroad National Historic Sites," Salem Chapel, National Underground Railroad Network to Freedom Program, National Park Service, published September 27, 2023, https://salemchapelbmechurch.ca/index.html.

15. Payne, *History of the African Methodist*, 252; Dickerson, *The African Methodist Episcopal Church*, 91.

16. "Meeting for the Promotion of Education," *Pennsylvania Freeman*, May 29, 1851.

17. Blackett, *The Captive's Quest for Freedom*.

18. *The Liberator*, April 5, 1850; Laura S. Havilland, *A Woman's Work: A Woman's Life Work: Including Thirty Years' Service on the Underground Railroad and in the War* (Grand Rapids, MI: S. B. Shaw, 1881), 178.

19. Payne, *History of the African Methodist*, 257.

20. Payne, *History of the African Methodist*, 259.

21. Payne, *History of the African Methodist*, 256.
22. Daniel A. Payne, *Sermons and Addresses 1853–1891* (New York: Arno Press, 1972), 271.
23. Payne, *Sermons and Addresses*, 271–73.
24. Payne, *Recollections of Seventy Years*, 109.
25. Lee, *Religious Experience and Journal*.
26. "William Paul Quinn, Bishop's Address" in C. S. Smith, ed., *A History of the African Methodist Episcopal Church*, 24; Martha S. Jones, *All Bound Up Together: The Woman Question in African American Public Culture, 1830–1900* (Chapel Hill: University of North Carolina Press, 2007), 108.
27. "The Ninth General Conference in New York City Refuses to License Women to Preach," in Handy, *Scraps of African Methodist Episcopal History*, 189.
28. Jones, *All Bound Up Together*, 109; Payne, *History of the African Methodist*, 27–73.
29. Julius H. Bailey, *Around the Family Altar: Domesticity in the African Methodist Episcopal Church 1865–1900* (Gainesville: University Press of Florida, 2005), 41.
30. Daniel A. Payne, *A Treatise on Domestic Education* (Cincinnati: Cranston and Stowe, 1885), 109.
31. Handy, *Scraps of African Methodist Episcopal History*; Payne, *History of the African Methodist*, 229.
32. Daniel A. Payne, *Semi-centenary and the Retrospection*; Wayman, *My Recollection of African M. E. Ministers*, 51; Payne, *History of the African Methodist*, 256; Payne, *Sermons and Addresses*, 274.
33. Payne, *Sermons and Addresses*, 274.
34. Handy, *Scraps of African Methodist Episcopal History*, 193.
35. Payne, *Recollections of Seventy Years*, 120.
36. Early, *Life and Labors of Rev. Jordan*, 38–39.
37. Payne, *Recollections of Seventy Years*, 128–29.
38. Early, *Life and Labors of Rev. Jordan*, 38–39; "An Act Respecting Slaves, Free Negroes and Mulattoes, 1847," Missouri Secretary of State, accessed November 19, 2023, https://www.sos.mo.gov/CMSImages/MDH/AnActRespectingSlaves,1847.pdf.

For a good understanding of the pre–Civil War racial climate in St. Louis, see p. 8 of "The African American Experience, a Preservation Plan for St. Louis, Part I: Historic Contexts," Missouri Secretary of State, accessed November 19, 2023, https://www.stlouismo.gov/government/departments/planning/cultural-resources/preservation-plan/Part-I-African-American-Experience.cfm.

39. Smith and Payne, *A Biography of Rev. David Smith*, 99.
40. L. C. Rudolph, *Hoosier Faiths* (Bloomington: Indiana University Press, 1995), 563–64. Wilberforce University is about three and a half miles from Xenia, in Greene County, Ohio.
41. "The Four Horsemen of the Liberation Church: Allen, Quinn, Payne, Turner," *Philadelphia Tribune*, June 12, 1987.

42. Smith, *History of the African Methodist Episcopal Church*, 26.

43. Leslie Alexander, *Fear of a Black Republic: Haiti and the Birth of Black Internationalism in the United States* (Urbana: University of Illinois Press, 2023).

44. Howard Bell, "The Negro Emigration Movement, 1849–1854," *The Phylon Quarterly* 20, no. 2 (2nd Quarter, 1959): 132–42.

45. *The National Era*, October 12, 1854.

46. *The National Era*, October 12, 1854.

47. National Emigration Convention of Colored People Cleveland, *Proceedings of the National Emigration Convention of Colored People, Held at Cleveland, Ohio, Thursday, Friday and Saturday, the 24th, 25th and 26th of August 1854* (Pittsburgh: A. A. Henderson, 1854); William F. Cheek, "John Mercer Langston: Black Protest Leader and Abolitionist," *Civil War History* 16, no. 2 (1970): 101–20.

48. See *Frederick Douglass' Paper* published on the following dates: January 20, 1854; January 27, 1854; February 3, 1854; February 17, 1854; March 25, 1854; April 28, 1854; May 5, 1854; May 12, 1854; September 15, 1854; September 22, 1854; October 6, 1854; November 3, 1854; December 1, 1854; January 19, 1855; and January 26, 1855.

49. *Frederick Douglass' Paper*, April 21, 1854.

50. Christopher Robert Reed, *Black Chicago's First Century, Vol. 1, 1833–1900* (Columbia: University of Missouri Press, 2005); Larry A. McClellan, *Onward to Chicago: Freedom Seekers and the Underground Railroad in Northeastern Illinois* (Carbondale: Southern Illinois University, 2023).

51. *The Provincial Freeman* (Toronto), August 12, 1854.

52. *Frederick Douglass' Paper*, August 25, 1854; *The Provincial Freeman*, August 12, 1854.

53. "The South Again in Peril," *The National Era* (Washington, DC), November 9, 1854, https://chroniclingamerica.loc.gov/lccn/sn84026752/1854-11-09/ed-1/seq-2/.

54. "The South Again in Peril," *The National Era*, November 9, 1854.

55. Handy, *Scraps of African Methodist Episcopal History*, 211. Handy says the lesson came from St. John.

56. Handy, *Scraps of African Methodist Episcopal History*, 212; Payne, *Semi-centenary and the Retrospection*, 77; Wayman, *My Recollection of African M. E. Ministers*, 34.

57. Payne, *History of the African Methodist*, 375.

58. Smith, *History of the African Methodist Episcopal Church*.

59. "Bishop Nazrey and the B.M.E. Church in Canada," *The Christian Recorder*, February 8, 1862.

60. *The Christian Recorder*, October 12, 1861; Payne, *History of the African Methodist*, 374–75.

61. *Evansville Daily Journal*, February 22, 1858; *The Baltimore Sun*, February 22, 1858; "Still Another Savage and Sanguinary Assault—A Colored Bishop Cruelly Beaten and Robbed," *The Cincinnati Daily Enquirer*, February 19, 1858. The amount of $112 is worth just under $4,000 in 2023 dollars, but the current value of $50 in gold is not calculated.

62. "Still Another Savage and Sanguinary Assault—A Colored Bishop Cruelly Beaten and Robbed," *The Cincinnati Daily Enquirer*, February 19, 1858.

63. *Evansville Daily Journal*, February 22, 1858; *The Baltimore Sun*, February 22, 1858; "Still Another Savage and Sanguinary Assault," *The Cincinnati Daily Enquirer*, February 19, 1858.

64. *Evansville Daily Journal*, February 22, 1858; *The Baltimore Sun*, February 22, 1858; "Still Another Savage and Sanguinary Assault," *The Cincinnati Daily Enquirer*, February 19, 1858.

65. *Richmond Telegram*, March 7, 1873; *Richmond Palladium*, August 26, 1871; "Wayne, Indiana, United States, 1854–1856, Deeds, Vol. 19–21, DGS 008070048, Image 274 of 467, September 24th, 1855," FamilySearch, accessed March 3, 2024, https://www.familysearch.org/ark:/61903/3:1:3Q9M-CSNS-Y59B.

Quinn had land dealings with James M. Poe in 1855 and in 1871. Richmond did have a Mayor Poe. See "Henry, Indiana, United States, May 9, 1880, Dec. 1, 1880–May 27, 1881, May 1881–Dec., Deeds, Vol. 34–36, DGS 008071832, Image 805 of 913, March 15th, 1881," FamilySearch, accessed March 3, 2024, https://www.familysearch.org/ark:/61903/3:1:3Q9M-CSNW-X9Z2-5.

Quinn's land dealings with Samuel Bundy were in Henry County.

66. Richard C. Erd and Seymour S. Greenberg, *Minerals of Indiana*, Indiana Department of Conservation, Geological Survey, Bulletin No. 18:34, accessed March 3, 2024, https://core.ac.uk/download/pdf/213806797.pdf.

67. Handy, *Scraps of African Methodist Episcopal History*, 140; "African M. E. Conference," *The Evening Star* (Washington, DC), May 3, 1858; *The Evening Star* (Washington, DC), April 28, 1858.

68. Wayman, *My Recollection of African M. E. Ministers*, 70.

69. Payne, *Recollections of Seventy Years*, 1888. In 1856, Jabez Campbell began publishing *The Christian Recorder*, the long-running, still-existing journal of the AME church. As editor, Campbell ranked among the able editors who battled valiantly in the cause of abolition and equality for free Blacks.

70. "The Dred Scott Decision: Opinion of Chief Justice Taney," Library of Congress, accessed September 25, 2023, https://www.loc.gov/resource/llst.022/?sp=18&st=text.

71. "Is Dred Scott to Be Repudiated?" *The National Era* (Washington, DC), August 11, 1859; "The Dred Scott Decision in England," *The National Era* (Washington, DC), May 14, 1857.

72. Hannah N. Geffert, "John Brown and His Black Allies: An Ignored Alliance," *The Pennsylvania Magazine of History and Biography* 126, no. 4 (October 2002): 591–610.

Chapter 9: Pages 125–140

1. Smith, *History of the African Methodist Episcopal Church*, 47.
2. Early, *Life and Labors of Rev. Jordan*, 53.
3. Arnett, *In Memoriam*; Benjamin Quarles, *Black Abolitionists* (New York: Oxford University Press, 1969), 121. See also W. E. B. Du Bois, *The Religion of the American Negro* (New York: Harper & Row, 1970).

4. H. M. Turner, "Reminiscences of the Proclamation of Emancipation," A. M. E. Review 29, no. 3 (January 1913): 211–13, https://www.thehenrymcnealturnerproject.org/2017/08/reminiscences-of-proclamation-of.html.

5. Turner, "Reminiscences of the Proclamation"; *The Afro-American*, December 26, 1931.

6. Stephen W. Angell, "A Black Minister Befriends the 'Unquestioned Father of Civil Rights': Henry McNeal Turner, Charles Sumner, and the African-American Quest for Freedom," *The Georgia Historical Quarterly* 85, no. 1 (Spring 2001): 27–58.

7. "Meetings of Annual Conferences," *The Christian Recorder*, February 1, 1862.

8. Turner, "Reminiscences of the Proclamation," 212.

9. Cromwell, "First Negro Churches," 69; Andre E. Johnson, *The Forgotten Prophet: Bishop Henry McNeal Turner and the African American Prophetic Tradition* (Lanham, MD: Lexington Books, 2012).

10. Arnett, *In Memoriam*, 25.

11. *The Christian Recorder*, July 19, 1862.

12. Arnett, *In Memoriam*, 25; Letter from Brother Strother, *The Christian Recorder*, August 2, 1862.

13. "From Leavenworth Kansas," *The Christian Recorder*, August 16, 1862.

14. "From Leavenworth Kansas," *The Christian Recorder*, August 16, 1862.

15. "Bishop Quinn's Tour West on a Visit to the Churches," *The Christian Recorder*, August 16, 1862.

16. "Bethel AME Church, Leavenworth, Kansas (1861–1976)" in Gregg, *The African Methodist Episcopal Church, One Hundred Eighty-Eight Years*.

17. Brent M. S. Campney, *This Is Not Dixie: Racist Violence in Kansas 1861–1927* (Urbana: University of Illinois Press, 2015).

18. *Daily Times* (Leavenworth, KS), August 15, 1863, as cited in Vicki Betts, *Daily Times* (Leavenworth, KS), August 15, 1863–March 25, 1864 (posted 2016), https://scholarworks.uttyler.edu/cw_newstitles/48/.

19. *Daily Times*, August 15, 1863, as cited in Vicki Betts, *Daily Times*, August 15, 1863–March 25, 1864 .

20. Campney, *This is Not Dixie*; Tony O'Bryan, "Quindaro, Kansas," Civil War on the Western Border: The Missouri-Kansas Conflict, 1854–1865, The Kansas City Public Library, accessed October 17, 2017, http://www.civilwaronthewesternborder.org/encyclopedia/quindaro-kansas; Randy Mason, "KC Black History: Do You Know the Town That Was a Stop on the Underground Railroad?" *Kansas City Star*, March 9, 2022; *The Leavenworth Times*, March 5, 1862.

21. United States War Records Office, *The War of the Rebellion: A Compilation of the Official Records of the Union and Confederate Armies*, vol. 13, series 1 (Washington, DC: Government Printing Office: 1880–1901), 10, https://babel.hathitrust.org/cgi/pt?id=coo.31924079609578&view=1up&seq=235&q1=Kansas.

22. United States War Records Office, *The War of the Rebellion*, 12–13; Frederick H. Dyer, *A Compendium of the War of the Rebellion, Volume II* (New York: Thomas

Yoseloff, 1959), 725, https://babel.hathitrust.org/cgi/pt?id=uc1.32106010766977&seq=245.

23. Arnett, *In Memoriam*, 22.

24. Richard B. Sheridan, ed., *Freedom's Crucible: The Underground Railroad in Lawrence and Douglas County, Kansas, 1854–1865: A Reader* (Lawrence: University of Kansas, 1998); Timothy Patrick McCarthy and John Stauffer, eds., *Prophets of Protest: Reconsidering the History of American Abolitionism* (New York: The New Press, 2006), 157; "Kansas Battles—Battle of Island Mound; Battle of Cabin Creek; Battle of Honey Springs; Camden Expedition; Battle of Poison Spring," *The Christian Recorder*, August 16, 1862.

25. "Bishop Quinn's Tour West," *The Christian Recorder*, August 16, 1862; "Map of Lawrence, KS," Kansas Historical Society, accessed January 25, 2024, https://www.kshs.org/km/items/view/472457.

26. See United States War Records Office, *The War of the Rebellion*; Gaines M. Foster, "What's Not in a Name: The Naming of the American Civil War," *Journal of the Civil War Era* 8, no. 3 (September 2018): 416–54.

27. HistoryNet Staff, "America's Civil War: Missouri and Kansas," HistoryNet, published June 12, 2006, https://www.historynet.com/americas-civil-war-missouri-and-kansas/. The original 1862 church stood at 900 New York Street, in East Lawrence. The modern 1910 structure is located at the east end of the lot. See Charles Rush et al., Saint Luke African Methodist Episcopal Church, National Register of Historic Places Nomination Form, National Park Service, United States Department of the Interior, accessed June 12, 2023, https://npgallery.nps.gov/NRHP/GetAsset/NRHP/05001240_text.

28. Kim Warren, "Seeking the Promised Land: African American Migrations to Kansas," Civil War on the Western Border, The Missouri-Kansas Conflict 1854–1865, The Kansas City Public Library, accessed October 12, 2017, http://www.civilwaronthewesternborder.org/essay/seeking-promised-land-african-american-migrations-kansas.

29. "At Battle of Island Mound State Historic Site," Missouri State Parks, accessed August 4, 2023, https://mostateparks.com/page/60129/historic-site-history.

30. "The 1st Regiment Kansas Volunteer Infantry (African Descent)," accessed January 20, 2024, https://civilwar-history.fandom.com/wiki/1st_Regiment_Kansas_Volunteer_Infantry_(African_Descent).

31. "Bishop Quinn's Tour West on a Visit to the Churches," *The Christian Recorder*, August 16, 1862. As with so many other phases of Quinn's enigmatic life, further research should clear up elusive details of this phase of his life. Quinn's name and address were listed in the 1857, 1859, 1860, 1863, and 1870 *Richmond City Directories*.

32. "Bishop Quinn's Tour West," *The Christian Recorder*, August 16, 1862.

33. Jenifer, *Centennial Retrospect History*, 31.

34. *The Christian Recorder*, September 13, 1862; Charles Wesley, *Waiting at the Cross*, The African Methodist Episcopal Church Hymn Book (Brooklyn: George Hogarth, 1837) https://hymnary.org/hymnal/AMEC1837?page=1.

35. "Willis R. Revels, Methodist Minister," Encyclopedia of Indianapolis, accessed November 8, 2023, https://indyencyclopedia.org/willis-r-revels/.
36. Smith, *History of the African Methodist Episcopal Church*, 50.
37. "Emancipation Proclamation (1863)," Milestone Documents, National Archives, accessed January 24, 2024, https://www.archives.gov/milestone-documents/emancipation-proclamation#:~:text=%22That%20on%20the%20first%20day,forever%20free%3B%20and%20the%20Executive.
38. Turner, "Reminiscences of the Proclamation," 214.
39. Turner, "Reminiscences of the Proclamation."
40. John T. Hubbell, "Abraham Lincoln and the Recruitment of Black Soldiers," *Journal of the Abraham Lincoln Association* 2, no. 1 (1980): 6–21.
41. Smith, *History of the African Methodist Episcopal Church*, 50.
42. Wayman, *My Recollection of African M. E. Ministers*, 84.
43. "Henry McNeal Turner," *This Far by Faith*, PBS, accessed January 24, 2024, https://www.pbs.org/thisfarbyfaith/people/henry_mcneal_turner.html#:~:text=He%20was%20taken%20under%20wing,became%20the%20first%20black%20chaplain.
44. Angell, "A Black Minister Befriends."
45. "Washington Correspondence," *The Christian Recorder*, May 21, 1864.
46. "Ohio Conference," *The Christian Recorder*, May 2, 1863.
47. "Ohio Conference," *The Christian Recorder*, May 2, 1863.
48. Hallie Quinn Brown, *Encyclopedia of World Biography Supplement*, Volume 30 (Detroit: Gale Cengage Learning, 2010), 84.
49. B. W. Arnett and S. T. Mitchell, *The Wilberforce Alumnal: A Comprehensive Review of the Origin, Development, and Present Status of Wilberforce University* (Xenia, OH: Gazette Office, 1885).
50. Invisible Black. "Pen and Ink Sketches of the African General Conference. As Viewed from the Gallery of Bethel Church," *The Christian Recorder*, May 7, 1864.
51. "We Appeal to You," *The Christian Recorder*, July 30, 1864.
52. Theophilus Gould Steward, *Fifty Years in the Gospel Ministry from 1864 to 1914. Twenty-Seven Years in the Pastorate; Sixteen Years' Active Service as Chaplain in the U.S. Army; Seven Years Professor in Wilberforce University. Two Trips to Europe; A Trip in Mexico* (Philadelphia: A.M.E. Book Concern, 1921); "African M. E. Church General Conference," *Baltimore Sun*, May 4, 1864; Wayman, *My Recollection of African M. E. Ministers*, 96; Andrew Billingsley, *Yearning to Breathe Free: Robert Smalls of South Carolina and His Families* (Columbia: The University of South Carolina Press, 2007); "Robert Smalls: The Steamer 'Planter' and Her Captor," *Harpers Weekly*, June 14, 1862.
53. Gregg, *The African Methodist Episcopal Church, One Hundred Eighty-Eight Years*.
54. Gregg, *The African Methodist Episcopal Church, One Hundred Eighty-Eight Years*.
55. *The Leavenworth Times*, August 15, 1863; Richard B. Sheridan, "The Contrabands in Lawrence and Douglas County," in *Freedom's Crucible: The Underground*

Railroad in Lawrence and Douglas County, Kansas, 1854–1865: A Reader, ed. and comp., Richard B. Sheridan (Lawrence: University of Kansas, 1998), 105–13.

56. Bishop J. C. Embry, "In the Dusty Records of the Missouri Conference," *The Christian Recorder*, October 14, 1897; *African Repository and Colonial Journal*, Vol. 40 (Washington, DC: American Colonization Society, 1864), 350.

57. "Editorial Correspondence. Missouri Annual Conference," *The Christian Recorder*, September 10, 1864.

Chapter 10: Pages 141–156

1. Hallie Quinn Brown, ed. and comp., *Homespun Heroines and Other Women of Distinction* (Xenia, OH: Aldine Publishing, 1926), 148; *The Christian Recorder*, October 7, 1865.

2. Payne, *Recollections of Seventy Years*, 144; United States War Records Office, *The War of the Rebellion*, 816; W. A. Nichols, *Official Arrangements at Washington for the Funeral Solemnities of the Late Abraham Lincoln, President of the United States, Who Died at the Seat of Government, on Saturday, the 15th day of April, 1865* (Washington, DC: War Department, 1865).

3. Arnett, *In Memoriam*, 26.

4. Arnett, *In Memoriam*, 26; Julius H. Bailey, *Race Patriotism: Protest and Print Culture in the A.M.E. Church* (Knoxville: University of Tennessee Press, 2012).

5. Wayman, *My Recollection of African M. E. Ministers*, 115.

6. *The Christian Recorder*, September 23, 1865.

7. Early, *Life and Labors of Rev. Jordan*, 55–56.

8. Eric Foner, *The Second Founding: How the Civil War and Reconstruction Remade the Constitution* (New York: W. W. Norton, 2020), 39.

9. Abraham Lincoln first used the term "ultimate extinction" in a Jonesboro speech on September 15, 1858, during his Illinois Senate campaign; see James Oates, *Freedom National: The Destruction of Slavery in the United States, 1861–1865* (New York: W. W. Norton, 2013); *Galveston Daily News*, May 30, 1987; "Juneteenth Block Party, Hosted by Reedy Chapel A.M.E. Church," Reedy Chapel, accessed October 31, 2023, https://reedychapel.com/.

10. Kate Masur, *An Example for All the Land: Emancipation and the Struggle Over Equality in Washington, D.C.* (Chapel Hill: University of North Carolina Press, 2010); United States House of Representatives, "The First African American to Speak in the House Chamber, February 12, 1865," History, Art, & Archives, accessed October 31, 2023, https://history.house.gov/Historical-Highlights/1851-1900/The-first-African-American-to-speak-in-the-House-Chamber/.

11. Anthony B. Pinn, *Terror and Triumph: The Nature of Black Religion, 20th Anniversary Edition* (Minneapolis: Fortress Press, 2022).

12. Wesley John Gaines, *African Methodism in the South: Or Twenty-Five Years of Freedom* (Atlanta: Franklin, 1890).

13. Smith, *History of the African Methodist Episcopal Church*.

14. Smith, *History of the African Methodist Episcopal Church*.

15. "Bishop William Paul Quinn," *The Christian Recorder*, April 7, 1866.
16. "Bishop William Paul Quinn," *The Christian Recorder*, April 7, 1866.
17. *The Christian Recorder*, May 5, 1866; Wright, *Centennial Encyclopaedia of the African Methodist*.
18. *The Christian Recorder*, July 14, 1866; *Christian Recorder*, May 19, 1866.
19. Welch, *William Paul Quinn*.
20. Welch, *William Paul Quinn*, 31; Quinn may have had two children of his own who died in New York, but that will require further research. See the *Christian Recorder*, November 17, 1866.
21. Welch, *William Paul Quinn*, 31.
22. *Christian Recorder*, November 17, 1866.
23. *The Urbana Union*, April 3, 1867.
24. Turner, "African M. E. General Conference," *Weekly Georgia Telegraph*, May 15, 1868.
25. Turner, "African M. E. General Conference," *Weekly Georgia Telegraph*, May 15, 1868.
26. "Legacy of Thaddeus Stevens," Thaddeus Stevens college of Technology, last updated 2024, https://stevenscollege.edu/legacy-of-thaddeus-stevens/; "Visit of the African General Conference to Hon. Thaddeus Stevens, Addresses on Behalf of the Conference—Reply of Mr. Stevens, *Evening Star* (Washington, DC), May 11, 1868.
27. "Visit of the African General Conference to Hon. Thaddeus Stevens, Addresses on Behalf of the Conference—Reply of Mr. Stevens," *Evening Star* (Washington, DC), May 11, 1868; "Henry McNeal Turner," *This Far by Faith*, PBS.

Turner and fourteen other Black representatives were expelled from the Georgia legislature after White legislators combined in an 82–83 vote: "The rejection made Turner turn his back on the American political process."
28. National Park Service, "Thaddeus Stevens' Home and Law Office," National Underground Railroad Network to Freedom Application, Department of the Interior, submitted 2011; National Park Service, "Thaddeus Stevens' Caledonia Iron Furnace Monument," National Underground Railroad Network to Freedom Application, Department of the Interior, submitted 2008.
29. He was closer to eighty years old.
30. "African M. E. General Conference," News/Opinion, *Macon Weekly Telegraph*, May 15, 1868.
31. African Methodist Episcopal Church, *General Conference Journal* (Philadelphia: A.M.E. Book Concern, 1900), 297; Payne, *History of the African Methodist*.
32. Randolph Paul Runyon, *Delia Webster and the Underground Railroad* (Lexington: University Press of Kentucky, 2015), 33; Mary Ellen Snodgrass, *The Underground Railroad: An Encyclopedia of People, Places, and Operations* (New York: Routledge, 2015), 82; Alicestyne Turley, *The Gospel of Freedom: Black Evangelicals and the Underground Railroad* (Louisville: University Press of Kentucky, 2022).
33. "Landmark Legislation: The Fourteenth Amendment," United States Senate, accessed November 7, 2023, https://www.senate.gov/about/

origins-foundations/senate-and-constitution/14th-amendment.htm#:~:text=Passed %20by%%20of; Foner, *The Second Founding*, 34.

34. "St Mark to Dedicate New Edifice," *Milwaukee Star*, December 21, 1968.

35. *The Leavenworth Weekly Times*, August 25, 1870.

36. *The Leavenworth Weekly Times*, August 25, 1870; Donald G. Nieman, ed., *Black Southerners and the Law 1865–1900* (New York: Garland Publishing, 1994).

37. Julius Eric Thompson, "Hiram R. Revels, 1827–1901: A Biography," PhD diss., Princeton University, 1973.

38. "Allen Chapel African Methodist Episcopal Church," National Register of Historic Places Inventory, Nomination Form, United States Department of the Interior, National Park Service, written July 23, 1975, https://secure.in.gov/apps/dnr/shaard/r/27618/N /Allen_Chapel_AME_Church_Vigo_CO_Nom.pdf; Steve Kash, "Terre Haute's First Black Teacher Made History," *Tribune Star*, March 11, 2007; "Allen Chapel AME Church, Terre Haute," Indiana Crossroads: Hoosier Civil Rights, Ball State University, accessed November 13, 2023, https://digitalresearch.bsu.edu/digitalcivilrightsmuseum/items/show/97; Hiram R. Revels, "Autobiography of Hiram Revels," Carter Godwin Woodson Collection of Negro Papers and Related Documents, Box 11, Manuscript Division, Library of Congress, Washington, DC, 1865.

39. Payne, *History of the African Methodist*; Turley, *The Gospel of Freedom*.

40. Wayman, *Cyclopaedia of African Methodism* (Baltimore: Methodist Episcopal Book Depository, 1882); Elizabeth D. Leonard, *Men of Color to Arms!: Black Soldiers, Indian Wars, and the Quest for Equality* (New York: W. W. Norton, 2010); "Hiram Revels: A Featured Biography," United States Senate, accessed November 11, 2023, https://www.senate.gov/senators/FeaturedBios/Featured_Bio_Revels.htm.

41. *Richmond Palladium*, September 9, 1871.

42. "Proceedings of the Missouri Conference," *Christian Recorder*, September 3, 1870.

43. "Death of Bishop Quinn," *Morning Republican*, March 7, 1873.

44. "Death of Bishop Quinn," *Morning Republican*, March 7, 1873.

45. Handy, *Scraps of African Methodist Episcopal History*, 252; *Nashville Union and American*, May 7, 1872; *Christian Recorder*, June 1, 1872.

46. "Henry Wilson in Indiana," *Indianapolis Journal*, August 5, 1872.

47. Early, *Life and Labors of Rev. Jordan*, 85–87.

48. Early, *Life and Labor of Rev. Jordan s*, 85–87.

49. Wayman, *My Recollection of African M. E. Ministers*.

50. "Religious. Thirty-Third Annual Conference of the African M.E. Church, *The Evansville Journal*, August 23, 1872; "The Evansville Boneyard," Alexander Chapel AME Church, accessed October 13, 2023, http://web.usi.edu/boneyard/church.htm.

51. Wayman, *My Recollection of African M. E. Ministers*, 189.

52. "The Underground Railway—Review of the System by Which Many Thousands of Slaves Were Liberated," *The Freeman* (Indianapolis), February 24, 1900.

53. "Bishop Quinn," *Richmond Weekly Palladium* (Indiana), December 6, 1873.

54. Rev. J. C. Embry, "Communications, Synopsis of the Proceedings of the Missouri Conference," *Christian Recorder*, October 12, 1872.

55. Wayman, *My Recollection of African M. E. Ministers*, 189; "A.M.E. Church. Missouri Annual Conference, Assignments, Etc.," *Weekly Atchison Champion* (Kansas), October 5, 1872; "Bishop Quinn," *Richmond Weekly Palladium* (Indiana), December 6, 1873.

56. *Richmond Palladium* (Indiana), February 22, 1873; *Wilmington Daily Commercial*, February 27, 1873.

57. John R. Hawkins, *The Educator: Organ of the Educational Department of the A.M.E. Church* (Kittrell, NC: Educational Department of the A.M.E. Church, 1898), 9–13, https://iiif.lib.harvard.edu/manifests/view/drs:444725848$12i.

58. B. Denise Hawkins, "Echoes of Faith," *Diverse Issues in Higher Education* 29, no. 12 (July 2012): 14–15.

59. Hawkins, "Echoes of Faith"; "The Black Church: This Is Our Story, This Is Our Song," KERA News, https://www.kera.org/tv/blackchurch/north-texas-timeline/.

60. "The Four Horsemen of Liberation Church: Allen, Quinn, Payne, Turner," *Philadelphia Tribune*, June 12, 1987; Singleton, *The Romance of African Methodism*, 116.

61. Wayman, *My Recollection of African M. E. Ministers*, 190.

62. Arnett, *In Memoriam*, 25.

63. Richard Allen, ed., "A Silent March We Make toward the Silent Grave, Hymn XXXVII," in *A Collection of Spiritual Songs and Hymns* (Philadelphia: John Ormrod, 1801), https://hymnary.org/hymnal/CSSH1801; Arnett, *In Memoriam*, 25.

Chapter 11: Pages 157–163

1. Arnett, *In Memoriam*, 25; "Bishop Quinn," *Richmond Weekly Palladium* (Indiana), December 6, 1873.

2. Arnett, *In Memoriam*, 25.

3. Henry McNeal Turner, *The Genius and Theory of Methodist Polity, or the Machinery of Methodism* (Philadelphia: Publication Department of the AME Church, 1885), 113.

4. Smith, *History of the African Methodist Episcopal Church*, 117.

5. Arnett, *In Memoriam*, 25.

6. Arnett, *In Memoriam*.

7. Arnett, *In Memoriam*.

8. Payne, *Recollections of Seventy Years*, 213.

9. Levi Jennings Coppin, *Unwritten History* (Philadelphia: AME Book Concern, 1919), 340.

10. The *1865 Directory and Soldiers' Registry of Wayne County, Indiana*, and the 1870 census list his birth year as 1813. Both his headstone and the Find a Grave index list 1800 as the year of his birth. A caption accompanying his image in the

Benjamin Arnett, ed., *Proceedings of the Quarto-Centennial Conference of the African M. E. Church, of South Carolina, at Charleston, S.C., May 15, 16 and 17, 1889* records his birth year as about 1795. Most records identify 1788 as his birth year. See https://www.familysearch.org/ark:/61903/3:1:3Q9M-CSZK-72NV?cc=3754697&personaUrl=%2Fark%3A%2F61903%2F1%3A1%3A6ZBY-YL54 and https://www.familysearch.org/search/record/results?q.anyDate.from=1873&q.anyPlace=Richmond%2C%20Wayne%20Township%2C%20Wayne%2C%20Indiana%2C%20United%20States&q.givenName=William%20Paul&q.surname=Quinn.

11. Brown, "William Paul Quinn," 665; "Funeral of Bishop Quinn," *Richmond Weekly Palladium* (Indiana), March 1, 1873; "Death of Bishop Quinn," *Morning Republican*, originally published as *Little Rock Daily Republican*, March 7, 1873; "Bishop Quinn," *Richmond Weekly Palladium* (Indiana), December 6, 1873; *Alexandria Gazette*, February 25, 1873.

12. Arnett, *In Memoriam*.

13. Arnett, *In Memoriam*, vi.

14. "Mortuary Notice," *The Elevator* (San Francisco), March 15, 1873.

15. Arnett, *In Memoriam*; Brown, "William Paul Quinn," 666.

16. Arnett, *In Memoriam*, 43.

17. Arnett, *In Memoriam*, 43.

18. Arnett, *In Memoriam*, 43; Tanner, *An Outline of Our History*, 81–82; Gaye E. Gindy, *The Underground Railroad and Sylvania's Historic Lathrop House* (Bloomington, IN: AuthorHouse, 2008), 22.

19. Payne, *Recollections of Seventy Years*, 213.

20. Peters, *The Underground Railroad in Floyd*, 38, 187.

21. National Park Service, *Underground Railroad, Special Resources Study, Management Concepts/Environmental Assessment* (Washington, DC: United States Department of the Interior, 1995), 43; Smith and Payne, *A Biography of Rev. David Smith*.

22. Tanner, *An Apology for African Methodism*, 145.

23. Brown, "William Paul Quinn," 664; Garland Penn and John W. E. Bowen, *The United Negro: His Problems and His Progress, Containing the Addresses and Proceedings the Negro Young People's Christian and Educational Congress, Held August 6–11, 1902* (Atlanta: D. E. Luther Publishing, 1902), 308.

24. Brown, "William Paul Quinn," 664; *The Annual Cyclopedia: 1866* (New York: D. Appleton, 1867), 492; *The Annual Cyclopedia: 1876* (New York: D. Appleton, 1877), 532.

25. "A.M.E. Delegates Honor Deceased Dignitaries," *Richmond Palladium* (Indiana), September 18, 1920.

26. "St. Mark AME. Church of the Anvil," News/Opinion, *Milwaukee Star*, February 22, 1973.

27. "Death of Bishop Quinn," *Morning Republican*, originally published as *Little Rock Daily Republican*, March 7, 1873.

28. "Quinn Memorial Services," *The Christian Recorder*, May 18, 1876.

29. Arnett, *In Memoriam*, 10.

Afterword: Pages 165–169

1. In 1986 the church celebrated the two hundredth anniversary of the founding of the Free African Society in 1786. In 2016 the AME also celebrated the two hundredth anniversary of the founding of the denomination in 1816.

2. Bishop Vashti Murphy McKenzie, Washington National Cathedral, last updated 2012, https://web.archive.org/web/20120115175533/http://www.nationalcathedral.org/staff/PE-46ER5-V0000I.shtml; The AME Exclusive at the 50th Session of the General Conference with Bishop Anne Henning Byfield, YouTube video, posted 2016, https://www.youtube.com/watch?v=VSKjinXcwBw.

3. H. J. Jackson, "AME Celebrates 200th Year by Honoring Heroes," *The Courier* (Waterloo, Iowa), May 29, 1988, Newspapers.com. https://www.newspapers.com/article/the-courier-4-horseman-29may1988-200th-a/137599275/.

4. Jackson, "AME Celebrates 200th."

5. Newman, *Freedom's Prophet*, 242.

6. Allen and Tapsico, *The Doctrines and Discipline*, 91.

7. Bishop J. M. Brown, "William Paul Quinn." In *Lives of Methodist Bishops*," edited by Theodore L. Flood and John W. Hamilton (New York: Phillips & Hunt, 1882), 661, https://archive.org/details/livesofmethodist0000floo/page/16/mode/2up?q=%22Lives+of+methodist+bishops%22&view=theater.

8. Benjamin Arnett. *In Memoriam: Funeral Services for Rev. William Paul Quinn; Late Senior Bishop of the African M.E. Church, Held at Warren Chapel, Toledo, Ohio, March 9th, 1873* (Toledo: Warren Chapel, 1973), 16. https://babel.hathitrust.org/cgi/pt?id=wu.89097214688&view=1up&seq=24&q1=Kansas.

9. Talbert, *The Sons of Allen*, 31.

Bibliography

"African American Perspectives: Pamphlets from the Daniel A. Murray Collection, 1818–1907." Library of Congress. Accessed December 4, 2022. https://www.loc.gov/resource/lcrbmrp.t0d02/?sp=24&st=image&r=0.162,0.922,0.755,0.371,0.

"African Methodist Episcopal Church Conference, 1840." *A.M.E. Church Magazine* (Brooklyn), September 1, 1841.

African Methodist Episcopal Church. *General Conference Journal*. Philadelphia: A.M.E. Book Concern, 1900.

African Methodist Episcopal Church, South Carolina Conference, Duke University Libraries / Internet Archives.

African Repository and Colonial Journal, Vol. 40. Washington, DC: American Colonization Society, 1864.

Alexander, Leslie M. *African or American? Black Identity and Political Activism in New York City, 1784–1861*. Urbana: University of Illinois Press, 2012.

———. *Fear of a Black Republic: Haiti and the Birth of Black Internationalism in the United States*. Urbana: University of Illinois Press, 2023.

"Allen Chapel African Methodist Episcopal Church," National Register of Historic Places Inventory, Nomination Form, United States Department of the Interior, National Park Service, written July 23, 1975, https://secure.in.gov/apps/dnr/shaard/r/27618/N/Allen_Chapel_AME_Church_Vigo_CO_Nom.pdf.

"Allen Chapel AME Church, Terre Haute." Indiana Crossroads: Hoosier Civil Rights, Ball State University. Accessed November 13, 2023. https://digitalresearch.bsu.edu/digitalcivilrightsmuseum/items/show/97.

Allen, Richard, ed. *A Collection of Spiritual Songs and Hymns*. Philadelphia: John Ormrod, 1801. https://hymnary.org/hymnal/CSSH1801.

———. *The Life, Experience, and Gospel Labours of the Rt. Rev. Richard Allen. To Which is Annexed the Rise and Progress of the African Methodist Episcopal Church in the United States of America. Containing a Narrative of the Yellow Fever in the Year of Our Lord 1793: With an Address to the People of Colour in the United States.* New York: Abingdon Press, 1960. First published 1833 by Martin & Boden.

Allen, Richard, and Jacob Tapsico. *The Doctrines and Discipline of the African Methodist Episcopal Church.* 1st ed. Philadelphia: The African Methodist Connection in the United States, 1817.

Anbinder, Tyler. *Five Points: The 19th-Century New York City Neighborhood That Invented Tap Dance, Stole Elections, and Became the World's Most Notorious Slum.* New York: Plume, 2002.

Andreas, Alfred Theodore. *The History of Chicago from the Earliest Period to the Present Time in Three Volumes. Volume I—Ending with the Year 1857.* Chicago: A. T. Andreas, 1884.

Angell, Stephen W. "Black Methodist Preachers in the South Carolina Upcountry, 1840–1866: Isaac (Counts) Cook, James Porter, and Henry McNeal Turner." In *Ain't Gonna Lay My 'Ligion Down: African American Roots in Southern Religion*, edited by Alonzo Johnson and Paul Jersild, 88–90. Columbia: University of South Carolina Press, 1996.

———. "A Black Minister Befriends the 'Unquestioned Father of Civil Rights': Henry McNeal Turner, Charles Sumner, and the African-American Quest for Freedom." *The Georgia Historical Quarterly* 85, no. 1 (Spring 2001): 27–58.

———. "'The Shadows of the Evening Stretched Out': Richard Robinson and the Shaping of African Methodist Identity, 1823–1862." *Journal of Africana Religions* 3, no. 3 (2015): 227–50.

The Annual Cyclopedia: 1866. New York: D. Appleton, 1867.

The Annual Cyclopedia: 1876. New York: D. Appleton, 1877.

"Annual Report of the African Dorcas Association." In *History of the New York African Free Schools, from Their Establishment in 1787, to the Present Time: Embracing A Period of More than Forty Years Also a Brief Account of the Successful Labors of the New-York Manumission Society: With an Appendix*, edited by Charles C. Andrews, 105. New York: Mahlon Day, 1830. https://digitalcollections.nypl.org/items/510d47e4-123b-a3d9-e040-e00a18064a99/book#page/1/mode/2up.

Appiah, Kwame Anthony, and Henry Louis Gates Jr., eds. *Africana: The Encyclopedia of the African and African American Experience.* New York: Basic Books, 1999.

Aptheker, Herbert. "Militant Abolitionism." *The Journal of Negro History* 26, no. 4 (October 1941): 438–84.

———, ed. *A Documentary History of the Negro People in the United States, Vol. I.* New York: Citadel Press, 1990.

Arnett, Benjamin. *In Memoriam: Funeral Services for Rev. William Paul Quinn; Late Senior Bishop of the African M.E. Church, Held at Warren Chapel, Toledo, Ohio, March 9th, 1873.* Toledo: Warren Chapel, 1873. https://babel.hathitrust.org/cgi/pt?id=wu.89097214688&view=1up&seq=24&q1=Kansas.

———. *Proceedings of the African Methodist Episcopal Church of Cincinnati, Held in Allen Temple, February 8th, 9th, and 10th, 1874, with an Account of the Rise and Progress of the Colored Schools; Also a List of the Charitable and Benevolent Societies of the City*. Cincinnati: H. Watkin, 1874.

———, ed. *The Budget: Containing the Annual Reports of the General Officers of the African M.E. Church of the United States of America*. Xenia, OH: Torchlight Publishing, 1881.

———, ed. *Proceedings of the Quarto-Centennial Conference of the African M. E. Church, of South Carolina, at Charleston, S.C., May 15, 16 and 17, 1889*. https://archive.org/details/proceedingsofqua01afri/page/n3/mode/2up.

Arnett, B. W., and S. T. Mitchell. *The Wilberforce Alumnal: A Comprehensive Review of the Origin, Development, and Present Status of Wilberforce University*. Xenia, OH: Gazette Office, 1885.

Bailey, Julius H. *Around the Family Altar: Domesticity in the African Methodist Episcopal Church 1865–1900*. Gainesville: University of Florida Press, 2005.

———. *Race Patriotism: Protest and Print Culture in the A.M.E. Church*. Knoxville: University of Tennessee Press, 2012.

Baldwin, Lewis V. *"Invisible" Strands in African Methodism: A History of the African Union Methodist Protestant and Union American Methodist Episcopal Churches, 1805–1980*. Metuchen, NJ: Scarecrow Press, 1983.

———. *The Mark of a Man: Peter Spencer and the African Union Methodist Tradition: The Man, the Movement, the Message, and the Legacy*. Lanham, MD: University Press of America, 1987.

Barnes, Gilbert H., and Dwight L. Dumond, eds. *Letters of Theodore Dwight Weld, Angelina Grimké Weld and Sarah Grimké 1822–1844*. New York: D. Appleton-Century Company, 1934.

Bell, Howard. "The Negro Emigration Movement, 1849–1854." *The Phylon Quarterly* 20, no. 2 (2nd Quarter, 1959): 132–42.

Bell, Richard. *Stolen: Five Free Boys Kidnapped into Slavery and Their Astonishing Odyssey Home*. New York: 37INK, 2019.

Bensalem African Methodist Episcopal Church, Historic American Building Survey, Department of the Interior, 1982. Accessed August 6, 2023. https://tile.loc.gov/storageservices/master/pnp /habshaer/pa/pa1700/pa1729/data/pa1729data.pdf.

Bernhard, Karl (Duke of Saxe Weimar-Eisenach). *Travels through North America, Vol. I*. London: Carey, Lea, & Carey, 1826.

Berry, L. L. *Century of Missions of the African Methodist Episcopal Church, 1840–1940*. New York: Gutenberg Printing, 1942.

Best, Wallace D. "Passionately Human. No Less Divine: Racial Ideology and Religious Culture in the Black Churches of Chicago, 1915–1963." PhD diss., Northwestern University, 2000. ProQuest Dissertations & Theses Global (304634498). https://www.proquest.com/dissertations-theses/passionately-human-no-less-divine-racial-ideology/docview/304634498/se-2.

Bethel A.M.E. Church, National Register of Historic Places Inventory—Nomination Form, United States Department of the Interior, National Park Service, September 1975. https://www.iowa-city.org/WebLink/0/edoc/1887924/Bethel%20AME%20form.pdf.

Billingsley, Andrew. *Yearning to Breathe Free: Robert Smalls of South Carolina and His Families*. Columbia: University of South Carolina Press, 2007.

Bishops of the AME Church. *The Quadrennial Address of the Bishops of the A.M.E. Church to the General Conference*. Wilmington, NC, 1896.

Blackett, R. J. M. *The Captive's Quest for Freedom: Fugitive Slaves, the 1850 Fugitive Slave Law, and the Politics of Slavery*. New York: Cambridge University Press, 2018.

Blakinger, Mary. "'It's Going to Get Done' Perseverance, Faith and Dollars Help Minister Restore Black Church." *Preservation News* (Cornell University), February 1, 1987.

Blanchard, Rufus. *Discovery and Conquests of the North-West, with the History of Chicago in Two Volumes, Vol. II*. Chicago: R. Blanchard, 1900.

Blassingame, John. *Frederick Douglass: The Clarion Voice*. Washington, DC: Division of Publications, National Park Service, US Department of the Interior, 1976.

Blockson, Charles. *The Underground Railroad in Pennsylvania*. Jacksonville, NC: Flame International, 1981.

———. "Escape from Slavery. The Underground Railroad." *National Geographic Magazine* 166, no. 1 (July 1984): 3–39.

Bordewich, Fergus. *Bound for Canaan: The Underground Railroad and the War for the Soul of America*. Amistad/HarperCollins, 2005.

Boromé, Joseph A., Jacob C. White, Robert B. Ayres, and J. M. McKim. "The Vigilant Committee of Philadelphia." *The Pennsylvania Magazine of History and Biography* 92, no. 3 (July 1968): 320–51.

Bradford, Sarah. *Scenes in the Life of Harriet Tubman*. Auburn, NY: W. J. Moses, 1869. https://docsouth.unc.edu/neh/bradford/bradford.html.

Bragg, George F. *Richard Allen and Absalom Jones*. Baltimore: Church Advocate Press, 1915.

———. *The First Negro Organization: The Free African Society, Established on April 12th, 1787*. Baltimore: G. F. Bragg, 1924.

Branagan, Thomas. "A Preliminary Essay on the Oppression of the Exiled Sons of Africa. Consisting of Animadversions of the Impolicy and Barbarity of the Deleterious Commerce and Subsequent Slavery of the Human Species: To Which Is Added, A Desultory Letter Written to Napoleon Bonaparte, Anno Domini, 1801." Philadelphia: John W. Scott, 1804. https://www.google.com/books/edition/A_Preliminary_Essay_on_the_Oppression_of/U5QSAAAAIAAJ?hl=en&gbpv=1&bsq=hint%20to%20congress.

Brands, H. W. *Andrew Jackson: A Life and Times*. New York: Doubleday, 2006.

Brekus, Catherine Anne. "'Let Your Women Keep Silence in the Churches': Female Preaching and Evangelical Religion in America, 1740–1845." PhD diss., Yale University, 1993. ProQuest Dissertations & Theses Global (304065506). https://www

.proquest.com/dissertations-theses/let-your-women-keep-silence-churches-female/docview/304065506/se-2.

Brewer, Herbert. "Chesapeake Free Blacks and the Origins of the Liberian State, 1776–1848." PhD diss., University of Maryland, 2017, https://api.drum.lib.umd.edu/server/api/core/bitstreams/6d014c7f-eb02-4f93-8ca5-f8db93c07414/content.

Brown, Bishop John M. "William Paul Quinn." In *Lives of Methodist Bishops,*" edited by Theodore L. Flood and John W. Hamilton, 658–66. New York: Phillips & Hunt, 1882. https://archive.org/details/livesofmethodist0000floo/page/16/mode/2up?q=%22Lives+of+methodist+bishops%22&view=theater.

Brown, Hallie Quinn. *Encyclopedia of World Biography Supplement, Volume 30.* Detroit: Gale Cengage Learning, 2010.

———, ed. and comp. *Homespun Heroines and Other Women of Distinction.* Xenia, OH: Aldine Publishing, 1926.

Campbell, James T. *Songs of Zion: The African Methodist Episcopal Church in the United States and South Africa.* New York: Oxford University Press, 1995.

Campney, Brent M. S. *Hostile Heartland: Racism, Repression, and Resistance in the Midwest.* Urbana–Champaign: University of Illinois Press, 2019.

———. *This Is Not Dixie: Racist Violence in Kansas 1861–1927.* Urbana: University of Illinois Press, 2015.

Carey, Brycchan, and Geoffrey Gilbert Plank, eds. *The Essential Elias Hicks: Quakers and Abolition.* Nerberg, OR: Inner Light Books, 2013.

Carrigan, William Dean. "Between South and West: Race, Violence, and Power in Central Texas, 1836–1916." PhD diss., Emory University, ProQuest Dissertations Publishing, 1999.

Cha-Jua, Sundiata Keita. *America's First Black Town: Brooklyn, Illinois 1830–1915.* Urbana: University of Illinois Press, 2000.

———. "Founded by Chance / Sustained by Courage: Black Power, Class, and Dependency in Brooklyn, Illinois, 1830–1915." PhD diss., University of Illinois at Urbana–Champaign, 1993. ProQuest Dissertations & Theses Global (304039609). https://www.proquest.com/dissertations-theses/founded-chance-sustained-courage-black-power/docview/304039609/se-2.

Cheek, William F., and Aimee Lee Cheek. *John Mercer Langston and the Fight for Black Freedom, 1829–65.* Champaign: University of Illinois Press, 1996.

Cheek, William F. "John Mercer Langston: Black Protest Leader and Abolitionist," *Civil War History* 16, no. 2 (1970): 101–20.

Clark, Elmer T., J. Manning Potts, and Jacob S. Payton. *The Journal and Letters of Francis Asbury in Three Volumes, Vol. II, The Journal 1794–1816.* London: Epworth Press; Nashville: Abingdon Press, 1958, 598. https://media.sabda.org/alkitab-6/wh3-ref/aj-v2.pdf.

Coffin, Levi. *Reminiscences of Levi Coffin, the Reputed President of the Underground Railroad; Being a Brief History of the Labors of a Lifetime in Behalf of the Slave, with the Stories of Numerous Fugitives, Who Gained Their Freedom through His Instrumentality, and Many Other Incidents.* Cincinnati: Western Tract Society, 1879.

Cone, James H. *A Black Theology of Liberation: 50th Anniversary Edition*. Maryknoll: NY: ORBIS, 2020.

Coon, Diane P. "Early African-American Congregations North Central Kentucky." Academia. Published April 12, 2024. https://www.academia.edu/14439494/Early_African_American_Congregations_North_Central_Kentucky.

Cooper, Richard, and Eric R. Jackson. *Cincinnati's Underground Railroad*. Charleston, SC: Arcadia Publishing, 2014.

Coppin, Levi Jennings. *Unwritten History*. Philadelphia: AME Book Concern, 1919.

Corey, Mary F. "Daniel Coker." In *African American Lives*, edited by Henry Louis Gates Jr. and Evelyn Brooks Higginbotham, 177–78. New York: Oxford University Press, 2004.

Cromwell, John W. "First Negro Churches in the District of Columbia." *Journal of Negro History* 7, no. 1 (January 1922): 64–106.

———. *The Early Negro Convention Movement*. Washington, DC: The American Negro Academy, 1904. https://www.gutenberg.org/files/31328/31328-h/31328-h.htm.

———. *The Negro in American History*. Washington, DC: The American Negro Academy, 1914.

Crummell, Alexander. *Eulogium on Henry Highland Garnet, D. D. Presbyterian Minister, Late Minister Resident of the US to the Republic of Liberia, Delivered under the Auspices of the Union Bethel Literary and Historical Association in the Nineteenth Street Baptist Church, Mar 4, 1882*. United States, 1882.

Dickerson-Cousin, Christina. *Black Indians & Freedmen: The African Methodist Episcopal Church & Indigenous Americans, 1816–1916*. Urbana: University of Illinois Press, 2021.

Dickerson, Dennis. *The African Methodist Episcopal Church: A History*. New York: Cambridge University Press, 2020.

Dickson, Moses. *Manual of the International Order of Twelve Knights and Daughters of Tabor*. St. Louis: A. R. Fleming, 1891.

Diggins, Milt. *Stealing Freedom along the Mason Dixon Line*. Baltimore: The Maryland Center for History and Culture, 2016.

Dinius, Marcy J. "Notes." In *The Textual Effects of David Walker's "Appeal": Print-Based Activism against Slavery, Racism, and Discrimination, 1829–1851*, 241–84. Philadelphia: University of Pennsylvania Press, 2022. https://doi.org/10.2307/j.ctv1q6bn79.11.

The Doctrines and Discipline of the African Methodist Episcopal Church. Philadelphia: Richard Allen and Jacob Tapsico, 1817. https://docsouth.unc.edu/church/ame/ame.html.

Dodson, Jualynne E. *Engendering Church: Women, Power, and the AME Church*. Lanham, MD: Rowman & Littlefield, 2002.

———. "Jarena Lee." In *African American Lives*, edited by Henry Louis Gates Jr. and Evelyn Brooks Higginbotham, 522–24. New York: Oxford University Press, 2004.

Dolinar, Brian, ed. *The Negro in Illinois, The WPA Papers*. Champaign: University of Illinois Press, 2015.

Douglass, William. *Annals of the First African Church, in the United States of America, Now Styled the African Episcopal Church of St. Thomas, Philadelphia, in Its Connection with the Early Struggles of the Colored People to Improve Their Conditions, with the Co-operation of Friends, and Other Philanthropists; Partly Derived from the Minutes of a Beneficial Society, Established by Absalom Jones, Richard Allen and Others in 1787, and Partly from the Minutes of the Aforesaid Church*. Philadelphia: King & Baird, 1862.

Drew, Benjamin. *The Refugee: Narratives of Fugitive Slaves in Canada*. Boston: John P. Jewett, 1856.

Du Bois, W. E. B. *The Religion of the American Negro*. New York: Harper & Row, 1970.

Dunphy, John J. *From Christmas to Twelfth Night in Southern Illinois*. Charleston, SC: The History Press, 2010.

Durst, Dennis L. "The Reverend John Berry Meachum (1789–1854) of St. Louis: Prophet and Entrepreneurial Black Educator in Historiographical Perspective." *The North Star* 7, no. 2 (Spring 2004). https://www.princeton.edu/~jweisenf/northstar/volume7/durst.html.

Dyer, Frederick H. *A Compendium of the War of the Rebellion, Volume II*. New York: Thomas Yoseloff, 1959. https://babel.hathitrust.org/cgi/pt?id=uc1.32106010766977&seq=8.

Early, Sarah J. W. *Life and Labors of Rev. Jordan W. Early: One of the Pioneers of African Methodism in the West and South*. Freeport, NY: Books for Libraries Press, 1971. First published 1894 by A.M.E. Church Sunday School Union.

Egerton, Douglas R. *He Shall Go Out Free: The Lives of Denmark Vesey*. Revised edition. Lanham, MD: Rowman & Littlefield, 2004. First published 1999 by Madison House Publishers.

Erd, Richard C., and Seymour S. Greenberg. *Minerals of Indiana*. Indiana Department of Conservation, Geological Survey, Bulletin No. 18:34. Accessed March 3, 2024. https://core.ac.uk/download/pdf/213806797.pdf.

Farish, Hunter Dickinson. *The Circuit Rider Dismounts: A Social History of Southern Methodism 1865–1900*. Richmond, VA: The Deitz Press, 1938.

Finkelman, Paul, ed. *Fugitive Slaves and American Courts: The Pamphlet Literature*. 4 Vols. Clark, NJ: The Lawbook Exchange, 2013. First published 1988 by Garland Publishers.

First Annual Report of the American Anti-Slavery Society with the Speeches Delivered at the Anniversary Meeting, Held in Chatham-Street Chapel, in the City of New York, on the Sixth of May, 1834. New York: Dorr and Butterfield, 1834.

Flood, Theodore. *Lives of Methodist Bishops*. New York: Phillips & Hunt, 1882.

Foner, Eric. *Gateway to Freedom: The Hidden History of the Underground Railroad*. New York: W. W. Norton, 2015.

———. *The Second Founding: How the Civil War and Reconstruction Remade the Constitution*. New York: W. W. Norton, 2020.

Foote, Julia A. J. *A Brand Plucked from the Fire: An Autobiographical Sketch*. New York: George Hughes, 1879.

Foster, Gaines M. "What's Not in a Name: The Naming of the American Civil War." *Journal of the Civil War Era* 8, no. 3 (September 2018): 416–54.

Fox, Tim, ed. *Where We Live: A Guide to St. Louis Communities*. St. Louis: Missouri Historical Society Press, 1995.

Frey, Sylvia, and Thomas E. Carney, "African Methodist Episcopal Church." Oxford African American Studies Center. Published December 1, 2006. https://doi-org.proxy-um.researchport.umd.edu/10.1093/acref/9780195301731.013.44522.

Gaines, Wesley John. *African Methodism in the South: Or Twenty-Five Years of Freedom*. Atlanta: Franklin, 1890.

Gara, Larry. *Liberty Line: The Legend of the Underground Railroad*. Lexington: University Press of Kentucky, 1961.

Garnet, Henry Highland. *Garnet's Memorial Discourse*. Philadelphia: Joseph M. Wilson, 1865.

Garnet, Henry Highland, and James M. Smith. *A Memorial Discourse by Henry Highland Garnet Delivered in the House of Representatives, Washington, DC*. Philadelphia: Joseph M. Wilson, 1865.

Geffert, Hannah N. "John Brown and His Black Allies: An Ignored Alliance." *The Pennsylvania Magazine of History and Biography* 126, no. 4 (October 2002): 591–610.

Getz, Lynne Marie. "Partners in Motion: Gender, Migration, and Reform in Antebellum Ohio and Kansas." *Frontiers: A Journal of Women Studies* 27, no. 2 (2006): 102–35.

Gindy, Gaye E. *The Underground Railroad and Sylvania's Historic Lathrop House*. Bloomington, IN: AuthorHouse, 2008.

Glasco, Laurence A., ed. *The WPA History of the Negro in Pittsburgh*. Pittsburgh: University of Pittsburgh Press, 2004.

Goodspeed, Weston A., and Daniel D. Healy. *History of Cook County, Illinois—Being a General Survey of Cook Country History, Including a Condensed History of Chicago and Special Account of Districts Outside the City Limits; from the Earliest Settlement to the Present Time. Volume I*. Chicago: Goodspeed Historical Association, 1909.

Gordon, Ernest L. "The Legacy and Contributions of Bishop Morris Brown." *The A.M.E. Church Review* 119, no. 391 (July–September 2003): 27–32.

Green, Augustus R. *The Life of the Rev. Dandridge F. Davis, of the African M.E. Church, with a Brief Account of His Conversion and Ministerial Labors, from August 1834, till March 1847. Also, a Brief Sketch of the Life of the Rev. David Conyou, of the A.M.E.C. and His Ministerial Labors. To Which Is Annexed the Funeral Discourse Delivered at the Ohio Conference, in Zanesville, on the Decease of the Rev. D. F. Davis, by the Author*. Pittsburgh: Ohio Conference, 1850. https://docsouth.unc.edu/neh/greena/greena.html.

Gregg, Howard. *The African Methodist Episcopal Church, One Hundred Eighty-Eight Years of Progress, Our Beginning*. https://centerforurbanstudies.ap.buffalo.edu

/wp-content/uploads/sites/16/2020/02/BAME_1976-01-01_Books_The_African_Methodist_Episcopal_Church_Our_Beginning.pdf.

Gregg, Howard D. *History of the African Methodist Episcopal Church (The Black Church in Action)*. Nashville: The African Methodist Episcopal Church, 1980.

Griffin, Eunice. *The Rise of American Missions, The African Methodist Episcopal Church*. New York: Coker Books, 1960.

Griffler, Kenneth. *Front Line of Freedom: African Americans and the Forging of the Underground Railroad in the Ohio Valley*. Lexington: University Press of Kentucky, 2004.

Gross, Bella. "Freedom's Journal and the Rights of All." *The Journal of Negro History* 17, no. 3 (July 1932): 241–86. https://doi.org/10.2307/2714274.

———. "Life and Times of Theodore S. Wright, 1797–1847." *Negro History Bulletin* 3, no. 9 (June 1940): 133–38.

Guzman, Richard R., ed. "John Jones (1816–1879)." In *Black Writing from Chicago: In the World, Not of It?*, edited by Richard Guzman, 3–8. Carbondale: Southern Illinois University, 2006.

Handy, James A. *Scraps of African Methodist Episcopal History*. Philadelphia: AME Book Concern, 1902. https://docsouth.unc.edu/church/handy/handy.html#p189.

Harbour, Jennifer. "Mary Jane Richardson Jones, Emancipation and Women's Suffrage Activist." National Park Service, Department of the Interior. Accessed January 23, 2024. https://www.nps.gov/articles/000/mary-jane-richardson-jones.htm#:~:text=Mary%20.

Harris, Leslie M. *In the Shadow of Slavery: African Americans in New York City, 1626–1863*. Chicago: University of Chicago Press, 2003.

Harrold, Stanley. *Subversives: The Anti-slavery Community in Washington, D.C., 1828–1865*. Baton Rouge: Louisiana State University, 2003.

Harrold, Stanley, and Randall M. Miller, eds. *The Denmark Vesey Affair: A Documentary History*, edited by Douglas R. Egerton and Robert L. Paquette. Gainesville: University Press of Florida, 2017.

Haviland, Laura S. *A Woman's Life Work: Including Thirty Years' Service on the Underground Railroad and in the War*. Grand Rapids, MI: S. B. Shaw, 1881.

Hawkins, B. Denise. "Echoes of Faith." *Diverse Issues in Higher Education* 29, no. 12 (July 2012): 14–15.

Hawkins, John R. *The Educator: Organ of the Educational Department of the A.M.E. Church*. Kittrell, NC: Educational Department of the A.M.E. Church, 1898. https://iiif.lib.harvard.edu/manifests/view/drs:444725848$1i.

Heintze, Michael R. *Private Black Colleges in Texas 1865–1954*. College Station: Texas A&M University Press, 1985.

Hicks, Elias. *Journal of the Life and Religious Labours of Elias Hicks*. New York: Elias Hopper, 1832.

Hinks, Peter. *To Awaken My Afflicted Brethren: David Walker and the Problem of Antebellum Slave Resistance*. University Park: Pennsylvania State University Press, 1997.

"Hiram Revels: A Featured Biography." United States Senate. Accessed November 11, 2023. https://www.senate.gov/senators/FeaturedBios/Featured_Bio_Revels.htm.

Hodges, Graham Russell, ed. *Black Itinerants of the Gospel: The Narratives of John Jea and George White*. Madison: Madison House Publishers, 1993.

Hood, J. W. *Sketch of the Early History of the African Methodist Episcopal Zion Church with Jubilee Souvenir and Appendix*. Charlotte, NC: A.M.E. Zion Publishing House, 1914. http://docsouth.unc.edu/church/hood/hood.html.

Hoover, Dorothy E. *A Layman Looks with Love at Her Church*. Philadelphia: Dorrance, 1970.

Hubbell, John T. "Abraham Lincoln and the Recruitment of Black Soldiers." *Journal of the Abraham Lincoln Association* 2, no. 1 (1980): 6–21. https://quod.lib.umich.edu/j/jala/2629860.0002.103/--abraham-lincoln-and-the-recruitment-of-black-soldiers?rgn=main;view=fulltext#:~:text=.

Hudson, J. Blaine. *Encyclopedia of the Underground Railroad*. Jefferson, NC: McFarland, 2006.

———. "'Upon This Rock'—The Free African American Community of Antebellum Louisville, Kentucky." *The Register of the Kentucky Historical Society* 109, no. 3/4 (2011): 295–326, http://www.jstor.org.proxy-um.researchport.umd.edu/stable/23388023.

Irma and Paul Milstein Division of United States History, Local History and Genealogy, The New York Public Library. *New York City Directory*. Published 1831. New York Public Library Digital Collections. https://digitalcollections.nypl.org/items/d3f992a0-2b8c-0136-1c46-532b55be5aa0.

Jenifer, J. T. *Centennial Retrospect History of the African Methodist Episcopal Church*. Philadelphia: Sunday School Union Press, 1916.

J. H. Colton & Co. "City of Louisville." Ball State University Digital Media Repository, created 1855, https://dmr.bsu.edu/digital/collection/AmrcnCtyHis/id/31/rec/3.

Johnson, Andre E. *The Forgotten Prophet: Bishop Henry McNeal Turner and the African American Prophetic Tradition*. Lanham, MD: Lexington Books, 2012.

Johnson, Leland R., and Charles E. Parrish. *Triumph of the Falls: The Louisville and Portland Canal*. Louisville, KY: Louisville District U.S. Army Corps of Engineers, 2007. https://www.lrl.usace.army.mil/Portals/64/docs/Ops/Navigation/TriumphAtTheFalls.pdf.

Johnson, Melissa A. "The Making of Race and Place in Nineteenth-Century British Honduras," *Environmental History* 8, no. 4 (October 2003): 598–617.

Johnson, Michael P., and James L. Roark. *Black Masters: A Free Family of Color in the Old South*. New York: W. W. Norton, 1984.

Jones, Martha S. *All Bound Up Together: The Woman Question in African American Public Culture, 1830–1900*. Chapel Hill: University of North Carolina Press, 2007.

Jordan, Amos M., comp. *Compiled History of the African Wesleyan Methodist Episcopal Church, Inc.* Brooklyn: Board of Trustees, 1973.

"Journal of Jarena Lee." *African Methodist Episcopal Church Magazine* (Brooklyn), September/October, 1841.

Kerstetter, Earl E. "The Glorious Camp Meetings of the Nineteenth Century." Lycoming College. Accessed March 11, 2024. https://umarch.lycoming.edu/chronicles/1993/4.%20KERSTET.pdf.

Killian, Charles D. "Bishop Daniel A. Payne: Black Spokesman for Reform." PhD diss., Indiana University, 1971. ProQuest Dissertations & Theses Global (302471619). https://www.proquest.com/dissertations-theses/bishop-daniel-payne-black-spokesman-reform/docview/302471619/se-2.

Knight, Frederick. "The Many Names for Jarena Lee." *The Pennsylvania Magazine of History and Biography* 141, no. 1 (January 2017): 59–68.

Lamb, George N, ed. *The Mahogany Book*, Chicago: Mahogany Association, 1947.

Lampl, Elizabeth Jo, and Clare Lise Kelly. "A Harvest in the Open for Saving Souls": The Camp Meetings of Montgomery County. Historic context report. Montgomery County Planning Department, Historic Preservation Section. Maryland Historical Trust, 2004. https://montgomeryplanning.org/historic/resources/documents/CampMeetingReport.pdf.

Lampton, Edward W. *Digest of the Rulings and Decisions of the Bishops of the African Methodist Episcopal Church from 1847 to 1907*. Washington, DC: The Record Publishing Company, 1907.

LaRoche, Cheryl Janifer. *Free Black Communities and the Underground Railroad: The Geography of Resistance*. Urbana: University of Illinois Press, 2014.

Latrobe, Benjamin Henry. *Journal of Benjamin Latrobe, August 23, 1806–August 8, 1809*. Latrobe Papers, Manuscript Department, Maryland Center for History and Culture, Baltimore. http://www.loc.gov/exhibits/religion/rel07.html.

Lee, Jarena. *Religious Experience and Journal of Mrs. Jarena Lee Giving an Account of Her Call to Preach the Gospel*. Project Gutenberg. Released December 16, 2021. https://www.gutenberg.org/files/66953/66953-h/66953-h.htm.

"Legislative Acts / Legal Proceedings." *Emancipator and Republican* no. 11 (July 9, 1845): 44.

Leonard, Elizabeth D. *Men of Color to Arms!: Black Soldiers, Indian Wars, and the Quest for Equality*. New York: W. W. Norton, 2010.

Lesick, Lawrence Thomas. *The Lane Rebels: Evangelicalism and Antislavery in Antebellum America*. Metuchen, NJ: The Scarecrow Press, 1980.

Levine, Robert S., ed. *Martin Delany: A Documentary Reader*. Chapel Hill: The University of North Carolina Press, 2003.

Lionel Pincus and Princess Firyal Map Division, The New York Public Library. "A New Map of the City of New York: Comprising All the Late Improvements, Compiled and Corrected from Authentic Documents, Designed to Accompany the Description of New York." New York Public Library Digital Collections. Accessed July 10, 2024. https://digitalcollections.nypl.org/items/510d47da-f075-a3d9-e040-e00a18064a99.

Lobb, John, ed. "Editorial Note in Uncle Tom's Story of His Life." In *An Autobiography of the Rev. Josiah Henson (Mrs. Harriet Beecher Stowe's "Uncle Tom"). From 1789 to 1876*, edited by John Lobb, 5–11. London: Christian Age Office, 1877.

Masur, Kate. *An Example for All the Land: Emancipation and the Struggle Over Equality in Washington, D.C.* Chapel Hill: University of North Carolina Press, 2010.

McCarthy, Timothy Patrick, and John Stauffer, eds., *Prophets of Protest: Reconsidering the History of American Abolitionism*. New York: The New Press, 2006.

McClellan, Larry A. *Onward to Chicago: Freedom Seekers and the Underground Railroad in Northeastern Illinois*. Carbondale: Southern Illinois University, 2023.

McDougall, Marion Gleason. *Fugitive Slaves (1619–1865)*. New York: Bergman Publishers, 1969. First published 1891 by Ginn.

McDougle, Ivan E. "The Legal Status of Slavery." *The Journal of Negro History* 3, no. 3 (July 1918): 211–328.

Melton, J. Gordon. *A Will to Choose: The Origins of African American Methodism*. Lanham, MD: Rowman & Littlefield, 2007.

Memorial of Elizabeth H. Walker, *Memorials Concerning Deceased Friends, Published by Direction of the Yearly Meeting of New York*. New York: James Egbert, 1859.

Missouri Secretary of State. "Missouri's Early Slave Laws: A History in Documents." Missouri Digital Heritage. Accessed February 13, 2023. https://www.sos.mo.gov/archives/education/aahi/earlyslavelaws/slavelaws.asp.

"Missouri State Law Banning the Teaching of Reading and Writing to Black Missourians," Accessed July 11, 2024, https://www.sos.mo.gov/CMSImages/MDH/AnActRespectingSlaves,1847.pdf.

Morales, R. Isabela. *Happy Dreams of Liberty: An American Family in Slavery and Freedom*. New York: Oxford University Press, 2022. https://doi-org.proxy-um.researchport.umd.edu/10.1093/oso/9780197531792.001.0001.

Morgan, Joseph H. *Morgan's History of the New Jersey Conference of the A.M.E. Church, from 1872 to 1887: And of the Several Churches, as Far as Possible, from Date of Organization, with Biographical Sketches of Members of the Conference*. Camden, NJ: S. Chew, 1887.

Nash, Gary B. "Reverberations of Haiti in the American North: Black Saint Dominguans in Philadelphia." *Pennsylvania History: A Journal of Mid-Atlantic Studies* 65 (1998): 44–73. https://www.jstor.org/stable/27774161.

National Emigration Convention of Colored People Cleveland. *Proceedings of the National Emigration Convention of Colored People, Held at Cleveland, Ohio, Thursday, Friday and Saturday, the 24th, 25th and 26th of August 1854*. Pittsburgh: A. A. Henderson, 1854.

National Park Service. "Thaddeus Stevens' Caledonia Iron Furnace Monument." National Underground Railroad Network to Freedom Application, Department of the Interior. Submitted 2008. http://undergroundrroriginspa.org/wp-content/uploads/2017/03/Caledonia-Stevens-Iron-Works-NTF-2008.pdf.

National Park Service. "Thaddeus Stevens' Home and Law Office." National Underground Railroad Network to Freedom Application, Department of the Interior. Submitted 2011. http://undergroundrroriginspa.org/wp-content/uploads/2016/10/StevensHouseOfficeNPSFinal1-2011.pdf

National Park Service. *The Underground Railroad: Essays on the Network to Freedom.* Washington, DC: United States Department of the Interior, 2024.

National Park Service. *Underground Railroad, Special Resources Study, Management Concepts/Environmental Assessment.* Washington, DC: United States Department of the Interior, 1995.

Newell, Maurice. "This Is Bethel—Reading. Come Ride the Underground Railroad, Where Culture and History Come to Life." Central Pennsylvania African American Museum, Reading, PA. Museum Exhibition.

Newman, Richard S. *Freedom's Prophet: Bishop Richard Allen, the AME Church, and the Black Founding Fathers.* New York: New York University Press, 2008.

Newsome, Effie Lee. "Early Figures in Haitian Methodism." *Phylon* 5, no. 1 (Quarter 1, 1944): 51–61.

New York Probate Records, 1659–1999, for Margaret Quinn, box 8-28694, vol. 0027-0028, 1830–1836. Accessed January 30, 2024. https://www.ancestryheritagequest.com/imageviewer/collections/8800/images/005522086_00945?treeid=&personid=&queryId=a2f72889-e9b0-4ce1-827b-58d97884ab1a&usePUB=true&_phsrc=Ujy2&_phstart=successSource&pId=721963.

Nichols, W. A. *Official Arrangements at Washington for the Funeral Solemnities of the Late Abraham Lincoln, President of the United States, Who Died at the Seat of Government, on Saturday, the 15th day of April, 1865.* Washington, DC: War Department, 1865. https://natedsanders.com/ItemImages/000008/38381_lg.jpeg; https://natedsanders.com/ItemImages/000008/8386b_lg.jpeg.

Nieman, Donald G., ed., *Black Southerners and the Law 1865–1900.* New York: Garland Publishing, 1994.

Oates, James. *Freedom National: The Destruction of Slavery in the United States, 1861–1865.* New York: W. W. Norton, 2013.

O'Bryan, Tony. "Quindaro, Kansas." Civil War on the Western Border: The Missouri-Kansas Conflict, 1854–1865, The Kansas City Public Library. Accessed October 17, 2017. http://www.civilwaronthewesternborder.org/encyclopedia/quindaro-kansas.

O'Neall, John Belton. *The Negro Law of South Carolina Collected and Digested.* London: Forgotten Books, 2016. http://genealogytrails.com/scar/negro_law2.htm.

Ohio Anti-slavery Society. *Report on the Condition of the People of Color in the State of Ohio, with Interesting Anecdotes.* Boston: Isaac Knapp, 1839. https://www.loc.gov/resource/gdclccn.12002909/?sp=5&st=image.

Owens, A. Nevell. *Formation of the African Methodist Episcopal Church in the Nineteenth Century: Rhetoric of Identification.* New York: Palgrave Macmillan, 2014.

Palmer, Ronald D. "AME Bishop William Paul Quinn—Notes toward a Biographical Chronology of an American Original." *The A.M.E. Church Review* 120, no. 395: (July–September 2004): 40–61.

Papson, Don, and Tom Calarco. *Secret Lives of the Underground Railroad in New York City: Sydney Howard Gay, Louis Napoleon and the "Record of Fugitives."* Jefferson, NC: McFarland, 2015.

Paquette, Robert L., and Manisha Sinha. "Revisiting Denmark Vesey's Church." In *Fugitive Movements: Commemorating the Denmark Vesey Affair and Black Radical Antislavery in the Atlantic World,* edited by James O'Neil Spady, 179–96. Columbia: University of South Carolina Press, 2022. https://doi.org/10.2307/j.ctv1n35799.15.

Payne, Daniel A. *A Treatise on Domestic Education.* Cincinnati: Cranston and Stowe, 1885.

———. *History of the African Methodist Episcopal Church.* Edited by C. S. Smith. Nashville: Publishing House of the A.M.E. Sunday School Union, 1891. https://docsouth.unc.edu/church/payne/payne.html.

———. "Morris Brown." In *Lives of Methodist Bishops,* edited by Theodore L. Flood and John W. Hamilton, 668–74. New York: Phillips & Hunt, 1882.

———. *Recollections of Seventy Years.* New York: Arno Press, 1969. First published 1888 by A.M.E. Sunday School Union.

———. *Semi-centenary and the Retrospection of the African Methodist Episcopal Church in America.* Baltimore: Sherwood, 1866. https://babel.hathitrust.org/cgi/pt?id=emu.010002588604&seq=1.

———. *Sermons and Addresses 1853–1891.* New York: Arno Press, 1972.

Penn, Garland, and John W. E. Bowen. *The United Negro: His Problems and His Progress, Containing the Addresses and Proceedings the Negro Young People's Christian and Educational Congress, Held August 6–11, 1902.* Atlanta: D. E. Luther Publishing, 1902.

Peters, Pamela R. *The Underground Railroad in Floyd County, Indiana.* Jefferson, NC: McFarland, 2001.

Phillips, Christopher. *Freedom's Port: The African American Community of Baltimore, 1790–1860.* Urbana: University of Illinois Press, 1997.

Pinn, Anthony B. *Terror and Triumph: The Nature of Black Religion,* 20th Anniversary Edition. Minneapolis: Fortress Press, 2022.

Porter, Dorothy B. "The Organized Educational Activities of Negro Literary Societies, 1828–1846." *The Journal of Negro Education* 5, no. 4 (1936): 555–78. https://doi.org/10.2307/2292029.

———, ed. "Minutes of the Four Last Annual Conferences of the African Methodist Episcopal Church Held at Pittsburg, Pa., Washington, D.C., Philadelphia, and New York 1833-4." In *Early Negro Writing, 1760–1837,* edited by Dorothy Porter, 189–99. Baltimore: Black Classic Press, 1995. First published 1834 by Joseph M. Corr.

———, ed. *Early Negro Writing 1760–1837*. Baltimore: The Black Classic Press, 1995.
Power, J. C., ed. *Directory and Soldier's Register of Wayne County, Indiana*. Richmond, IN: W. H. Lanthurn, 1865.
Quarles, Benjamin. *Black Abolitionists*. New York: Oxford University Press, 1969.
"Quinn Chapel African Methodist Episcopal Church." *Underground Ohio* (blog). https://undergroundoh.com/churches/.
Quinn, Willliam Paul. "The Origin, Horrors and Results of Slavery, Faithfully and Minutely Described in a Series of Facts, and Its Advocates Pathetically Addressed." In *Early Negro Writing, 1760–1837*, edited by Dorothy Porter, 614–36. Baltimore: Black Classic Press, 1995.
"The Railroad to Freedom," WPA Papers, Vivian Harsh Collection, Chicago Public Library, Box 7, Folder 2.
Reed, Christopher Robert. *Black Chicago's First Century, Vol. 1, 1833–1900*. Columbia: University of Missouri Press, 2005.
Revels, Hiram R. "Autobiography of Hiram Revels." Carter Godwin Woodson Collection of Negro Papers and Related Documents. Box 11, Manuscript Division, Library of Congress, Washington, DC, 1865.
Ripley, C. Peter, ed. *Black Abolitionist Papers 3*. Chapel Hill: University of North Carolina Press, 2015.
Rose, William Ganson. *Cleveland: The Making of a City*. Kent, OH: Kent State University Press, 1990.
Rosen, Marty. "Gateway to Freedom." *Louisville Magazine* 63, no. 10 (October 2012): 42–45.
Rudolph, L. C. *Hoosier Faiths*. Bloomington: Indiana University Press, 1995.
Runyon, Randolph Paul. *Delia Webster and the Underground Railroad*. Lexington: University Press of Kentucky, 2015.
Rush, Charles, William Robinson, Abraham Cole, and James Simmons. Saint Luke African Methodist Episcopal Church, National Register of Historic Places Nomination Form, National Park Service, United States Department of the Interior. Accessed June 12, 2023. https://npgallery.nps.gov/NRHP/GetAsset/NRHP/05001240_text.
Rush, Christopher. *A Short Account of the Rise and Progress of the African M. E. Church in America, Written by Christopher Rush, Superintendent of the Connexion, with the Aid of George Collins. Also, a Concise View of Church Order or Government, from Scripture, and from Some of the Best Authors on the Subject of Church Government, Relative to Episcopacy*. New York: published by the author, 1843.
Schipper, Jeremy. "On Such Texts Comment Is Unnecessary." *Journal of the American Academy of Religion* 85, no. 4 (December 2017): 1032–49. https://www.jstor.org/stable/10.2307/48556266.
Schor, Joel. *Henry Highland Garnet: A Voice of Black Radicalism in the Nineteenth Century*. Westport, CT: Greenwood Press, 1944.

Sernett, Milton C. *Black Religion and American Evangelicalism: White Protestants, Plantation Missions, and the Flowering of Negro Christianity, 1787–1865*. Metuchen, NJ: Scarecrow Press, 1975.

"Seventh General Conference." *African Methodist Episcopal Church Magazine*, June 1844.

Sheridan, Richard B., ed. *Freedom's Crucible: The Underground Railroad in Lawrence and Douglas County, Kansas, 1854–1865: A Reader*. Lawrence: University of Kansas, 1998.

———. "From Slavery in Missouri to Freedom in Kansas: The Influx of Black Fugitives and Contrabands into Kansas, 1854–1865." *Kansas History* 12, no. 1 (Spring 1989): 28–47.

Shreve, Dorothy Shadd. *The AfriCanadian Church: A Stabilizer*. Jordan Station, Ontario: Paideia Press, 1983.

Siebert, Wilbur H. *The Underground Railroad from Slavery to Freedom*. New York: The Macmillan Company, 1898.

———. "Underground Routes of Indiana by Prof. W. H. Siebert." Ohio History Center, Wilbur H. Siebert Underground Railroad Collection, ca. 1888. https://ohiomemory.org/digital/collection/siebert/id/9123.

Simmons, William J. *Men of Mark: Eminent, Progressive and Rising*. Cleveland: Geo. M. Rewell, 1887.

Simpson, Donald George. "Negroes in Ontario from Early Times to 1870." PhD diss., University of Western Ontario, 1971. https://www.proquest.com/dissertations-theses/negroes-ontario-early-times-1870/docview/1445211241/se-2.

Singleton, George A. *The Romance of African Methodism: A Study of the African Methodist Episcopal Church*. New York: Exposition Press, 1952.

———. "Sarah Allen: A Portrait of a Heroine Mother of African Methodism." *The African M. E. Church Review*. Written 1960. Accessed March 20, 2023. https://archive.org/details/sarahallenportra00sing /page/n1/mode/2up?q=Quinn Internet archives.

Sinha, Manisha. *The Slave's Cause: A History of Abolition*. New Haven: Yale University Press, 2016.

Slider, John Wesley. *Essays on American History: Historical Studies*. Scotts Valley, CA: CreateSpace Independent Publishing Platform, 2013.

Smith, C. S., ed. *History of the African Methodist Episcopal Church: Being a Volume Supplemental to a History of the African Methodist Episcopal Church, by Daniel Alexander Payne, D. D., LL. D., Late One of Its Bishops: Chronicling the Principal Events in the Advance of the African Methodist Episcopal Church from 1856 to 1922*. Philadelphia: Book Concern of the AME Church, 1922.

———. *History of the African Methodist Episcopal Church*. Nashville: Publishing House of the AME Sunday School Union, 1891.

Smith, David, and Daniel Payne. *A Biography of Rev. David Smith of the A.M.E. Church; Being a Complete History, Embracing over Sixty Years' Labor in the*

Advancement of the Redeemer's Kingdom on Earth. Including "The History of the Origin and Development of Wilberforce University." Xenia, OH, 1881.

Smith, William. *The Works of William Smith, D.D. Late Provost of The College and Academy of Philadelphia*, Vol. II. Philadelphia: Hugh Maxwell and William Fry, 1803.

Snethen, Worthington G. *The Black Code of the District of Columbia in Force September 1st, 1848*. New York: A&F Anti-slavery Society, 1948. https://archive.org/details/0823eecd-d5d9-4017-99b9-2d4a01141fbb/page/n3/mode/2up?view=theater.

Snodgrass, Mary Ellen. *The Underground Railroad: An Encyclopedia of People, Places, and Operations*. New York: Routledge, 2015.

Spady, James O'Neil. *Fugitive Movements: Commemorating the Denmark Vesey Affair and Black Radical Antislavery in the Atlantic World*. Columbia: University of South Carolina Press, 2022.

Stevens, Abel. *History of the Methodist Episcopal Church in the United States of America*. Vol. 4, bk. 5. Ann Arbor: University of Michigan Library, 1866. https://archive.org/details/historyofmethodi04instev/mode/2up.

Steward, Theophilus Gould. *Fifty Years in the Gospel Ministry from 1864 to 1914. Twenty-Seven Years in the Pastorate; Sixteen Years' Active Service as Chaplain in the U.S. Army; Seven Years Professor in Wilberforce University. Two Trips to Europe; A Trip in Mexico*. Philadelphia: A.M.E. Book Concern, 1921.

Still, William. *The Underground Rail Road: A Record of Facts, Authentic Narratives, Letters, &c., Narrating the Hardships, Hair-breadth Escapes, and Death Struggles of the Slaves in Their Efforts for Freedom, as Related by Themselves and Others or Witnessed by the Author: Together with Sketches of Some of the Largest Stockholders and Most Liberal Aiders and Advisers of the Road*. Philadelphia: Porter & Coates, 1872. https://www.loc.gov/item/31024984/.

Strobert, Nelson T. "Education for Liberation: Daniel Alexander Payne." In *Critical Voices of Black Liberation: Resistance and Representations in the Americas*, edited by Kimberley L. Phillips, Hermine D. Pinson, Lorenzo Thomas, and Hanna Wallinger, 115–25. New Brunswick, Canada: Transaction Publishers, 2003.

Stovall, Katherine E. "The Development of an Educated Clergy within the African Methodist Episcopal Church," Master's thesis, Trinity International University, 2015. ProQuest Dissertations & Theses Global (1712864843). https://www.proquest.com/dissertations-theses/development-educated-clergy-within-african/docview/1712864843/se-2.

Switala, William J. *Underground Railroad in New York and New Jersey*. Mechanicsburg, PA: Stackpole Books, 2006.

Talbert, Horace. *The Sons of Allen: Together with a Sketch of the Rise and Progress of Wilberforce University, Wilberforce, Ohio*. Xenia, OH: Aldine Press, 1906. https://docsouth.unc.edu/church/talbert/talbert.html.

Tanner, Benjamin T. *An Apology for African Methodism*. Baltimore, 1867.

———. *An Outline of Our History and Government for African Methodist Churchmen, Ministerial and Lay: In Catechetical Form: Two Parts with Appendix.* Philadelphia: Grant, Faires & Rodgers, 1884.

Tappan, Lewis. *The Life of Arthur Tappan.* New York: Hurd & Houghton, 1870.

Taylor, Nikki Marie. *Frontiers of Freedom: Cincinnati's Black Community, 1802–1868.* Athens: Ohio University Press, 2005.

Thirteenth General Conference of the AME Church. 1868. Photograph. Payne Theological Seminary. https://archive.org/details/thirteenthgenera00unse/mode/2up.

Thomas, Benjamin. *Theodore Weld: Crusader for Freedom.* New Brunswick: Rutgers University Press, 1950.

Thompson, Rev. Alfred L. *The History of St. Paul AME.* 1999.

Thompson, Julius Eric. "Hiram R. Revels, 1827–1901: A Biography." PhD diss., Princeton University, 1973. ProQuest Dissertations & Theses Global (302658049). https://www.proquest.com/dissertations-theses/hiram-r-revels-1827-1901-biography/docview/302658049/se-2.

Turley, Alicestyne. *The Gospel of Freedom: Black Evangelicals and the Underground Railroad.* Louisville: University Press of Kentucky, 2022.

Turner, Glenette Tilley. *The Underground Railroad in Illinois.* Glen Ellyn, IL: Newman Educational Publishing, 2001.

Turner, Henry McNeal. *The Genius and Theory of Methodist Polity, or the Machinery of Methodism.* Philadelphia: Publication Department of the AME Church, 1885.

Turner, H. M. "Reminiscences of the Proclamation of Emancipation." *A.M.E. Review* 29, no. 3 (January 1913): 211–13. https://www.thehenrymcnealturnerproject.org/2017/08/reminiscences-of-proclamation-of.html.

248th Anniversary Souvenir Journal. Brooklyn: Bridge Street AWME Church, 2014.

United States Federal Census of 1810, Westtown, Chester, Pennsylvania.

United States House of Representatives. "The First African American to Speak in the House Chamber, February 12, 1865." History, Art, & Archives. Accessed October 31, 2023. https://history.house.gov/Historical-Highlights/1851-1900/The-first-African-American-to-speak-in-the-House-Chamber/.

United States War Records Office. *The War of the Rebellion: A Compilation of the Official Records of the Union and Confederate Armies.* Vol. 13, series 1. Washington, DC: Government Printing Office, 1880–1901. https://babel.hathitrust.org/cgi/pt?id=coo.31924079609578&view=1up&seq=235&q1=Kansas.

Walker, Clarence E. *A Rock in a Weary Land: The African Methodist Episcopal Church during the Civil War and Reconstruction.* Baton Rouge: Louisiana State University Press, 1982.

Walker, David. *Walker's Appeal, in Four Articles; Together with a Preamble, to the Coloured Citizens of the World, but in Particular, and Very Expressly, to Those of the United States of America, Written in Boston, State of Massachusetts, September 28, 1829.* Boston: printed by the author, 1830.

Walker, Henry D. *History of the Town of Flushing, Long Island, New York.* Flushing, NY: J. H. Ridenour, 1899.

Walker, Timothy D., ed. *Sailing to Freedom: Maritime Dimensions of the Underground Railroad*. Amherst: University Press of Massachusetts, 2021.

Walkes, Joseph A., Jr. *Black Square and Compass: 200 Years of Prince Hall Freemasonry*. Richmond, VA: Macoy, 1979.

Wallace, Howard. *Historical Sketch of the Underground Railroad from Uniontown to Pittsburgh*. N.p., 1903.

Wallace, J. P. Q. "Unique Biographical Sketch of a Pioneer Missionary." In *A Century of Missions of the African Methodist Episcopal Church, 1840–1940*, edited by L. L. Berry, 49–55. New York: Gutenberg Printing, 1942.

Walls, William J. *The African Methodist Episcopal Zion Church: Reality of the Black Church*. Charlotte, NC: A.M.E. Zion Publishing House, 1974.

Ward, Samuel Ringgold. *Autobiography of a Fugitive Negro: His Anti-slavery Labours in the United States, Canada, & England*. London: John Snow, 1855. https://docsouth.unc.edu/neh/wards/ward.html.

Warren, Kim. "Seeking the Promised Land: African American Migrations to Kansas." Civil War on the Western Border: The Missouri-Kansas Conflict 1854–1865, The Kansas City Public Library. Accessed October 12, 2017. http://www.civilwaronthewesternborder.org/essay/seeking-promised-land-african-american-migrations-kansas.

Warren, Stanley. "The Bethel African Methodist Episcopal Church." *Traces of Indiana and Midwestern History* 19, no. 3 (Summer 2007): 32–38. https://images.indianahistory.org/digital/collection/p16797coll39/id/3306.

Washington, Booker T. *The Story of the Negro: The Rise of the Race from Slavery*. New York: Barnes and Noble, 2009. First published 1909 by Doubleday.

Watkins, Ralph Craig. "The Institutionalization of the African Methodist Episcopal Church." PhD diss., University of Pittsburgh, 1997. ProQuest Dissertations & Theses Global (304424872). https://www.proquest.com/dissertations-theses/institutionalization-african-methodist-episcopal/docview/304424872/se-2.

Wayman, Alexander Walker. *Cyclopaedia of African Methodism*. Baltimore: Methodist Episcopal Book Depository, 1882.

———. *My Recollection of African M. E. Ministers, or Forty Years' Experience in the African Methodist Episcopal Church*. Philadelphia: A.M.E. Book Rooms, 1881.

Wayne County Deed Books. Wayne County Recorder of Deeds, Land Records, Richmond, Indiana.

Weeden, H. C., ed. and comp. *Weeden's History of The Colored People of Louisville*. Louisville, KY, 1897.

Welch, Elaine. *William Paul Quinn, A Militant Churchman: A Biographical Sketch*. Chicago: n.p., 1933.

Wellman, Judith. *Brooklyn's Promised Land: The Free Black Community of Weeksville, New York*. New York: New York University Press, 2014.

Wesley, Charles. *Waiting at the Cross, The African Methodist Episcopal Church Hymn Book*. Brooklyn: George Hogarth, 1837. https://hymnary.org/hymnal/AMEC1837?page=1.

Wesley, Charles H. *Richard Allen: An Apostle of Freedom.* Washington, DC: Associated Publishers, 1935.

William Paul Quinn Certificate, Affidavit by M. M. Clarke in Respect of Reverend William Paul Quinn's Parentage and National Origin, February 12, 1851. Pittsburgh, PA, DR 14-312, deposited at Wayne County, Indiana, Courthouse on October 28, 1851.

Willis, Arlette Ingram. *Anti-Black Literacy Laws and Policies.* New York: Routledge, 2023.

Wilson, Joseph. *Sketches of the Higher Classes of Colored Society in Philadelphia.* Philadelphia: Merrihew and Thompson, 1841.

Wingert, Cooper H. *Slavery & the Underground Railroad in South Central Pennsylvania.* Charleston, SC: The History Press, 2016.

Winks, Robin W. *The Blacks in Canada: A History.* 2nd ed. Montreal: McGill-Queen's University Press, 1997.

Woodson, Bryan W., Sr. *A President in the Family: Thomas Jefferson, Sally Hemmings, and Thomas Woodson.* Westport, CT: Praeger, 2001.

Woodson, Carter Goodwin. *Free Negro Heads of Families in the United States in 1830.* Washington, DC: The Association for the Study of Negro Life and History, 1925.

Wright, Richard R. *Centennial Encyclopaedia of the African Methodist Episcopal Church. Containing Principally the Biographies of the Men and Women, Both Ministers and Laymen, Whose Labors during a Hundred Years, Helped Make the A.M.E. Church What It Is; Also Short Historical Sketches of Annual Conferences, Educational Institutions, General Departments, Missionary Societies of the A.M.E. Church, and General Information about African Methodism and the Christian Church in General; Being a Literary Contribution to the Celebration of the One Hundredth Anniversary of the Formation of the African Methodist Episcopal Church Denomination by Richard Allen and Others, at Philadelphia, Penna., in 1816.* Philadelphia: Book Concern of the A.M.E. Church, 1916. https://docsouth.unc.edu/church/wright/wright.html.

Young, Henry J. *Major Black Religious Leaders: 1755–1940.* Nashville: Parthenon Press, 1977.

Websites

All websites were accessed between January 2023 and July 2024.

"A Century of Missions of the A.M.E. Church." HathiTrust. https://babel.hathitrust.org/cgi/pt?id=wu.89077022952&view=1up&format=plaintext&seq=58&skin=2021&q1=Quinn.

"The African Methodist Episcopal Church." Underground Railroad, Oxford African American Studies Center. http://aasc.oupexplore.com/undergroundrailroad/-!/event/african-methodist-episcopal-church.

Alfini, Michelle. "Cincinnati's Historic AME Church Keeps Community Connected During Pandemic." Spectrum News 1. Published February 8, 2021. https://

spectrumnews1.com/oh/columbus/news/2021/02/08/cincinnati-s-historic-ame-church-keeps-community-connected-during-pandemic.

"Allen Temple A.M.E. Church." *Underground Ohio* (blog). https://undergroundoh.com/churches/.

"The AME Exclusive at the 50th Session of the General Conference with Bishop Anne Henning Byfield." YouTube video. Posted 2016. https://www.youtube.com/watch?v=VSKjinXcwBw.

"An Act Respecting Slaves, Free Negroes and Mulattoes, 1847." Missouri Secretary of State. Accessed November 19, 2023. https://www.sos.mo.gov/CMSImages/MDH/AnActRespectingSlaves,1847.pdf.

"Article XIII of the 1851 Indiana Constitution." IndianaHistory.org. Accessed December 7, 2022. https://indianahistory.org/wp-content/uploads/NHD Exhibit - 1851 IN Constitution.pdf.

"At Battle of Island Mound State Historic Site." Missouri State Parks. Accessed August 4, 2023. https://mostateparks.com/page/60129/historic-site-history.

"Being Black in Indiana." Indiana Historical Bureau. https://www.in.gov/history/for-educators/download-issues-of-the-indiana-historian/indiana-emigrants-to-liberia/being-black-in-indiana/.

Bethel AME Church. "Aboard the Underground Railroad." National Park Service. Accessed October 9, 2023. https://www.nps.gov/nr/travel/underground/in1.htm.

"Bibliography." Colored Conventions Project. https://coloredconventions.org/bibliography/.

"Bishop Vashti Murphy McKenzie." Washington National Cathedral. Last updated 2012. https://web.archive.org/web/20120115175533/http://www.nationalcathedral.org/staff/PE-46ER5-V0000I.shtml.

"Bishop William Paul Quinn (1806?–1873)." Morrisson-Reeves Library, Richmond, IN. Accessed October 10, 2023, https://mrlinfo.org/history/biography/quinn.htm.

"The Black Church: This Is Our Story, This Is Our Song." KERA News. https://www.kera.org/tv/blackchurch/north-texas-timeline/.

Bowens, Lisa. "A Biographical Reflection of Theodore Sedgwick Wright." Princeton Theological Seminary. Published October 14, 2021. https://www.ptsem.edu/news/biographical-reflection.

"Bridge Street AWME Church," MAAP, Mapping the African American Past. Accessed August 26, 2022. https://maap.columbia.edu/place/11.html.

"The Cathedral at St. Paul AME Church Annual Report 2021." St. Paul AME Church. Accessed October 9, 2023.https://stpaulamestl.net/church-history.

"Constitution of 1851 as Originally Written." Indiana Historical Bureau. Accessed March 2, 2024. https://www.in.gov/history/about-indiana-history-and-trivia/explore-indiana-history-by-topic/indiana-documents-leading-to-statehood/constitution-of-1851/.

Davenport, Nora. "Bethel AME Wins Back Land and Has Exciting Restorative Development Plans for Pittsburgh." Regional Housing Legal Services (RHLS).

Published May 24, 2023. https://www.rhls.org/2023/05/bethel-ame-wins-back-land-and-has-exciting-restorative-development-plans-for-pittsburgh/.

"The Dred Scott Decision: Opinion of Chief Justice Taney." Library of Congress. Accessed September 25, 2023. https://www.loc.gov/resource/llst.022/?sp=18&st=text.

"Dred Scott versus John F. A. Sandford." Milestone Documents, National Archives. https://www.archives.gov/milestone-documents/dred-scott-v-sandford#:~:text=They%20had%%20lawfully%20be.

"Denmark Vesey." *This Far by Faith*, PBS. Accessed January 24, 2024. http://www.pbs.org/thisfarbyfaith/people/denmark_vesey.html.

"Emancipation Proclamation (1863)." Milestone Documents, National Archives. Accessed January 24, 2024. https://www.archives.gov/milestone-documents/emancipation-proclamation#:~:text=%22That%20on%20the%20first%20day,forever%20free%3B%20and%20the%20Executive.

"The Evansville Boneyard." Alexander Chapel AME Church. Accessed October 13, 2023. http://web.usi.edu/boneyard/church.htm.

"The 1st Regiment Kansas Volunteer Infantry (African Descent)." Accessed January 20, 2024. https://civilwarhistory.fandom.com/wiki/1st_Regiment_Kansas_Volunteer_Infantry_(African_Descent).

"Foreword by Diane Miller." Underground Railroad Online Handbook. https://housedivided.dickinson.edu/sites/ugrr/overview-essays/foreword-miller/.

Headsman. "1829: Richard Johnson and Catherine Cashiere, the Last Public Hangings in New York City." ExecutedToday. Published May 7, 2015. http://www.executedtoday.com/2015/05/07/1829-richard-johnson-and-catharine-cashiere/.

Hedlin, Chris. "How Did Pittsburgh's Oldest Black Church Form? What Was Its Role in the Underground Railroad and Fighting Slavery?" PublicSource. Published January 31, 2022. https://www.publicsource.org/pittsburgh-faith-race-place-oldest-black-church-underground-railroad-anti-slavery/.

"Henry Highland Garnet." Examination Days, The New York African Free School Collection. Accessed February 16, 2024. https://www.nyhistory.org/web/africanfreeschool/bios/henry-highland-garnet.html.

"Henry, Indiana, United States, May 9, 1880, Dec. 1, 1880–May 27, 1881, May 1881–Dec., Deeds, Vol. 34–36, DGS 008071832, Image 805 of 913, March 15th, 1881." FamilySearch. Accessed March 3, 2024. https://www.familysearch.org/ark:/61903/3:1:3Q9M-CSNW-X9Z2-5.

"Henry McNeal Turner." *This Far by Faith*, PBS. Accessed January 24, 2024. https://www.pbs.org/thisfarbyfaith/people/henry_mcneal_turner.html#:~:text=He%20was%20taken%20under%20wing,became%20the%20first%20black%20chaplain

HistoryNet Staff. "America's Civil War: Missouri and Kansas." HistoryNet. Published June 12, 2006. https://www.historynet.com/americas-civil-war-missouri-and-kansas/.

"History of Quinn Chapel African Methodist Episcopal Church, Frederick Maryland, 1800–Present." Quinn Chapel AME. Accessed August 16, 2022. https://www.quinnamefrederick.org/history/.

"Home." Underground Railroad Online Handbook. https://housedivided.dickinson.edu/sites/ugrr/.

"Image 18 of the Dred Scott Decision: Opinion of Chief Justice Taney." Library of Congress. https://www.loc.gov/resource/llst.022/?sp=18&st=text.

Indiana Historical Society. "Article XIII of the 1851 Indiana Constitution." We Do History. https://www.in.gov/history/about-indiana-history-and-trivia/explore-indiana-history-by-topic/indiana-documents-leading-to-statehood/constitution-of-1851/article-13-negroes-and-mulattoes/.

"Juneteenth Block Party, Hosted by Reedy Chapel A.M.E. Church." Reedy Chapel. Accessed October 31, 2023. https://reedychapel.com/.

Kirkland, Talia. "Members of Bethel AME Church Continue Working on Deal to Recover Land." WPXI-TV. Published November 18, 2022. https://www.wpxi.com/news/local/members-bethel-ame-church-continue-working-deal-recover-land/3SMTBIGJNFDQDPBE4O4DSPFF4I/.

"Landmark Legislation: The Fourteenth Amendment." United States Senate. Accessed November 7, 2023. https://www.senate.gov/about/origins-foundations/senate-and-constitution/14th-amendment.htm#:~:text=Passed%20by%20of.

"Legacy of Thaddeus Stevens." Thaddeus Stevens College of Technology. Last updated 2024. https://stevenscollege.edu/legacy-of-thaddeus-stevens/.

"Levi & Catharine Coffin State Historic Site & Interpretive Center." Visit. Discover. Explore. Richmond. Accessed March 2, 2024. https://visitrichmond.org/listing/levi-catharine-coffin-state-historic-site-interpretive-center#:~:text=The%20Underground%20Railroad%20safety.

"Let Your Motto Be Resistance." The Legacy of Henry Highland Garnet. Accessed December 2, 2023. https://kentcountyhistory.org/wp-content/uploads/2018/08/Henry-Highland-Garnet.pdf.

"Map of Lawrence, KS." Kansas Historical Society. Accessed January 25, 2024. https://www.kshs.org/km/items/view/472457.

Melton, Gordon, comp. "African American Methodists in the Antebellum and Reconstruction Periods: A Timetable, 1760–1876." African American Methodists, Historic St. George's United Methodist Church. Published 2013. http://www.historicstgeorges.org/african-american-methodists.

"Missouri Compromise: Date, Definition & 1820." History. Accessed March 13, 2024. https://www.history.com/topics/slavery/missouri-compromise.

"Missouri Prohibits Education of Black People." Equal Justice Initiative. https://calendar.eji.org/racial-injustice/feb/16

Missouri Secretary of State. "Missouri's Early Slave Laws: A History in Documents, Missouri State Archives." Missouri Digital Heritage. https://www.sos.mo.gov/archives/education/aahi/earlyslavelaws/slavelaws.

"National Underground Railroad Network to Freedom Act of 1998. Public Law 105-203—July 21, 1998." Accessed July 26, 2024. https://www.congress.gov/105/plaws/publ203/PLAW-105publ203.pdf.

"New Sectional Map of the State of Illinois: Compiled from the United States Surveys." Historical Maps Online, Illinois Library Digital Collections. Accessed March 16, 2024. https://digital.library.illinois.edu/items/a6ade740-994e-0134 -2096-0050569601ca-6.

"New-York African Free School Records, 1817–1832, Vol. 2." New-York Historical Society. Accessed August 20, 2022. https://digitalcollections.nyhistory.org/ islandora/object/islandora%3A139453#page/36/mode/1up.

"New York City Directory, 1831–32." New York Public Library Digital Collections, Irma and Paul Milstein Division of United States History, Local History and Genealogy, The New York Public Library. Accessed December 27, 2021. https:// digitalcollections.nypl.org/items/f58e2a30-2b8c-0136-d580-0f70555aba17.

"1,200 at St. John's A.M.E. Mark 100th Anniversary." ClevelandMemory.org. Accessed August 21, 2022. https://clevelandmemory.contentdm.oclc.org/digital/ collection/press/id/2477.

"People & Ideas: Richard Allen." WETA, PBS. Published October 11, 2010. https:// www.pbs.org/wgbh/pages/frontline/godinamerica/people/richard-allen.html.

"Primary Resources for the Study of Southern History, Literature, and Culture." Documenting American South. https://docsouth.unc.edu/.

Quann, Peg. "Bensalem AME Church to Honor Founder Richard Allen." *Bucks County Courier Times*, February 11, 2016, buckscountycouriertimes.com/article /20160211/news/302119907.

"Reedy Chapel 1848–Present." Reedy Chapel. https://reedychapel.com/.

"Richmond City Directory 1865." FamilySearch. Accessed March 14, 2024. https://www.familysearch.org/ark:/61903/3:1:3Q9M-CSZK-72NV?cc=3754697 &personaUrl=%2Fark%3A%2F61903%2F1%3A1%3A6ZBY-YL54.

"Rt. Rev. Wm. Paul Quinn. Senior Bishop A.M.E. Church, 1848–1873." New York Public Library. https://digitalcollections.nypl.org/items/510d47da-7659-a3d9-e040 -e00a18064a99.

"Salem Chapel BME Church Harriet Tubman Underground Railroad National Historic Sites." Salem Chapel, National Underground Railroad Network to Freedom Program, National Park Service. Published September 27, 2023. https://www .salemchapelbmechurch.ca/index.html.

"St. John African Methodist Episcopal (AME) Church." Encyclopedia of Cleveland History, Case Western Reserve University. https://case.edu/ech/articles/s/st-johns -african-methodist-episcopal-ame-church.

"Session Laws 1831, Vol. 213, 448." Archives of Maryland Online. Last updated October 6, 2023. https://msa.maryland.gov/megafile/msa/speccol/sc2900/sc2908 /000001/000213/html/am213--445.html.

"Sketch of the Harbor of St Louis Reduced From Captn Lee's Map of 1837." Barry Lawrence Ruderman. https://www.raremaps.com/gallery/detail/47576/ sketch-of-the-harbor-of-st-louis-reduced-fromcaptn-lees-united-states-bureau-of -topographical-engineers.

"Slave Codes 1690–1865." South Carolina Encyclopedia. Last updated August 23, 2022. https://www.scencyclopedia.org/sce/entries/slave-codes/.

"Throwback Thursday: Lane Theological Seminary." Walnut Hills Redevelopment Foundation. Published February 7, 2013. https://walnuthillsrf.org/throwback-thursday-lane-theological-seminary/.

Underground Railroad in Canada. "Religious Institutions." Parks Canada. http://www.pc.gc.ca/canada/proj/cfc-ugrr/itm2-com/pg13_e.asp.

"The Underground Railroad in Chillicothe/Ross County, Historic Underground Railroad Site." The Historical Marker Database. https://www.hmdb.org/m.asp?m=118737.

Vieira, Imani. "'Separate but Equal': From the African Free Schools to the New York City Public School System." Arts, Culture, Community, Lower East Side. Accessed February 27, 2024. https://www.fabnyc.org/2022/02/03/4481/

Wayne, Indiana, United States, 1854–1856, Deeds, Vol. 19–21, DGS 008070048, Image 274 of 467, September 24th, 1855." FamilySearch. Accessed March 3, 2024. https://www.familysearch.org/ark:/61903/3:1:3Q9M-CSNS-Y59B.

"What Is the Underground Railroad?" Underground Railroad, National Park Service. Accessed July 6, 2024. https://www.nps.gov/subjects/undergroundrailroad/what-is-the-underground-railroad.htm.

"Willis R. Revels, Methodist Minister." Encyclopedia of Indianapolis. Accessed November 8, 2023. https://indyencyclopedia.org/willis-r-revels/.

Newspapers

The Afro-American. December 26, 1931.

Alexandria Gazette. February 25, 1873.

American and Commercial Daily Advertiser. August 25, 1842.

The Baltimore Afro-American. "Golden Achievements of the Women's Missionary Society." June 13, 1987.

The Baltimore Sun. "African M. E. Church General Conference." May 4, 1864.

———. February 22, 1858.

———. July 11, 1848.

Bucks County Courier Times. February 11, 2016. buckscountycouriertimes.com/article/20160211/news/302119907

———. "Historic South Side church celebrates 160 years of ministry." *Chicago Defender*, July 18, 2007.

Cambridge Chronicle. August 16, 1824

———. August 27, 1825.

The Charleroi Mail (PA). June 2, 1938.

Chicago Daily Journal. October 3, 1850.

Chicago Defender. Calloway, Earl. "Quinn AME Church Presents Its Historic 'June Rose Concert' Sunday." June 12, 2004.

———. Calloway, Earl. "Historic South Side Church Celebrates 160 Years of Ministry." July 2007.
The Christian Recorder. Bishop James A. Shorter. "One of the Bishops of The A.M.E. Church." May 17, 1887.
———. "Bishop Nazrey and the B.M.E. Church in Canada." February 8, 1862.
———. "Bishop Quinn's Tour West on a Visit to the Churches." August 16, 1862.
———. "Bishop William Paul Quinn." April 7, 1866.
———. "Editorial Correspondence. Missouri Annual Conference." September 10, 1864.
———. Embry, Bishop J. C. "In the Dusty Records of the Missouri Conference." October 14, 1897.
———. Embry, Rev. J. C. "Communications, Synopsis of the Proceedings of the Missouri Conference." October 12, 1872.
———. "From Leavenworth Kansas." August 16, 1862.
———. Henry Highland Garnet. "Pioneers of the A.M.E. Church. No III." March 13, 1869.
———. Invisible Black. "Pen and Ink Sketches of the African General Conference. As Viewed from the Gallery of Bethel Church." May 7, 1864.
———. "Kansas Battles—Battle of Island Mound; Battle of Cabin Creek; Battle of Honey Springs; Camden Expedition; Battle of Poison Spring." August 16, 1862.
———. "Letter from Brother Strother." August 2, 1862.
———. "Meetings of Annual Conferences." February 1, 1862.
———. October 12, 1861–June 1, 1872.
———. "Ohio Conference." May 2, 1863.
———. "Payne, Daniel A., to Dr. Garnett. Rev. H. H. Garnet, D. D." April 10, 1873.
———. "Proceedings of the Missouri Conference." September 3, 1870.
———. "Quinn Memorial Services." May 18, 1876.
———. "The Virginia Conference of the A.M.E. Church." May 25, 1867.
———. "Washington Correspondence." May 21, 1864.
———. "We Appeal to You." July 30, 1864.
The Cincinnati Daily Enquirer. "Still Another Savage and Sanguinary Assault—A Colored Bishop Cruelly Beaten and Robbed." February 19, 1858.
Cleveland Call and Post. "First Negro Church Was St. John's AME." June 24, 1961.
Colored American. August 31, 1839.
———. March 17, 1838.
Courier (Waterloo, Iowa). Jackson, H. J. "AME Celebrates 200th Year by Honoring Heroes." May 29, 1988. https://www.newspapers.com/article/the-courier-4-horseman-29may1988-200th-a/137599275/.
The Daily Kansas Tribune (Lawrence, KS). August 12, 1870.
Daily National Intelligencer. August 8, 1831.
Daily Times (Leavenworth, KS). Betts, Vicki. August 15, 1863–March 25, 1864 (posted 2016). https://scholarworks.uttyler.edu/cw_newstitles/48/.

The Elevator (San Francisco). "Mortuary Notice." March 15, 1873.
Emancipator and Weekly Chronicle. "Gen. Jackson." July 9, 1845.
Evansville Daily Journal. February 22, 1858.
The Evansville Journal. "Religious. Thirty-Third Annual Conference of the African M.E. Church." August 23, 1872.
Evening Post. "Worthy of Attention." January 7, 1826.
The Evening Star (New York). "Worthy of Attention, for Sale." January 7, 1826.
The Evening Star (Washington, DC). April 28, 1858.
———. "African M. E. Conference." May 3, 1858.
———. "Visit of the African General Conference to Hon. Thaddeus Stevens, Addresses on Behalf of the Conference—Reply of Mr. Stevens." May 11, 1868.
Flushing Daily Times. "Macedonia A.M.E. Church." June 6, 1903.
Frederick Douglass' Papers. January 20, 1854–January 26, 1855. https://www.loc.gov/collections/frederick-douglass-newspapers/?q=Quinn.
Freedom's Journal (New York). April 27, 1827.
———. December 31, 1827.
———. July 6, 1827.
———. "Land of Liberty." December 5, 1828.
———. May 4, 1827.
———. "Notice." February 1, 1828.
———. April 27, 1827.
The Freeman (Indianapolis). "The Underground Railway—Review of the System by Which Many Thousands of Slaves Were Liberated." February 24, 1900.
Galveston Daily News. May 30, 1987.
Genius of Universal Emancipation. July 14, 1827.
Harper's Bazaar. January 6, 1883.
Harpers Weekly. "Robert Smalls: The Steamer 'Planter' and Her Captor." June 14, 1862.
Indianapolis Indiana State Sentinel. March 7, 1843.
Indianapolis Journal. September 28, 1891.
———. "Henry Wilson in Indiana." August 5, 1872. https://newspapers.library.in.gov/?a=d&d=IJ18720805&e=-------en-20--1--txt-txIN-------.
Indianapolis Recorder. "History of the Negro in Hoosier State." April 15, 1916.
Indianapolis Times. "Negroes Start Church." October 1, 1936.
Indianapolis World. February 23, 1893.
Indiana True Republican. May 4, 1865.
The Inter Ocean. "Death of John Jones." May 22, 1879.
Kansas City Star. Mason, Randy. "KC Black History: Do You Know the Town That Was a Stop on the Underground Railroad?" March 9, 2022. https://www.kansascity.com/news/your-kcq/article258753333.html#storylink=cpy.
The Leavenworth Times. August 15, 1863.
———. March 5, 1862. https://www.newspapers.com/image/382046493/?terms=solid%20ice&match=1.

The Leavenworth Weekly Times. August 25, 1870. https://chroniclingamerica.loc.gov/lccn/sn84027691/1870-08-25/ed-1/seq-3/.

The Liberator. "Affairs in Pittsburg—Fugitive Slaves." October 4, 1840. http://fair-use.org/the-liberator/1850/10/04/the-liberator-20-40.pdf.

———. April 5, 1850.

———. December 20, 1834.

———. "The Fugitive Slave Bill." September 27, 1850. http://fair-use.org/the-liberator/1850/09/27/the-liberator-20-39.pdf.

———. January 5, 1833.

———. October 12, 1833.

Long Island Star. "African Camp Meeting." August 7, 1828.

———. August 23, 1826.

———. October 4, 1817.

Macon Weekly Telegraph. "African M. E. General Conference." News/Opinion. May 15, 1868.

Milwaukee Daily Free Democrat. October 12, 1850.

Milwaukee Star. "St. Mark AME. Church of the Anvil." News/Opinion. February 22, 1873.

———. "St Mark to Dedicate New Edifice." December 21, 1968.

Mirror of Liberty. January 1839.

The Morning News. August 26, 1889.

Morning Republican. Originally published as *Little Rock Daily Republican*. "Death of Bishop Quinn." March 7, 1873.

Nashville Union and American. May 7, 1872.

The National Era (Washington, DC). "The Dred Scott Decision in England." May 14, 1857.

———. "Is Dred Scott to Be Repudiated?" August 11, 1859.

———. July 13, 1848.

———. October 12, 1854.

———. "The South Again in Peril." November 9, 1854.

National Intelligencer. November 13, 1809

Newbern Gazette. August 15, 1800.

North Star. "Mass Meeting of Colored Citizens." July 11, 1850. https://www.loc.gov/resource/sn84026365/1850-07-11/ed-1/?dl=issue&sp=2&r=0,0.037,0.417,0.235,0.

Pennsylvania Freeman. "Meeting for the Promotion of Education." May 29, 1851, https://infoweb-newsbank-com.proxy-um.researchport.umd.edu/apps/readex/doc?p=EANX&sort=YMD_date%3AA&fld-base20185140Communicated.%2BMeeting %2Bfor%2Bthe%2BPromotion%2Bof%2BEducation.

Philadelphia Tribune. "The Four Horsemen of the Liberation Church: Allen, Quinn, Payne, Turner." June 12, 1987.

Pittsburgh Commercial Gazette. "Obituary." January 15, 1878.

Pittsburgh Courier. "AME Churches in Rural Area Meet Community Challenges." August 8, 1953.

The Provincial Freeman (Toronto). August 12, 1854.

Richmond Palladium (Indiana). "A.M.E. Delegates Honor Deceased Dignitaries." September 18, 1920.

———. August 26, 1871. https://newspapers.library.in.gov/?a=d&d=RPW18710826.1.3&e=-------en-20--1--txt-txIN-------.

———. February 21, 1867.

———. February 22, 1873.

———. June 8, 1869.

———. September 9, 1871.

Richmond Telegram. "Bishop Paul Quinn, Death of a Distinguished Colored Divine—A Brief Sketch of His Eventful Career." February 28, 1873.

———. March 7, 1873.

Richmond Weekly Palladium (Indiana). "Bishop Quinn." December 6, 1873.

———. "Funeral of Bishop Quinn." March 1, 1873.

St. Louis Daily Globe-Democrat. "'Mother' Baltimore's Burial." December 4, 1882.

———. "Secrets of the Underground Railway Told by a St. Louis Director." February 4, 1900.

St. Louis Star. "Moses Dickson: The Great Negro Organizer and Fraternal Society Leader." April 1902.

Steubenville Herald-Star. April 23, 1960.

———. May 8, 1908.

The Topeka Daily Press (Topeka, Kansas). August 12, 1890.

Tribune Star. Kash, Steve. "Terre Haute's First Black Teacher Made History." March 11, 2007. https://www.tribstar.com/news/lifestyles/terre-haute-s-first-black-teacher-made-history/article_56dea70f-ed94-54b3-8d39-85aca84fd655.html.

The Urbana Union. April 3, 1867.

Vermont Stateman. "The Executions." May 20, 1829.

Washington DC National Intelligencer. November 13, 1809.

Weekly Advocate. January 14, 1837.

Weekly Atchison Champion (Kansas). "A.M.E. Church. Missouri Annual Conference, Assignments, Etc." October 5, 1872.

Weekly Georgia Telegraph. Turner. "African M. E. General Conference." May 15, 1868.

Wilmington Daily Commercial. February 27, 1873.

Index

abolition. *See* slavery, abolition of
Africa, xi, xiii, 29, 54, 64, 105, 115–16, 140, 160, 165, 167, 169
African Americans, xv, xx, 2–6, 8, 10–12, 25–27, 29, 35, 38, 42, 46, 48–49, 51, 54, 56, 59–60, 63, 66, 71, 76–77, 79, 85, 92–93, 107–8, 113–15, 117, 124, 127, 131, 133–34, 136–38, 140, 143, 148, 150, 156, 162, 166
African Dorcas Association, 38
African Free Methodist Society, 36–37, 40
African Free School, 35–36, 38–40, 42, 45, 48, 52, 54–55
African Methodist Bethel Society, 8
African Methodist Episcopal (AME) Church: AME Connection, xix, 2, 7, 9, 17–18, 20–22, 25, 28, 33–34, 36, 41, 43, 45, 48, 50, 53–56, 59, 61–62, 67, 69, 73, 79, 86, 88, 91, 98, 100, 102, 110, 120, 126, 144, 161, 168; Connectional Lay Organization, 165. *See also* African Methodist Episcopal (AME) conferences; British Methodist Episcopal (BME) Church; *The Christian Recorder*; Black church; Methodism; Methodist Episcopal Church; specific AME Church congregations
African Methodist Episcopal (AME) conferences: Baltimore conference, 19, 23, 29, 65–68, 99, 100, 107, 123, 126–27, 141, 145; California conference, 144; Canadian conference, xv, 96–97, 99, 120; general conference, 13, 31, 44, 53–54, 81, 87, 89, 91–95, 100–2, 110–13, 120, 138–40, 147, 149, 152–53, 165–66; Illinois conference, 151; Indiana conference, 86, 91–92, 105, 119, 135–36, 138, 149–51, 153; Liberia conference, 140; Louisiana conference, 144; Missouri conference, 126, 128, 135, 140, 150, 153–54; New Jersey conference, 162; New York conference, 23, 34–35, 42–43, 53, 56, 63, 81, 95–97, 99–100, 108–11, 144, 189n7, 194n40; Ohio conference, 52, 56–57, 59, 61, 86, 98–99, 137, 142, 151;

Philadelphia conference, 7, 17–19, 23–24, 29, 34, 42, 52, 80, 95, 98, 101, 103, 106, 115, 123, 142, 145, 151–52. *See also* African Methodist Episcopal (AME) Church
Aldridge, Ira, 48
Allegheny Mountains, 18, 23–24, 27, 29, 49, 57, 89, 160
Allegheny River, 29
Allen, Richard, xiii, xvii–xix, 4–9, 11, 13–15, 17–19, 21–25, 27, 29, 33–37, 41–44, 48–49, 52–53, 61–63, 74, 79, 86, 92, 95, 101, 103, 110–11, 138–40, 142, 150–51, 160, 165, 167–69, 183n30, 185n3, 188n54
Allen, Sarah, 23, 103
American Anti-Slavery Society, 45. *See also* slavery, antislavery
American Colonization Society, 115
Anderson, Vinton R., 166–67
Angel, Stephen, xiv
Arkansas, 134, 140, 144
Arnett, Benjamin William, 61, 76, 90, 129, 132–33, 138, 142, 147, 157–58, 160, 163
arson, 131, 139, 141
arrest, xvii, 46, 77, 82, 109, 113, 132, 161; of ministers, 77, 109, 113, 161
Asbury, Francis, xix, 4, 7, 34, 158, 189
Avery, Charles, 112

Bailey, Julius, 111
Baltimore, Maryland, 4, 7–8, 19–20, 22–23, 29–31, 33–34, 36, 42, 49, 65–67, 76, 79, 81, 87, 89, 92, 97–100, 102, 107, 110–12, 120, 123, 126–27, 141, 145, 148, 162, 183n30
Baltimore, Priscilla, xv, 49–50, 82–83, 85, 92, 113, 126, 161
Bensalem, Pennsylvania, 9–10, 48
Belize, xii, 123
Berry, L. L., 41, 53
Bibb, Henry, 115–16

Bibb, Mary, 115–16
the Bible, xi, xiv, 3, 9, 11, 20, 22, 24, 31, 62, 65, 71, 97, 114, 120; Old Testament, 20
the Black Atlantic, xi, 30, 114–15, 151
Black churches, xiii, xv–xvi, 4–6, 8, 12, 14, 20, 25, 27, 29–30, 33, 38–39, 54, 62, 68, 74, 78, 90, 119, 126–27, 138, 160, 162, 166–67, 190n15
Black liberation theology, 30
Black codes, xiv, 53–54, 59, 71, 87, 202
Black laws. *See* Black codes
Bonner, James D., 116–18
Branagan, Thomas, 64–65
British Methodist Episcopal (BME) Church, 108, 120–21. *See also* African Methodist Episcopal (AME) Church; Methodism; Methodist Episcopal Church
Brooklyn, New York City, 34–35, 43, 190n9, 194n40. *See also* New York City
Brooklyn, Illinois, 49–51, 82–84, 113, 126, 128; Brooklyn's Bethel AME Church, 50
Brown, John, 117, 125, 161
Brown, John Mifflin, 7, 15, 22–23, 63, 90, 99, 147–49, 159–60, 199n10
Brown, Morris, xvii, xix, 19–22, 25, 29, 35, 41–42, 44, 49, 52–53, 56–58, 68, 81, 86, 89, 92, 94–100, 102–3, 110–11, 117, 123, 161, 165, 168

California, xiv, 102, 105, 125, 144, 148
Campbell, Jabez, 107, 136, 139, 142, 144, 148–49, 151, 158–60, 209n69
Canada, xi, xiii–xvi, 11, 14, 24, 27, 31, 35, 42, 60–61, 63, 71, 73–74, 80–82, 86, 96–97, 99–100, 105–16, 118–21, 128, 133, 139, 149, 151
Cane Ridge Revival, 9
Cape May, New Jersey, 25–26

the Caribbean, xi–xii, 160, 179
Cashiere, Catharine, 44, 56
Central America, xi–xiii, 2
Cha-Jua, Sundiata Keita, 50, 82
Charlston, South Carolina, 19–21, 23, 90, 139, 144, 146; Mother Emanual AME Church, 20, 186n12
Chicago, Illinois, xvii, 69, 96, 101, 106, 116–18, 128, 136–38, 151, 161; Chicago's Quinn Chapel AME Church, xvii, 96, 106, 116, 137, 180n9, 201n41
Chillicothe, Ohio, 27, 62, 154, 187n42; Chillicothe's Quinn Chapel AME Church, 27
The Christian Recorder, xix, 39, 66, 128–30, 132–34, 136, 138–39, 142, 145, 209n69
Cincinnati, Ohio, 30, 58–63, 73–74, 99, 120–21, 128, 132, 137; Allen Temple AME Church, 30, 61–62; Cincinnati's Bethel AME Church, 62; Lane Seminary, 59–63
civil rights, xiv, 5
Civil War. *See* United States, Civil War
Clarke, M. M., 107, 116, 143, 206n12
Clarkson, Thomas, 38
Cleveland, Ohio, 51, 115, 128; St. John AME Church, 51, 194n32
Coffin, Catherine, 72–73
Coffin, Levi, 72–74
Coker, Daniel, 4, 7–8, 25, 34, 54, 183n30, 185n3
Collins, Samuel, 1–2, 7–9, 18, 23, 28–29, 48, 52, 57, 181n3
Colored Methodist Society, 51
Compromise of 1850, 105, 124
Cone, James H., 14, 98
Coppin, Levi, 159
Cornish, Samuel Eli, 37, 41, 45, 54–55
Crummell, Alexander, 48, 54, 56
Crummell, Boston, 56

Cuba, 48

Dallas, Texas, xix, 154–55, 168
Daughters of the Conference, 38, 103
Delany, Martin, 66–67, 115, 141
Delaware, 7–8, 12, 26, 43–44, 47–48, 54, 136, 142–43
Delaware River, 12, 48
Detroit, Michigan, 69, 116, 128
Dickerson, Dennis, xii, 13, 20, 179n1
Dickson, Hannah, 69
Dickson, Moses, xv, 69, 153–54, 161, 163
Dinius, Marcy, 64
District of Colombia. *See* Washington DC
Dodson, Jualynne, 92
Douglass, Frederick, 45, 99, 116–17, 119. *See also Frederick Douglass' Paper*
Downing, Thomas, 56
the Dred Scott decision, 124–25, 127; *Dred Scott v Sanford*, 124
Du Bois, W. E. B., 126

Early, Jordan Winston, 50, 83, 100, 113, 126, 142, 152–53, 161
education, xiii–xiv, xix, 22, 35, 38–39, 41, 54, 56, 59–61, 63–65, 71, 79, 85, 90, 93–94, 98, 107–9, 112, 114, 124, 137–38, 142–43, 154–55, 159, 166–68, 195n6, 197n24, 198–99n2, 203n17
the Emancipation Proclamation, 135–37, 139, 143. *See also* slavery, emancipation from
England, 2–3, 80, 147
Europe, xi
exhorter, 2–3, 11–12, 28, 46, 95

Fairbank, Calvin, xv, 109
the Fifteenth Amendment, 150
financial literacy, xiv, 142
Floating Freedom School, 85

Flushing, New York City, 35, 37, 43, 189–90n7; Flushing's Macedonia AME Church, 35, 37, 189n7. *See also* New York City
Foner, Eric, 45, 47, 143
Foote, Julia, 89, 95
Forten, James, 87
Fountain City, Indiana, 72–74, 81, 199n5
Frederick Douglass' Paper, 116–18
Frederick, Maryland, 7, 18; Frederick's Quinn Chapel AME Church, 18
Free African Society, 4, 6, 36, 166, 218n1
freedom, xi, xiv–xvi, xix, 6, 11–15, 18, 20, 23, 26, 29–30, 35–37, 39–40, 45, 48–49, 51–53, 55, 61–62, 64, 66, 68–69, 73–74, 76–78, 82, 85–86, 96, 99–100, 103, 106–9, 112, 116, 118–19, 129–36, 139–40, 142–43, 147–49, 151, 153, 161, 166–68, 180n7; fighter, 119, 129; physical, xiv, 168; religious, xi, 6, 11, 153, 166
freedom seekers, xv–xvi, 12, 18, 26, 35, 45, 51–52, 55, 61–62, 69, 73–74, 77–78, 82, 85–86, 96, 99, 103, 106, 108, 112, 116, 118, 130–36, 139, 148, 161
Freedom's Journal, 36–37, 39–40, 45, 55, 66
Freemasonry, 40, 69, 74, 94, 101, 199n9
Fugitive Slave Act (1850), xii, 105–9, 115, 124–25. *See also* slavery, fugitives

Galbreath, George, 103
Garnet, Eliza, 46–48, 193n21
Garnet, George, 46, 48, 193n21
Garnet, Henry Highland, xv, xvii–xviii, 39–40, 45, 47–49, 54, 58–59, 87, 93, 115, 143, 192–93n14, 193n21
Garrett, Thomas, 47
Garrison, William Lloyd, 54, 60–61
Gettysburg, Pennsylvania, 93
Gloucester, John, 9–10, 13

Haiti, xiii–xiv, 21, 30, 42, 89, 105, 115–16
harassment, 6, 19, 126
Harper, Frances Watkins, 138
Harpers Ferry, West Virginia, 125
Haviland, Laura, 109
Henry, Thomas, 100
Henson, Josiah, 96–98, 108, 203–4n27
Hicks, Elias, xiii, 2, 206n12
Honduras, xi–xii, 1–2, 28, 38, 107, 123, 206n12
Hopper, Isaac T., 45, 192n14
Hudson, Blaine, 76

Illinois, xiv–xv, xviii, 49–51, 54, 68–69, 71, 79, 81–86, 88, 91–92, 106, 113, 126, 135, 145, 149, 151, 153, 213n9
immediatism, 60
India, xi, 115, 167
Indiana, xiv, xvi, xviii–xix, 27, 54, 68–69, 71–74, 76–77, 79–81, 86–87, 91–92, 105, 107, 109, 111–13, 115, 119, 123, 128, 135, 138, 145, 149–53, 156, 158, 161–62, 166, 180n9, 195n6, 198–99n2, 206n12
Indianapolis, Indiana, 80–81, 87, 123, 128–31, 135, 150–51; Indianapolis's Bethel AME Church, 81, 135, 138, 151
Iowa, xiv, 79, 133, 198, 218

Jackson, Andrew, xviii, 66–68
the Jim Lane Trail, 133. *See also* Lane, Jim
Jocelyn, Simeon S. 56
Johnson, Richard, 44, 147
Jones, Absalom, xiii, 4–6
Jones, John, xv, 96, 106, 116–17, 161, 203–4n26
Jones, Mary Richardson, 96, 203–4n26
justice, xi–xii, xix, 47, 65, 74, 83, 91, 124, 153

Index 253

Kansas, xiv, xvi, 125, 129–36, 139–40, 149
Kansas River, 131–33
Kentucky, xiv–xv, 21, 27, 61, 68–69, 71, 76–79, 82, 88, 91, 108–9, 116, 136, 140, 146, 151
kidnapping, 2, 20, 27, 47–48, 82, 86, 107, 134
King, James, 61–62, 162
Knights of Liberty, 69

Lake Michigan, 66, 96
Lambert, William, 34, 116
land ownership, 6, 25, 72, 79, 88, 98, 122, 155, 188n54, 209n65
Lane, Jim, 134. *See also* Cincinnati, Ohio, Lane Seminary; the Jim Lane Trail
Lawnside (Snow Hill), New Jersey, 25; Mt. Pisgah AME Church, 25
leadership, xi, xiii, xx, 5, 9, 24, 34, 37–39, 52, 59, 73, 87, 93–94, 102, 110–11, 115, 119–20, 138, 140, 162; Black leaders, xviii, xx, 56, 62, 136
Leavenworth, Kansas, 130–33, 149; Leavenworth's Bethel AME Church, 130
Lee, Jarena, 8, 35, 42, 95, 111, 165–66
liberation, xi, xiv, xix, 11, 20, 22, 30, 35, 116, 138, 154, 156, 165–68
The Liberator, 54–55, 60
Liberia, 115, 140, 169
Lincoln, Abraham, 69, 135–37, 141–43, 213n9
Louisiana, xiv, 21, 71, 91, 119, 144, 161
Louisville, Kentucky, 69, 76–79, 88, 109, 113, 140, 144, 148, 150–51; Louisville's Bethel AME Church (later Quinn Chapel), 77–78

Manumission Society, 39–40
manstealing. *See* kidnapping

Maryland, xiv, 2, 7, 10, 12, 18, 26–27, 46–48, 53–54, 66–67, 91, 99, 108, 126, 136, 151
Mason-Dixon Line, 24. *See also* Missouri Compromise (1820)
Massachusetts, xiv, 23, 107, 116, 152
McKenzie, Vashti, 165–66
Meachum, John Berry, 84–85
Methodism, xii–xiii, xix, 1, 3, 5, 7–9, 11–15, 19, 25, 27, 51, 53–54, 76, 82, 85, 92, 97, 99, 102, 105, 113, 144, 156, 163, 169. *See also* African Methodist Episcopal (AME) Church; British Methodist Episcopal (BME) Church; Methodist Episcopal Church; Wesley, John
Methodist Episcopal Church, xii, 2–5, 7, 10, 14, 19, 25, 30, 34, 51, 83, 90–91, 97, 101, 110, 114, 118–20, 127, 137, 140, 146, 151, 154, 158, 162, 165–67. *See also* African Methodist Episcopal (AME) Church; British Methodist Episcopal (BME) Church; Methodism
Michigan, xiv, 65–66, 69, 71, 91, 96, 199n10
missionaries, xii–xiv, 1, 19–24, 28–31, 34, 38, 51, 56–57, 59, 69, 71, 78, 80–82, 85–87, 91–92, 96, 122, 128, 140, 144–45, 162, 168–69, 187n31
Mississippi, 24, 107, 113, 144, 151, 161
Mississippi River, 49, 76, 82–85, 156; Bloody Island, 83–84; Duncan Island, 83–84
Missouri, xiv–xv, xviii, 11, 21, 24, 51, 69, 71, 82–86, 88, 91, 113, 123, 126, 128, 130–36, 139–40, 144–45, 149–51, 153–54, 195n6
Missouri Compromise (1820), 24. *See also* Mason-Dixon Line
Missouri River, 130–33
Monongahela River, 24, 58

moral suasion, 49
Mother Baltimore. *See* Baltimore, Priscilla

Nash, Gary, 5–6
Nazrey, Willis, 81, 86–87, 110, 112–13, 115, 120–21, 137, 139–40, 149
New Bedford, Massachusetts, xiv, 23, 190n7
New England, 112, 123, 134, 145
New Jersey, xiv, 7, 12, 25–27, 47, 55, 91, 107, 162, 187n38
New Orleans, 58, 79, 105, 110, 119, 142, 144, 148, 151, 161
New York, xiii–xv, 2, 8, 22–23, 33–56, 62–63, 72, 80–81, 87, 89, 91, 95–97, 99, 107–9, 111–12, 116, 123
New York City, New York, xii, 7, 12, 22, 26, 31, 33–56, 71, 74, 97, 101, 103, 110, 123, 143, 145, 189–90nn7–10, 192n14, 193n25, 194n40; AME Zion Church, 33–34, 38, 44, 103; Elizabeth Street Bethel AME Church, 37, 189n7; New York Committee of Vigilance, 45. *See also* Brooklyn, New York City; Flushing, New York City
Nickens, David, 62
North America, xi, 2, 82, 121, 147, 206n12
Northwest Ordinance, 91

Oberlin College, 63, 93
Ohio, 9, 23–24, 27–30, 33, 49, 51–52, 54, 56–59, 61–63, 68, 71, 73–74, 81, 86, 91, 97–99, 107, 111, 114, 120, 126, 128, 137, 142, 145, 147–48, 151, 154, 160–61, 195–96n6, 207n40
Ohio River, 68, 74, 76–77; Corn Island, 77–78; Falls of the Ohio, 76–77
Ontario, Canada, 31, 108
oppression, xix, 13, 15, 19, 31, 64, 103, 108, 116, 121, 133, 168

Paul, Benjamin, 41
Payne, Daniel, xvii–xix, 1, 22, 41, 43, 45, 52–53, 57, 81, 86–87, 89–90, 92–94, 101–3, 108, 110–14, 118–21, 123, 126–27, 129, 136–42, 144–45, 148–49, 156–62, 165, 167–68, 206n12
Pennington, J. W. C., 112
Pennsylvania, xiv, 1–2, 7–9, 12, 18, 23, 26–27, 30, 33, 35, 48–49, 56, 58, 91–92, 107, 145, 147–48, 156
Philadelphia, Pennsylvania, xiii, xix, 4, 6–8, 13, 17–19, 21–25, 29, 31, 33–34, 36, 42–43, 47, 49, 52–53, 56, 58, 72, 80, 86–87, 89, 92, 95, 97–98, 100–103, 106, 108, 111–12, 115–16, 118, 120, 122–23, 139, 142, 145, 151–52, 162, 165, 167, 183n30, 206n12; African Church of St. Thomas, 5; Philadelphia's Bethel AME Church, 4–7, 31, 101–3, 108, 120, 139; St. George's AME Church, xiii, 4, 6; Union AME Church, 142
Pinn, Anthony, xiv
Pittsburgh, Pennsylvania, 18, 23, 27, 29–30, 52, 57–58, 64, 66, 71, 89, 91–92, 94–95, 106, 108, 115, 128, 144, 157, 206n12; Brown Chapel, 30; Chartiers Street AME Church, 30; St. James AME Church, 30; St. Paul's AME Church, 30; Trinity AME Church, 30; Wylie Street Bethel AME Church, 29–30, 106, 114, 188n54
Porter, Dorothy, 64–65
Portland, Maine, xiv, 161
Potts, Margaretta (Margaret, Marguarite). *See* Quinn, Margaretta (Margaret, Marguarite) R.
prejudice, xiii, 3, 45, 57, 109, 118, 142

Quakerism, xii–xiii, xvi, xix, 1–2, 13, 38, 47, 72, 74, 80, 158–59, 192n14, 206n12

Quantrill, William, 139–40
Quarles, Benjamin, 124
Quinn Chapel, xvii, 18, 27, 77–78, 96, 106, 116, 137, 171–74, 180n9, 3.2n41 *See also* Appendix and specific Quinn Chapels by city
Quinn, Margaretta (Margaret, Marguarite) R., xii, 38, 47, 51, 145, 191n21, 194n34
Quinn, Mary Jane Simms, 145–56, 159, 179n1
Quinn, William Paul, xi–15, 17–31, 33–69, 71–74, 76–87, 89–103, 105–23, 125–30, 132–63, 165–68, 179n1, 180n9, 181n3, 181n15, 185n3, 188n56, 191n34, 193n25, 194n44, 199n9, 201n41, 206n12, 209n65, 211n31, 214n20, 216n10

racism, xiv, 4, 114–15, 124, 131, 118, 150
Reading, Pennsylvania, 9–10; Bethel AME Church of Reading, 10
Reason, Charles, 48
Reconstruction, 143, 147, 156, 169
resistance, xi, xv, 5, 127
Revels, Hiram, 81, 150–51
Revels, Willis, 81, 130, 135, 150–51, 161
Richmond, Indiana, xvi, xix, 69, 71–74, 113, 123, 128–29, 136, 138, 145, 150–52, 156, 158–61, 179n1, 199n5, 199n9, 206n12, 209n65; Richmond's Bethel AME Church, 71, 158, 161
Riker, Richard, 46–47
Robinson, Richard, 28–30, 89–90, 108
Rush, Christopher, 34, 41, 45, 56, 103
Russwurm, John, 37, 39–40

Sabbath Schools, 35, 61–62, 91, 94, 114, 130, 138

Salem, New Jersey, 7, 25–27, 183n30
salvation, xiv, xix, 9, 13, 22, 29, 160
schisms, 60, 93, 97–98, 115, 204n33
Sernett, Milton, 65
Shadd, Mary Ann, 118–19
Shorter, James A., 141, 148–49, 156–60
Siebert, Wilber H., 73–74, 187n38
Sierra Leone, 115
Singleton, George, xix
slavery, xi–xiii, xv–xix, 2, 4, 7, 10–12, 14, 18, 20, 24–30, 33, 37, 39, 45–49, 51, 55, 59–65, 69, 72, 74, 77, 82, 85–87, 97–98, 100, 103, 105–10, 114–16, 118, 121, 124–26, 128–31, 133–34, 136–38, 140–43, 150, 154, 167–68, 197n24; abolition of, xv, 45, 49, 63, 65, 76, 78–80, 83, 106, 127, 136, 138, 143, 209n69; antislavery, xiii, xvi, 2–3, 19, 27, 29–30, 49, 54, 60–62, 80, 82, 85, 117, 119, 131, 147; emancipation from, 2, 14, 20, 38, 116, 135–37, 139, 142–43; escape from, xvi–xvii, 18, 48, 74, 108, 116, 118, 142, 180n7, 181n11; fugitives, xii, 10, 45–46, 51, 59, 63, 84, 105–9, 115, 124–25, 133; slave catchers, 26, 46, 48, 76, 106. *See also* the Dred Scott Decision; the Compromise of 1850; the Emancipation Proclamation; Fugitive Slave Act (1850); Missouri Compromise (1820); Underground Railroad
Smalls, Robert, 139
Smith, David, 9, 18, 21, 25, 34, 41–43, 54, 56, 76, 100
Smith, James McCune, 48, 54
Society for the Colonization of Free People of Color, 54
Society of Friends. *See* Quakerism
South Carolina, 19–21, 23, 41, 44, 64, 90, 94, 103, 107, 125, 127, 144, 146, 203n17

256 ~ Index

Spencer, Peter, 43–44, 183n30
Spencer, William, 46–48, 183n30
Springtown, New Jersey, 25–27, 183n30; Springtown's Bethel AME Church, 26–27
St. Catharines, Canada, 14, 63, 108, 118–19, 121; St. Catharines's Salem Chapel, 14, 108, 121
Stevens, Thaddeus, 129, 147–48
Still, William, 26
Stowe, Harriet Beecher, 59, 96, 98, 125, 203–4n27
Steubenville, Ohio, 30, 187n42; Quinn Memorial AME Church, 30
suffrage, 147
Sumner, Charles, 129, 136–37
Switala, William, 27

Talbert, Horace, 169
Taney, Roger, 124
Tappan, Arthur, 56
Tennessee, xiv, 88, 140
Terre Haute, Indiana, 74, 95, 113, 123, 128, 130, 150–51; Allen Chapel, 74, 95, 150–51
Texas, xix, 143–44, 154–55, 168
the Thirteenth Amendment, 143
Thomas, Nathan, 46–47
Tilley, Pamela, 165
Toledo, Ohio, 128, 160–61; Warren Chapel, 160–61
Toronto, Canada, 31, 81, 96–97, 113, 118–19
Tubman, Harriet, 63, 107–8
Turner, Augustus, 80
Turner, Henry McNeal, xix, 80, 127, 129, 135–37, 143, 147, 156–57, 165, 167–69, 214n27

Uncle Tom's Cabin (Stowe), 96, 98, 125, 203–4n27

Underground Railroad, xi, xv–xvii, 10, 12, 14, 17–18, 25–27, 29–30, 35, 45, 47–48, 55, 57, 59, 61–63, 69, 72–75, 77–78, 80, 83, 85–87, 96, 100, 108–9, 112, 115–18, 125, 127, 129–31, 133–35, 137, 139, 148, 151, 154, 161–62, 180n7, 199n5, 199n10, 203–4n26
United States, xii–xiii, xvi, 2, 5–8, 14, 23, 29–31, 35, 38, 41–42, 48, 50, 53, 67, 69, 81–82, 87, 90, 96, 99–100, 105–9, 114–15, 117–18, 121, 129, 135, 137, 143–44, 147–50, 162; Civil War, xi, xiii, xv–xvii, 14, 21, 24, 27, 61, 69, 78, 87, 90, 114, 117, 124–35, 137, 139, 141–43, 147–48, 150–51, 169, 180n7, 207n38

Vesey, Denmark, 14, 20–21, 103
Virginia, 1, 58, 60, 160

Waco, Texas, 154–55; Paul Quinn College, xix, 154–55, 168
Walker, David, 45, 60, 63–64, 87
Walker, Elizabeth H., xii–xiii, 1, 72, 181n1
Wallace, J. P. Q., 18, 21, 186n19
Ward, Samuel Ringgold, 26, 48, 51, 55, 102, 105, 148–49, 205n1
Washington, Booker T., 69, 198n52
Washington DC, 12, 18, 48, 66–67, 87, 99, 107, 127–29, 135, 137, 141–43, 145, 147, 149; Israel Bethel AME Church, 107, 129, 135, 145, 147; Union Bethel AME Church, 87, 127
Waters, Edward, 52, 86, 97–99, 100, 111
Wattles, Augustus, xv, 59–61, 63
Wayman, Alexander, 5, 123, 136, 139, 144, 148–49, 153–54, 156–57, 160–61

Welch, Elaine, xvi–xvii, 18, 24, 28, 33, 56, 65–66, 72, 74, 79–80, 85, 91, 106, 123, 145, 180n9
Weld, Theodore, xv, 59–62
Wells, Samuel, 62
Wesley, Charles, 37
Wesley, John, 9, 97
Wilberforce Society, 38
Wilberforce, William, 114. *See also* Wilberforce Society; Wilberforce University
Wilberforce University, 114, 137–38, 141, 168, 207n40
Williams, Peter, 39–40, 56
Wilmington, Delaware, 7, 44, 47, 144, 183n30; African Union Church, 43–44
Wisconsin, xiv, 79, 149
Wilson, Henry C., 129, 152
Woodson, Lewis, 27, 29–30, 52, 59, 62, 81
Wright, Richard R., xvi, 35
Wright, Theodore S., xv, 40–41, 44–45, 48, 54, 56

About the Author

Historical archaeologist Cheryl Janifer LaRoche, a noted scholar of the Underground Railroad, has written extensively on the subject of escape from slavery. Her first book, *Free Black Communities and the Underground Railroad: The Geography of Resistance*, was published in 2014. She is an associate research professor in historic preservation in the School of Architecture at the University of Maryland College Park.